JESUS— THE PORTRAIT AND INSCRIPTION OF GOD

*"what is now and
what will take place later"*

GEORGE PAKI

TEACH Services, Inc.
P U B L I S H I N G
www.TEACHServices.com • (800) 367-1844

World rights reserved. This book or any portion thereof may not be copied or reproduced in any form or manner whatever, except as provided by law, without the written permission of the publisher, except by a reviewer who may quote brief passages in a review.

The author assumes full responsibility for the accuracy of all facts and quotations as cited in this book. The opinions expressed in this book are the author's personal views and interpretations, and do not necessarily reflect those of the publisher.

This book is provided with the understanding that the publisher is not engaged in giving spiritual, legal, medical, or other professional advice. If authoritative advice is needed, the reader should seek the counsel of a competent professional.

Copyright © 2021 George Paki
Copyright © 2021 TEACH Services, Inc.
ISBN-13: 978-1-4796-1043-3 (Paperback)
ISBN-13: 978-1-4796-1049-5 (Hardback)
ISBN-13: 978-1-4796-1044-0 (ePub)
Library of Congress Control Number: 2020925802

Scripture taken from the New King James Version®. Copyright © 1982 by Thomas Nelson. Used by permission. All rights reserved.

THE HOLY BIBLE, NEW INTERNATIONAL VERSION®, NIV® Copyright © 1973, 1978, 1984 by International Bible Society.® Used by permission. All rights reserved worldwide.

Published by

www.TEACHServices.com • (800) 367-1844

TABLE OF CONTENTS

Acknowledgment . . . . *viii*
Introduction . . . . *ix*

PART 1:
METHODOLOGY, AUTHORSHIP, AND LITERARY RELATIONSHIPS

1. **APPROACHES TO REVELATION.** 14
   Introduction 14
   Methods of Interpretation 15
   Analysis of Methods. 18
   Criteria for a Modified Historicism (Dual-Intentionalism). 27
   Dual-Intentionalism and Conclusion. 39

2. **THE AUTHORSHIP OF THE JOHANNINE BOOKS** 40
   Johannine Books. 40
   Authorship. 43
   Order in Which the Johannine Books Were Written 50

3. **THE RELATIONSHIP AMONG THE JOHANNINE BOOKS.** . . 52
   The Gospel and Epistles of John 52
   Revelation 1–3 and 1 John 53
   Gospel of John and Revelation 4–22 59
   Conclusion 66

PART 2:
JESUS, GOD, SPIRITS OF GOD, AND DUALISM (REVELATION 1:1–9)

4. **REVELATION OF JESUS CHRIST** 70
   Introduction 70
   Definition and Significance 70
   What Is Now and What Will Take Place Later
      (Revelation 1–3 and 4–22) 73
   The Word of God, Testimony of Jesus, and Believers. 78
   Literary, Contextual, and Theological Reflections 81

5. **CHRIST AND CONCEPT OF TIME IN REVELATION** 84
   Concept and Urgency of Time 84
   Literary, Contextual, and Theological Reflections 106

6. **THE COMMUNICATION OF CHRIST** 109
   Introduction 109
   Communication and Writing Processes 109
   Implications on Structure and Content 113
   Critical Scholarship 113

7. **JESUS AND GOD** 115
   Introduction 115
   Structure and Analysis of the Text 116
   Jesus as God 118
   Literary, Contextual, and Theological Implications. 122

8. **JESUS AND THE SPIRITS** 125
   The Holy Spirit and the Text 125
   Analysis of the Seven Spirits and the Lamb 128
   The Spirits of God and Contextual Issues 130
   The "Spirits" and "Jesus" in Johannine Literature 138
   The "Spirits," "Jesus," and Old Testament Prophets 140
   Analysis and Summary 144

9. **JESUS CHRIST** 146
   Introduction 146
   Jesus' Names and Titles 147
   Theological Implications 152

Summary Statement: Chapters 1–9. 153
Conclusion 156

10. DUAL FOCUS OF THE WORD OF GOD 157
John and His Brothers. 157
The Word of God and the Testimony of Jesus. 158
The Word of God 161
Dual Focus of the Word and Commandments of God 168
Summary 179

11. THE DUAL FOCUS OF THE TESTIMONY OF JESUS 180
Introduction 180
Usage of The Phrase "Testimony of Jesus" 180
Nature and Type of Testimonies 182
Testimony of Jesus as The Spirit of Prophecy 186
Testimonies of Jesus Then and Now 189
Conclusion 192

12. DUAL FOCUS IN REVELATION, 1 JOHN,
AND THE GOSPEL OF JOHN 193
Dual Meanings in Revelation 193
Dual Meanings in 1 John 215
Dual Meanings in The Gospel of John 223
Conclusion 224

PART 3:
JESUS, THE ONE LIKE THE SON OF MAN
(REVELATION 1:10–3:22)

13. THE SON OF MAN, PART I 228
Introduction 229
Preincarnate Christ 231
Post-Ascension and Future Roles of Jesus 238
Composite Divine Figures in New Testament Writings 242
Conclusion 244

14. THE SON OF MAN, PART II 246
Review: Assumptions and Objectives of This Study 246
Theological Implications 247

    Contextual Implications 252
    Conclusion 253

15. EPHESUS: HIM WHO HOLDS THE SEVEN STARS 254
    Jesus in Ephesus 254
    Opponents in Ephesus 261
    Relationship Between Revelation 1–3 and 4–22 268

16. SMYRNA: HIM WHO IS THE FIRST AND LAST 269
    Jesus in Smyrna and the Implication 269
    Contextual and Theological Issues 279
    Opponents in Smyrna 289
    Relationship Between Revelation 1–3 and 4–22 291

17. PERGAMUM: HIM WHO HAS A SHARP, DOUBLE-EDGED SWORD 294
    Jesus in Pergamum 294
    Opponents 307
    Rewards for Faithfulness 309
    Relationship Between Revelation 1–3 and 4–22 311

18. THYATIRA: SON OF GOD, WHOSE EYES ARE LIKE BLAZING FIRE 313
    Jesus in Thyatira 314
    Opponents and their Significance 322
    Relationship Between Revelation 1–3 and 4–22 330
    Conclusion 331

19. SARDIS, PART I: HIM WHO HOLDS THE SEVEN SPIRITS AND STARS 332
    Christ in Sardis 332
    Christ, Spirits, Angels, and the Seven Churches 344
    Contextual Issues: Christ and Angels 349

20. SARDIS, PART II 353
    Angels, Moses, and Jesus in Hebrews 353
    Angels, Moses, and Jesus in Old Testament Context 356
    "Another Mighty Angel" of Revelation 10: Angel or Christ? 362

    Characters and Issues 367
    Relationship Between Revelation 1–3 and 4–22. 379
    Summary 380

21. PHILADELPHIA, PART I: HIM WHO IS HOLY, TRUE, AND HOLDS THE KEYS OF DAVID **384**
    Introduction 385
    Jesus Christ in Philadelphia. 385

22. PHILADELPHIA, PART II **398**
    Characters and Issues 398
    Promises and Rewards. 409
    Relationship Between Revelation 1–3 and 4–22. 426
    Comprehensibility and Applicability 428

23. LAODICEA, PART I: THE AMEN, FAITHFUL, TRUE WITNESS, THE RULER OF GOD'S CREATION **430**
    Jesus Christ in Laodicea. 430
    Analysis and Conclusion 448

24. LAODICEA, PART II **449**
    Contextual Issues 449
    Textual Analysis 455
    Promises and Rewards. 467
    Relationship Between Revelation 1–3 and 4–22. 471

PART 4:
EPILOGUE

25. CONCLUSION AND RECOMMENDATIONS **476**
    Aims and Purposes of the Study 476
    Results of the Study 477
    Recommendations for Future Study 481

Bibliography *483*

ACKNOWLEDGMENT

What began as a journey with a series of rough notes in a basement in Berrien Springs has ended up as a 490-page book in Port Moresby. Along the way, many joined in, starting with Melissa and Clyde Morgan who showed interest in the original manuscript and poured many long hours in editing it. Dr. Kayle de Waal's feedback was invaluable in allowing me to refine the work. McKeruzza Paugari's input after reading the draft helped me polish the work. Moses Palipe, Paiyo Bale and Fred Angoman's consistent support ensured that I lacked nothing in this journey. I am indebted to these and a host of many others who read the manuscript and offered helpful insights and encouragements during this experience.

I am also grateful to my wife and kids who sacrificed a lot of family time which enabled me to stay focused on this journey.

Now I wish to invite you to join us. As you journey through the pages of this book, may you, in spite of my inadequacies, clearly see the Apocalyptic Christ—*The Portrait and Inscription of God*.

INTRODUCTION

This study aims to achieve four main objectives:

i. **Validate a dual-focus approach to Revelation**—to see the text through a dualistic method of interpretation, as opposed to preterist, futurist, idealist, or historical methods. A dual-focus method is not totally new, but a slightly modified version of the historical method, which sees the prophecies of Revelation being fulfilled both in the first century and today (see chapter 1).[1]

ii. **Investigate the dual-focus method in Revelation and other Johannine books**—to show that the prophetic messages of Revelation were read, understood, and applicable to those who first received the document. Additionally, as dual-intentionalism suggests, the same prophecies spoke throughout history and today as well. In order for this to happen, this study assumes that all key words, concepts, characters, dates, names, places, and events in the Apocalypse to have a dual meaning, purpose, and application (see chapters 10–12).

iii. **Analyze the relationship between Revelation 1–3 and 4–22**—to determine the nature and extent of the relationship that exists between the materials of Revelation 1–3 and 4–22. Furthermore, the relationship

---

[1] In this study, the dual-focused approach will also be called bi-intentionalism or dual-intentionalism in order to maximize clarity and avoid confusion between this method and other dualistic methods of interpretations. In current scholarship, the platform of dualism is used in gnostic and prophetic literature to push for certain controversial interpretations. However, whenever the term "dualism," "dualistic method," or "dual-focus" is used here, it simply means that the prophecies of Revelation were read and understood by and applicable to the early readers and us. These terms are interchangeably used to avoid monotony.

between Revelation and other Johannine books (1, 2, and 3 John and the Gospel of John) and Hebrews will be assessed. This is important for two reasons. First, the current approach that attempts to divide the apocalyptic book into two sections (chapters 1–3 and 4–22) ignores textual evidences that suggests otherwise.[2] Second, the book of Revelation must first be read within the historical and textual context in which it was conceived (see chapters 15–24).

iv. **Recognize how the dual-focus method enhances the reader's understanding and appreciation of the apocalyptic Christ** ... and more importantly, see Jesus as John of Patmos saw Him. If the author described the apocalyptic book as the "Revelation of Jesus Christ" and assured us that we shall "see him as he [really] is" (Rev. 1:1; 1 John 3:2), then it beckons the question, *Whom* did John see? And what was He really like? (see chapters 5–24).

This book consists of twenty-five chapters that are divided into three parts. Part 1 has three chapters that discusses the methodology adopted in this study (chapter 1), the authorship (chapter 2), and Revelation's literary relationship to other Johannine works (chapter 3). The main aim of these chapters is to show that the prophecies of Revelation were originally intended to address pressing issues the early church grappled with. Contrary to popular opinion, Revelation is not a semi-closed book, where certain parts were applicable to the early church (chs. 1–3) while other parts (chs. 4–22) are to remain closed until a later time.[3]

Parts 2 and 3 discuss the main text (Rev. 1:1–3:22). Part 2 assesses the prologue and other introductory materials (1:1–9). This portion not only attempts to introduce Revelation but also functions as the synopsis of the entire text. Therefore, the nine chapters (4–12) in Part 2 attempt

---

[2] See an interesting study by Clinton Wahlen "Letters to the seven churches: historical or prophetic?" *Ministry*. November 2007, pp. 12–15. The current work builds on Wahlen's study and attempts to show that Revelation 1–3 and 4–22 contain essentially the same material. However, if there are any differences, they are more stylistic in nature, not in substance.

[3] This is the majority view held by all historicists.

to determine the intrinsic relationships that exist between this section and the main text. The main aim of this section is to show that John and his audience read and understood the prophecies of Revelation (particularly 4–22).

Part 3 comprises the two subsections of Revelation 1:10–3:22. The first subsection discusses the vision of "one like the son of man" (chapters 13, 14), and the second analyzes each of the seven messages (chapters 15–25). The studies in Part 3 attempt to 1) paint the portrait of Jesus as presented in each of the seven oracles (Rev. 1:10–3:22), 2) demonstrate any relationship that may exist between Revelation 1–3 and 4–22, 3) show how the entire text addresses the issues the early church encountered, and 4) demonstrate the author and his initial audiences' comprehension and appreciation of the entire book. The primary aim of this is to show how God uses the same prophecies to speak to the early church and the contemporary church.

> *Contrary to popular opinion, Revelation is not a semi-closed book, where certain parts were applicable to the early church (chs. 1–3) and other parts (chs. 4–22) are to remain closed until a later time.*

PART 1:

METHODOLOGY, AUTHORSHIP, AND LITERARY RELATIONSHIPS

1.
APPROACHES TO REVELATION

INTRODUCTION

Scholars use one of four methods—preterism, futurism, idealism, or historicism—to interpret the book of Revelation.[4] One may not typically state the method he or she espouses, but it functions, more or less, like a window through which the scholar views the text. Therefore, the chosen method has a direct bearing on the way the text is read, assessed, and interpreted. This, perhaps, is one reason why a lack of unanimity exists on most aspects of Revelation. Given this scenario, the process of selecting an appropriate method of interpretation is critically important.

It is for these reasons that this chapter briefly discusses the four approaches and proposes a modified historicism. For classification purposes, the method adapted in this study is called *dual-focus, dual-intentionalism*, or the *dualistic method*. The dualistic method is essentially a modified historicism—an approach that combines certain core tenets of preteristic and historical methods of study.[5] This method proposes that the

---

[4] To further explore these methods of interpretation, see Ranko Stefanovic, *Revelation of Jesus Christ: Commentary on the Book of Revelation*, 2nd ed. (Berrien Springs, MI: Andrews University Press, 2009), pp. 11–14; Kenneth A. Strand, "Foundational Principles of Interpretation," in *Symposium on Revelation—Book I*, pp. 4–7; Jon Paulien, "The End of Historicism? Reflections on the Adventist Approach to Biblical Apocalyptic—Part One," *Journal of the Adventist Theological Society* 11 (Fall, 2003): pp. 15–43; Hans K. LaRondelle, "Babylon: Anti-Christian Empire," in *Symposium on Revelation—Book II*, pp. 151–176; William G. Johnsson, "The Saints' End-Time Victory over the Forces of Evil," in *Symposium on Revelation—Book II*, pp. 6–10.

[5] Other scholars have offered similar propositions. Jon Paulien argued for a modified historicism in "The End of Historicism? Reflections on the Adventist Approach to Biblical Apocalyptic—Part One," whereas Alden Thompson suggested an applied historicism. Erwin R. Gane, in his book

entire prophecies of Revelation spoke to John and his audience, the same prophecies also speak to us today—and attempts to demonstrate that. In this way, the dual-focused method will also be called dual-intentionalism; that the author (or God) intended the text to have a double interpretation or application. Then in the remainder of this book, we will demonstrate the dualistic method in Revelation 1–3.[6]

METHODS OF INTERPRETATION

Preterism

Pretersism or the preteristic approach states that Revelation primarily addressed immediate issues of the author and his audience.[7] Although preterists (those who adhere to this view) agree that predictive elements occur in the text, these elements are limited in scope, geography, and application, and these prophetic messages were relevant only to those who lived during the first century. They insist that a modern reader should treat the text purely as a historical account and proceed to find events, dates, and key characters in that era to substantiate their claims. The proponents of this view have done a masterful job of demonstrating the text's

---

Trumpet After Trumpet, proposed a dualistic approach to the trumpets section. The differences among Gane's dualism, the church's position, and this study are as follows: (1) Gane is of the opinion that the seven trumpets were fulfilled in the past and will sound again before the end. (2) The church sees the trumpet beginning in the first century and will continue until second coming. The church's view is not sensitive to the views of the document's primary readers. It can be summarized this way: "Whether the early church understood or not is irrelevant, the document was written primarily for and to us." (3) Therefore, the dualistic approach proposed in this study first attempts to see the prophecies the way the early church might have seen them, then show how the same prophecies could apply to us (i.e., throughout history and today). See Alberto Treiyer's review of Gane's book on his website (https://1ref.us/10g, September, 2012, accessed February 13, 2020), pp. 1–4.

[6] In later works, a similar attempt will be made with the remainder of Revelation (chs. 4–22).

[7] Preterism sees the prophecies of Revelation as being fulfilled in and around AD70. See Bob L. Ross, *The Historical background of Modern Preterism or AD 70ism* (Pasadena, Texas: n.d. This is one of many short monographs which can be accessed via http://members.aol.com/pilgrimpub/pretrist.htm. See also Dennie M. Swanson, "International Preterist Association: Reformation or Retrogression?," *The Master's Seminary Journal* 15/1 (Spring 2004), 39–58.

applicability to believers in the early church. Most modern scholars subscribe to this view.[8] The following diagram illustrates this method.

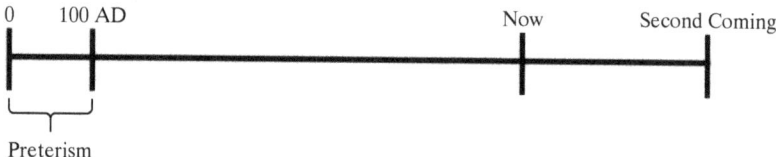

The natural conclusion of this thesis is the denial of any revelatory messages the book may have for those living after the first century. The preterists do not think that the same prophecies that spoke to the early believers could also speak to those living in later times. Such denials, especially in the face of demonstrable prophetic landmarks punctuated throughout church history and today, seriously challenge the validity of this method.

Futurism

The opposite of preterism is futurism, which primarily views Revelation as a prophetic book and denies its historical relevance and the ongoing fulfillment of its prophecies. Instead, it suggests that all predictive messages of Revelation will be fulfilled at the very end, just before Jesus returns. The inference is that the book currently does not have any relevance. Futurists may as well have us "close up and seal the words of this scroll until the time of the end" (Dan. 12:4).[9]

---

[8] Jon Paulien understands that the historical method of interpretation has been marginalized for "dispensationalist futurism" and "scholarly preterism." Prior to the Great Disappointment of 1844, the historical method was the dominant method used for interpreting Daniel and Revelation, but after the Great Disappointment, that method lost its dominance, and in the twentieth and twenty-first centuries, futurism and preterism are gaining momentum. See "The End of Historicism? Reflections on the Adventist Approach to Biblical Apocalyptic—Part One," *Journal of the Adventist Theological Society* 11 (Fall, 2003): pp. 15–43. For further examples of preterism, see Noe, John. "An Exegetical Basis for a Preterist-Idealist Understanding of the Book of Revelation." *Journal of the Evangelical Theological Society* 49, no. 4 (December 2006): 767–96; Preston, Don K. "Full Preterism and the Millennium." *Criswell Theological Review* 11, no. 1 (Fall 2013): 121–36.

[9] Hitchcock, Mark L. "A Critique of the Preterist View of Revelation 17:9–11 and Nero." *Bibliotheca Sacra* 164, no. 656 (2007): 472–85. Tan, Christine Joy. "A Futurist View of the Two Witnesses in Revelation 11." *Bibliotheca Sacra* 171, no. 684 (October 2014): 452–71.

This method poses two problems. First, this view opposes the text itself. The book literally urges the saints to read and even pronounces blessings on those doing it (1:1–3; 22:7, 10, 18, 19). Unlike Daniel, Revelation declares, "Do not seal up the words of the prophecy of this book, because the time is near" (22:10). Second, if the prophecies were for the "last days," then how will we determine when that time ("last days") actually begins? The following diagram represents the futuristic method of interpretation.

Idealism

Similar to preterism, idealism denies the predictive nature of Revelation. However, unlike preterism and futurism, idealism idealizes the book by emphasizing the timeless moral principles that it may contain. Idealists argue that the messages of Revelation were written for all people and times.[10] Although this is true, it seriously conflicts with the volume of details—dates, names, characters, and events—that endorse the apocalyptic nature of the text. The chronological order and arrangement of the book do not support an idealistic approach.

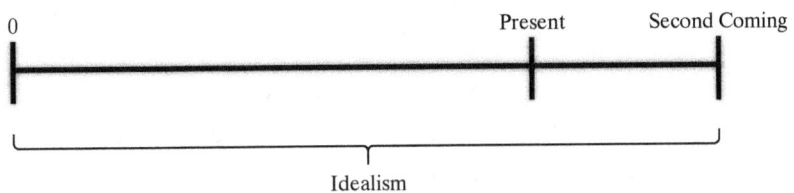

---

[10] For a comparative discussion on Idealism and other other competing views, see: Noe, John. "An Exegetical Basis for a Preterist-Idealist Understanding of the Book of Revelation." *Journal of the Evangelical Theological Society* 49, no. 4 (December 2006): 767–96.

Historicism

Historicism is a method of interpretation that sees the prophetic messages of Revelation from John's time to our time and beyond. This method has some similarities with the other three. First, similar to futurism, historicism sees the contents of Revelation as predictive in nature. However, it differs in that historicism sees those predictive elements being fulfilled in the past, present, and future; whereas futurism holds that the prophecies have no relevance in the past and present. Second, this method shares some common features with preterism too. Although they differ on Revelation 4–22, they agree that chapters 1–3 spoke to the saints living in the first century. Also, historicists may not deny the fulfillment of certain predictive elements of Revelation 4–22 in the early church, but stress the broader and ultimate fulfillment of the same prophecies throughout history and into the present age.

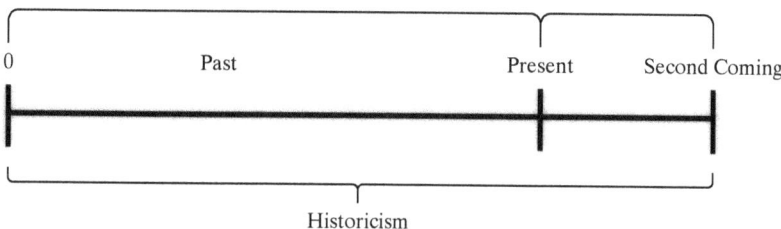

ANALYSIS OF METHODS

A Case for the Historical Method

<u>Imminent Return of Jesus Christ</u>. A question that arises is, Which method did John and his audience likely use? Preterism appears to be the most likely one. The early church did not think the world would last another 2,000 years. They thought they were living in the "last days" and expected Christ to return in their own lifetime. Thus, the text is punctuated with a deep sense of urgency. Consider the following examples:

1. A mighty angel "swore by him who lives for ever and ever," saying, "There will be no more delay!" (10:6).
2. In numerous places, Christ declares, "Behold I am coming quickly" (22:7, 12).
3. With regards to the element of time, a number of passages clearly teach that "time is [indeed] short" (1:3; 12:12).
4. The saints are urged to read, hear, and keep the "word of God and the testimony of Jesus" as presented in Revelation because the time of the end is near (1:1–3; 14:12).
5. By the time Revelation is read, some saints have already died; and others would die in the immediate future. However, the text does not say that all would die. Some among the saints would remain alive to see Jesus return (6:9–11; 14:10–12). This is not an isolated view held by the seven churches of Revelation. Paul and other New Testament (NT) writers shared the same view (see 1 Thess. 4:13–17).
6. Christ's imminent return is likened to a "thief" (3:3; 16:15).

Therefore, arguing that the early church may have understood concepts such as "soon," "no more delay," "coming quickly," and "time is short" differently than we understand today is to not merely challenge their reading abilities but their intelligence as well. Besides, unlike Daniel, John concludes with the words, "Amen, Come, Lord Jesus" (22:20).

> *The early church did not conceive the world would last another 2,000 years.*

The Delay. Since John and his addressees have died and Christ has not yet returned in the last 2,000 years, we are forced to reinterpret the prophecies. Perhaps the predictive elements that begin with 1:1 and 19 and 4:1 must be restudied. This is where the historical method comes in.

The historical method makes a compelling case for two reasons: 1) Since Revelation builds on the prophetic messages of Daniel, one appropriately sees a correlation between the two books. The fact that the prophecies of Daniel began with his time (Babylonian empire) and progressively revealed events of succeeding generations, allows a historicist to conclude that the materials in Revelation must follow the same tradition because it encompasses the birth of Jesus in old Jerusalem to the "marriage supper of the Lamb" in the New Jerusalem;[11] 2) This method therefore attempts to identify which materials constitutes our past, which are being fulfilled presently, and which will come to pass in the future.

The Critique on the Historical Method

Of the four methods, historicism presents fewer problems than do the others. However, there are two areas that bring historicism into question. These areas are discussed below.

<u>Tension Between Biblical Principle for Exegesis and Historicism</u>. The main issue is an exegetical one and apparent in Ranko Stefanovic's commentary, *Revelation of Jesus Christ*. Stefanovic makes the following observations:

> Biblical exegesis involves Two basic steps. The first involves determining **what the text meant** for the time when it was written. Before we try to discover the relevance of the biblical text for us today, we must understand what its author intended to convey to the readers of his time. This phase of exegesis seeks to determine both *what* the inspired author tried to say to the original readers, and *why* he said it ... The second step of exegesis analysis is to ask **what the text means** for the reader today.[12]

---

[11] While this is generally true, I think Paulien is correct in challenging this assumption. In a footnote he writes this: "The book of Daniel clearly exhibits a series of historical events running from the prophet's time to the end. The Book of Revelation quotes Daniel and is similar in style to Daniel, therefore, the sevenfold series of Revelation are also to be understood as historical series running from the time of the prophet until the end. This argument by itself is not satisfactory."—See "The End of Historicism? Reflections on the Adventist Approach to Biblical Apocalyptic—Part One," *Journal of the Adventist Theological Society* 11 (Fall, 2003): p. 37.

[12] Stefanovic, *Revelation of Jesus Christ*, pp. 10, 11. For an analysis of Revelation 1:19, refer to chapter 4 of this book.

These two steps are at the core of any biblical exegesis. Step one is a prerequisite to step two. However, Stefanovic attempts to slightly bend these exegetical principles in order to accommodate or make historicism work.

<u>Text Divisional Issue</u>. In the section dealing with "How to interpret the book of Revelation," Stefanovic makes several statements to this effect:

1. First, based on 1:1 and 19 and 4:1, he divides Revelation into two sections—the "things which are [Rev. 1–3]" and the "things which are about to take place after this [Rev. 4–22]." Although Revelation 1–3 contains certain predictive elements, the core messages in this section were written to the original readers during John's time, addressing concerns and issues they faced. The prophetic elements contained in this section "were intended to help those congregations in their immediate situations." In essence, Revelation 1–3 consists primarily of "things which are."[13]
2. Revelation 4–22, however, may contain certain historical messages (from John's standpoint, chapters 4, 5, and 12), but the bulk of the messages were for the future. Stefanovic heavily uses the divine invitation of Revelation 4:1 ("Come up here, and I will show you what must take place after this") as evidence to support this division.

For various reasons, Stefanovic states:

> Christians of the time of John and the succeeding 200 years no doubt would have found contemporary relevance in the material of Revelation 4[:1]–22:5... However, no matter what the applications and relevance Christians of John's day and the succeeding century might have seen in the symbols of Revelation 4[:1]–22:5, it is essential that we discover John's intentions and purpose in recording the visions he saw, for he states clearly that they looked *beyond the first century* (cf. 4:1). It is essential for a

---

[13] Ibid., p. 15.

responsible interpretation of Revelation 4[:1]–22:5, particularly in view of the fact that the language of the book is often highly figurative, that we discover, first of all, *what John meant* in the text, and, then, what meaning the book might have conveyed to the readers to whom it was originally addressed... But to focus only and exclusively on how the *first-century Christians might have interpreted and applied the messages of Revelation 4–22:5 to their immediate situation would be clearly contrary to the intention and purpose of the inspired author.*[14] (emphasis supplied)

Stefanovic attempts to accomplish three things here. First, he affirms that the original readers may have "found contemporary relevance in the material of Revelation 4[:1]–22:5," but then suggests that what the original readers understood may not have been exactly synonymous with the author's (John's) "intention and purpose." Second, the material in Revelation 4:1–22:5 may have some relevance in the "time of John [first century] and the succeeding 200 years [through the third century]," but 4:1 clearly indicates they "looked beyond the first [or by implication, third] century." Third, he reiterates that exclusively focusing on how the "first-century Christians might have interpreted and applied the messages of Revelation 4[:1]–22:5 to their immediate situation [aimed at preterism] ... would be clearly contrary to the intention and purpose of the inspired author."

<u>Analysis of the Issue</u>. Stefanovic seems to be saying that 1) "what John [actually] meant" in Revelation 4:1–22:5 is different from "what the text meant to the original audience" and 2) because John was the "inspired author," he somehow understood that the messages of Revelation 4:1–22:5 were for the distant future (addressing those living beyond the third century). Therefore, any attempt to discover "what the text meant to the original audience" is contrary to the *actual* intent and purpose of the text and its author. This line of reasoning entails several problems.

---

[14] Ibid., pp. 14–16; Stefanovic, *Plain Language* (Berrien Springs, MI: Andrew University Press, 2013), p. 4; William G. Johnsson, "The Saint's End-Time Victory over the Forces of Evil," in *Symposium on Revelation—Book II*, p. 22.

Author's Intent Versus Audience's Interpretation. First, Stefanovic's attempt to differentiate between the "author's intent" and his "audience's interpretation" poses some real challenges. The text is clear that John, who wrote Revelation, was merely a penman.[15] The thoughts did not originate from or with him, for "prophecy never had its origin in the will of man" (2 Pet. 1:21). Paulien is correct when he states that Revelation's "contents came directly from God."[16] The apostle was basically told to "write," and write he did. However, to suggest that as an "inspired author," he had access to some type of privileged information cannot be supported textually. If John "wept" in Revelation 5 because there was none "worthy," was clueless when "one of the four elders" asked about the identity of those dressed in "white" (ch. 7), and reprimanded for being "astonished" at the prostitute (ch. 17), then these demonstrate that he was not privy to any additional information.[17] Furthermore, the "inspired" Bible authors wrote things that they themselves did not fully understand. Daniel, for instance, was as inspired as John was, but his writings do not reflect that he had access to privileged information. He continuously wrestled with the information he received in his own visions. He wrote, "I heard but I did not understand. So I asked, 'My lord, what will be the outcome of all these be?'" (Dan. 12:8). This is why Ellen G. White wrote, "Of the spiritual truths spoken by the [Old Testament] prophets [the disciples] had a clearer understanding than had the original writers themselves."[18]

Issues of Revelation 4:1. The second issue concerns the incorrect use of Revelation 4:1. The text does say that the prophecies of 4:1–22:5 are for the future. For Stefanovic, the future here does not begin until after AD 300. This conclusion is partly correct because the "future" in contention begins with John's future and ends with Jesus' return. In this sense,

---

[15] Stefanovic does acknowledge this. He actually provides a statement saying that by "author's purpose/intent" he is doing so for conveniences. See *Revelation of Jesus Christ*, p. 23.

[16] Jon Paulien, "Simply Revelation—A Beginner's Guide to the Most Challenging Book of the Bible—Part 1," p. 8. (All Paulien books or articles that do not have any publishing details are copies of the original manuscripts sold separately on his website).

[17] Therefore, it is better to assume that the author and his initial audience had a similar understanding of the prophecies of Revelation.

[18] Ellen G. White, *The Desire of Ages*, (Mountain View, CA: Pacific Press, 1898), p. 494.

it includes both the immediate and distant future. However, Stefanovic's push for a distant future—one that is beyond the third century—is not supported by the text. Understanding these issues, Paulien writes, "In applying a historicist approach to Revelation ... it is not necessary to claim that John himself, or any of the other writers of the New Testament, foresaw the enormous length of the Christian era, the time between the first and second advents of Jesus. If the Parousia had occurred in the first century, no one would have been troubled on account of any statement in the New Testament. The finality of the Christ event is such that looking beyond the first century was not conceivable, even for the apostles."[19] He then cautions; "It is not appropriate to force a text into the historicist mode if that was not the intention of the text. We must allow the characteristics and purposes of each text to emerge out of the text. Only then can we accurately determine whether the chapter has the marks of historical apocalyptic or not."[20]

<u>Historical Method Versus Principles of Exegesis</u>. Finally, while arguing for the historical method, Stefanovic asserts the following: "No matter what applications the Christians of John's time or later might have seen in Revelation, the fulfillment of the book's prophecies were reserved for the future from John's perspective."[21] If true exegesis attempts to investigate what the text meant to the original readers, then the tone and dismissive language here betray that principle.

<u>Summary</u>. These examples demonstrate a tension between proper exegesis and the historical method of interpretation. Jon Paulien acknowledges this tension when he writes that when proper "methods of exegesis, carefully carried out, yield a reasonably clear understanding of most NT books. But in Revelation they produce an unsatisfying result ... Thus, a

---

[19] Jon Paulien, "The End of Historicism? Reflections on the Adventist Approach to Biblical Apocalyptic—Part One," *Journal of the Adventist Theological Society* 11 (Fall 2003): pp 15–44.

[20] Paulien, "The End of Historicism? Reflections on the Adventist Approach to Biblical Apocalyptic—Part Two," *Journal of the Adventist Theological Society* 12 (Fall, 2006), 93, 94.

[21] Stefanovic, *Revelation of Jesus Christ*, p. 13. Many contemporary scholars hold and share the same view. See *Symposium on Revelation—Book I* and *Book II*. William G. Johnsson and other historicists hold a similar view. See "The Saint's End-time victory over the forces of Evil," in *Symposium on Revelation—Book II*, p. 10.

broader more theological method of exegesis is necessary to do justice to the Apocalypse."[22] Although historicism presents fewer problems than the other three methods do, these inconsistencies cast doubts on it. Paulien is blunt; "But if a historicist approach to Revelation is to have any validity, it must be demonstrated from the text, not assumed from long tradition."[23] Therefore, a proper exegesis of Revelation must take into account Paulien's counsel:

> But regardless of John's own perception of time, the question here is whether or not John saw the future in terms of a sequence of events or purely in the immediate terms typical of the OT Day of the Lord prophecies. Time has continued far past John's expectation. If John's Apocalypse is a genuine revelation the question becomes whether or not *God used the immediate intention of a human writer, who thought he was close to the End, to say anything substantive about the events that lay beyond his time.*[24] (emphasis supplied)

Comprehensibility of the Text

Even if it is unclear to us, it is safer to assume the entire messages and prophecies of Revelation were not only comprehensible, but also addressed the immediate issues of the first-century church.[25] This is because the nature of the text, the author's reaction to the visions, and the theological

---

[22] Jon Paulien, "Interpreting Revelation's Symbols," in *Symposium on Revelation—Book I*, p. 82.

[23] "The End of Historicism—Part One," p. 38.

[24] Jon Paulien, "The End of Historicism? Reflections on the Adventist Approach to Biblical Apocalyptic—Part One," *Journal of the Adventist Theological Society* 11 (Fall 2003): pp. 15–43. While discussing the relationship between the Jezebel of Revelation 2 and the 'false prophet' of Revelation 13 and 16, Kyle B. de Waal argues for a similar position. See, Kayle B. de Waal, "The Two Witnesses and the Land Beast in the Book of Revelation," *Andrews University Seminary Studies* 53, no 1 (Spr 2015), p. 166, 168.

[25] Jon Paulien is of the opinion that the first-century church did read and hear the prophecies of Revelation "with understanding," "Simply Revelation: A Beginner's Guide to the Most Challenging Book of the Bible—Part One," *A Seminar*, p. 3.

(particularly Christological) issues discussed in the book endorse such an understanding. Each of these three aspects is discussed as follows:

<u>Comprehensibility and Applicability of the Text</u>. Unlike 4:1, there are three passages that show that Revelation was comprehensible to the early church. First, the seven churches are warned, "do not seal up the words of this prophecy" (22:10). Further, a triple blessing is pronounced on those who "read, hear and keep" the words of this prophecy (1:3). Finally, "I, Jesus, have sent my angel to give you this testimony *for* the churches" (22:16, emphasis supplied). Undoubtedly, "the churches" referred to here must begin with the "seven [literal] churches" of Revelation 1–3 and note that the phrase "this testimony" refers to the entire book of Revelation. These evidences suggest that the initial readers could not only understand the materials, but even saw the book as primarily *for* them.

> *John's emotional reaction, whether he "wept," "fell," was "astonished," or "worshiped" during the visions of Revelation, demonstrates a high degree of comprehensibility on his part.*

If, for argument's sake, Revelation was only for those living centuries later, it would have been a futile exercise trying to read a document that had no relevance to them. He who told another prophet hundreds of years earlier to "Go your way, Daniel, because the words are closed up and sealed until the end of time" would have also said the same to John and his audience. However, He did not. He instead did the complete opposite when He urged them to read. Therefore, if we insist that the prophecies of Revelation 4:1–22:5 were not applicable to the first-century church, then the text itself would castigate us.

<u>Author's Emotional Engagement</u>. Nearly all the prophetic messages of Revelation 4:1–22:5 appear to be comprehensible to the author. Unlike Daniel (whose endless questions "frustrated" even the angelic guide), John did not ask even a single question. In most cases, it is either an elder or angel who typically asked a rhetorical question before supplying the

answer (see 5:2–5; 7:13–17). John's silence could mean that he either understood the visions or simply displayed dumbness.

However, John's emotional reaction, whether he "wept," "fell," was "astonished," or "worshiped" during the visions of Revelation, demonstrates a high degree of comprehensibility on his part (see 5:4; 7:14; 17:6–7; 19:10; 22:8, 9, 20). Conversely, only in two places is the reader asked to summon "wisdom," perhaps a tacit indication that the prophetic messages indeed spoke to John and his audience (see 13:18; 17:9).

Revelation as a Divine Response to the Struggles of the Early Church. Revelation was obviously not given in a vacuum. As we shall see later, the prophecies were given in response to the struggles, prayers, and issues the early church encountered.[26] Therefore, a valid approach to Revelation must take these contextual issues into consideration.

CRITERIA FOR A MODIFIED HISTORICISM (DUAL-INTENTIONALISM)

Criteria for Dual-Intentionalism

If the first readers saw most predictive prophecies as being fulfilled in their time, and the same prophecies can be applied to our time and beyond, perhaps they carry a *dual* application. They had immediate fulfillment in the first hundred years and then a much broader fulfillment throughout church history, today, and beyond.

1) <u>Dual Focus of Words, Concepts, and Characters</u>. This means the same languages, concepts, imageries, characters, dates, issues, and events *must* have two or more meanings. In chapters 10–12 of this book, we have documented and discussed all the key words and concepts that have either a dual definition or application. Chapters 10 and 11 discuss the "Word of God" and "Testimony of Jesus," respectively. Then in chapter 12, nearly all key terms, concepts, imageries, and characters from Revelation and

---

[26] Kenneth A. Strand, "Foundational Principles of Interpretation," in *Symposium on Revelation—Book I*, p. 13.

other Johannine books are discussed. As we shall see later, an analysis of these concepts and characters strongly suggests that the prophecies of Revelation could have a dual intent, a dual application, or a dual fulfillment, and the Johannine author seemed to be aware of this literary mechanism. However, for our purposes here, we use two problematic passages to illustrate this point:

1. "Their bodies will lie in the street of the great city, which is figuratively called Sodom and Egypt, where *also* their Lord was crucified" (Rev. 11:8, emphasis supplied). Note that the "great city" is figuratively called "Sodom and Egypt," but the phrase "where also their Lord was crucified" is literal. With that said, is the "great city" the same as "Babylon the Great"? Or is it Jerusalem?[27]
2. "The seven heads are seven hills on which the woman sits. They are *also* seven kings" (Rev. 17:9, 10, emphasis supplied). Which is it? Are the seven heads "seven hills" or "seven kings"? Or do they represent one and the same entity?[28]

The current approach to such complex passages is to see the entities in each of these passages as referring to a single concept, object, or character.

---

[27] The conjunction "also" indicates an additional or secondary identification of the "great city." Since the "Lord was crucified" in Jerusalem, one would conclude that the "great city" that is "figuratively called Sodom and Egypt" is Jerusalem as well. However, the problem arises when one considers the time of the two witnesses' death. The beast from the Abyss kills them "when they had finished their testimony." That would be any time after the "1,260 [prophetic] days" (Rev 11:7, 2, 3). For further discussion, refer to chapter 12 of this study.

[28] We include two more examples here: 1) "And I will give power to my two witnesses... These are two olive trees and the two lampstands that stand before the Lord of the earth" (Rev. 11:3, 4). Are the two witnesses "two olive trees" or "two lampstands"? Or do we treat them as referring to one and the same thing? Are they "Moses and Elijah" (Law and the Prophets/Old Testament Scriptures), Old and the New Testaments, or something else? 2) "He also forced everyone... to receive a mark... which is the name of the beast or the number of his name ... If anyone has insight, let him calculate the number of the beast, for it is man's number. His number is 666" (Rev. 13:16–18). Is the "mark" the "name of the beast" or "the number of his name"? Or is it both (the name and the number)?

Therefore, Stefanovic and others could argue that the "seven hills" and "seven kings" refer to one and the same thing (Rev. 17:9, 10). They also equate the "great city [Sodom and Egypt]" (11:8) to the "Babylon" of Revelation 17.[29] In this line of reasoning, the italicized conjunctions ("and," "also," "or") are seen as facilitating an equational relationship between the joined clauses. However, as discussed in chapter 12, such approaches are unnatural. This is because the types of conjunctions used (coordinate conjunctions) do not warrant an equational relationship.[30] Such texts favor a dual significance. In his book *7 Heads and 10 Horns in Daniel and the Revelation*, Edwin de Kock correctly points out that "[t]he heads have a dual application ..."[31] As we shall see later, the "great city" of Revelation 11 also has a dual application. If these passages are seen in the light of the materials discussed in chapter 12, then most of the exegetical issues could be minimized.

2) <u>Immediate, Distant, and Dual Application of Prophecies</u>. However, certain prophetic elements that were specific to their time may not have any bearing on our time. Conversely, the opposite can also be true. That is, other elements of the prophecies may not have had immediate application in John's time but are relevant to our time. To illustrate this point, let us consider the prophecies of Matthew 24:

---

[29] See the discussions on Stefanovic, *The Revelation of Jesus Christ*, pp. 354, 355, 524, 525.

[30] In other words, the place where "their Lord was crucified" and the "seven kings" are not dependent clauses. They are independent clauses held together by the conjunctions. For more discussion on this, see Daniel B. Wallace, *The Basics of New Testament Syntax* (Grand Rapids, MI: Zondervan, 2000), pp. 293, 294.

[31] Unlike Stefanovic and others, Edwin de Kock thinks that the "seven hills" represent Rome in John's time, and the "seven kings" represent past, current, and future political powers. See *7 Heads and 10 Horns in Daniel and the Revelation* (Edinburg, TX: Edwin de Kock, 2012), pp. 37, 83, 84. Kayle de Waal not only sees a relationship between the "Jezebel" and the "false prophet" of Revelation 13 and 16, but he also favors a dual application of the same. He writes; "The symbol of Jezebel in particular functions as the local embodiment of false prophecy just as the symbol of the land beast functions as a false prophet in an eschatological sense. The notion of a false prophet therefore has both a local and eschatological setting with John ingeniously causing the local or historical to impact and influence the eschatological." See, Kayle de Waal, p.166.

Immediate Future	**Distant Future**	Single/Dual application
Destruction of temple (v. 2)	–	Single
False prophets (4–5, 11, 24, 25)	False prophets (4–5, 11, 24, 25)	Dual
Wars (6–8)	Wars (6–8)	Dual
"famines and earthquakes" (7)	"famines and earthquakes" (7)	Dual
Persecution (9, 10)	Persecution (9, 10)	Dual
"gospel as a testimony to all nations and then the end will come" (14)	"gospel as a testimony to all nations and then the end will come" (14)	Dual
"great distress"	"great distress" (great tribulation)	Dual
–	"sun will be darkened, and the moon will not give light and the stars will fall from the sky" (29)	Dual
"pray that your flight will not take place in winter or on the Sabbath" (20)	–	Early church

At the time Jesus uttered the words of Matthew 24, they were mostly predictive in nature. However, for these prophecies to be properly understood, one must decide which of these prophecies fall into any of the following categories: a) prophecies that were fulfilled in the first century only, b) the ones that were fulfilled throughout church history and the "last days" only, and c) the ones that have a *dual* application and apply to both periods. Concerning the signs of Matthew 24, Ekkehardt Mueller writes, "These signs were fulfilled before the destruction of Jerusalem." Then in a "secondary sense," he continues, "the signs mentioned above also apply to the time before Christ's second coming." Mueller agrees that most of the signs of Matthew 24 served a dual purpose. He says Jesus answered a "double question" "simultaneously without informing them [His audience] that the two events [destruction of Jerusalem and the second coming of Jesus] were not directly connected."[32] The same maybe

---

[32] Ekkehardt Mueller, "Signs of the Times," *Biblical Research Institute of the General Conference of Seventh-day Adventists* 1. (April, 2006), p. 1. C. Mervyn Maxwell is also of the same opinion (see *God Cares: The Message of Revelation for You and Your Family*, vol. 2, p. 19).

true for certain aspects of Revelation. Therefore, first having a mental awareness of this fact and then identifying such passages is crucial for a proper interpretation of the prophecies.[33]

3) <u>Fulfilled, Contemporaneous, and Yet-to-be-fulfilled Prophecies</u>. The third criterion is to determine if the fulfillment of certain prophecies was contemporaneous. In other words, at the time Christ spoke them, these events were still in the future, but one wonders if some of these prophecies had or were being fulfilled at the time the apostles began to write them down. The "false prophets," according to Matthew and John, will be used here to illustrate this point:

Matthew 24	1 John 2
"Many false prophets will appear and deceive many people. ... For false christs and false prophets will appear and perform great signs and miracles to deceive. *See, I have told you ahead of time*" (vss. 11, 24, 25, *emphasis supplied*).	"Dear children, this is the last hour; and as you have heard that the antichrist [false prophets, lairs] is coming, *even now many antichrists have come*" (vv. 18, *emphasis supplied*; see also 19–27; 4:1–3; 2 John 7–11).

Matthew simply stated the prophetic words that Christ had uttered during His earthly ministry. He said that Christ had told His disciples "ahead of time" about the false prophets, but John clearly taught that "even now many antichrist [false prophets] have [already] come." Therefore, what was initially a prophecy told merely "ahead of time" was being fulfilled when John wrote his letters. This is an important key toward unlocking some of the most difficult parts of the prophecies in Revelation. This principle will help us determine exactly where the first readers saw themselves.[34] Kenneth A. Strand writes, "All system of interpreting

---

[33] For example, consider Acts 2:16–21. To explain the Pentecost, Peter quoted Joel 2:28–32. Although the entire passage is included, the part that was fulfilled (at least at Pentecost) was Acts 2:16–18. The latter half found its fulfillment centuries later. However, both are given as if they were to be fulfilled at the same time. This does not mean that the Pentecost experience cannot occur today. The outpouring of the Spirit of God can occur in a more powerful way in our time.

[34] Especially in the series of seven seals, trumpets, etc., we must determine in which era John and his audience saw themselves.

Revelation must begin by locating its several segments in the past, present or future timeframes."[35]

We will use another example from Revelation to illustrate this criterion. Concerning the meaning of the "seven heads" of the beast of chapter 17, the text reads, "They are also seven kings. Five have fallen, one is, the other has not yet come" (v. 10). When interpreting this, most scholars agree that the timing and identity of these kings must begin with the "one is" or the sixth head. "The sixth head seems ... to refer to John's time, that is, the first century A.D."[36] This means that the fallen five consist of John's past, the sixth is the current power from his standpoint, and the seventh king is still in his future.

This interpretation is reasonable, and nearly all historicists subscribe to it. However, the question that demands an answer is, Can we apply the same principle when interpreting the seven seals and seven trumpets? How many of those seals/trumpets were in John's past, which one was his "one is," and which ones were still in his future? If the prophecies of Revelation were relevant and applicable to John and his audience—and they were—then these questions must be answered.[37]

4) <u>OT and NT Contextual Issues</u>. Of all NT books, Revelation is infused with OT sights, sounds, echoes, allusions, themes, and characters. Because of this, scholars have done the responsible thing by allowing the OT to shed light on the prophecies of Revelation.[38] However, this may have an

---

[35] Kenneth A. Strand, "Foundational Principles of Interpretation," *Symposium on Revelation—Book I*, p. 3. Although Strand talks about the later fulfillment, he is referring to *our* time—past, present, and future—not the early church's. That will help us locate where they were as far as the prophecies were concerned.

[36] Ekkehardt Mueller, "The Beast of Revelation 17—A Suggestion," *Biblical Research Institute* 7 (https://1ref.us/10h, accessed February 13, 2020). See Stefanovic, *Revelation of Jesus Christ*, p. 525; *Plain Revelation*, p. 209.

[37] God willing, these questions can be fully explored in another project. However, this writer is of the opinion that the first through fourth seals consisted of John's past, the fifth seal was his "one is," and the sixth and seventh seals were in his future. It's the same with the trumpets.

[38] Scholars agree that the Old Testament is indispensable for a proper interpretation of the book of Revelation. See for example, G. K. Beale, "John's Use of the Old Testament," *JSOTSup* 166 (Sheffield, UK: Sheffield Academic Press, 1998). Stefanovic, *Revelation of Jesus Christ*, pp. 18–19. John Paulien, *What the Bible Says About the End-Time*. (Hagerstown, MD: Review and Herald, 1994), p. 135. Kayle B.

unintended side effect. Because of the volume of OT material in Revelation, scholars tend to dwell heavily on the OT to help interpret the prophecies of Revelation, but at the expense of the immediate NT writings and context.

Importance of the Immediate Context. The NT, especially the writings of John, must provide the context, set the boundaries, define the issues, and identify the opponents of Revelation before we go to the OT. In other words, one must resist the urge to jump from an obscure passage in Revelation to an identical one in the OT. Stefanovic says that in "order to unlock the symbols of Revelation, the reader today must search for the most appropriate Old Testament background."[39] Since Revelation was born in the cradle of the NT context and issues, the same must also guide the interpretation. The interpretation of the OT imageries and allusions in the prophecies of Revelation must always be done through the prism of the known NT text and history. The neglect of this has given birth to most exegetical and interpretive issues today. We shall use the vision of Revelation 4 and 5 as an example to illustrate this point.

> *One must resist the urge to jump from an obscure passage in Revelation to an identical one in the OT. Since Revelation was born in the cradle of the NT context and issues, the same must also guide the interpretation.*

Enthronement or Judgment (an example). The scholars are divided over the interpretation of Revelation 4 and 5. Some see the "open door," "throne," "him who sat on it," the scroll in His right hand, the setting, and those in attendance and conclude this vision as the enthronement of Jesus Christ in AD 31,[40] while others see the same and conclude that the vision

---

de Waal is of the same opinion too. "The Two Witnesses and the Land Beast in the Book of Revelation," *Andrews University Seminary Studies* 53, no 1 (Spr 2015). See *Revelation of Jesus Christ*, p. 19.

[39] See *Revelation of Jesus Christ*, p. 19.

[40] See Jon Paulien, "Seals and Trumpets: Some Current Discussions." *Symposium on Revelation—Book I*, pp. 186, 187; "The Role of the Hebrew Cultus, Sanctuary, and Temple in the Plot and Structure of Revelation," (although this was published in AUSS, I used a copy of the original manuscript),

is about the end-time judgment that began in AD 1844.[41] Which view is the correct one? Traditionally, the church subscribed to the judgment theory, but more recently the enthronement view has attracted a significant following.

Alberto Treiyer, a proponent of the judgment view, writes concerning the enthronement theory. This proposition "is primarily based not on what John really saw, but on what the author ... presupposes John to have seen."[42] In other words, he says that we allow the OT "kingly background" to basically supply the investiture, crowning, and sitting at the right hand of Christ—all of which do not take place in Revelation 5.[43] Treiyer's assessment is correct because what we know from the OT background is superimposed on Revelation 5.

Treiyer then does an elaborate work to show that Revelation 4 and 5 discuss the final court and judgment. He heavily uses the writings of Ellen White and the OT text to support his view. Although he uses Revelation, he does so loosely and broadly. In other words, just like the enthronement theory, the judgment theory is not based on a proper exegesis of Revelation 4 and 5.[44] Therefore, Stefanovic is correct when he says that "nothing in the text indicates that Revelation 4–5 is a judgment scene."[45] The core issue with both of these approaches is that they neglect the immediate NT context.[46] No serious effort is made to understand the text from the early church's viewpoint. Sadly, we assume the text was written exclusively for and to us. This is the common problem shared by the proponents of both views.[47]

---

pp. 9–14; Stefanovic, *Revelation of Jesus Christ*, pp. 163–215; *Plain Revelation*, pp. 56–76; Ekkehardt Mueller, "Jesus and His Second Coming," *Journal of the Adventist Theological Society* 11/12 (200?), p. 206.

[41] Alberto R. Treiyer, *The final Crisis in Revelation 4–5* (Santo Domingo: Biblical Projections, 1998).
[42] Ibid., p. 220.
[43] Ibid., p. 224.
[44] Ibid.
[45] Stefanovic, *Revelation of Jesus Christ*, p. 168.
[46] On the proper use of E. G. White for Revelation 4–6, see Jon Paulien, "Ellen G. White and Revelation 4–6," *Symposium on Revelation—Book I*, pp. 363–373.
[47] It is not our intention to develop the significance of Revelation 4 and 5 now. We merely employ this to illustrate the exegetical issues into which we run when we ignore the immediate NT context of

The Dangers to Avoid. By the very act of labeling this event as "enthronement" or "judgment," readers have just imposed their own opinions on the text. The crucial questions, however, should be, What did Revelation 4 and 5 mean to John and his audience? How did these chapters speak hope and courage to a fledgling church in the first century? Or did they speak to the early church at all? If John wept when there was none worthy to receive the scroll and fell on his knees in adoration to the Lamb after He took the scroll, then he must have fully understood the implications of the events in Revelation 4 and 5. Therefore, it is necessary for us to investigate these contextual issues, but if we insist that the text is discussing coronation or judgment, then we must also show that either of them was a controversial issue in the first-century church.[48]

Priority of the Immediate NT Context. It is for this reason that our current study on Revelation 1–3 will be placed where it belongs—in the NT context. As much as practical, we will allow Revelation 4–22, the three epistles of John, and his Gospel to help us interpret Revelation 1–3. Hebrews, Acts, and the rest of the NT books will provide the general context for our study. If we have to consult the OT—and we must—then that should be dictated by the findings of the immediate NT contexts, not the other way around.

Perhaps Jesus had this principle in mind when He said, "Therefore every teacher of the law who has been instructed about the kingdom of heaven is like the owner of a house who brings out of his storeroom new treasures as well as old" (Matt. 13:52).[49] Therefore, the "new" and "old"

Revelation. Hopefully in a future project, we can explore Revelation 4 and 5. At this stage, however, refer to some contextual issues scattered in this volume. See especially the nature of the Holy Spirit in chapter 8 and the summary of Christ's titles in chapter 23 (the specific contextual information is in a footnote under a paragraph entitled "Jesus and the Courtroom").

[48] Otherwise, this theological slugfest over many parts of Revelation will continue, unless we decide to ask the fundamental question: What did the text—in this case, Revelation 5—really mean to John and his audience? If we neglect this important exegetical question, then any winds of doctrine that come our way will sweep us either back to the past (AD 31, 1844) or into the future.

[49] The "teacher of the law" in this context is the disciples. Earlier in the chapter (vv. 11, 12), Christ said to the same disciples, "The knowledge of the secret of the kingdom of heaven has been given to you, but not to them."

that John brings out in Revelation must be first read within the context of the NT settings. However, attempting to interpret Revelation through the OT context alone is like a merchant trying to "pour new wine into the old wineskins" (Matt. 9:17).

Comparative Analysis of Dual-Intentionalism, Preterism, and Historicism

<u>Comparative Analysis of Preterism, Historicism, and the Dual-Intentionalism</u>. The double-focused method of interpretation or dual-intentionalsim attempts to combine preterism and historicism and concurs with preterism in that all the prophecies of Revelation were comprehensible by and applicable to those living in the first century. However, unlike preterism, dualism also sees the same prophecies as having relevance to those living beyond AD 100. In this sense, it is similar to historicism.

Nevertheless, historicism isolates Revelation 1–3 as having relevance to the first century saints, whereas the rest of Revelation contains predictive elements for a later time. The dualistic method differs with historicism in a number of ways: 1) Both Revelation 1–3 and 4–22 had an immediate, more literal, and local application to the early church and also has a more distant, broader, and global application; 2) Revelation 1–3 and 4–22 contain exactly the same message and speak to both the "local" and "global" churches. However, their differences lie in the genre, form, and style of the text. Revelation 1–3 is epistolary in nature and heavily features direct approach in which the Orator is actively speaking *to* His subjects. Revelation 4–22 is apocalyptic in form and features a less direct approach. As we shall see, the linguistic, visual, conceptual, theological, and Christological relationships between these two sections is overwhelming.[50] The following table compares and contrasts the three methods of interpretation:

---

[50] Examples of these are presented in this study, especially in the messages to the seven churches (See chapters 15–24). The type of relationship between Revelation 1–3 and 4–22 is similar to John's three epistles and Gospel. Paki, George. *The Structural and Thematic Analysis of 1 John*, Study Notes.

Methodology	Predictive Part	Comprehensibility/ Applicability	Nature of Prophecy
Preterism	Revelation 1–22	First century only	Past, historical
Historicism	Revelation 4–22	First century – second coming	Progressive, linear
Dual-Intentionalism	Revelation 1–22	First century + history – second coming	Dualistic [immediate, local + distance, global]

Comparative Analysis of Classical and Apocalyptic Prophecies

The OT prophecies of Ezekiel, Isaiah, Amos, and others are described as "classical" or "general" prophecies, while the prophecies of Daniel and Revelation are classified as "apocalyptic" prophecies. Jon Paulien enlists a total of six differences between these two types of prophecies:

1. General prophecies are mostly conditional in nature, while the apocalyptic prophecies are not.
2. General prophecies feature a mixture of present and end-time events, while apocalyptic prophecies present a series of historical events leading up to and culminating with the end-time judgment.
3. The focus of general prophecy is on the immediate time and context, while the focus of apocalyptic prophecy is on the distant, broader, and global context.
4. Certain aspects of general prophecies can have "dual fulfillment," while apocalyptic prophecies have a "single fulfillment."
5. General prophecies mostly feature a "short-range view," while apocalyptic prophecies mainly feature a "long-range view."
6. General prophecies view the local situation, while apocalyptic prophecies view the "whole span of history."

How do general and apocalyptic prophecies relate to the dualistic method as espoused in this thesis? Dual-intentioalism combines tendencies of both types of prophecies. Revelation's focus is both immediate and distant, and as we shall see later, most of the prophecies have dual fulfillment. The prophecies of Revelation feature both a "short-range view" and "long-range view," but all these prophecies are not conditional. Revelation does address the local context, but the very same prophetic materials speak to the wider context. Therefore, with the exception of the conditional aspect (which heavily characterizes general prophecies), the rest of the characteristics of both general and apocalyptic prophecies apply to the prophecies of Revelation. The following table summarizes these discussions:

Aspect	Classical	Apocalyptic	Dual-intentionalism
Focus	Immediate	Distant	Both
Range	Short-range view	Long-range view	Both
Conditionality	Conditional	Unconditional	Unconditional
Context	Local context	Wider context	Both
Time	Present + Immediate Future	History + Present + Future	Both
Fulfillment	Some dual	Mostly single	Mostly dual

One may object to this theory in that such a method is foreign to biblical prophetic norms and traditions, especially in that this dual-focused prophecy cannot be corroborated with the types of prophecies as recorded in the biblical data. While this objection is valid, it is wrong to assume that God cannot work outside of *established* methods of communication. He who used general and apocalyptic methods to communicate prophecies in the past is not bound by those methods. He could easily use another method or a combination of them to communicate to the final generation. Further, instead of trying to fit the prophecies of Revelation into a known mold, we should do well to let the text lead us to the kind of mold in which it fits. In other words, one should avoid trying to force "new wine into the old wineskins."

DUAL-INTENTIONALISM AND CONCLUSION

Representation of Dual-Intentionalism

The following diagram shows the dual-focused method of interpretation:

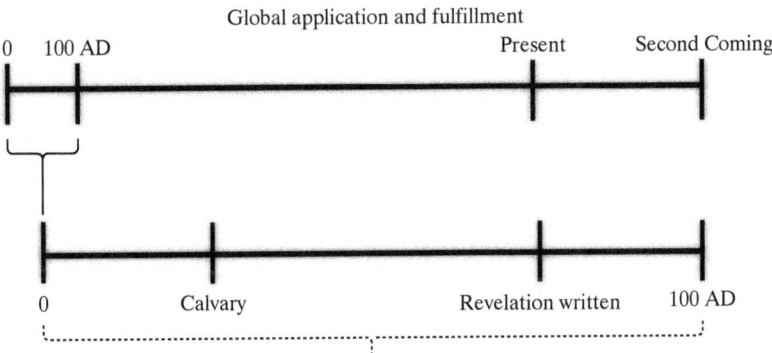

Conclusion

This representation captures the essence of what Jon Paulien says: "Time has continued far past John's expectation. If John's Apocalypse is a genuine revelation the question becomes whether or not God used the immediate intention of a human writer, who thought he was close to the End, to say anything substantive about the events that lay beyond his time."[51] The dual-focused or modified historical method, therefore, assumes that the prophetic messages of Revelation spoke to both the early church and the churches thereafter.[52] The predictive elements in Revelation, therefore, serve a dual purpose.

---

[51] Jon Paulien, "The End of Historicism? Reflections on the Adventist Approach to Biblical Apocalyptic—Part One," *Journal of the Adventist Theological Society* 11 (Fall 2003): pp. 15–43.

[52] Daniel Wysong and Steve Case, *Finding Jesus in the Book of Revelation* (Carmichael, CA: Involve Youth, 2014), p. 21. In this book, Case and Wysong briefly discuss the four "traditional methods of interpretation" but refuse to subscribe to any of them. The reason they offer is that the same prophecies that spoke to John and his audience still speak to our times. Although they do not offer an alternative method of interpretation, their "free" spirit can find expression in the dualistic method as discussed in this study.

2.

THE AUTHORSHIP OF THE JOHANNINE BOOKS

JOHANNINE BOOKS

An elaborate introduction at this stage is necessary for what will follow next. This is because if the John who wrote Revelation is the same person behind the three letters and Gospel, then it is important that we consider all books together in order to obtain a richer glimpse of the author and the Jesus whom he presents.[53]

Introduction

Revelation, the three letters of John, and his Gospel are referred to as the "Johannine Corpus." The scholarly world contains a myriad of theories concerning the origin, authenticity, authorship, and sequence in which these books were written.[54] It is not the intention of this writer to argue for or against these theories, but to allow the internal evidences mined from these pages to guide us toward a conclusion. The sole purpose

---

[53] In this study, several names and designations will be used for each of the Johannine books. "Revelation" and "Apocalypse" will be used interchangeably to refer to the last book in the NT. The Gospel of John will be also called "the fourth Gospel," "the Gospel," and sometimes "Gospel John." Similarly, the epistles of John will be called "epistles," "letters," "letters of John," and "epistles of John."

[54] Regardless of these ongoing debates, the majority of Bible students are attracted to these books because of the manner in which Jesus is presented in them.

of this work is to allow these books to paint a picture of "One like the Son of Man" so that "we may see Him as He [really] is" (Rev 1:13; 1 John 3:2). Before journeying into the events of the Apocalypse, we will address three pertinent issues.

The Book of Hebrews

The first concerns the authorship of Hebrews. Most scholars hold that the apostle Paul, Luke, Apollos, or someone else authored this book.[55] The evidences supporting this view (especially Pauline authorship) are brief but crucial. For example, this epistle mentions "Timothy" and "Italy" (Heb. 13:22, 23). Timothy was a core member of the Pauline team, and there is sufficient evidence that Paul either visited or wrote from Rome. Additionally, the author seems to imply that he was not an eyewitness of Jesus (Heb. 2:3). These evidences support *non-disciplic* authorship. However, the overwhelming number of similarities that exists between Hebrews and the Johannine books challenges this and other competing interpretations.[56] Therefore, a case exists for Johannine authorship of

---

[55] For Pauline authorship see; Black, David Alan. "On the Pauline Authorship of Hebrews (Part 1): Overlooked Affinities between Hebrews and Paul." *Faith and Mission* 16, no. 2 (Spr 1999): 32–51. Black, David Alan. "On the Pauline Authorship of Hebrews (Part 2): The External Evidence Reconsidered." *Faith and Mission* 16, no. 3 (Sum 1999): 78–86. For Lukan authorship, see; "The Authorship of Hebrews: The Lukan Proposal." *Faith and Mission* 18, no. 2 (Spr 2001): 27–40. And for Apollos, Priscilla, Barnabas or others refer to; Torrey, Charles Cutler. "The Authorship and Character of the So-Called 'Epistle to the Hebrews.'" *Journal of Biblical Literature* 30, no. 2 (1911): 137–56.

[56] Several scholars have carried out linguistic and stylistic analysis to determine the Hebraic authorship. For example, David L. Allen lists a series of linguistic/stylistic similarities between Luke-Acts and Hebrews and concludes Lukan authorship of Hebrews. He writes; "The cumulative effect of these lexical and stylistic similarities serves as a forceful argument in favor of Lukan authorship of Hebrews," p. 32. See, Allen, David Lewis. "The Authorship of Hebrews: The Lukan Proposal." *Faith and Mission* 18, no. 2 (Spr 2001): 27–40. David A. Black, however, does the same with Pauline letters and Hebrews and finds even greater number of similar words, styles and concepts and concludes Paul as the author. See; Black, David Alan. "On the Pauline Authorship of Hebrews (Part 1): Overlooked Affinities between Hebrews and Paul." *Faith and Mission* 16, no. 2

Hebrews. Theologically—or more specifically, Christologically—Hebrews is much closer to the Johannine books than the Pauline epistles.[57] The semantics, styles, imagery, themes, and even the entire structure of Hebrews closely resemble the NT books that bears John's name. These evidences will be explored later.[58]

Order

The second concern is related to the reasons for discussing the Apocalypse first. This is done for two reasons. First, it has the authorial details (name, location, and circumstances) and the recipients' geographical and topographical information. Second, sufficient internal evidence suggests the Apocalypse was the first of the Johannine books (including Hebrews). A separate section will discuss the chronology of these writings.

(Spr 1999): 32–51. Similarly, Frederic Gardiner does a comparative word count between Paul, Luke, John and others and endorses Paul as the author. See; Gardiner, Frederic. "The Language of the Epistle to the Hebrews as Bearing upon Its Authorship." *Journal of the Society of Biblical Literature and Exegesis, Including the Papers Read and Abstract of Proceedings For 7*, no. 1 (June 1887): 1–27. These samples of scholarly investigation shows that most of the internal evidences used are either linguistic or stylistic in nature. There is no strong theological, thematic and structural argument in favor of either Lukan or Pauline authorship. This explains why other scholars have even proposed Barnabas, Apollos, Timothy, and others as possible contenders for this authorship issue.

[57] For a thorough discussion on this refer to chapters 13–14 and 19–20 of this book. There, this author proposes that the Christology developed in chapters 13–14 is advanced in chapter 20. In this scheme, Hebrews reinforces the arguments John made in his earlier works; especially Revelation and Gospel of John.

[58] The similarities that exist between the Johannine books and Hebrews will be highlighted in the discussion of the main text. However, for a discussion on Christ's superiority, see chapters 20 and 21. For a discussion on the structure, see George Paki, *The Textual and Structural Analysis of 1 John*, Study Notes.

Assumptions

For a wide variety of reasons, this author assumes the following:

Aspects	Adopted Assumptions
Author	John Zebedee, the youngest of the twelve apostles, wrote all of these books, including Hebrews. There was no further "editorial" work done by an extra hand either during his time or at a later date.
Order Written	Revelation was written first. This was followed by the three epistles (1–3 John), then the Gospel of John, and finally Hebrews.
Issues and Addressees	Generally, the Johannine books (including Revelation) address the same issues (Judaism) as do the Synoptic Gospels, Acts, and Pauline epistles. Revelation was addressed to the "seven churches in the province of Asia," whereas the epistles and Gospel of John were written to one of the seven churches, addressing a particular issue (or two) that threatened that church.[59] Hebrews was the final book written to another faith community of a more Jewish composition.
Textual Inter-dependence	The Gospel of John also plays a complementary role to the Apocalypse. That is, the Gospel attempts to address specific issues that may have risen from the Apocalypse. Of particular interest is John 4 and 16:16–33 (these will be discussed later).

This author's failure to prove these claims (at least at this stage) will justifiably invite righteous indignation from scholars and students of the Bible. However, the discussion on the contents of the books will hopefully aid in reinforcing and substantiating the stated assumptions. Having said that, we will briefly discuss the authorship, sequence, and other relationships these books share.

AUTHORSHIP

To avoid duplication of material, we offer a comparative discussion of all Johannine books (including Hebrews). The author of the Apocalypse

---

[59] See Daniel R. Streett, They Went Out from Us: *The Identify of the Opponents in First John* (Ann Arbor, MI: UMI Dissertation Publishing, 2008), pp. xi–xii. Daniel Streett argues that the Gospel and letters of John addressed Jewish apostasy. This writer agrees that the two books addressed the same issues/audience, but the audience was not totally of Jewish descent. This is because the writings are infused with geographical and ceremonial information. If the audience were mostly of Jewish descent, such background information would not have been necessary.

identified himself as John (1:1, 9). Whoever this John may have been, certain internal evidence suggests that he was an apostolic figure in the early church.

Apostle John as the Author

<u>John, the addressees, NT church, and Apostle Paul</u>. The author identified himself in this way: "I, John your brother and companion" (Rev. 1:9). Apart from his name and the nature of his relationship with his audience, he also provided the time, location, and circumstances in which "the words of this prophecy" were written (v. 3). The author's brotherhood and companionship were not with an individual or a family, but with the "seven churches [Ephesus, Smyrna, Pergamum, Thyatira, Sardis, Philadelphia, and Laodicea] in the province of Asia." If the author saw himself as a brother and companion to several churches in a large territory, he may have been a well-known figure and someone as apostolic as Paul was, especially since Paul acknowledged what Jew and Gentile churches knew to be an irrefutable fact—that the apostle John was one of the "pillars" of the church (Gal. 2:9).

> *If the author saw himself as a brother and companion to several churches in a large territory, he may have been a well-known figure and someone as apostolic as Paul was, especially since Paul acknowledged what Jew and Gentile churches knew to be an irrefutable fact—that the apostle John was one of the "pillars" of the church*

<u>The Author's Name, Titles, and Office</u>. To the seven churches, the author (John) saw himself as a "brother" and "companion" (Rev. 1:4). However, in relation to heaven, he described himself as a "servant" of Jesus Christ (vv. 1, 2). How did heaven view him? The angel of Revelation 19:10 addressed John as his "fellow servant." The same angel also referred to him as a prophet in the likeness of Daniel and others (see also 1:1; 6:11). Regardless of the angle from which he was viewed, John

was a "brother," "companion," "servant," "fellow servant," an "elder," "prophet," and a reputable "pillar" in the NT church.

<u>The Author and Martyrs of Revelation 6:9–11</u>. Revelation 6:11 adds a different dimension to this. In response to the "how long" cry of verse 10, a heavenly voice is heard saying, "they [those who were slain] were told to wait a little longer, until the number of their fellow servants and brothers who were to be killed, as they had been was completed." This does not state that *all* believers were to be killed. However, it specifically refers to a certain "number" of "servants and brothers," most of whom (by the time the author wrote Revelation) had died for their faith. And those remaining would soon die in order to make the number "complete." Two factors suggest that this number of servants and brothers could refer specifically to the twelve disciples.

First, it is true that most of the surviving addressees may have identified themselves with the "servants and brothers" of Revelation 6:9–11. However, as indicated, the divine voice seems to have a specific group in mind. The similarity in language between "the fellow servants and brothers" in 6:9–11 with that of 19:10 serves to narrow the identity of those "yet to be killed." In 19:10, John was referred to as a "fellow servant" to the angel and a "brother" to "the prophets." This raises the question as to whether those already slain consisted predominantly of John's "fellow servants [and] brothers"—the martyred apostles. If this has any merit, then he could be numbered among those who must die.[60]

Second, there are sufficient examples in the NT text that seem to endorse this rendering. We cite two examples here: 1) With the urging of Peter, the early church appointed Mathias to replace Judas. Concerning this event, the text says that Judas "was one of our *number* and shared in this ministry." However, after his death, Mathias "was added to the eleven apostles" in order to make the number complete again (Acts 1:17, 26, emphasis supplied); 2) Concerning Nicodemus' membership to the Sanhedrin Council, John wrote, "Nicodemus, who had gone to Jesus

---

[60] Refer to chapter 12 for more discussion on the two types of "brothers and servants" in Revelation.

earlier and who was one of their own number ..." (John 7:50; see also Acts 20:30).

The linguistic and conceptual similarities here seem to validate the existence of a specific number of servants and brothers of which John was one—and would die soon. As if to reinforce the same, the divine Voice is again heard saying, "Write, Blessed are the dead who die in the Lord from now on" (Rev. 14:13). This is like John writing his own obituary! Why, then, is this important to our discussion on the authorship of Revelation?

<u>Apocalyptic Author, Synoptic Gospels, and the Fourth Gospel</u>. The disclaimer of John 21:20–24 in this context makes absolute sense. In response to Peter's query concerning John, Jesus had replied, "If I want him to remain alive until I return, what is that to you?" John admitted, "Because of this, the rumor [*logos*] spread among the brothers that this disciple [John] would not die." Note that this rumor was not spread by a few fanatics in the early church, but treated as the *logos* and proclaimed by the apostles, beginning with Peter. Perhaps John himself may have also believed the same. However, when the Voice declared that the number must be completed, John understood that he would die.[61] Therefore, when he penned his Gospel afterward, John corrected his error, stating, "Jesus did not say that he [John] would not die; he only said 'If I want him to remain alive until I return, what is that to you?'"[62]

<u>The Author and the Epistles of John</u>. In the epistles, the author simply identified himself as "the elder" (2 John 1; 3 John 1), a clear reference to his seniority, position, or both. This is reinforced by the fact that "the elder" called his audience "my [little] children" throughout the epistles

---

[61] Jon Paulien, however, thinks that the same is an indication of a later edition by an editor. He is of the opinion that this happened after John's death. See "The Rhetorical Purpose of the Fourth Gospel," *Chicago Society for Biblical Research*, April 21, 1990, at Trinity Evangelical Divinity School, Deerfield, IL., pp. 8, 9.

[62] Matthew does not name names, but perhaps he had John in mind when he wrote that "some who are standing here will not taste death before they see the Son of Man coming in his kingdom" (Matt. 16:28). This may have been a reference to the "transfiguration" of chapter 17, but it is possible that the apostles may have also seen this in light of John 21.

(1 John 2:1; 2:18; 3:7, 18). However, in both 1 John and the Gospel of John, the author did not include his name, title, identity of his audience, or even salutations, which raises the question, If the apocalyptic John also authored the epistles and Gospel, why did he not simply say "John"? Why was "the elder" used in 2 and 3 John and not in 1 John and the Gospel? As is evidenced, the book of Hebrews is similar to 1 John and the Gospel in that it lacks any information about the author, recipients, and introductory salutations, which is uncharacteristic of Paul. However, the threads that bind these books together and to the Apocalypse (and thus to the apostle John) is much stronger than the absence of a name or a title.

The Author and His Literary Masterpiece

As far as the person and number are concerned, three aspects will be discussed.

The Author Switching Between First and Second Person. In Revelation, the author identified himself as "John." Whenever he inserted himself in the book, he did so in the first person singular. For instance, "I, John," "I was in the Spirit on the Lord's day," "I wept," "I saw … I marveled," "I fell down to worship him," etc. (1:9, 12, 17; 4:1; 5:1–6). He also employed the third person singular when writing about himself. For instance, "he [Jesus] made it known by sending his angel to *his servant John*; who testifies to everything he saw" (1:1, 2, emphasis added). The epistles and Gospel use the same literary feature (moving from "I-John" to "he-John"). In 1 John, for instance, the author used the first person plural ("we have seen," "our hands have touched," "we declare to you"). Then in the body of the letter, the author reverted to the first person singular ["my little children, I write these things to you," (1 John 2:1; 2:12–14, 15; 2–3 John)]. In the Gospel of John, the author moved from the first person plural ["dwelt among us, and we beheld his glory" (John 1:14)] to the third person singular ["the disciple whom He loved" (19:26–27; 21:7); "the other disciple whom Jesus loved" (20:2)].

<u>The Author Moving from First Person Plural to Second Singular</u>. The author went a step further and identified himself with his audience in the first person plural (we), then wrote about himself in third person singular. For instance, "This is the disciple who testifies to these thing … and we know that his testimony is true" (21:24). A similar construction exists in 3 John 12: "Demetrius has a good testimony from all … And we also bear witness, and you know that our testimony is true," although he moved from the first person plural to the first person singular.

<u>From Third Person Singular to Exclusion</u>. If the same author is behind all of these books, then a deliberate progression—all aimed at the author trying to make himself less apparent—is emerging in the discourses. In Revelation, where the author identified himself as "John," he consistently used the first person singular. Then in the two smaller letters, the author substituted a title ("the elder") for his name before using the first person singular. However, in the larger epistle, the author omitted all introductory salutations, including his identity, "John" and "elder." This style continues in the Gospel of John (and Hebrews). However, on most occasions, he referenced himself in the third person singular. If this is true, and John also authored Hebrews (which this author thinks he did), then he finally removed himself from the book and left no trace of himself (in what this author thinks is his final book).

The author's closest reference to himself is in Hebrews 2:1–4. In verses 1 and 2, the author's tone is inclusive as he identified himself with his audience. In verse 3, the author continued his inclusivity but excluded himself from the apostleship. The text reads, "This salvation, which was first announced by the Lord, was confirmed to us by those who heard him." This text seems to suggest a non-apostolic authorship of Hebrews. To a large degree, this text is seen conclusively as endorsing Paul or someone else as the author of Hebrews. However, the problem arises regarding Paul's own writings. Nowhere does he mention that he was one of those who received his message from "those who first heard the Lord." Paul emphatically wrote that "those men [the apostles] added nothing to my message" (Gal. 2:6).

Incidentally, in Hebrews 3:1, the author designated "Jesus [as] the apostle." Perhaps this was an intentional attempt by the last surviving apostle who knew that he would not live to see Jesus return trying to commit the church to the Living Apostle before his departure. In his closing days, the apostle Peter attempted the same: "And I will make every effort to see that after my departure you will always be able to remember these things" (2 Peter 1:15). How do these observations all factor into the authorship issue? We present two considerations.

Literary Style in Revelation

The previously mentioned literary style first appears in Revelation 1–3. The seven oracles begin with the vision of 1:10–20. The vision basically describes "One like the Son of Man"—His physicality and immediate environment. The messages to the seven churches consist of Jesus' narration. Consider the manner in which He discloses Himself. For instance, He says to the church at Ephesus, "These are the words of Him who holds the seven stars in his right hand," as if He is referring to someone else. However, the Narrator immediately switches to first person singular: "I know your deeds." Then to the church at Laodicea, He says, "These are the words of the Amen ... I know your deeds" (2:1; 3:14).

Note how the person and number change in these constructions, beginning with the third person and reverting to the first person singular. By the time the apocalyptic audience arrive at the end of chapter 3, they know the third person singular and first person singular refer to the same Person. If Revelation was written first, it is highly likely that the author learned such literary art from the Master and utilized it in his later works (the epistles, Gospel, and Hebrews).

Absence of Conventional Epistolary Formula in Johannine Writings

New Testament authors typically began and ended with the conventional epistolary formula, in which one explicitly identified himself and his audience in the prologue and pronounced blessings in the epilogue. The authorial name is not only for identification but more so for authentication. However, the Johannine author differs in that his name appears only four times in the introductory material of the Apocalypse (1:1, 4, 9; 22:8). Somewhat ambiguous titles such as "the elder" appear in the two smaller epistles. Then there is no such information in the first epistle, Gospel, and Hebrews.

Despite these, the author still provided sufficient information to show that he was a well-known character in the early church. The audience was well aware of his impeccable character, the veracity of his speech, reliability of his testimony, his fearless and unwavering commitment to Jesus Christ, devotion and duty to "One like the Son of Man," and fierce opposition to opponents and falsehood.

After all, if the author was John, his subjects and peers considered him to be "one of the pillars" of the early church. Even Jesus' public commendation of the same was already in the public domain before John began writing his books (see John 21:22, 23). If John wrote his books after most of the apostles had died, the rumor that John would "remain alive until [Jesus] return[s]" had entered the public domain, and the NT church had nicknamed him "the disciple whom Jesus loved," then perhaps he needed no introduction. It was as if the very second coming of Jesus Christ hinged on his life!

ORDER IN WHICH THE JOHANNINE BOOKS WERE WRITTEN

Assumptions

The relationship between Revelation, the epistles, the fourth Gospel, and Hebrews is so overwhelming and multifaceted that it beckons the question, Which one was written first? Do these similarities speak of John's own cultivated writing styles, or was he using a "borrowed" template?

The author set out to write all books as an "eyewitness." In the epistles, he was one of those who "have looked at ... and touched" Jesus with his own hands (1 John 1–2). In the Gospel, he wrote of himself, saying, "the man who saw it has given testimony" (John 19:35). Then in Hebrews, he acknowledged that God "has spoken to us by his Son" (Heb. 1:2). In writing in the third person, he stated that the "salvation ... first announced by the Lord, was confirmed to us by those who heard him" (2:3). In these books, the author was at liberty to select, organize, and present his material to achieve his goals (John 20:30–31; 21:25). In this process, he also chose the format and arrangement that best communicated his message.

However, the Apocalypse differs on many fronts. The author was commanded to "write on a scroll what you see and send it to the seven churches" (1:11). His role, therefore, was limited to the choice of the scroll, the color of inks, and the words. He had less influence on the content, arrangement, and structure in which the prophecy was presented to him. This is because, as a penman, he basically wrote what he saw and heard. Unlike the other Johannine writings, the content and structure of Revelation were of the Revealer and not the writer.

> *If John felt that the arrangement and presentation of the Apocalypse was effective, he may have adopted these features in his later works.*

If John felt that the arrangement and presentation of the Apocalypse was effective, he may have adopted these features in his later works. In other words, if the literary, thematic and structural relationship between Revelation and other Johannine works can be established, then that could indicate; (i). John adopting the patterns of heaven/Revelation in his later works more feasible, (ii). that Revelation was one of John's earlier works. The nature of these relations is discussed in the next chapter.

3.
THE RELATIONSHIP AMONG THE JOHANNINE BOOKS

THE GOSPEL AND EPISTLES OF JOHN

The relationship that exists between the Gospel and epistles of John has been well documented. Apart from the linguistics, themes, and nearly identical prologues in both books, the Gospel of John and 1 John have essentially the same purposes.[63] If the purpose of a document reveals the core intention of the author, then in both books *that* core intention does not change (Christology: 1 John 5:13, John 20:30, 31; Love-hate: 1 John 2:9–11; 3:11–23; John 15:1–16:4; 10:1–21). Unlike the Synoptic Gospels, the author injects himself throughout the fourth Gospel as he does in his three letters.[64] Finally, if every observation (linguistic, literary, stylistic, tonal, visual, thematic, theological) indicates that a relationship between these two documents and the core issues (authorial intention, themes, and

---

[63] Scholars who believe that the first epistle and Gospel of John addressed two different audiences at different times attempt to offer a superficial distinction between the purposes of the two documents. Westcott, for example, wrote that 1 John argues that "the Christ is Jesus," while in the Gospel of John, "Jesus is the Christ" (see Westcott's *The Epistles of St. John*, pp. xliii–xlvi). Similarly, Brown holds that 1 John stressed a "lower Christology," whereas the Gospel of John stressed a "higher Christology" (see *The Epistles of John*, pp. 25–27). The difference, if any, is not so apparent. One must intentionally inflate the issues in order make them appear different.

[64] In the Synoptic Gospels, for instance, when Matthew documented his own conversion, he did not provide a "clue" indicating that he was the author (see Matt. 9:9–13). Luke only referred to the research that he had evidently done (see Luke 1:1–4).

Christological issues) remains constant, then a methodological difference is feasible.[65]

Is it possible that the author could have written two different letters to a single church addressing the same issues but using two different literary approaches?[66] The obvious difference between the epistles and Gospel of John is that the epistles are direct—similar to the "I" writing to "you" approach[67] of Revelation 1–3—while the Gospel approaches the same issues, but in an indirect (or more symbolic) manner patterned after Revelation 4–22.

REVELATION 1–3 AND 1 JOHN

Scholars have struggled to describe the genre of Revelation because it possesses a "formal epistolary framework in Rev 1:1–3:22 and Rev 22:10–21" but the larger "prophetic portion [4:1–22:5]" consists of a "series of episodic vision narratives introduced with a heavenly journey."[68] However,

---

[65] Those who think the purposes of the two are different struggle to differentiate the issues and reconstruct the community life, context, opponents, the entire time it took to write, and the *authors* who wrote them. If the similarities in purposes are accepted as they are, then all these exercises will prove futile. Here, Ockham's razor should stigmatize such approaches: one should not multiply theories when it is not necessary. For a linguistic and stylistic relationship between the Gospel of John and the epistles, see Westcott, *The Epistles of St. John*, pp. xxxix–xliii.

[66] The current predominant view suggests that there are either two different communities or two different stages of community life in a single community. Scholars have yet to propose a convincing reconstruction of such a community. They also claim to see the Gospel of John as written in different stages by different hands at different times. However, no scholar has yet produced a manuscript demonstrating the stages the Gospel underwent. See A. T. Mattill, Jr., "Johannine Communities Behind the Fourth Gospel: Georg Richter's Analysis," *Theological Studies* 38, no. 2 (1977), p. 297; Raymond E. Brown, *The Community of the Beloved Disciple: The Life, Loves, and Hates of an Individual Church in New Testament Times* (New York: Paulist Press, 1979), p. ?.

[67] In defense of his "circular letter" theory, D.W. Burdick recognizes the personal nature of 1 John. To illustrate this, he coins the "I" to "you" concept [see *The Letters of John the Apostle: An In-Depth Commentary* (Chicago: Moody Press, 1985), p. 69].

[68] Ranko Stefanovic, *Revelation of Jesus Christ*, pp. 81–84, 90–92. See also David E. Aune, *Revelation 1–5*, ed. Ralph P. Martin, *Word Biblical Commentary*, vol. 52A (Dallas, Texas: Word Books, 1982), p. lxxii. For a detailed discussion on the genre of Revelation, see Aune, pp. lxx–xc.

in this study, we attempt to demonstrate the literary, material, tonal, and stylistic dependence of the Gospel and epistles of John on Revelation.[69] The similarities between these two letters are many, but we will consider only four.[70]

The Format

The manner or format, as Stefanovic describes, of Revelation 1–3 shares a striking similarity with 1 John. Stefanovic identifies a total of six common features in each address. They begin with the identification of the addressees, followed by a brief description of Christ, then an analysis of the spiritual condition of the communities addressed. This proceeds to counsels and warnings, which are followed by a proclamation and conclusion with a promise of a reward to the overcomer.[71] However, in each of these oracles, no attempt is made to call to repentance those who have intentionally aligned themselves with the evil one. They are dismissed as belonging to Satan. The same literary styles are heavily featured in 1 John. The following compares the first message of Revelation (2:1–11) with a selection of 1 John.[72]

---

[69] Many reputable scholars not only deny any relationship between the Apocalypse and the remaining Johannine books (the Gospel and three letters), but also assert that the Apocalypse was written by "another John," not the son of Zebedee. For instance, see Brown, *The Community of the Beloved Disciple*, p. 6; Aune, *Revelation 1–5*, p. xxx; E. S. Fiorenza, "The Quest for the Johannine School: The Apocalypse and the Fourth Gospel," *New Testament Studies* 23 (1976–1977), pp. 402–427.

[70] For a thorough linguistic and literary relationship, read R. W. Yarborough, *1–3 John*, pp. 17–21. Yarborough summarizes two earlier works by Trebilco (2004) and Schnabel (2004). After consulting these two primary authors, the view of the current author is reviewed on the genre because these sources were discovered after completing the first draft.

[71] Stefanovic, *Revelation of Jesus Christ*, pp. 81–84, 90–92. Aune lists eight features: The addressees, a command to write, the "thus said" formula, Christological predications, narrative, warning, proclamation formula, and promise to the victor (pp. 119–124).

[72] Only in a few cases will other passages be used.

Features	Revelation 1–3	1 John
Christ	The one who "walks among the seven golden lampstands" (2:1)	"light" (1:5), "advocate" (2:1), "atoning sacrifice" (2:2), "righteous" (2:29; 3:7)
Compliments	"I know your deeds, your hard work … and have not grown weary," "You hate the practices of the Nicolaitans," (2:2, 3, 6)	"you have known him" (2:13a, 13c), "you have overcome the evil one" (2:13b), "you have an anointing from the Holy One, and all of you know the truth" (2:20).
Diagnosis of Weaknesses	"Yet I hold this against you; You have forsaken your first love" (2:4) "'You say, I am rich…' [b]ut you do not realize that you are wretched, pitiful, poor…" (3:17)	"if we claim to be without sin,, we deceive ourselves" (1:8)[73] "The man who says, 'I know him, but does not do what he commands is a liar" (1 John 2:3), "If anyone says, 'I love God,' yet hates his brother, he is a liar" (1 John 4:19)
Remedy	"Repent and do the things you did at first" (2:5b)	"walk in the light" (1:7), you "must walk as Jesus did" (2:6), love your brother (2:9–10; 3:10), be righteous and do "what is right" (2:29; 3:7), be pure (3:3), "believe in the name of his Son Jesus Christ" (3:23)
Rebukes/ Warnings	"if you do not repent, I will come to you and remove your lampstand from its place" (2:5c).	If we love another we will "have confidence on the day of judgment" and not fear (4:17, 18)
Promise to Overcomer	"to him who overcomes, I will give the right to eat from the tree of life" (2:7)	"everyone born of God overcomes the world" (5:4) "when he appears, we shall be like him, for we shall see him as he is" (3:2)
Enemies and Their Diabolical Teachings	"wicked men," false "apostles," "practices of the Nicolaitans" (2:2, 6)	"antichrists," "deceivers," "liars," "false prophets," "Cain," "the world," "children of the devil" (2:15–24, 4:1–6; 5:16; 2 John 7–11)

---

[73] Although the series of "if" statements in 1 John is not identical to the "I know" declarations of Revelation 2–3, statements such as "if any claim," "if anyone says," or "if we claim" presuppose that the author is fully aware of those who are making such claims. In both cases, the narrator-author knows those who are responsible but refrains from calling them by names.

Direct Address

Both 1 John and Revelation 1–3 heavily feature active interactions between the author-narrator and the audience. While commenting on 1 John, Jan A. Du Rand states, "The narrative is in the I-style which indicates that the author-narrator is not outside the narration."[74] The same is also true in Revelation 1–3, in which the glorified Christ is repeatedly seen saying, "I know you," "I have this against you," "I will come and take the lampstand," and "repent."

Strategic Introduction of Jesus

> *To each of the seven churches, Christ's self-identification consists of various aspects of the vision of Revelation 1:12–20. Each of these details is strategically chosen to draw a corresponding application from it.*

Both texts introduce Christ strategically. To each of the seven churches, Christ's self-identification consists of various aspects of the vision of Revelation 1:12–20. Each of these details is strategically chosen to draw a corresponding application from it.[75] For instance, to the church in Ephesus, Christ is introduced as the one who "holds the seven stars in his right hand and walks amongst the seven golden lampstands" (2:1). Thus, His ability to know, accurately diagnose, offer a remedy, and issue a warning stems from the fact that He "walks amongst the lampstands." Similarly, in 1 John 1:5–2:11, Jesus is referred to as the "atoning sacrifice," "advocate,"

---

[74] Jan A. du Rand, *Johannine Perspective: Introduction to the Johannine Writtings—Part I* (New York: Orion, 1991), p. 148.

[75] David Arthur DeSilva, "Out of Our Minds? Appeals to Reason (Logos) in the Seven Oracles of Revelation 2–3," *Journal for the Study of the New Testament* 31, no. 2 (December 1, 2008), p. 130.

"righteous" one, "pure," and referred to as "the light."[76] These are not mere theological statements for ideological purposes, but similar to Revelation 1–3, the applications are drawn directly from them, and the audiences are urged to "walk in the light," "be righteous," and "be pure as He is pure."[77]

The Authority of the Author

Both the epistles and Gospel show the author as someone having and exercising *authority*.[78] The radical rhetoric, choice of language, tone, and style in all of the Johannine books demonstrate this. DeSilva describes the "seven oracles of Rev 2–3" as using an enthymemic construction.[79] He differentiates an enthymeme (an argument without an explicit premise) from a maxim (a conclusion without a reason) and syllogism (a formal argument having a scientific premise in which the conclusions are made for the audience) as a "maxim with a reason" or an "informal syllogism," which subtly enlists "the hearer's aid and partnership, in effect, in the construction and completion of the argumentation." This is done where "the orator assumes the hearers can and will supply the missing link that makes the logical transference within the syllogism viable."[80] He further notes

---

[76] Some scholars contest that "the pure" and "the righteous" of 1 John 3 are references to God (the Father). However, as will be demonstrated later, all these attributes consistently speak of Christ.

[77] Some may rightly object that in the Apocalypse, Jesus was the one who was narrating, whereas in the epistles, John was the one who was writing. Others may further see differences in the nature of referents: in the Apocalypse, the Christ's self-disclosures consist of His material or physical attributes, whereas in 1 John, they consist of His qualitative attributes. Although these differences do exist, they do not affect the similarity in literary style, tone, rhetoric, or argumentation.

[78] The author was forthright and conclusive in his logic and language. He set the rules and stated that those who live by them "have eternal life" and those who do not "are already condemned." There is no middle ground. This is characteristic of Paul, who was even willing to "curse" an "angel" if he delivered a different gospel from the one he preached! In other words, the force of the discourse is as if they "possessed the keys to the kingdom."

[79] DeSilva, pp. 126, 127. See also *Ancient Literary Criticism: The Principal Texts in New Testament Translations*, ed. D. A. Russell and M. Winterbottom (Oxford: Claredon Press, 1972), pp. 147–150, 175–184.

[80] DeSilva, pp. 127, 128

that in order for enthymemic rhetoric to work, the orator and hearers must have a shared experience and subscribe to the same set of values.[81]

Given this literary device, DeSilva analyzes the seven oracles. In the address to the church in Ephesus, for example, he identifies the core issue to be Revelation 2:4–5: "Yet I hold this against you: you have forsaken your first love. Remember the height from which you have fallen. Repent and do the things you did at first!" To show the enthymemic nature of this argumentation, DeSilva highlights three important features. First, the Orator does not provide a list to show how or from where the Ephesians have fallen. Second, by appealing to them to "remember," He is inviting his audience to supply "that list." Finally, the authority of the oracle emanates from the validity of the testimony and the credibility of the One who says it.[82]

The epistle is replete with similar literary constructions. In the prologue, the author alluded to his own experience, but without providing any detail of those encounters (see 1 John 1:1–4). Similarly, in 1 John 2:12–14, the author reminded his audience of their knowledge of the one "who is from the beginning," but he does not identify who the beginning one is. Further, in verses 20–26, he told his audience, "you know the truth," but failed to show of what that truth consisted. Altogether, the author not only assumed familiarity on the part of his audience but also enlisted his audience to provide those details. Thus, the force of his persuasion is not dependent on either the logic of the argument or the weight of the evidence, but on the validity of the shared experience and the authority of the author.[83]

---

[81] Ibid., pp. 127, 129.

[82] Ibid., p. 132.

[83] A similar relationship exists between Revelation 19:9, John 21:23–24, and 3 John 12. In Revelation 19:9, the angel instructed John to write, "Blessed are those who are invited to the wedding supper of the Lamb!" Then the angel added, "These are the true words of God." In 3 John 12, "We also speak well of him, and you know that our testimony is true." In John 21:24, "We know that his testimony is true." Just like the angel of Revelation 19 who testified to the validity of the statement of the "words of God," in 3 John and the Gospel, the references are possibly to the author and his associates. However, if he wrote to an audience "who know[s] the truth" (2 John 1), then they would agree to the validity of the testimonies and the credibility of the author.

Literary, Theological, and Exegetical Evidences in Chapter 12 of this Study

The similarities are still tentative for we have merely taken similar words from different parts of 1 John to argue for a literary relationship with Revelation 1–3. This is a valid objection, as such appearances of similarities must be strengthened by thematic and exegetical evidences. To this, we point the reader to the thematic and exegetical evidences documented in other parts of this book. Consider particularly chapter 12, where further literary and thematic relationships between Revelation and 1 John are discussed. It is hoped that the volume and quality of evidences discussed there and elsewhere will serve to reinforce the relationship between these two documents.

GOSPEL OF JOHN AND REVELATION 4–22

Similarly, the tone, literary style, material,[84] form, and overall approach in the Gospel shares marked similarities with the second part of Revelation (chapters 4–22).[85]

Indirect Address

If the messages in both sections (Revelation 1–3 and 4–22) were intended to address the issues of the original recipients, then the manner

---

[84] As we shall see, the Apocalypse and Gospel of John do have a fair amount of materials (not merely language, literary styles, etc.) in common. In this study, we will identify such and use the word "material" because any thematic or theological relationship is another issue.

[85] Revelation 1:9–11 states that the entire book was written to the seven churches. However, as noted earlier, the interaction that we see in chapters 1–3 is absent in chapters 4–21. Some may rightly wonder if the messages in Revelation 4–21 also addressed their situation. Or do we suppose that the initial recipients were mere custodians of prophecies that had no relevance to their condition? If any of what occurs in Revelation 4–21 is applicable to the recipients of that book, it is neither stressed nor applied directly. One of the important clues to this issue is the reactions and attitudes of the author. John's reactions, enquiries, and attitudes testify to the clarity and relevance of its contents to him and those being addressed in his time.

in which this was to be achieved would differ. As previously demonstrated, Revelation 1–3 heavily features a direct approach, whereas 4–22 addresses the concerns of the addressees indirectly. Similar to Revelation 4–22, the Gospel addresses the audience indirectly. Unlike 1 John and Revelation 1–3, there is no direct interaction between the author-narrator and his addressees. In both books (Revelation 4–22 and the Gospel of John), the original recipients assumed a silent-audience status in the narratives that follow.

The author provides several clues to this reality. First, Christ's prayer for His disciples reads, "My prayer is not for them alone. I pray also for those who will believe in me through their message" (John 17:20). The second passage reads, "Then Jesus told him [Thomas], 'Because you have seen me, you have believed; blessed are those who have not seen and yet have believed" (20:19).[86] Both passages attempt to make the Gospel of John relevant and applicable to "those who have not seen" but "believed through [the disciples'] message." Thus, similar to Revelation 4–22, the Gospel is tailored to indirectly address their issues.

Miracles, Signs, and Wonders Serve as Prelude

In both cases, a series of highly dramatized events serves as a prelude to the discourses that follow. In the Apocalypse, it is the sanctuary visions or signs and wonders that pave the way for the discourses, whereas the discourses in the Gospel are prefaced by a series of "miraculous signs" (John 2:11; 20:30). These visions and miraculous signs serve to dramatize the issues with which the recipients in both books grappled. Thus, the setting, imageries employed, words uttered, conflicts and confrontations are all carefully crafted to indirectly address the issues of those who first received the documents.

---

[86] Brendan Byrne, "The Faith of the Beloved Disciple and the Community in John 20," *Journal for the Study of the New Testament* 23 (1985), pp. 88–90. Here, Byrne suggests that the beloved disciple accounted his own faith journey of his own time to nourish those of the later community, which we argue to be the recipients of the Gospel of John.

For example, the "how long" cry of Revelation 6:9–11, allegedly from the "souls of those who had been slain," merely echoed or mirrored the longing and anxiety of those being addressed as evident in all New Testament writings (see Matt. 24:14; Acts 1:6–8; 1 Thess. 4:13–5:11; 2 Thess. 2:1–12; 2 Peter 3:3–10).[87] If the response "wait a little longer [*chronon mikron*]" was intended to address that issue, then some likely felt that "a little longer" (which literally means "a little time, or a little while") was too vague and lacked specificity. Thus, in the Gospel (and Hebrews), the author made another attempt to address this issue in John 16:16–33.[88]

However, this time, it is not the blood of the martyrs but "his disciples" who are seen asking, "What does he mean by 'in a little while [*mikron*]?'" (John 16:17, 18).[89] The author seems to be saying that even though this particular concern was already addressed (in Rev. 6), they kept asking.[90] The same concept is reiterated in Hebrews: "For in just a very little while [*mikron*], 'He who is coming will come and will not delay'" (10:37).

---

[87] These passages reveal that the early church began with an "imminent" return of the Lord's proclamation, but with the passage of time and as the apostles began to die out, these authors found different ways to address that issue. Mark completely ignored the issue and left it "open," and Matthew and Luke adopted a similar view. Their position can be summarized in this way: the day of the lord is ushered in by the proclamation of the gospel (see Matt. 24:24, 36). Paul and Peter, however, adopted a thief-like metaphor, while John used the phrase "in a little while" (Rev. 6:9–11, John 16:17–33).

[88] Scholars dispute whether this "little while" reference was to His resurrection or the *Parousia*. No doubt, it had a double meaning, a feature that is highly consistent with the Gospel. However, this passage was primarily intended to answer the issue that arose from Revelation 6:9–11 and 17:9–12, pertaining to the *Parousia*. See D. A. Carson, The Gospel According to John (Grand Rapids, MI: Wm. B. Eerdsman Pub. Co., 1991), pp. 542, 543.

[89] Concerning the structure of the Gospel of John, scholars have acknowledged that the narrative ends abruptly at 14:31 and is picked up at 18:1. Thus, they have postulated many theories to account for the lengthy "farewell speech" that covers chapters 15, 16, and 17. Similar to John 10, chapter 15 addresses the "love-hate" issue of 1 John (John 15:1–16:4), whereas a large part of chapter 16 addresses certain issues (in particular, *Parousia*) that arose from Revelation 6:9–11 and 17:9–12 (John 16:16–33), and chapter 17 is a prayer "not for them [his disciples] alone," but also "for those who will believe in me through their message" (John 17:20).

[90] For another example, consider the different aspects in which the author admonishes the idolaters. Towards the end of Revelation 22, John testified to seeing "idolaters," among others, "outside" the city (vv. 14, 15). Although what he saw is true, it was a subtle way of urging the recipients to keep away "from idols" (1 John 5:22).

Historical and Symbolic Key Players

Unlike the author/narrator-audience interactions in 1 John and Revelation 1–3, the Gospel and Revelation 4–22 feature diverse key players. In the Apocalypse, the key players are characteristically symbolic, whereas in the Gospel, the players and events are historical. For instance, the lamb, enthroned one, dragon, horses, beasts, women, and many waters symbolically represent the main characters. In the Gospel, the key players are Jesus, the Jews, disciples, Judas, and the crowd. In both cases, the issues are dramatized and the addressees are the audiences.

Symbolism and Figure of Speech

Similar to the Apocalypse (Rev. 1:1—"he made is known [by signs]"), the Gospel also has a high degree of symbolism, or in the author's own words, "figures of speech" (John 16:29).[91] For instance, there are those with double meanings (see John 3, 4, and 6) and those that have a clear symbolic cloak (see 8:1–13; 13:1–17). However, the one that shows a clear relationship between these two books is found in John 4.[92] When Jesus asked the Samaritan woman to invite her husband, the woman responded, "I have no husband [*andra*]." Jesus affirmed her response and then added, "in fact you have had five husbands [*pente gar andras esches*], the one that you have now is not your husband [*anēr*]" (vv. 16–18).

Regarding the significance of this narrative, scholars are divided into one of two competing camps. One group claims to see this as an allegorical reference to the seven foreign gods of 2 Kings 17:19–34. Most, however, reject this because the historical facts surrounding the allegorical interpretation do not harmonize, for in one account, there are "seven"

---

[91] Brown also recognizes these metaphors but sees them as equivalent to "parables" in the Synoptic Gospels, or in certain cases, thinks they have a dual meaning, "literal" and "spiritual/sacramental" [*The Gospel and Epistles of John: A Concise Commentary* (Collegeville, Minnesota: The Liturgical Press, 1988), pp. 17, 18].

[92] Carson, pp. 221, 232, 233. Lincoln, pp. 175, 176.

gods, whereas in the other, there are six men. Therefore, most posit a literal interpretation of the passage. Konstenberger, a representative of this view, thinks that the story highlights the woman's violation of a rabbinical law that restricted an individual from marrying more than three times.[93] If that rabbinical law did exist, then the Mosaic and NT records seriously conflict with it because the questions by the Sadducees concerning marriage at the resurrection presupposes that a woman (or a man) *could* marry up to at least seven times (see Luke 20:27–40; Mark 12:18–27).[94]

Since the word for "husband" is the same term used for "man," Keener wonders if there is a word play here. The fact that Jesus' double affirmation of the woman's basic admission ("I have no *andra*") indicates that the woman may have known five *andras* (men) previously, but that does not necessarily translate into five husbands. She could have possibly been a "serial fornicator" and the current man was her sixth one.[95] Keener's take on this passage is consistent with the text, context, and nature of the narrative on a number of levels.

Apart from the narrative being an authentic historical event, John's symbolic intent in this instance is apparent. A few important clues indicate the author's use of a historical account with a symbolic twist. First, this narrative is preceded by the Baptist's declaration that the "bride belongs to the bridegroom [Jesus]" (John 3:29). Note that the concept of marriage, harlotry, and especially Jesus as the Bridegroom is heavily featured in Revelation 17, 19, and 21 as well.

---

[93] Andreas J. Konstenberger, *John*, ed. Robert Yarbrough and Robert H. Stein, Baker Exegetical Commentary on the New Testament (Grand Rapids, MI: Baker Academic, 2004), p. 152. See also Lincoln, pp. 174–176.

[94] Note that the Sadducees referred to the Mosaic law to frame their question. In other words, their question was consistent with the marital laws of Moses.

[95] Andreas J. Konstenberger concurs with Keener that the author is employing a word play here. Since *andra* can either mean "man" or "husband", and if the sixth "man" is not her legal "husband," then there is a possibility that she may have had "five men", thus openly living as a "serial fornicator." See Konstenberger, pp. 152, 153.

Second, the language Jesus utters in John 4 is taken directly from Revelation 17:9–11, where a prostitute is seen sitting on a seven-headed beast. The angel tells John, "The seven heads are ... seven kings. Five have fallen, one is, and the other has not yet come, but when he does come he must remain for a little while" (vv. 9, 10). Now consider the Samaritan woman's records. She had known five men and is now with the sixth man. The obvious objection here is that in Revelation, there are seven men, whereas in John there are six. How do we reconcile this? The total number of men the women in both accounts had known in the past *and* present are same—six. That is the focus in this discussion. Revelation, however, proceeds to add the seventh man.

> *The details of Revelation 17 and Ezekiel 23 are remarkably similar. Ezekiel named three of Israel's former lovers as Egypt, Assyria, and Babylon. Medo-Persia and Greece followed the Babylonian empires (see Dan. 2 and 7). By the time Revelation and the Gospel of John were written, the Jews had allied themselves with Rome in persecuting Christ and His followers.*

Third, both the apocalyptic and Samaritan women continue and add a seventh man each. The apocalyptic woman does not repent from her adulterous life and will marry a seventh man. The Samaritan woman also continued and added a seventh man. However, her seventh man, according to the narrative, was Jesus, who at last, is the Bridegroom and her real husband.

Fourth, who are these men and women? To those who first read the documents, the Samaritan woman undoubtedly represents Samaria, whereas the apocalyptic woman represents the Jewish nation. They both have had a shared history. They have fallen and risen together under different political regimes. Stated differently, they both had fallen in and out of love with the same men. Both have had and known five men and now share the sixth men. The Scripture paints a graphic picture of Israel (with Samaria) as the one who:

> Gave herself as a prostitute to ... the Assyrians ... She did not give up the prostitution she began in Egypt, when during her youth [Egyptian] men slept with her ... But she carried her prostitution still further. She saw men portrayed on a wall, figures of Chaldeans ... all of them looked like Babylonian chariot officers, natives of Chaldea. As soon as she saw them, she lusted after them and sent messengers to them in Chaldea. Then the Babylonians came to her, to the bed of love, and in their lust they defiled her ... Therefore ... this is what the Sovereign Lord says: I will stir up your lovers against you. (Ezekiel 23:7, 8, 14–17, 22)

The details of Revelation 17 and Ezekiel 23 are remarkably similar. Ezekiel named three of Israel's former lovers as Egypt, Assyria, and Babylon. Medo-Persia and Greece followed the Babylonian empires (see Dan. 2 and 7). By the time Revelation and the Gospel of John were written, the Jews had allied themselves with Rome in persecuting Christ and His followers. Thus, she (Israel and Samaria) had known five men (Egypt, Assyria, Babylon, Medo-Persia, Greece) and is now with the sixth man (Rome).[96] The text does not indicate if any of the six men was her actual

---

[96] A relationship also exists in the symbolic nature of the two books. For examples, all dates and times in Revelation are given in "days" and "months," or in some cases, "in a little while" or a "short time" (see 6:11; 7:4; 8:1; 12:6; 13:5, 18). In the Gospel of John, the author also provided certain numerical details: the paralytic of "38 years" (see ch. 5) and the "153 fish" (see ch. 21). Scholars have rightly identified the "38 years" as a symbolic reference to the time it took from Kadesh Barnea to the Valley of Zered (see Deut. 2:14). See also Carpenter, *The Johannine writings*, pp. 244, 245; Lincoln, p. 193.

However, the "153 fish" continue to perplex the scholars. Various views have been suggested regarding the significance of this detail. See Lincoln, pp. 512, 513; Carpenter, pp. 245–249. We think the "153" is a symbolic reference to the total number of members John was addressing. The context also seems to favor this interpretation. First, the word for "haul" (21:6) is also translated "to draw" elsewhere (see 6:44; 12:32). In 6:44, it is the Father "drawing" people to Jesus, whereas in 12:32, when the Son is lifted up, that act of lifting will "draw" people to Himself. In the latter part of 21:6, the disciples "haul" it toward Jesus. Second, Peter was admonished to "feed" His lambs/sheep, indicating

husband. However, the reader is left with the strong impression that Jesus is the Bridegroom and real Husband.

Old Testament Allusions

As in Revelation, the Gospel does not possess any direct OT quotations but is impregnated with allusions in veiled references to the word, light, ladder of Jacob, and lamb in John 1, the bridegroom in chapter 2, and being lifted up as Moses lifted up the serpent in chapter 3. The author attempted to present Jesus as the realization of all OT prophecies and the embodiment of all Jewish imageries, rituals, feasts, and characters (see John 1:44; 5:45–47).[97]

Dual Focus

Revelation and the Gospel of John also have a dual concept in common. Certain words, imageries, concepts, and characters having dual or double meanings are also another common occurrence between these two books. For a further discussion on this, refer to the section "Dual Meaning in the Gospel of John" in chapter 12 of this volume.

CONCLUSION

If the literary, stylistic, methodological, and material dependence on the Apocalypse can be established in the Gospel of John and 1 John, then four conclusions are possible. First, the same author who wrote Revelation was behind the Gospel and epistles. Second, similar to Revelation 1–3 and 4–22, which addressed the same audience but used two different literary approaches, it is possible that both the Gospel and epistles of John

---

the very intent of the document (Gospel of John). Third, a large volume of fish did not break the net, perhaps hinting at the impact on the church and all the issues it was facing.

[97] Space does not allow documenting the linguistics, literary nature, imagery, and length of both documents or the climactic nature of the composition.

addressed the same issues in a specific church but used two different literary approaches. Third, it is obvious that the epistles of John are patterned after Revelation 1–3, whereas the literary approaches of the Gospel are similar to Revelation 4–22. Finally, every indication thus far (and as we shall see later) points to another possible explanation that Revelation was written before the epistles and the Gospel of John.

PART 2:
JESUS, GOD, SPIRITS OF GOD, AND DUALISM (REVELATION 1:1–9)

4.
REVELATION OF JESUS CHRIST

INTRODUCTION

In Revelation 1:11, the one "like the Son of Man" urged John, "write on a scroll what you see" and send it to the seven churches (see also v. 13; 19:9). What John actually "heard and saw" (22:8) began with 1:9 and ended with 22:5. This means that the prologue (1:1–8) and epilogue (22:6–21) comprise the author's own summation of and reflections on the prophecies. As such, they serve a critical role in revealing the authorial views and insights on the main text (1:9–22:6). Therefore, a thorough analysis of the prologue and epilogue will enable us to see the prophecies of Revelation as John saw them.

> The revelation from Jesus Christ, which God gave him to show his servants what must soon take place. He made it known by sending his angel to his servant John, who testifies to everything he saw—that is, the word of God and the testimony of Jesus Christ. Blessed is the one who reads aloud the words of this prophecy, and blessed are those who hear it and take to heart what is written in it, because the time is near. (Revelation 1:1-3)

DEFINITION AND SIGNIFICANCE

Revelation

<u>Definition</u>. The word "revelation" originates from the compound Greek word *apokalupsis*, which is translated to mean "unveiling or

removing the covering" with an intent to expose an object, concept, or person. The "revelation of Jesus," therefore, claims to "reveal," "unmask," "unveil," or "disclose" hidden things about or concerning Jesus Christ.

The same concept is repeated in the epilogue (22:10), but there it uses the verbal form of the antonym of *apokalupsis*—*sphragizō*. "Do not seal up [*spragisēs*, from its verb *sphragizō*], the words of the prophecy of this book, because the time is near." The term *sphragizō*, which means to "seal up," "cover," or "shut up," functions as the opposite of the term "*apokalupsis*." The same verb (*sphragizō*) is also used in Revelation 10:4 and 20:3. In 10:4, John was told to "seal up [*sphragizō*] what the seven thunders said and do not write it down," whereas in 20:3, Satan was thrown into the Abyss, which was "locked and sealed [*esphragisen*]" to prevent him from "deceiving the nations anymore."

The noun form of *sphragizō* is *sphragis*, which refers to the instrument used for sealing or closing. This is the term used to describe the "seven seals" of Revelation 5–8:1 and the "seal of God" in 7:3. This noun carries various nuances. For example, the reason for having a seal on a scroll is for authentication and to avoid tempering, while putting a "seal of the living God" on a person is to show ownership. Therefore, apart from the 144,000 having the "seal of God," Jesus is set apart as the only emissary who has God's "seal of approval" (John 6:27). The apostle Paul also saw the indwelling Spirit of God as the "seal of ownership" (2 Cor. 1:22).

Revelation of Jesus Christ

The Greek phrase "of Jesus Christ" is *Iēsou Christou*, which is the genitive masculine singular and can be translated either "from Jesus" or "about Jesus." The phrase "from Jesus" could mean that Jesus is either the source or transmitter of the "words of this prophecy," whereas "about or concerning Jesus" could signify Him as the main subject or content of the prophetic book. Revelation and other Johannine writings show that both positions are possible.

Revelation Is Both "from" and "about" Jesus. Since "God gave him [Jesus] to show his servants," the context appears to support Jesus as either the "transmitter," "channel," or "conduit" of the messages of Revelation (see 1:1–3). The seven messages, seven seals, seven trumpets, and other sections also provide sufficient evidence that support this view (see Heb. 1:1, 2; John 1:17). However, the same also presents Jesus Christ as the essence of the main messages. For instance, the messages to the seven churches (Rev. 2 and 3) proceed from the vision of 1:10–20, a vision that is essentially *about* Jesus, which makes Him the actual content of the messages. Then notice that Jesus is also the One orating these messages. This makes Him both the *content* and the *channel* through whom the word of prophecy came.

> *The Lamb that opens the "first of the seven seals" is also "the rider" on the "white horse" (6:1, 2). Similarly, the Lamb opens the sixth seal to reveal the scene that concerns the "wrath of the lamb" (vv. 12–17). Therefore, the overall design of the text supports Revelation as being both "from" and "about" Christ.*

Further Examples of "from" and "about" Jesus. The vision of Revelation 4–5 is about Jesus. Here, He is introduced as the "root of David," "lion of the tribe of Judah," and seven-horned and seven-eyed "lamb" at the center of the throne. However, in the scenes that follow (see chs. 6–11), Jesus acts as the medium through which those messages are communicated. For instance, the voice that invited John to come and see and the Lamb that he actually saw are both one and the same character (see 4:1). In the seals section, Jesus is both the One involved in breaking and opening the seals and the main character inside each of the seals. Consider the first seal as an example. The Lamb that opens the "first of the seven seals" is also "the rider" on the "white horse" (6:1, 2). Similarly, the Lamb opens the sixth seal to reveal the scene that concerns the "wrath of the lamb" (vv. 12–17). Therefore, the overall design of the text supports Revelation as being both "from" and "about" Christ.

WHAT IS NOW AND WHAT WILL TAKE PLACE LATER (REVELATION 1–3 AND 4–22)

Revelation and Prophecy

"Show his servants what must take place soon." The contents of the "revelation of Jesus Christ" are described in various ways. In two places, Revelation is described as "the words of this prophecy"—one in the prologue and the other in the epilogue (1:3; 22:7). These two passages should guide our reading of the text.

The "words of [the] prophecy" primarily concern "what must take place soon" (1:1). This same concept is repeated in 4:1: "Come up here, and I will show you what must take place after this." Then a third passage is sandwiched between these two references: "Write, therefore, what you have seen, what is now and what will take place later" (1:19).

An analysis of these pages reveals two things. First, the prologue, epilogue, and Revelation 4:1 state that this book addresses future events—that is, the future from John's time. Second, 1:19 consists of two elements: the "what is now" and the "what will take place later."

Differences Between Revelation 1–3 and 4–22

Scholars interpret "what is now" and "what will take place later" to mean the "present" and "imminent future" aspect of the prophecies, respectively (Rev. 1:19). Some even use these two temporal elements to divide the book into two sections—1–3 ("what is now") and 4–22 ("what will take place later"). Stefanovic, for instance, writes:

> "The things which are" refer to the situation and needs of the seven local churches of his own time. "The things which

are about to take place after these things" refer to the visions described in chapter 4 through 22. This section describes the ongoing great controversy between the forces of good and evil that is moving towards the end ...[98]

Aune sees a problem with this interpretation because there are historical materials in Revelation 4–22 (e.g., ch. 12).[99] In such situations, one can either dismiss the differences as insignificant and go with Stefanovic or seek to reinterpret Revelation 1:19. We shall do the latter, and for the following reasons.

Similarities Between Revelation 1–3 and 4–22

First, the structure Stefanovic proposes is based on the *past-present* (Rev. 1–3) and *future-prophetic* (4–22) natures of the prophecies, but as discussed, the actual materials contained in these two sections do not endorse such a proposition. Apart from Revelation 12, there are considerable predictive materials in chapters 2 and 3 (e.g., 2:10, 16, 22–24) and historical materials in 4–22 (e.g., 4 and 5).

Second, these two elements, as agreed by most scholars, could refer to the historical and predictive natures of the prophecies. However, if the validity of this interpretation is dependent on the two-part structure as proposed by Stefanovic (and others), then we have some serious contextual issues (which are discussed in the next section).

At this point, the reader will notice that this issue is actually at the heart of this study. The third aim of the current study, as outlined at the beginning, was to address this very issue. Based on the facts that there are significant historical and predictive elements on either sides of the book and the volume of shared material is high, we proposed that the

---

[98] Stefanovic, The Revelation of Jesus Christ, pp. 107, 187; Plain Revelation (Berrien Springs, MI: Andrews University Press, 2013), p. 4.

[99] David E. Aune, Revelation 1–5, p. 105. Stefanovic also sees Revelation 4, 5, and 12 as "historical events."

"two books" contain essentially the same material.[100] However, if there are any differences, then those differences are more stylistic in nature, not in substance. Therefore, if John and his audience did understand Revelation 1–3, then it is highly likely that they could have understood 4–22 as well (refer to the seven oracles in Part 3 of this volume for more discussion).

With that said, the question is, How do we then read the "what is now" and "what will take place later" of Revelation 1:19? If this passage is not discussing the structure or historical-predictive nature of the book, then to what is it referring?

Alternate Meanings for "what is now" and "what will take place later"

In analyzing Revelation 1:19, there are several facts that need to be highlighted. First, the immediate context shows that the two elements of this verse refer back to the vision of 1:10–20, especially the divine command to write in verse 10. Let us compare these two passages: "Write on a scroll what you see and send to the seven churches" (v. 10). "Write, therefore, what you have seen, what is now, and what will take place later" (v. 19). As we can see, verse 19 is a reiteration of verse 10, but with some additional details. The additional information includes "what is now" and "what will take place later."

Second, the key words for both passages are "write" and "see," and the focus is on the act of writing on a scroll things already shown and things yet to be shown. The events and visions that John is about to see and write may contain historical and/or predictive elements, but they are not the focus in these two passages.

---

[100] Because the purpose of this study is to make a case for a "dual approach" to Revelation, deciding exactly what part (of chapters 1–3 and 4–22) consists of historical, current, and future events is crucial. As Kenneth A. Strand also notes, "All systems of interpreting Revelation must begin by locating its several segments in past, present or future time frames" ("Foundational Principles of Interpretation," in Synopsis on Revelation—Book I, p. 3).

Third, notice that the "what you have seen" of 1:19 consists of two things—"what is now" and "what will take place later." The popular view attempts to equate "what is now" to Revelation 2 and 3, but the problem with this interpretation is that these chapters cannot fall into the "what is now" section of the structure. This is because, by the time John saw or wrote 1:19, Revelation 2 and 3 were still in the future—or in the "what will take place later" section—for he had not yet seen them. What John saw thus far is limited to 1:10–20.

Finally, the vision of the "one like the son of man" is sandwiched in between these two texts. In 1:10, John was invited to write what he was *about* to see, but by the time the initial command is reiterated in 1:19, Christ had already given (or was still giving) the first of many visions. John was urged to write what he saw, which consists of "what is now" and "what will take place later."

Therefore, the context indicates that "what is now" could simply refer to the vision John had already received or was still in the process of receiving (1:10–20), and "what will take place later" could refer to the number of visions or materials he was yet to receive (i.e., chs. 2–22). Therefore, there is a possibility that Revelation 1:19 could refer to the *number*, *volume*, or *amount* of materials already shown, and those that are yet to be shown, rather than to the *type*, *nature*, or *significance* of the shown materials.

Similar Literary Construction of Revelation 1:19 in the Johannine Writings

Notice that John frequently uses this literary style in other places too. The table below lists three of the main ones:

Texts	Details
"He made it known ... to his servant John, who testifies to *everything he saw—that is the word of God and the testimony of Jesus Christ*" (Rev. 1:1, 2, emphasis supplied).	"everything he saw" consists of two things: the "word of God" and the "testimony of Jesus"

Texts	Details
"They are also seven kings. Five have fallen, *one is*, the other has yet to come" (Rev. 17:10, emphasis supplied).	Total number of kings is "seven," which is followed by its breakup in this order: 5-1-1. Notice that the "one is" is currently in power.
"You are right when you say you have no husband. The fact is, you have had five husbands, and the man you *now* have is not your husband" (John 4:17, 18, emphasis supplied).	Total number of husbands or men the woman had known or knows is six. She had "five" in the past and is living with the sixth man now.

Notice the following similarities between these passages. First, in all these passages, John provided the summation before listing their individual components. In Revelation 1:19, "what you have seen" consists of "what is now" and "what will take place later." The same is true with the above texts. In 17:10, "seven kings" is divided into "five have fallen," "one is," and the "other has yet to come." In 1:1–2, "everything" is equal to the "word of God" plus the "testimony of Jesus." Then in John 4, we see the reverse of this—the Samaritan woman told Jesus that she had "no husbands." He affirmed the woman's claim by saying that "you have had five husbands" and "the man you now have" is "*not* your husband," which means that she has "no husbands."

Second, all these passages do contain both historical and predictive materials, but that is not their primary focus. All temporal elements in the aforementioned passages are better understood as having a more literal and sequential significance. For instance, $2 = 1 + 1$ (Rev. 1:2, 3), $2 = 1 + 1$ (v. 19), $7 = 5 + 1 + 1$ (17:10), and $5 + 1 - 6 = 0$ (John 4:17, 18). Therefore, trying to use these passages as having some sort of a symbolic or structural significance is actually saying more than what they warrant.

Third, in Revelation 1:1–2, John summarized the entire messages of Revelation as the "word of God" and "testimony of Jesus." Then 1:19 summarizes what Christ has already revealed (vv. 10–20) and what is about to be revealed (chs. 2–22). All of these constitute the "words of this prophecy" (1:3; 22:7), and the prophecies may contain past, present, or future events. Therefore, any attempt to divide the book along historical and predictive lines is an artificial exercise.

Finally, trying to use Revelation 1:19 as a guide for the structure of Revelation is just like trying to use verses 1 and 2 ("everything he saw—that is the word of God and the testimony of Jesus Christ") for the same purpose. Verses 1 and 2 cannot be used for any structural purpose because the discussion on the two elements—"word of God" and "testimony of Jesus"—are scattered everywhere in the text, and as demonstrated, the same is true for verse 19. The volume of historical and predictive materials is scattered on both sides of Revelation (1–3 and 4–22), which makes the popular rendering of Revelation 1:19 an impossible proposition.

However, instead of Revelation 1:19 ("what you have seen, what is now, and what will take place later") serving as a clue to the structure and the past-future aspect of the prophecies, it can actually mean something totally different. If "what you have seen" refers to the entire contents of Revelation (1:9–22:6), and that that consists of "what is now" and "what will take place" later, it could simply refer to the dual nature of the prophecies. Making the prophecies of Revelation true and applicable to John and his audience ("what is now") and the same will also speak to future generations ("what will take place later"). This interpretation is actually closer to the spirit of the text than the other two interpretations. This is the reason why this passage is used as the sub-title for this book.

THE WORD OF GOD, TESTIMONY OF JESUS, AND BELIEVERS

"Everything he saw; that is, the word of God and the testimony of Jesus Christ"

Here, we elucidate a few items. First, as the term "saw" suggests, the messages of Revelation were "shown" to John (1:1; 4:1), before he was told to "write what you see and hear." Therefore, Revelation consists of a series of theophanies in which John was not merely the audience but also an active participant.

The usage of the word "everything" carries two significances. First, it reveals the author's duty of care. John carefully recorded "everything" that he saw and heard, including his own reactions and those things he was shown but told "not to write" (10:4). What he recorded concerns future events, particularly as they relate to "the word of God" and "the testimony of Jesus Christ." As mentioned earlier, Revelation is both "from" and "about" Jesus. This passage now defines the two key aspects of Revelation as the word of God and testimony of Jesus. As we shall see later, "Jesus," "the word of God," and "the testimony of Jesus" are not separate entities. The word of God and the testimony of Jesus are intended to describe, explain, or elaborate on the person of Christ.

Second, the term "everything" used here reveals John's comprehensibility of the contents of Revelation. The term "everything," which consists of the "word of God" and the "testimony of Jesus," is not part of the actual vision (see Rev. 1:9–22:6). As pointed out in the introduction, the concept of "everything" is John's own assessment or summation of the contents of Revelation. In other words, if John summarized "everything" in Revelation as "the word of God and testimony of Jesus," then this suggests that he probably had a clearer understanding of the entire contents of the book.

"The word of God and the testimony of Jesus." "The word of God and the testimony of Jesus" are either closely identified with the saints of God or something that they possess (see also Rev. 1:9; 6:9; 12:17; 14:12; 20:4). The "Word of God," "the commandments of God," and "the testimony of Jesus" are discussed separately in chapters 10–12 of this volume.

"Blessed are those who read, hear, and keep." A threefold blessing is pronounced on those who read, hear, and keep those things written in Revelation. In the epilogue, however, only the *keeping* aspect is reiterated: "Blessed is he who keeps the words of the prophecy in this book" (22:7). Although those reading and hearing are blessed, the emphasis is placed more on those keeping the words of this prophecy.

Keeping is Obeying or Doing. The Greek word for "keep" or "keeping" is *tēs tēpountēs* from the root word *tērouō*, which means to "hold onto or keep." It is the same word used in Revelation 12:17 and 14:12, where the people of God are identified as "those who keep the commandments of

God and have the testimony of Jesus" and "saints who obey [*tērountes*] God's commandment and remain faithful to Jesus," respectively. The concept of "keeping" is associated with "obeying," or "doing." "Behold, I am coming soon! My reward is with me, and I will give to everyone according to what he has done" (22:12). Although blessings are pronounced on those who "read, hear, and keep [obey/do]," the ultimate reward or punishment is based on "what [one] has done." In the Gospel, John wrote, "Now that you know these things, you will be blessed if you *do* them" (John 13:17, emphasis supplied).

Keeping Involves Risk. In places where the term "keeping" is used in connection with the commandments of God and the testimony of Jesus, the ones keeping them typically do so by placing their own lives at risk. For instance, the saints who had suffered martyrdom (from John's past) had done so because they had maintained the commandments of God and the testimony of Jesus (see Rev. 6:9–12). Similarly, those who are about to die or will die (from John's perspective) will do so because of their faith in Jesus and keeping God's commandments (see 12:17; 14:12). Even John acknowledged that he was banished to the island of Patmos because he kept the word of God and the testimony of Jesus (see 1:9).

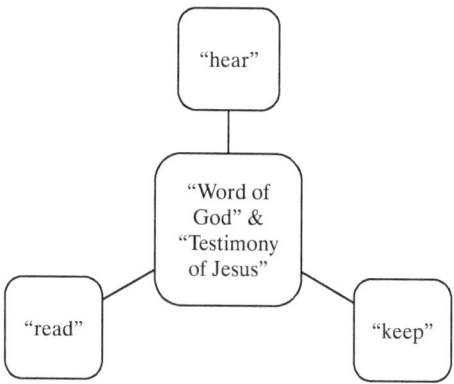

Therefore, those who read and hear do receive a blessing, but the ultimate blessing is bestowed on the one who actually keeps the word and commandments of God and has the testimony of Jesus.

LITERARY, CONTEXTUAL, AND THEOLOGICAL REFLECTIONS

The Structure of Revelation and Jesus

John entitled the book the "Revelation of Jesus," possibly because the main discourses on the three major sections (1–3, 4–11, and 12–22) are introduced by a Jesus vision. The vision of 1:9–20 features Jesus standing in the midst of the seven churches on earth. This vision serves as a prelude to the messages of 2:1–3:22. The second vision of chapters 4 and 5 features Jesus standing in the midst of the throne in heaven. Note that this vision not only serves to introduce the messages of chapters 6–11, but also provides the basis for it. The final vision of chapter 12 introduces Jesus as waging war against Satan. It also paves the way for the reminder of the book.

The Function of the Prologue/Epilogue

What the author wrote in the prologue and epilogue serves two purposes. First, because Revelation consists of what was shown to John, the prologue (1:1–8) and epilogue (22:7–21) preview and summarize the main text (1:9–22:6). Second, these previews and summations, therefore, show that the author actually understood the entire messages.[101] If John understood the materials, then

> *If John understood the materials, then it is possible to assume that these messages first addressed him and his audience in their time and context. This places a huge responsibility on the modern reader to first investigate what the messages actually meant to the early church before attempting to discover what they mean to us.*

---

[101] If someone else inserted those introductory and concluding remarks later, then the same is also true—that those who later did that did understand the prophecies.

it is possible to assume that these messages first addressed him and his audience in their time and context. This places a huge responsibility on the modern reader to first investigate what the messages actually meant to the early church before attempting to discover their contemporary relevance.

The "Revelation of Jesus" and Other Related Terms

The author used at least three other designations to describe the "revelation of Jesus" in 1:1–3: 1) The "words of this prophecy," 2) "what must take place soon," and 3) "the word of God and the testimony of Jesus." The first two designations refer to the predictive nature of the contents, whereas the third describes the essence of the actual messages. The phrase "word of God and the testimony of Jesus" appears in several crucial places in the book (1:2, 9; 6:9; 12:17; 14:12).

"What is now" and "what will take place later" (Revelation 1:19)

Revelation 1:19 is often used by scholars to divide the book into two sections—"what is now" (chs. 1–3) and "what will take place later" (chs. 4–22). They claim to see chapters 1–3 as containing mostly historical material, while chapters 4–22 containing predictive materials. However, the volume and quality of contextual, stylistic, and exegetical evidences show that the text has nothing to do with the structure of the book. Revelation 1:19 points back to or reiterates 1:10 for emphasis.[102]

The "word of God and the testimony of Jesus"

The "word of God" and the "testimony of Jesus" are the two crucial elements that the readers are urged to "read," "hear," and "keep." Definitions and details of these two entities will be explored later, but it is important to note that 1) John was imprisoned "on the island of Patmos because

---

[102] For further discussion on this, refer to the beginning of this chapter.

of the word of God and the testimony of Jesus" (Rev. 1:9), 2) the martyrs of 6:9–12 had been killed because of the "word of God and the testimony" of Jesus, 3) the end-time saints who invite the wrath of the enemy are also identified as being obedient to "the commandments of God" and in possession of the "testimony of Jesus" (12:17), 4) those who will die (in the future) will do so because of the "word of God" and the "testimony of Jesus" (14:12; 6:11; 12:17), and finally, 5) those who will come back to life and receive eternal life are those who have kept the word of God and testimony of Jesus (20:4).

Therefore, if keeping God's word/commandment and having the testimony/faith of Jesus forms the central focus of the great controversy, one must clearly define what these elements mean. For a detailed discussion of these topics, see the discussion on Revelation 1:9 in chapter 10 and 11 of this volume. However, if John and his audience saw their suffering in the light of the "word of God and the testimony of Jesus" in 1:9, is it possible that they also saw themselves in the struggles of 6:9–11, 12:17, 14:12, and 20:4?[103] Stated differently, if the core of the prophetic messages are "the word of God" and "the testimony of Jesus," and if John saw the same as the purpose for his and his audiences' suffering, then there is no reason to think that the messages of Revelation 4–22 were not applicable to him and his initial audience.

---

[103] In chapters 10 and 11 of this study, these two commodities (the word/commandments of God and testimony of Jesus) will be discussed. The study of these and other concepts will show that the entire book of Revelation was not only comprehensible but also applicable to John and his initial audience.

5.
CHRIST AND CONCEPT OF TIME IN REVELATION

> **Blessed is the one who reads aloud the words of this prophecy, and blessed are those who hear it and take to heart what is written in it, because the time is near. (Revelation 1:3)**

CONCEPT AND URGENCY OF TIME

Nearness of Time

The threefold blessing pronounced on those reading, hearing, and keeping God's commandments and Jesus' testimony was intended to serve as an incentive. However, the nearness of time ("because the time is near") stated here, reiterated in the epilogue (see 22:10), and appearing numerous times in the main text serves two other purposes: First, it functions as a mild warning to the saints who are living in sin and thus unprepared for Christ's return. Second, the concept is intended to provide assurance to those who are crying "how long" in the fifth seal (see 6:9–11) and elsewhere (see 10:6, 7; 12:12; 16:15). Thus, the book uses all possible means to persuade its readers into keeping the commandments of God and the testimony of Jesus. We begin the discussions by first tracing the occurrences and significances of the temporal element in Revelation.

Temporal References in the Main Text. As stated earlier, the prologue and epilogue reflect the authorial view on the main text. Thus, the phrase "time is near" in the prologue previews similar statements in the main text. Therefore, a survey of these passages are necessary.

Revelation 1–3. In Revelation 1:4 and 8, God is identified as the "one who is to come," but sandwiched in between these verses, Jesus is "coming with the clouds" (v. 7). Then in 3:3, Jesus is quoted as saying, "But if you do not wake up, I come like a thief, you will not know what time I will come to you." This passage is reiterated in 16:15. Obviously, the first is Christ's actual words (3:3), while the second was possibly a paraphrase by the author for emphasis. These passages carry two implications. First, if those addressed did wake up, they would come to know the time Jesus is going to come. Second, to those who do not wake up, Jesus' coming will be like a thief in the night and they will be caught unaware.

Revelation 4–11. The fifth seal constitutes the next passage. "They [the souls of the martyrs] called out in a loud voice, 'How long, Sovereign Lord, holy and true, until you judge the inhabitants of the earth and avenge our blood?'" (6:10). As if in response to this anguished question, we find these words in the midst of the sixth trumpet: "And he [the mighty angel of Rev. 10:1] swore by him who lives forever ... 'There will be no more delay! But in the days when the seventh angel is about to sound his trumpet, the mystery of God will be accomplished" (10:6, 7). Whatever the "mystery of God" may be, one thing is clear: that "there will be no more delay" does seem to respond to the "how long" question of the fifth seal. This is then followed by the "seventh trumpet," which announces that the "time has [finally] come" (11:18). Also, note that the sixth and seventh seals correspond with the seventh trumpet, where Jesus' second advent is in view in both places.

Revelation 12–22. Revelation 12:12 discusses Satan's wrath in the light of the "nearness of time." "He is filled with fury because he knows that his time is short." As in the sixth and seventh seals and seventh trumpet, chapter 14 describes Jesus as coming in "a white cloud." We have noted in 16:15 where Jesus is quoted as saying, "Behold, I come like a thief!" Then He finally comes riding on a "white horse" as the "King of kings and Lord of Lords" (see 19:11–16). Twice in the epilogue, John quoted Jesus as saying, "Behold I am coming soon!" and "Behold I am coming quickly ... [and] My reward is with me" (22:7, 12).

Analysis of the Temporal References. The temporal element in Revelation is crucial to a proper interpretation of the entire text. This literary feature serves two functions. First, the temporal signature provides cohesiveness to the text. These occurrences act as a literary adhesive and hold the entire text together. Second, the temporal elements provide crucial insights into the spiritual conditions of those who first received the messages. Since these two elements are directly related to one of the main objectives of this study, discussions on them are developed throughout the book. At this stage, however, certain important aspects about the temporal references will be explored.

Temporal References and the Second Coming

A Series of Second Comings in Revelation. First, there are two sets of events regarding the time signature that is repeated throughout the text. A reference concerning time is typically followed by either a description or vision of Jesus' second coming. This occurs five times in the main text, excluding the references in the prologue and epilogue (see 6:10/17; 10:6/11:18; 12:12/14:14; and 16:15/19:11–16). The following table lists these occurrences:

Temporal Reference	Vision or Description of Second Coming
"I will come like a thief" (3:3)	"Behold! I am coming quickly" (3:11)
"How long…?" (6:10)	"the great day of his wrath has come" (6:17)
"No more delay!" (10:6)	"time has come" (11:18)
Satan "knows that his time is short" (12:12)	"Son of Man" sitting on "white clouds" (14:14)
"Behold, I come like a thief" (16:15)	"King of Kings" riding on a white horse (19:11–16)

Analysis of the Temporal References and Second Comings. In the "seven messages" section, a reference to Jesus' coming "like a thief" is followed by a declaration of His actual coming. Next, the "great day" of God's wrath in the sixth seal is preceded by the "how long" cry of the slain saints in the fifth seal. In the trumpet section, the "time has come" announcement of the seventh trumpet is the realization of the oath ("no more delay") of the sixth trumpet (see 10:6). Following the "time is short" statement in Revelation 12:12, Jesus is seen coming in the clouds in 14:14. Finally, the King of kings mounted on a white horse in 19:11 comes after the manner of Jesus' coming described in 16:15.

Series of Second Comings. Further, as evidenced above, there is a series or cycle of second comings, each one stressing a particular aspect of the same event. Revelation 3:11 announces the imminent return of Christ, and the focus of 6:17 is on the fate of the wicked, while the focus of 11:18 is on the saints. However, in both occurrences, Christ's return is merely previewed but not fully consummated. His coming in the clouds and having a sharp sickle uses farming imagery to depict the judgment of both the wicked and righteous (see 14:14). Finally, in 19:11–16, Christ comes as a victorious Warrior-King. Note that all these are different facets of the same event. Let us consider a similar development in Matthew 24.

<u>A Series of Second Comings in Matthew 24</u>. Matthew 24 not only echoes most of the themes of Revelation, but also mimics its cycles of second comings. Like in Revelation, Matthew also features a series of second comings, each featuring a particular aspect of the same event. As shown below, the structure of Matthew 24 revolves around these cycles:

Matthew 24	Notes on Revelation
"end is still to come" (4–8)	Events described here are similar to the first five seals of Rev. 6:1–9—"wait a little longer"
"gospel into all the whole world ... then the end will come" (9–14)	Events here are similar to Rev. 10 and 14; after the bittersweet experience, the saints are to "prophesy again" the "testimony and the commandments" to all peoples and nations.
"days will be shortened" (15–22)	The "great tribulation" of the fifth seal and Rev. 12–17 is combined with shortening of days in Rev. 10.

Matthew 24	Notes on Revelation
Coming of Christ likened to "lightening"; Vultures will feast on the carcasses (23–28)	The events in the sixth seal and Rev. 19 are depicted here
"sign of [His] coming on the clouds" and angels gather the elect from the four winds (29–31)	Events here combine sixth seal, four angels of Rev. 7, and the coming in clouds of Rev. 14.
Coming of Christ likened to a thief in the night; The need to be ready is stressed here (32–51)	See the thief motif of Rev. 3:3 and 16:15; The second coming is heavily featured in the prologue/epilogue too

(a) End Is Still to Come. Notice that the statement "end is still to come" comes following a series of signs. The signs are wars, rumors of wars, famines and earthquakes in various places, nations against nations, and the coming of false prophets. These same events are described as the "beginning of birth pains," "but the end is still to come" (Matt. 24:4–8). The events portrayed here are similar to the first five seals of Revelation 6. For example, "take peace from the earth" and a "large sword" is given in the second and fourth seals, "famine" in the third and fourth seals, and "pestilence" in the fourth seal. Further, the language, especially "the end is still to come," suggests the following:

(i) Contrary to prevailing expectations, anguish, and longings, Matthew states that the end is still to come. Incidentally, this is similar to the divine response to the "how long" question of the fifth seal in Revelation 6. The divine response reads, "wait a little longer until the number of their fellow servants ... who were to be killed as they had been was completed" (6:11).

(ii) Apart from the deaths associated with "famine, sword, wars, and pestilence" (that is, those who died during the "beginning of birth pains" in Matthew 24 or those who died during the first five seals in Revelation 6), the text implies that there will be another wave of intensified tribulation and persecution just before the coming of the Lord. For instance, Matthew distinguishes the two as the "beginning of births pains" and the "great tribulation" (see 24:15–22). Revelation also speaks of two wars:

the first/current war in which the victims were crying "how long" and the impending war in which "those who were to be killed" will be killed (6:11). Like in Matthew 24, the second war is also described as "great tribulation" in Revelation 7 (For further study on these two wars, read chapter sixteen of this volume).

(iii) The text suggests that Matthew may have had a definitive prophetic timeline in mind, for how else could he have known exactly when or after which event the end would come? Paul also had something similar in mind when he insisted that the "man of lawlessness" must come first (2 Thess. 2:3). Note the relationship between Paul's lawless man and Matthew's "abomination of desolation." Both of these characters set themselves up against God and "in God's temple" (2 Thess. 2:4; Matt. 24:15); both continue to war against God and His saints up until the end; and both are destroyed by the splendor of Christ's coming.

(b) The End Will Come. In Matthew 24:9–14, a second wave of activities takes place, which includes an increased religious persecution, believers falling away from the faith, general increase in wickedness, and the rise of false prophets. It is in the midst of these setbacks that the gospel must be preached in "all the whole world as a testimony, and then the end will come" (v. 14). Note the following:

(i) The phrase "the end will come" stands opposed to the earlier declaration, "end is still to come," of Matthew 24:4–8.

(ii) The focus here is on the proclamation of the gospel. Notice that that proclamation comes in the midst of terrible afflictions and persecutions. These persecutions are fully discussed in Matt. 24:15–22.

(iii) Although Matthew wrote in passive language, it appears that he was almost urging the saints to preach as reflected in the "great commission" of chapter 28. The exact command to preach is mentioned in Revelation 10 and 14. In 10:11, the saints are commanded, "you must prophesy again." As in Matthew, notice that this command comes after or in the midst of their bittersweet experience. Then in 14:6–7, the great commission of Matthew 28 is magnified.

(c) Days Will Be Shortened. If the activities in Matthew 24:4–8 serve as the "beginning of birth pains," then the activities in verses 15–22, could be considered the "final push" that actually ushers in the second coming. As if to affirm this, the events in this passage are described as "dreadful" (v. 19) or "great distress, unequaled from the beginning of the world until now—and never will be equaled again" (v. 21). The persecutor in the great tribulation will be Daniel's "abomination of desolation." However, for the elects' sake, the duration of those dreadful "days will be shortened." Although it is not explicitly stated, the shortening of days implies the second coming. A couple things need to be pointed out here:

(i) The focus of Matthew 24:4–8 and 15–22 are on the two persecutions, while the focus of verses 9–14 is on the mission of the church. Notice that the return of Christ is ushered in by both the proclamation and great tribulation. As the persecution intensifies, the mission of the church should also intensify, as has been adequately demonstrated in history—the blood of martyrs is the seed of the church.

> As the persecution intensifies, the mission of the church should also intensify, as has been adequately demonstrated in history—the blood of martyrs is the seed of the church.

(ii) What Matthew implies here is perfectly captured in Revelation 13 and 14. Chapter 13 discloses the identity and persecuting activities of the two beasts. In the midst of these afflictions, the loud command to preach the eternal gospel is given in 14:6–7.

(d) Vultures Feast on Carcasses. The false prophets and their activities are featured in nearly all series, but here, their deceptive works are taken to a whole new level. Their final performance of signs and wonders are designed "to deceive even the elect." In the midst of their deceptive and diabolical works, Christ comes, and the glory of His coming slays the wicked, and their bodies are given to the vultures (see Matt 24:23–28). This is another second coming scene, with a focus on the punishment of the wicked.

Concerning the same, the apostle Paul wrote, "And then the lawless one will be revealed whom the Lord Jesus will overthrow with the breath of his mouth and destroy by the splendor of his coming" (2 Thess. 2:8). John made the same point in Revelation 19:17–18. Therefore, Christ's splendor destroying the opponents at His coming is a common occurrence that runs through Revelation 19, Matthew 24, and 2 Thessalonians 2. The striking similarities among these books seem to hint at the possibility that Revelation existed prior to the composition of the other two books.

(e) Coming on the Clouds. Immediately after the great distress, there will be signs in the heavenly bodies. Then the "sign of the Son of Man will appear" in the sky. The signs in the heavenly bodies and the sign of Christ's coming are taken straight from the sixth seal (see Rev. 6). Then Christ comes riding "on the clouds of the sky with power and glory." He sends His "angels to gather the saints from the four winds" (Matt. 24:31). Christ coming in the clouds is similar to the manner of His coming as depicted in Revelation 14, while the angels of the four winds are similar to the angels of 7:1–3.

As demonstrated above, Matthew's series are fully reflected in Revelation. At this stage, it is not clear if Matthew relied on a shared oral tradition or on Revelation. Whatever lays behind the text, no one knows, but what we do know is that both books feature an identical series of second comings. In some, the event is implied, while in others the same is explicitly stated. In some, only the "sign of his coming" is previewed, while in the others, the same is fully consummated. If this is not a reflection of literary dependence, then the similarities indicate that Matthew, Paul and John wrote to address similar contextual issues.[104]

---

[104] The similarities could reflect a shared tradition, but I suspect a textual dependence. It appears that someone did have access to an earlier document. And there is insufficient evidence to suggest that Mathew and Paul relied totally on Daniel and OT prophecies. Could it be that Revelation was written before Matthew and the letters to the Thessalonians? It definitely would make an interesting study in the future.

Temporal References and the Chiasmus

<u>Temporal References and the Fifth Seal</u>. Nearly all temporal elements are intended to respond to the "how long" question from a wide variety of angles. Consider the "Temporal Reference" section in a previous table. The "time is near" (Rev. 1:3) is intended to instill a sense of urgency and spur the fatigued audience into a right course of action. The use of the thief metaphor is intended to reinforce the same, particularly addressing those who have grown weary because of the apparent delay. The divine response to the "how long" question itself acknowledges a slight delay (see 6:10, 11).[105]

However, immediately after that, in Revelation 10:6, the One who had promised to come soon (see John 14:1–3) now reaffirms the same, but this time with an oath, saying that there will not be any "more delay." Then in 12:12, even Satan is employed to testify of the imminent return of Christ. In the seventh trumpet, the words "The time has come" (11:18) are both a response to the question in the fifth seal and the realization of the oath in 10:6. Because God (who does not lie) has now added an oath to His (previous) promise and even Satan confirms it, the onus is on the readers to "endure patiently," which is where Revelation 16:15 emerges. As stated earlier, this verse is borrowed from 3:3. The author attempted to stir the saints from their slumber, have their robes washed, and put them on, as summarized in the following table:[106]

---

[105] Matthew repeatedly addressed the apparent delay in the parables of the wicked servant, talents, and ten virgins (see Matt. 24:45–25:30). Peter taught the same (see 2 Peter 3:8–10).

[106] The historical interpretive landscape does not allow for such an approach to the text. If one believes that certain parts of the text are intended for a particular time period, similar passages cannot be accumulated and assessed together. However, it is unlikely that John and his audience read the text in such a way. They did not have a mental timeline ranging over two thousand years to determine which section fit into which era. They likely considered the letter (Revelation) as theirs and adapted a method similar to what is done here.

5. Christ and Concept of Time in Revelation

Nature	Aspects
"time is near" (1:3)	To instill a sense of urgency and spur the audience into righteous living
"like a thief, and you will not know at what time" (3:3)	Addressed to a "dead" church with "soiled" clothes; no sign of "external enemies"; possibly the result of the "delay."
"How long ...?" (6:10, 11)	The divine response "wait a little while" (v. 11) implies "delay"
"No more delay" (10:6)	Jesus had promised to return soon; now He "swears"; He who does not lie now adds an oath to a promise
"time has come" (10:17)	"time has come," follows the two previous statements: "wait a little while" and "no more delay," demonstrating a progression of thoughts
"his time is short" (12:12)	Satan used as a "witness" to support the claim that "time is short"
"I come like a thief" (16:15)	"stays awake, keeps his clothes"

Temporal References and Chiasm. When these passages are analyzed, a chiasm seems to emerge. A chiasm (chiasmus) or chiastic structure is an ancient literary or rhetorical technique that uses a unique repetition

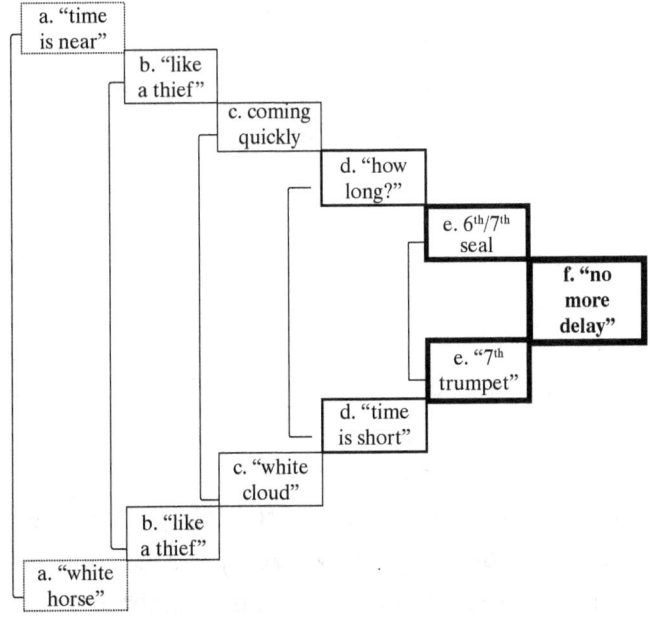

pattern to emphasize or clarify a concept. In our current discussion, the divine response ("no more delay") to the "how long" cry seems to be the central thought. The rest of the passages revolve around this. The previous diagram illustrates this structure.

How then does the chiasm work? The top "a" to "e" corresponds to the bottom "a" to "e." In this scheme, "f" constitutes the core message. The explanations of the chiasm are as follows:

1. *The Manner of Christ's Coming.* In the top "a," John saw Jesus coming, whereas in the bottom "a," Jesus actually comes riding on a white horse.
2. *No One Knows the Day or the Hour.* Both "bs" liken Jesus' coming as a thief, reinforcing the fact that "no one knows about that day or the hour" of His coming (Matt. 24:36). However, the same passage also seems to suggest that the saints "can know the time." This knowledge depends on two factors: staying awake and washing their soiled garments in the blood of the lamb. Therefore, the focus of the message here is the need to be ready.
3. *The Nearness and Manner of His Coming.* The top and bottom "cs" present Jesus as "standing at the door" and actually coming in the clouds, respectively. Standing at the door implies the terrible nearness of His return, again reinforcing the need to be ready.
4. *The Enemy and His victims Testify of His Coming.* In the top "d," the slain saints ask, "How long," whereas in the bottom "d," Satan is used to testify that the "time is short." Also note that in the bottom "d," his wrath and killing prowess is highlighted, whereas in the top "d," his victims are calling for divine intervention. If, as argued in this study, the "how long" cry emanates from the living saints, then the author and his audience saw themselves living in the fifth-seal period.
5. *The Last Seal and Trumpet.* The top "e" features the sixth and seventh seals, while the bottom "e" has the seventh trumpet in focus. Both of these passages provide a preview of Jesus' second coming. If, as argued earlier and elsewhere in this volume, the author and his first readers saw themselves as living in the "d" era in this scheme, then the only

hurdle that needs to be overcome is "e" (the final seal and trumpet era). After this, the delay is over, which leads us to "f."

6. *The "no more delay" Oath.* Finally, the divine character in "f" responds to the apparent delay, saying there is "no more delay." The immediate divine response to the "how long" question of Revelation 6:10 had been a vague "wait a little while." Now, "another mighty angel" announces with an oath, saying, "no more delay." However, both responses to the anguished cry lack specificity. Perhaps this was the reason why John addressed the same issue again in John 16 (For more discussion on this, refer to chapter 3 of this book).

Jesus had promised to return (see John 14:1–3), and the disciples could have believed that that coming would be in "this [or their] generation" (Matt. 24:34). However, that did not transpire. As the apostles began to die out, those who still clung to the promise of His coming were derided. Scoffers taunted, "Where is this 'coming' he [has] promised?" (2 Pet. 2:3). Given this onslaught, the believers in Asia were growing weary or falling way from the faith. To this group, the "mighty angel ... swore by him who lives for ever and ever" and said, "There shall be no more delay" (Rev. 10:6).

> *Given this onslaught, the believers in Asia were growing weary or falling way from the faith. To this group, the "mighty angel ... swore by him who lives for ever and ever" and said, "There shall be no more delay."*

An Oath After a Promise

Note that in this case, the "mighty angel" added an "oath" to a "promise" Jesus had made earlier (see John 14:1–3).[107] Addressing those

---

[107] This does not in any way mean that the Gospel of John was written before Revelation. What I am saying is that the events of John 14:1–3 happened before Revelation.

who have either "fallen away" or are at the verge of doing so (Heb. 6:6), the author[108] of Hebrews made the same point:

> When God made his promise to Abraham, since there was no one greater for him to swear by, he swore by himself, saying, "I will surely bless you and give you many descendants." And so after waiting patiently, Abraham received what was promised. People swear by someone greater than themselves, and the oath confirms what is said and puts an end to all argument. Because God wanted to make the unchanging nature of his purpose very clear to the heirs of what was promised, he confirmed it with an oath. God did this so that, by two unchangeable things in which it is impossible for God to lie, we who have fled to take hold of the hope set before us may be greatly encouraged. We have this hope as an anchor for the soul, firm and secure. It enters the inner sanctuary behind the curtain. (Hebrews 6:13–19)

If an oath *after* a (seemingly delayed) promise is intended to put "an end to all argument," then the "mighty angel" swearing by "him who lives for ever and ever" is also intended to conclusively "put an end to" the anxiety and frustration expressed in Revelation 6:9–11 and elsewhere (see 1:9; 5:8; 8:2–5; 14:12; 16:15).[109]

In his second letter, the apostle Peter made the same point:

> Above all, you must understand that in the last days scoffers will come, scoffing and following their own evil desires. They will say, "Where is this 'coming' he promised? ..." The Lord is not slow in keeping his promise, as some understand slowness.

---

[108] The introduction of this book suggests that John (not Paul) was the author of Hebrews. The evidences of the relationship between the Johannine books and the book of Hebrews are too abundant to list here.

[109] Note that a promise, especially an "oath," is irrevocably binding, even among the wicked. See the "oath" Herod made to Herodias' daughter that cost the life of the Baptizer (see Matt. 14:7–9).

Instead he is patient with you, not wanting anyone to perish, but everyone to come to repentance. But the day of the Lord will come like a thief. (2 Pet 3:3, 4, 9, 10).

Matthew used more than three parables to address different facets of the same issue: the wicked servant, ten virgins, and talents (see 24:45–25:30). Such shared issues place Revelation within the perimeter of the NT textual context.

Patient Endurance, Prayers of the Saints, and Cries of the Martyrs

Patient Endurance and Delay. A few more important points need to be highlighted at this stage. The first one concerns the concept of "patient endurance" that characterizes the saints of God in Revelation (see 1:9; 6:9–11; 14:12). Although the exact word is not used, the same concept is also implied in 12:17 and 17:14. The virtue of patient endurance can only be summoned if someone has either given up or is on the verge of giving up. Therefore, the text presents the saints of God as those who "endure to the end" (Matt. 24:13; see also 10:22) or are urged to endure. This would be logical if certain believers in the early church were fatigued by this "delay."

Prayers of the Saints *Versus* the Cries of the Martyrs. Is there any relationship between the "prayers of the saints" (Rev. 5:8; see also 8:2–5) and the cries of the martyrs in the fifth seal (see 6:9–11)? If there is, it is not so apparent. In fact, their differences are quite pronounced. First, one is described as "prayers," while the other is described as "cries." Second, the prayers are implied as coming from the living saints, while the cries in the fifth seal are from the dead saints. Third, the contents, nature, and details of the prayers of the saints are not provided, while the actual contents of the cries of the martyrs are explicitly stated. Finally, scholars generally hold that these two events took place at two different times.

Timing of the Prayers of the Saints and the Cries of the Martyrs. Ranko Stefanovic sees the events of Revelation 4 and 5 as taking place in AD 31.

This means that the "prayers of the saints," which form an integral part of the events of Revelation 4 and 5, also took place in AD 31.[110] Stefanovic then places the cries of the martyrs (see 6:9–11) centuries later. He writes that the "scenes of the fifth seal ... represents a later point in time."[111] By "later," he means after the "first millennium," particularly, during the "middle ages."[112] While such an approach may have some validity, it basically ignores the historical and textual context of the passage. It fails to ask the fundamental question: What did this passage—or the entire prophecies of Revelation, for that matter—mean to John and his audience? For only after seeing the text as John saw it, then can we decide what the same prophecies mean to us today.

<u>Prayers of the Saints</u> *Same as* <u>the Cries of the Martyrs</u>. While the "prayers of the saints" and the "cries of the martyrs" do have notable differences, the similarities they share outweigh the perceived differences.

The Dead Saints Vocalize the Living Saints' Concerns. First, the martyrs of the fifth seal must be taken symbolically. Since the dead do not know anything, their cries symbolically vocalize the concerns, frustrations,

---

[110] Stefanovic places the events of Revelation 4 and 5 in the "Pentecost" era. If these events occurred in AD 31, then that presents a substantial problem with the alleged timing of the "fifth seal." Note in particular the "prayers of the saints" in 5:8. With Stefanovic's theory, the prayers are of that era too. However, the nature and exact vocalization of those prayers are captured in the fifth seal, with the divine response in 8:3–4 and chapters 9–11. If the scenes of Revelation 4–5 occurred in and around AD 31, then how can the "prayers of the saints" of AD 31 (5:8) be reconciled with the prayers of the fifth seal (see 6:9–11) and the trumpets (see 8:3, 4)?

[111] I agree with this basic interpretation. However, it assumes that what took place in the fifth seal has no bearing on the author and his initial audience. I, therefore, would like to think that all the prophecies of Revelation were relevant to those who first read it, and the same prophecies also speak to us today.

[112] Stefanovic, Commentary, p. 254. This does not mean that the author takes issues with "historicism," but that the method of interpretation tends to place the fifth seal in the second millennium without any consideration of the Johannine world and context. Before applying what the text meant later in history, what the text meant to John and his initial audience must first be determined, which is where "dualism" comes in and is what this volume attempts to accomplish.

impatience, fears, and experiences of the *living* saints, especially those who first received the letter.[113]

The Relationship Between the "cries" and "prayers." Second, note that the "how long" cry of the martyrs is actually sandwiched in between two references to "the prayers of the saints" (Rev. 5:8 and 8:2–5). In Revelation 5:8, the twenty-four elders and four living creatures are seen "holding golden bowls full of incense, which are the prayers of the saints." In 8:2–5 (specifically v. 3), an angel "was given [possibly by the elders and the creatures] much incense ... with the prayers of all the saints" to offer to God (see also Ps. 141:2).[114] The different settings of these two prayer references (worship and judgment settings in heaven) may indicate differences in significance too.

However, the exact details or contents of those prayers are not provided. This is where the fifth seal comes in. The sentiments of the (living saints') prayers are perfectly captured in the "how long" cries of the martyrs.[115] Besides, the psalmist did equate the prayers of the living saints to bowl of tears: "O Lord God Almighty, how long will your anger smolder against the prayers of your people? ... you have made them drink tears by the bowlful" (Psalm 80:4, 5).

Martyrs' Cries Part of a Literary Device. Third, this concept (of the "dead" vocalizing the concerns of the living saints) is part of a literary device that is frequently used in Revelation. We cite a couple of examples to illustrate this point. The first concerns the loud voice of the mighty angel of Revelation 5. The angel asks, "Who is worthy ...?" The context

---

[113] Although Stefanovic asserts that both the "prayers" (Rev. 5:8; 8:3–5) and "cries" (Rev. 6:9–12) emanate from the "slain souls," rather than the living, he views the seven trumpets as a response to these "cries" and "prayers" (pp. 291, 292).

[114] A passive voice usually suggests divine action, but in this case, God is the recipient of these actions. That makes the elders and living creatures the ones involved in giving the incense and prayers to the angel.

[115] Further, instead of the "living saints," God uses those who have already made the ultimate sacrifice to vocalize the concerns of the living saints in John's time. The fact that the martyrs were given "white robes" and told to "wait a while" signified that their eternal destiny was secured. It is as if God is (indirectly) reminding the living saints to endure patiently, not shrink from death, and secure your own "white robes" too.

shows that the concerned angel already knew the answer. If he knew the answer, then for whose benefit does he scream? John's weeping and emotional response to the question shows that the mighty angel actually vocalized John's (and the living saints') thoughts.

The same is also true with "another mighty angel" of 10:1. This angel comes down from heaven, stands on both land and sea, raises his right hand toward heaven, and swears by "him who lives for ever and ever," saying, "There will be no more delay ..." (v. 6). This angel is not involved in some publicity stunt. He is addressing one of the principle concerns of the living saints. Therefore, whether it's a "loud voice" from a "mighty angel," "another mighty angel," or the martyrs, none is done in a vacuum. These heavenly shouts have a direct bearing on the living saints. Therefore, the heavenly voices either vocalized the living saints' concerns or provided answers to their anguished prayers.

The Seven Trumpets in Response to Both the "prayers" and the "cries." Finally, there is every indication that the seven trumpets (see Rev. 8–11) hurled down to the earth are in direct response to *both* the prayer of the saints (see 8:2–5) and the cries of the martyrs (see 6:9–11). For instance, as the "incense ... with the prayers of the saints" was offered to God from the "golden altar," the censer filled with "fire from the altar" was "mixed with blood" and hurled down to the earth (8:5–7).

Notice that the blood that was hurled down had its origin in the heavenly altar. The only other place we are told about the presence of blood near the altar is in the fifth seal: "I saw under the altar the souls of those who had been slain ..." crying out, "how long ...?"[116] Therefore, it is possible that the seven trumpets were administered in response to both the prayers of the saints and the blood of the martyrs. This suggests that the

---

[116] We understand the term used here is "soul" and not "blood." However, there are two reasons why we are using "blood" for "soul." First, elsewhere in the NT (and the OT), the spilled blood of the martyrs is presented as speaking or crying. In Hebrews 12:24, the sprinkled blood of both Jesus and Abel are speaking. The same is also true in Genesis 4:10. In this way, the "souls" of the martyrs can be understood as "blood" in Revelation 6:9–11. Second, the Bible consistently teaches that "life is in the blood." Therefore, "life" or "soul" can be equated to "blood."

"prayers of the [living] saints" and the "how long" cry of the slain martyrs are not two separate entities but one and the same.[117] And it is possible that John and his initial audience may have understood the text this way too.

The Timing of the Seven Trumpets. In the light of this, how do we address the timing of the divine response (see Rev. 8–11)? When did the events of the seven trumpets occur? There are usually two approaches when it comes to the prophecies of Revelation, particularly the seals and trumpets. The first method overemphasizes the nuances of the text—usually in favor of a historical method of interpretation—and downplays the literal fulfillment of these events. The second approach delights in removing any time element by promoting a more idealistic approach to the text.

No doubt these are logically sound responses, but the answer may lay in two other areas. First, acknowledging that these prophecies were written to the early church, who not only understood the contents, but also saw them as being applicable in its own time. Second, if the prophecies of Revelation (particularly the series of sevens) are presented in a sequential order, one must first determine where John and his audience saw themselves. In other words, which of the events constitute their past, which ones were still in their future, and which ones framed their present? This is one of the fundamental questions on which the main thesis of this study is built. Therefore, where applicable, we shall seek to respond to this question in the rest of the chapters.[118]

---

[117] In Revelation (as in the Gospel of John), the audiences who actually received these messages are not so apparent. Although these letters addressed their real and immediate concerns, they do not receive a mention. In Paul's letters, he addressed them directly, but in Revelation, the audiences take a muted position. They are like the "silent audience" in a movie. However, they know that the letter addresses their concerns. This comes through in two ways. First, concerning the "prayers," the text does not specify the "saints" who made those prayers. Second, regarding the fifth seal, it uses the martyred saints. This is consistent with what the author wrote elsewhere. See, for instance, Revelation 21:8 and 27. In these passages, the author made an appeal to the saints to abstain from idolatry, sexual immorality, magic, and other deceitful practices, but he did not make a direct appeal. He indirectly said who will enter the city of God and who will not.

[118] We will heavily use this principle when we come to Revelation 4–11. Note that the focus of this study is chapters 1–3, which means that in an upcoming study, we will see how this literary principle helps our studies in chapters 4–11.

The Focus of the Temporal References

Temporal References Spiral Up to the Return of Christ. There are many responses given in Revelation to explain the obvious delay in 6:9–11. In the immediate context, there are three divine responses to the "how long" question. First, to allow time for the saints who would be killed to be killed in order to make the number "complete" (see v. 11). Second, to allow time for the sealing of the saints to occur before God responds to their anguished cries (see 7:3). Third, to follow up with the "no more delay" shout from the "mighty angel" (10:6). These and other similar responses, confessions, and testimonies, either from humans (whether living or dead) or angels (holy or unholy), shed further light on the concerns of the fifth seal.

These responses capture various facets of the divine response to the basic question asked in the fifth seal. However, the primary focus of the temporal references in Revelation is the timing of Christ's return. As discussed earlier, each series or cycle-of-time reference spirals up and climaxes with the return of Christ.[119] The second coming of Christ is finally the ultimate response to the question (see 6:10). This is like a series of steps or a stairway that leads up to and climaxes with the return of Christ as shown in this diagram.

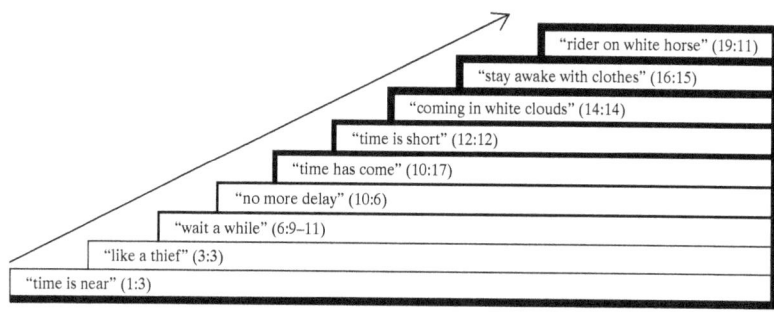

---

[119] The objection to this argument is the fact that at the end of each series of seven and in Revelation 14, the second coming of Christ is previewed. This reality favors a more cyclical order of events, rather than a linear order. While that is true, these instances of preview or flashes of the second coming finds its ultimate fulfillment in Revelation 19.

Temporal References in the Gospel of John

<u>Temporal References Climax with the Crucifixion.</u> A similar literary construction can be detected in the Gospel of John. Unlike the construction in Revelation, the one in John swells up and climaxes with the crucifixion of Jesus Christ. For instance, in John 2:4, Jesus says to his mother, "My time has not yet come." Further, in John 4:35, He tells His disciples, "Do you not say, 'four months more and then the harvest?'" A little later, when one of Jesus' unbelieving brothers challenges Him to go to Jerusalem, He replies, "My right time has not yet come" (7:6–8). Later in the chapter, He states, "I am with you only for a short time" (v. 33). The author then enlisted hard truths that Jesus proclaimed within the temple area, but "no one seized him because his time has not yet come" (8:20). "As long as it is day," Jesus states, "we must do the work of him who sent me. Night is coming when no man can work" (9:4). Note how the time changes from "not yet" to "four months" and further down to one "day" ("night" and "day" make up twenty-four hours).

Then in John 11:9, the time further drops to "twelve hours." When His disciples attempted to restrain Jesus from going to Jerusalem, He replied, "Are there not twelve hours of daylight?" Then when "some Greeks" requested "to see Jesus," He replied, "the hour has come for the Son of Man to be glorified" (12:23). Here, Jesus reaffirms His decision to face Calvary. "Now my soul is troubled, and what shall I say? 'Father, save me from this hour'? No, it was for this very reason I came to this hour" (v. 27). Finally, John said, "Jesus knew that the time had come for him to leave the world" (13:1). Compare this diagram with the previous one:

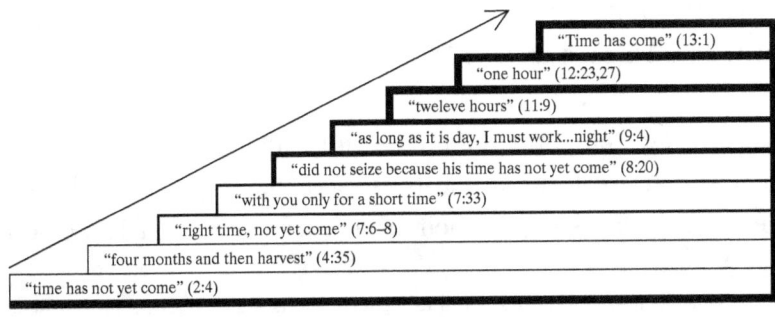

Analysis of the Diagram. The temporal references reflect a meticulous progression. There are three important points that need to be stressed.

First, they move from "time is not yet" to "time has come," and sandwiched in between these are "four months," "day and night [24 hours]," "twelve hours," and "one hour."

Second, three other temporal references appear in between the "four months" and "day and night" references, and they are "right time," "short time," and "time has not yet come." On the surface, these phrases appear to be a repetition of John 2:4. However, the context of each usage proves otherwise.

1. Note the "right time" reference, for instance. The reference to a "right time" is an anticipatory expression that Jesus would eventually go to Jerusalem as the Passover Lamb. When that time finally came, two groups of people attempted to hinder Him. First, His own disciples cautioned Him about the dangers of going back to Bethany, which is "less than two miles from Jerusalem" (John 11:8, 16, 19). Also, some Greeks' request to "see Jesus" was denied with the words "the hour has come" (12:20–23).
2. The next phrase "short time" plays a dual role, pointing to both Calvary (the "right time") and the ascension, events that are not far off.
3. Then the reference to "his time has not yet come" is used in either a failed attempt to arrest, seize, or stone Jesus. Soldiers had been dispatched to arrest Him, but no one had dared to seize or stone Him, even within the temple area, because "His time has not yet come" (7:32, 45–49; 8:20, 59). When the time finally did come, Jesus voluntarily gave Himself up (see 18:1–11).[120]

Third, these temporal references not only speak of the scheduled and timely death of Jesus, but also its sacrificial import. The Jews being unable to seize Jesus within their own gates shows that His death was

---

[120] The same is inferred when Jesus said to the high priest, "I always taught in synagogues or at the temple, where all the Jews come together" (John 18:20).

an intentionally sacrificial act on His part. John 10:17–18 captures this well: "The reason my Father loves me is that I lay down my own life—only to take is up again. No one takes it from me, but I lay it down on my own accord. I have authority to lay it down and authority to take it up again."

Even the nature of Jesus' death confirms this reality. "Jesus said, 'It is finished.' With that, he bowed his head and gave up his spirit" (John 19:30). His death is unique. In normal scenarios, one has to give up the spirit before bowing the head. However, Jesus breathed His last and died *after* bowing His head. This is a physiologically impossible phenomenon. This again speaks volumes of Jesus' intentional and sacrificial death.[121]

Therefore, a parallel exists between the usage and significance of the temporal elements in Revelation and the Gospel of John. One swells and climaxes with Jesus' death, whereas the other does so with His return.[122]

> *These temporal references not only speak of the scheduled and timely death of Jesus, but also its sacrificial import. The Jews being unable to seize Jesus within their own gates shows that His death was an intentionally sacrificial act on His part.*

---

[121] Elder Floyd Paua highlighted this insight during a series of lectures at The University of Papua New Guinea Church in January 2018.

[122] Another notable feature is that the references to Jesus' imminent return featured in the prologue and epilogue are as numerous as the ones in the main text. The prologue and epilogue feature four references each. In these sections, the references consist of either John's reflections or Jesus' own words. Nearly all references in these sections address Jesus as the One "who is to come" and "coming soon." The purpose of these usages appears to be to "spur" the "dying," "almost dead," and "sleeping" saints into a right course of action.

Prologue	Epilogue
"because the time is near" (1:3)	"Behold, I am coming soon!" (22:7)
"God who is to come" (v. 4)	"Behold, I am coming soon!" (v. 12)
"Look, he is coming with clouds" (v. 7)	"Yes, I am coming soon" (v. 20)
"God who is to come" (v. 8)	"Amen. Come, Lord Jesus" (v. 20)

LITERARY, CONTEXTUAL, AND THEOLOGICAL REFLECTIONS

Prophecy Not Given in a Vacuum

God did not give the prophecies of Revelation to John in a vacuum. The prophetic words (both 1–3 and 4–22) were revealed to respond to and address certain pressing concerns that the early church had. The assumption that the author and his readers served as mere custodians of a prophetic book that had no relevance to them is untenable. Stefanovic posits that the seven churches may have understood the messages of Revelation 4–22:5, but that their actual fulfillment was still in the future (approximately three hundred years later).[123]

Looking back from two thousand years later, what Stefanovic and others say seems to make sense. However, we must not do so at the expense of the text and what it particularly meant to the early church. If John knew that the application of these messages was to be in the future only, he would have told the seven churches to "seal and close up" the book. Instead, a triple blessing is pronounced on those who "read," "hear," and "keep" the things revealed in it. Therefore, it is safer to assume that the messages of Revelation did speak to John and his audience.

John, His Churches, and the Imminent Return of Jesus

John and his churches expected Jesus to return in their lifetime. They absolutely had no idea that people would still be living on earth 2,000 years

---

There are three references to Christ's second coming in the prologue (1:4, 7, 8) and another three in the epilogue (22:7, 12, 20). In 1:4, 7, and 8, the author's confession of Jesus' advent is layered between two references to God as the coming One (vv. 7 and 4 and 8, respectively). The three occurrences in the epilogue are direct quotes of Jesus ("Behold, I am coming soon") and identical to the statement in 1:7, except that the latter consists of John's declaration.

[123] See Ranko Stefanovic, *Revelation of Jesus Christ*, p. xx. Stefanovic offers Revelation 4:1 as evidence that the prophecies of chapters 4–22 were intended for a future generation. That reading is actually shaped by 2,000 years of history that stands in between us and John. This will be discussed more fully later.

later! If, as discussed, the prologue and epilogue consist of the authorial intent and reflections, then one would do well to take note of the "nearness of time" concept that saturates the text. In light of the "how long" cry (6:10), and with statements like the "time is near" (1:3), "there will be no more delay" (10:6), the "time has come" (11:18), and "he [Satan] knows that his time is short" (12:12), the seven churches saw Revelation (both 1–3 and 4–22) as very much applicable to their own time.

This does not mean that one must adopt a preterist method of approaching the text. What it does mean is that this should compel us to investigate what the text (chapters 4–22, in particular) actually meant to John and his readers. The "how long" cry could be indicative of their state of affairs. If they had expected Jesus to come in their lifetime (which they had), but were experiencing delays, then these passages were intended to first speak to their time.

The "how long" Cry

The anguished cry of Revelation 6:9–11 is stated as coming from the "souls of those who had been slain." If the Bible does not teach the immortality of the soul, then how can these conflicting thoughts be reconciled? Unless the martyrs are symbolically "voicing" the concern of the living saints (John and his readers), these passages are a minefield for interpretive and theological problems (For further discussion on these problems, see the end of 6:9–12).[124]

Revelation of Jesus: "The word of God and the Testimony of Jesus"

The concepts associated with terms like "word," "commandments of God," and "faith of Jesus" permeate the text. The author (John)

---

[124] Since the discussion in this book is limited to Revelation 1–3, studies based on passages like 6:9–12 and others will be included in an upcoming project.

acknowledged that he was on the "island of Patmos because of the word of God and the testimony of Jesus" (1:9). He addressed his readers as his "companions in suffering," possibly because of the same. He then presented those who had been slain (see 6:9–12) and those who will be slain (see 12:17; 14:12) because of the "word of God and the testimony of Jesus." If John and his audience identified themselves with those who kept the "word of God and the testimony of Jesus" in 1:1–3 and 9, would they not also see themselves in 6:9–11, 12:17, 14:12, and 20:4?

If they did, then these concepts would challenge those who neatly divide the text into two sections—chapters 1–3 dealing with John's time and 4–22 dealing with the future—in a number of ways. Although it is true that the messages of 4–22 has the future in focus, that does not mean that John and his readers had nothing to do with them. Especially if John and his audience considered that their suffering was related to the "word of God and the testimony of Jesus," they perhaps saw themselves as the ones who were being targeted in 12:17 and would die soon (see 6:9–11; 14:12). A thorough discussion on these will shed more light on the text, context, and other pertinent issues from which this and other Johannine books emerged (see also 1:9; 6:9–11; 12:17; 14:12).

6.

THE COMMUNICATION OF CHRIST

> God gave him [Jesus] to show his servants ... He made it known by sending his angel to his servant John. (Revelation 1:1)

INTRODUCTION

In this chapter, we will discuss the way Revelation was communicated to the seven churches. To accomplish this, we shall consider the follow areas: 1). The communication, writing process and their implication on the book's accuracy, 2). The writing process and its implication on the content and structure, 3). The writing process and its Implication on critical scholarship.[125]

COMMUNICATION AND WRITING PROCESSES

The Manner in which Revelation Was Given and Its Implication on Accuracy

The messages of Revelation as they were given to John have less room for error. Although all Scripture is inspired (see 2 Tim. 3:16) and was

---

[125] 1) In Revelation 4–5, God gives the sealed "scroll" to Jesus, and chapters 6–22 constitute the "unsealing" and "eating" of the actual content of that scrolled-message. 2) Jesus delivers the prophetic words to "the servants" in the seven churches through the "angel" and "John." Thus, the message that originated from God was given to Jesus, who plays a key role in both the revelation and dissemination processes. Jesus is also the chief protagonist figure in the numerous war scenes in chapters 12–19. The angel, however, assumes a very critical role in this revealing process. He is the personal guide who explains and clarifies, asks rhetorical questions, responds to queries, and affirms and confirms the things John "sees and hears."

written when holy men were moved by the Spirit of God (see 2 Peter 1:21), the messages of Revelation have a high degree of divine control. Three reasons support this idea.

First, it is impossible for the One who gave (God), the One who received (Jesus), and the angel who explained to err on their part. John was told to only "write what he saw and heard." Apart from the author's own personal reaction to what he saw and heard (see Rev. 1:17; 5:4; 19:10) and the angelic guide's commentaries, the remaining text (1:10–22:6) essentially contains the things he saw and heard.

Second, prior to John's involvement, he was thoroughly quarantined. Note that he was "in the Spirit" on the "Lord's day" when he received the vision. After he saw the one "like the Son of Man," he "fell as though dead." However, the glorified Christ "placed his right hand on" him and supernaturally strengthened him (1:9–17). In other words, being in the Spirit on the Lord's day and beholding the glorified Christ, being smitten by the presence of God and His right hand being placed on him, and being resuscitated and commissioned to write all show heavy, divine presence and involvement with John during the writing process. In such a tightly controlled atmosphere, one would naturally expect less room for error.

Third, what John saw, heard, and wrote was carefully guided. For instance, he was restrained from writing about the seven thunders (see 10:3–5), the veracity of certain things he wrote were stressed (see 19:9; 22:6), and if any of the heavenly beings felt certain parts of the visions needed clarification, they intervened (see 5:5; 7:13–17; 17:7–18). This also attests to the fact that Revelation was not only *of* Christ, but also *by* Christ.

How and When John Actually Wrote Revelation

When did John write the book of Revelation? Did he write while still within each vision or did he write after coming out of his vision? Either is possible. Most, if not all, biblical prophecies were written after coming out of the vision. Certain times when the prophet was still praying, the angel of the Lord communicated with him and the prophet would write it afterwards (see Dan. 9–12). What follows next is a discussion on all available evidences so that the reader can make his/her own decision.

Revelation Written in and During Vision. First, like Daniel, John was conscious and "in the Spirit" during the divine encounter (see Rev 1:9, 10). Second, the instruction to "write [*graphon*] on a scroll what you see" is in imperative aorist, meaning that John was urged upon or almost commanded to start writing and not stop until the task was completed. Each time he was told to write, the same tense, voice, and mood are used (see vv. 10, 19; 19:9). The consistent choice of the language is only possible if the writer was actually engaged in writing during the vision.

Third, concerning the seven thunders, John wrote, "When he [the mighty angel] shouted, the voices of the seven thunders spoke. And when the seven thunders spoke, I was about to write, but I heard a voice from heaven say, 'seal up what the seven thunders have said and do not write it down'" (10:3, 4). Note that John was about to write what the seven thunders spoke when the heavenly voice stopped him. It does not appear that the visions he saw and the actual writing took place at separate times. The prophet likely wrote Revelation while still in vision (see also 19:9, 10).[126] Why is this important? Why is John writing while in vision or merely what was shown to him important? If the text is embraced as it appears, it would put a multitude of human-generated controversies to rest. Such suggestions might seem too simplistic to serious Bible students, but regarding matters of faith, it is better to take the text as it reads.[127]

---

[126] See the narrative of Peter's imprisonment and release and how an angel led him out (Acts 12:8–11).

[127] It is possible that John may have written Revelation after coming out of the vision because God would have enabled His servant to bring to memory all that he had seen in the visions. All the theory proposed in this study is challenged by the fact that John was not just playing a "sedentary" role in the vision; he actually travelled to heaven (4:1, 2), walked to receive the little scroll (10:8–11), and bowed and worshiped (19:9, 10).

Revelation Written After the Vision. There are a couple of objections to this thesis. The first one is that John must have had a scroll and ink readily available at the time of the vision for this to happen. If not, he must have received the visions in his place of residence. The second objection is that John does not appear to be sitting at one place with a scroll and ink in hand during the visions. This is because he is seen travelling extensively and participating in the visions.

For instance, Revelation 1–3 takes place while he is on Patmos Island, but in chapter 4, he is invited to come up higher to heaven. Other times, the author is either standing or walking on the beach (see 10:9–11). Still other passages show that John is actively participating and interacting with the characters in the visions (where he is involved in either eating the scrolls or worshiping the angels [see chs. 10, 17]). Therefore, his movements and participation in and during the vision would make writing during vision almost impossible. Therefore, it is also possible that John may have written Revelation after coming out from the visions, and the fact is that either method is possible with God.

Both Scenarios Are Possible. The apostle Peter's prison escape story might shed some light on this dilemma. "Intending to persecute," King Herod "proceeded to seize Peter" and imprisoned him (Acts 12:1, 3). "But the church was earnestly praying to God for him" (v. 5). In response to prayer, an angel of the Lord came in, woke him up, and led him out. The text describes Peter's experience this way: "Peter followed him [the angel] out of the prison, but he had no idea that what the angel was doing was really happening; he thought he was seeing a vision" (v. 9). It was after passing several guarded gates, and after "the angel left him," that "Peter came to himself" (vv. 10, 11) and realized that his escape was real.

Here is a situation where Peter thought he was "seeing a vision," but it was actually happening. It is possible that the same could have happened in Revelation, where the author *thought* he was writing in a vision, but it could have been very real. Although we do not have sufficient evidence to conclusively put this issue to rest, it is important to bear in mind that either scenario is possible with God.

IMPLICATIONS ON STRUCTURE AND CONTENT

The Implication of "write what you see and hear"

If John wrote "what he saw and heard," then did he write them down in the order in which they were revealed, or did he rearrange the materials? In other words, did he have any control of the content, sequence, design, and structure of the book? Certain literary features show that John wrote the prophetic visions in the order and manner in which they were presented to him.

First, as mentioned earlier, the prologue and epilogue consist of the author's own summation, assessment, and reflections (see Rev. 1:1–9; 22:7–21). However, the main text begins with the vision of the glorified Christ and ends with a description of New Jerusalem (see 1:10–20; 21:1–22:6). Between these two visions are four series of septets: seven churches (2:1–3:22), seven seals (6:1–8:1), seven trumpets (8:2–11:19), and seven plagues (16–18). The fact that these series of sevens are enumerated as "first," "second," "third," etc. suggests that they were recorded in the exact order in which they were shown. This means John had less control over the content and structure of Revelation 1–3, 6–11, and 16–18.

Second, the remaining chapters are closely related to these septets in a profound way. For instance, chapters 4 and 5 serve as a prelude to the seven seals (6–11), and 12–15 provides the ground for what follows in the seven plagues (16–18).

Third, each of the scenes, either happening in heaven, earth, or the sea begins with phrases such as "after this I saw," "then I saw," "then I saw another," or "after this I heard." These phrases indicate the chronological and sequential order in which John saw and wrote the scenes. Therefore, these literary features suggest that the messages and structure of Revelation had its origin in heaven as well.

CRITICAL SCHOLARSHIP

Critical scholarship would consider our discussion on the revelation process as being too simplistic. A critical scholar would contest any

> *If Revelation as we have it today went through different stages of editorial work, then one would expect to find earlier copies that demonstrate those changes. Thus far, none has done that. Therefore, we are compelled to work with the actual document as we have it.*

claim to inspiration or accuracy of the contents, order, and even the process. For various reasons, such a scholar would also reject the notion that Revelation was written by a single author in one sitting. These are proper areas of enquiry and as such expected. However, this author refuses to engage in those conversations because critical scholarship has yet to produce an evidentiary document substantiating their own theories. For instance, if Revelation as we have it today went through different stages of editorial work, then one would expect to find earlier copies that demonstrate those changes. Thus far, no one has done that. Therefore, we are compelled to work with the *actual* document as we have it.

7.

JESUS AND GOD

INTRODUCTION

This section of the prologue accomplishes two things. First, similar to any Greco-Roman epistle of that era, it identifies the author, recipients, and their location, and includes general salutations. Second, it provides a preview of the major sections of the text. Therefore, to avoid repetition, we reserve the detailed analysis for those sections in the main text. Here, however, we make certain important observations.

> John, to the seven churches in the province of Asia: Grace and peace to you from him who is, and who was, and who is to come, and from the seven spirits before his throne, and from Jesus Christ, who is the faithful witness, the firstborn from the dead, and the ruler of the kings of the earth. To him who loves us and has freed us from our sins by his blood, and has made us to be a kingdom and priests to serve his God and Father—to him be glory and power for ever and ever! Amen. "Look, he is coming with the clouds," and "every eye will see him, even those who pierced him"; and all peoples on earth "will mourn because of him." So shall it be! Amen. "I am the Alpha and the Omega," says the Lord God, "who is, and who was, and who is to come, the Almighty. (Revelation 1:4–8)

STRUCTURE AND ANALYSIS OF THE TEXT

Structure

Revelation 1:4–8 has two main sections: 1) the general greetings (v. 4a–b) and 2) the pronouncement of the blessings from the members of the triune God (v. 4c–8). These two sections are further divided into several subdivisions as follows:

> General Greetings
> i. *Author (4a)*
> ii. *Addressees (4b)*
> Pronouncement of Blessings
> iii. *From God (4c)*
> iv. *From the Holy Spirit (4d)*
> v. *From Jesus (5–7)*
> vi. *From God (8)*

The first section identifies the author and his readers. The second section pronounces a blessing of "grace and peace" from the three members of the Godhead. Of the three, God opens and closes the blessings, and those from the Holy Spirit and Jesus Christ are sandwiched in between.

Analysis of the Text

The Trinity and God as the Coming One. In this triune blessing, the Holy Spirit is described as the "seven spirits before the throne." God is mentioned twice. These passages begin and end with the tripartite reference to God as the One "who is, and who was, and who is to come" (vv. 4c, 8). Note that He who "is to come" is God, not Jesus. However, in verse 7, Jesus receives a brief mention as "coming with the clouds," thus implicating both the Father and the Son as the "coming one." Following a brief reference to the Father and the Spirit, the bulk of the passages describe Jesus Christ.

The Multiplicity and Emphatic use of Jesus' Name. A number of varying names, titles, and descriptions—more than twelve in all—are accorded to Jesus in Revelation 1:5–7: "Jesus," "Christ," "the faithful witness," "the firstborn from the dead," "the ruler of the kings of the earth," "him who loves us," him who "has freed us from our sins by his blood," "his blood," "has made us to be a kingdom," has made us to be "priests to serve his God and Father," the "Amen," "he is coming with the clouds," "every eye will see him, even those who pierced him," and "will mourn because of him." We have noted how the author had described the book as "the Revelation of Jesus Christ." Therefore, this introductory passage only serves to reinforce Jesus as the central character in the book. We will note the following points.

First, if this introductory passage is not part of the main visions that John received, then he was providing his own reflections on the main text. He may have attempted to even cluster the notable names, titles, and accomplishments of Jesus that are featured in the main text. For example, in Revelation 2 and 3, Jesus uses most of these titles to introduce Himself to the seven churches. Second, regardless of when John wrote this passage (i.e., after or below the main text, or even if someone else did), the author's use of these divine titles is intended to set the general tone and introduce the main text. Third, the multiplicity and emphatic use of "Jesus Christ" could also provide relevant clues to the background issues addressed in this book. The details of these will be discussed in chapters 7–9.

> *Note that He who "is to come" is God, not Jesus. However, in verse 7, Jesus receives a brief mention as "coming with the clouds," thus implicating both the Father and the Son as the "coming one." Following a brief reference to the Father and the Spirit, the bulk of the passages heavily describe Jesus Christ.*

Authorship. "John, to the seven churches in the province of Asia." Scholars have debated the actual identity of John.[128] Tradition identifies this John as the brother of James, one of the "sons of thunder." Others have suggested either John Mark or another John as the author. We adopt the view that John, the son of Zebedee, is the author of Revelation. This is because the volume of internal evidence proving Johannine authorship is far more convincing than are those that suggest otherwise. For further comments on the issue of authorship and other related issues, refer to the discussion in chapter 2.

Authorship and the Order in Which the Johannine Books Were Written. When discussing authorship, the date, place, and other related issues, Revelation cannot be discussed in isolation. It is important to discuss all Johannine books together. These books include the three letters (1, 2, and 3 John) and the Gospel of John. In the two smaller epistles (2 and 3 John), the author is identified only as "the elder." Then in 1 John and the fourth Gospel, the books do not provide any information about his or his readers' identity. Here, scholarship has utilized internal, external, and other available evidences to reconstruct those missing pieces. For more information on this, refer to chapter 3.

JESUS AS GOD

The One "who is, who was and who is to come"

God as the One "who is, who was and who is to come." This threefold title for God first appears in Revelation 1:4 and is reiterated in verse 8: "'I am the Alpha and Omega' says the Lord God, 'who is, and who was, and who is to come; the Almighty.'" John was undoubtedly alluding to at least three places in the main text. The first is uttered by the four living creatures in a worship setting in 4:8: "the Lord God Almighty, who was, and is, and is to come." The

---

[128] MacKenzie, Robert K. *The Author of the Apocalypse: A Review of the Prevailing Hypothesis of Jewish-Christian Authorship*. Mellen Biblical Press Series 51. Lewiston, NY: Edwin Mellen Pr, 1997. See also, a review of MacKenzie's book by Farmer, Ronald L. "The Author of the Apocalypse: A Review of the Prevailing Hypothesis of Jewish-Christian Authorship." *Journal of Biblical Literature* 117, no. 4 (Wint 1998): 756–58.

second utterance is also in a worship setting but this time, from the twenty-four elders. "We give thanks to you," they cried, "Lord God Almighty, the One who is and who was" (11:17). The third occurrence is in response to God's judgment on the wicked. The "angel in charge of the waters" is heard saying, "You are just in these judgments; you who are and who were, the Holy One" (16:5). Note that in 11:16–17 and 16:5, the phrase "who is to come" is omitted.

Jesus as the "one who is, who was and who is to come." The same titles are also attributed to Jesus. Initially, the One "like the Son of Man" is quoted as saying, "Do not be afraid. I am the First and the Last ... I was dead, and behold I am alive forever and ever" (1:17, 18). The phrases "I was dead" and "I am alive forevermore" are conceptually identical to the phrases "who was" and "who is," respectively. As indicated earlier, only in Revelation 1:8 and 4:8 is the phrase "who is to come" used in reference to God. However, in 11:16–17 and 16:5, this phrase is dropped, but not entirely. It ("who is to come") is then increasingly applied to Jesus in more than five places (see 1:7; 14:14–16; 16:15; 19:11–16; 22:7, 11). Is this usage merely accidental or by design?[129] The evidence shows that this literary brilliance is intentional. Revelation and other Johannine books are actually replete with this type of literary construction. To appreciate this device, we explore the following examples:

A Literary Crescendo: Divine Titles for God Attributed to Jesus

From God as the "Alpha and the Omega" to Jesus as the "Alpha and the Omega." In Revelation 1:8, the Lord God is quoted as saying, "I am the Alpha and the Omega." Literally, *"alpha"* and *"omega"* are the first and the last letters of the Greek Alphabet. John was obviously alluding to 21:6, where God describes Himself saying, "I am the Alpha and the Omega." Similar to the phrase "who was, is and is to come," this title assumes a similar development where the author first referred to God as the "Alpha and Omega," and then he incrementally transferred these titles to Jesus.

---

[129] Ekkehardt Mueller observes the same, but he thinks the phrase "is to come" is omitted "in this text because God will have come at that time." See "Jesus and His Second Coming in the Apocalypse," *Journal of the Adventist Theological Society*, 11/12, p. 207.

God as the "Alpha and the Omega." In Revelation 21:6, where there are actually two sets of titles for God: "the Alpha and the Omega and the Beginning and the End [*egō to Alpha kai to ō, hē apchē kai to telos*]." In 1:8, however, John quoted only the "Alpha and Omega" title and omitted "the Beginning and the End." Also, notice that these two sets of divine titles are semantically different but conceptually identical:

Αλφα, *Alpha* – "Alpha"	Ομεγα, *Omega* – "Omega"
Αρχη, *Archē* – "Beginning"	Τελος, *Telos* – "End"

Jesus as the "Alpha and the Omega." Only nine verses after Revelation 1:8, Jesus introduces himself as "the First and the Last [*ho prōtos kai ho eschatos*]" (v. 17). The same is repeated in 2:8. Lexically, the designation "First and the Last" for Jesus differs from the ones used for God ("Alpha-Omega" and "Beginning-End"), but conceptually, these designations convey a similar meaning. Therefore, it appears that the use of the designations "the First and the Last" for Jesus Christ are intended to maintain a distinction (between Jesus Christ and God) at this initial stage. However, as we approach the end of the book, both sets of designations for God—"Alpha and Omega" and the "Beginning and the End"—and Jesus' own designation—"First and the Last"—are all attributed to Jesus Christ: "I am (Jesus Christ) the Alpha and the Omega. The First and the Last, the Beginning and the End [*egō to Alpha kai to ō, ho prōtos kai ho eschatos, hē archē kai to telos*]" (22:13). If such literary constructions were intentional, one must seek to discover the contextual and theological rationale behind such approaches.

"One who is to come"		"Alpha and Omega"	
God	Jesus	God	Jesus
1:4, 8	1:7	1:8	1:17, 18
4:8	14:14–16	21:6	22:12, 13
11:16, 17	16:15		
16:5 (*omitted*)	19:11–16		
	22:7, 11		

We also offer further examples from other Johannine books to demonstrate this literary feature.

Jesus as "eternal life" in 1 John. The term "eternal life" appears five times in 1 John (2:25; 3:15; 5:11, 13, 20). The author began by presenting the concept of eternal life as a *separate* entity being promised by Jesus Christ (2:25). In this context, the term has an eschatological overtone. In 1 John 3:15, the term "eternal life" is presented as an entity that a believer can possess here and now. In chapter 5, eternal life is portrayed as something that is contained in the person of Christ: "God has given us eternal life, and this life is in his Son" (v. 12). A single verse later, the author showed how one can possess eternal life (see also 3:15).[130] Finally, in 5:20, eternal life is *likened* to Christ ("He [Jesus Christ] is the true God and eternal life"). As with the previous designations for God, here John used "eternal life," one of God's attributes, to equate Jesus to God.

Jesus as "God" in 1 John. The same is also true using the relational term of Jesus—"the Son"—in 1 John. Initially, "the Son" is presented as Someone distinct from God the Father (see 1:3, 7; 2:1). He is then portrayed as someone closely related or identical to God (see 2:22–25). Eventually, the author asserted that "He [Son/Christ] is the true God" (5:20).

"eternal life"		"the Son"	
Text	*Relationship to Jesus*	*Text*	*Relationship to God*
2:25	separate entity	1:3, 4; 2:1	separate and distinct from God
3:15	an entity that believers can possess here and now	2:22–25	related to or identical with God
5:12	eternal life and Jesus are inseparable	5:20	Son/Jesus is God
5:13, 15	how and who can possess		
5:20	eternal life is Jesus		

---

[130] Also, note the dualism here. Two groups of people are said to "have" or "possess eternal life." In 1 John 3:14–15, it's not the brother-hater but the brother-lover who has "eternal life," whereas in 5:13, those who "believe in the name of the son of God" have eternal life. This interpretation is consistent with what we have seen so far.

As in Revelation, John initially associated the concept of eternal life to God, but then transfers the title over to Jesus Christ. Then with the title "the Son," John does the opposite. He used this title for Jesus but later makes the son become God.

This literary construction is consistently used to transfer certain divine titles—namely "who is to come," "Alpha-Omega," and "eternal life"—from God to Jesus. Among others, the literary device is aimed at making Jesus equal to or identical with God. The author first assigned each of these designations to God and then gradually transferred the designations to Jesus, thus making Him nearly identical to God. Such a literary masterpiece begs the question, Why? Is it merely a display of the author's literary craftsmanship, or is he tiptoeing around certain underlying issues? The intentionality and consistency in the use of these divine attributes may actually serve to reveal certain theological and contextual issues in the Johannine world. We will turn to these now.

LITERARY, CONTEXTUAL, AND THEOLOGICAL IMPLICATIONS

A Literary Crescendo

What we find in these four examples is a *literary crescendo*. A literary crescendo is a piece of writing in which there is a gradual increase in intensity, force, and volume leading up to a climactic finish. In each of these examples, the text *initially* presents Jesus as Someone who is distinct, separate, and/or somewhat inferior to (or not exactly the same as) God the Father. However, a careful reading of the text increasingly evidences that Jesus is likened to God. At the end of the text, He is declaratively stated as the "true God"! This Johannine literary style can be summarized as follows:

<u>Literary and Designation Transformation</u>. Initially in the text, the above titles ("Alpha-Omega," "beginning and the end," "who was, is and is come," "eternal life") are attributed to God, but as the text progresses,

the same titles undergo a literary transformation where they are finally associated with or attributed to Jesus Christ. Similarly, the designation of Jesus as the "Son of God" begins as Someone distinct, separate, and somewhat inferior to God. However, in the end, the Son is described as the "true God."

> *The designation of Jesus as the "Son of God" begins as Someone distinct, separate, and somewhat inferior to God. However, in the end, the Son is described as the "true God."*

<u>From the Agreed to the Disputed</u>. The author engineered the discourses to demonstrate that Jesus is God, or that Jesus the Son and God the Father "are one." To advance his argument, he began his discourses by progressing from the agreed to the disputed. The following diagram summarizes these discussions:

God's titles	Jesus as God	Jesus' titles
"alpha-omega"	"alpha-omega"	
	"the true God"	"Son"
"beginning-end"	"beginning-end"	
→	"first-last"	← "first-last"
"eternal life"	"eternal life"	
	"eternal life"	"Jesus"
"coming one"	"coming one"	

Contextual and Theological Implications

<u>The Literary Approach and the Core Issues</u>. This implies that Jesus' identity and authority, particularly His Christology and divinity, may have been challenged or questioned. All the NT writers actually dealt with Jesus' Christology and divinity. This is well illustrated in the way in which John wrote his purpose statement: "Jesus performed many other signs ... But these are written that you may believe that Jesus is the Messiah, the

Son of God" (John 20:30, 31). In fact, Jesus was crucified because of these claims (see 19:7; Matt. 26:63–66; 27:40–43). However, Christ's tormentors had no issue with God. While rejecting Jesus of Nazareth as the Son of God, they themselves boasted of being the *children of God* (see John 8:41). In fact, they thought crucifying the Son of God was an acceptable "service to God" (16:2). If such were the case in the early church, then these issues may have possibly influenced the language, concepts, content, and literary style of Revelation and other Johannine books.

If this literary construction was a consistent device used in the Johannine books to advance the Christology and divinity of Jesus, then it could serve as a clue to the theological backdrop against which these books were conceived. The next two chapters (8 and 9) further develop this thesis.

8.

JESUS AND THE SPIRITS

THE HOLY SPIRIT AND THE TEXT

Introduction to Spirits

"And from the seven spirits before his throne." The seven spirits are presented as being in the presence of God. References to the spirits, whether from God or the devil permeate the apocalyptic book.[131] Those usages can generally be categorized into several groups: 1) the Holy Spirit and the Trinity, 2) the Holy Spirit's relationship to the saints of God, 3) the Holy Spirit's relationship to Jesus Christ, and 4) the evil spirits and their activities. We will now explore these categories.

The Holy Spirit and the Trinity

In Revelation 1:4–8, the author presented the greetings as being from all three members of the Godhead (the "Lord God, Almighty," the "seven spirits," and "Jesus Christ"). The same members of the Trinity are again featured in 5:6, where the "lamb" having the "seven spirits of God" comes and takes the scroll from "him who sat on the throne." Another place in the NT where the Trinity is predominant is in Matthew 28:19. The great commission reads, "Therefore, go and make disciples of all nations, baptizing them in the name of the Father, and the Son and the Holy Spirit."

---

[131] The topic of the Holy Spirit is discussed heavily in this volume in the following three places: chapters 8 (relationship between Christ and the "seven spirits before the throne"), 18 (Christ's fiery eyes), and 19 ("seven spirits and seven angels" in the hand of Christ).

Then in Acts we read, "God has raised this Jesus to life ... Exalted to the right hand of God, he has received from the Father the promised Holy Spirit and has poured out what you see and hear" (2:32, 33).

Concerning the Holy Spirit's relationship with the Father and Jesus Christ, two inferences can be gleaned from this passage. First, it emphasizes Jesus' relationship to and with the Father in that "God raised *this* Jesus," "exalted" Him (Jesus), and gave Him the Holy Spirit. Second, Jesus' relationship to and with the Holy Spirit is similarly emphasized in that the exalted Christ "received from the Father" the "Holy Spirit" and poured Him out to us. Although these passages differ in methodology and style, what Luke wrote in Acts 2:32–33 is identical to what John saw in Revelation 5:6. If this is an indication of any Trinity-related issue in the early church, it is unclear at this stage.

The Holy Spirit and the Saints of God

The Spirit of God is mentioned twice in relation to the saints of God. Without any form of qualification, in both cases, John referred to being "in the Spirit" in Revelation 1:10 and 4:1 (see also 17:3; 21:10). He perhaps assumed that his audience knew what he meant. Unfortunately, his meaning is unclear to us today.

Then in Revelation 2 and 3, the One like the "Son of Man" is the Orator addressing the "seven churches." However, each message ends with an appeal that is allegedly from the Spirit: "He who has ear, let him hear what the Spirit says to the churches" (Rev 2:7, 11, 17, 29; 3:6, 13, 22). Therefore, the question arises as to who is actually speaking to the seven churches? Is it the Son of Man or the Spirit? The answer, of course, is again not clear. However, when one gets to chapters 4 and 5, the issue is compounded.

The Holy Spirit and Jesus Christ

In Revelation 4:5, the "seven spirits [are] blazing before the throne," but notice the change that takes place in the next chapter. "Then I saw a lamb," wrote John, "looking as if he had been slain, standing in the center of the throne. ... He had seven horns and seven eyes, which are the seven Spirits of God sent out into all the earth" (5:6). In one place, the "seven spirits of God" are "before the throne" (1:4–8; 4:5), but in the other, the seven spirits form a part of the Lamb. Do they represent two different sets of seven spirits or the same entity? If they are the same, then what are they really like? Are they "seven lamps ... blazing before the throne" (4:5; see also 1:4) or the "seven eyes of the lamb" that is at the "center of the throne"?

Consider Revelation 3:1, in which Jesus introduces Himself as the One "hold[ing] the seven spirits of God" in His hand. If this verse is alluding to the vision of 1:9–20, then this presents another problem. In that vision, Jesus only has the seven stars—not seven spirits—in His hands. What could possibly be going on here? If this tortured language indicates certain controversies surrounding the relationship between Jesus and the Holy Spirit during John's time, then what were they? Whatever the problems may have been, it is better to follow the textual trail and see where it leads us.

> *What could possibly be going on here? If this tortured language indicates certain controversies surrounding the relationship between Jesus and the Holy Spirit during John's time, then what were they? Whatever the problems may have been, it is better to follow the textual trail and see where it leads us.*

To do that, two pertinent points must be addressed: 1) to make sense of Revelation's teaching on the Holy Spirit, particularly as it relates to the Trinity and the saints of God, and 2) to determine the contextual issue John and his readers may have likely encountered.

ANALYSIS OF THE SEVEN SPIRITS AND THE LAMB

"Spirits of God" and "Jesus"

The Apocalypse seeks to accomplish two goals. First, it presents the third member of the Godhead as being either the "Spirit" or the "spirits of God," "blazing" like "lamps" and being present "before the throne" (1:4; 4:5; 5:6; 22:6). These descriptions identify the Spirit as belonging to or having its origin from God. The language here is clear and straightforward. Second, the text makes numerous attempts to closely link Jesus to the ministry of the Spirit of God. As seen in the following, the text attempts to make the spirits of God subservient to Jesus Christ:

1. *The Seven Spirits Submit to Jesus*. The seven spirits of God are presented as being "before the throne" (Rev. 1:4). In 4:5, the same spirits are described as "blazing lamps" "before the throne." Note that in these two references, the spirits are separate from and independent of Jesus. Then in 3:1, John saw the same "seven spirits" in the "hand" of Jesus. Being in His hand could make the spirits of God as instruments or agents of Jesus Christ. Finally, in 5:6, the spirits become the "seven eyes" of the Lamb. Note how the spirits of God move from being in the "presence of God" to becoming an essential part of the Lamb. Either in the hand or on the head of Jesus, the text makes it abundantly clear that the spirits of God are intricately related to Jesus and function in harmony with or submission to Him.
2. *The Seven Sprits Given by Jesus*. Revelation 5:6 states that the "seven eyes, are the seven Spirits of God, sent out into all the earth." Although the passive language suggests that the One sending the spirits is God, the context favors Jesus as the sender. a) As discussed, the spirits are in Jesus' hand (see 3:1), b) If the Lamb alone was worthy to receive the scroll, break the seals, and make it known to the saints of God, then the same could also make Him worthy of receiving the seven spirits of God and sending them into all the earth. This interpretation is consistent with other NT writings: "God has raised this Jesus to life." "Exalted at the right hand of God, he has received from the

Father the promised Holy Spirit and has poured out what you now see and hear" (Acts 2:32, 33; John 16:6, 7).

3. *Jesus and the Spirit are One.* As mentioned earlier, Jesus, who holds the seven spirits in His hand, is the Orator of the messages of Revelation 2 and 3. Each address concludes with the appeal to "hear what the Spirit says." The book ends with another invitation: "The Spirit and the Bride say, 'Come!'" (22:17). The implication here seems to be that the Spirit is not only subservient to Jesus, but also that they are one, just as the Father and Son are one. John quoted Jesus as saying, "The Spirit gives life; the flesh counts for nothing. The words I have spoken to you are Spirit and they are life" (John 6:63). Here, Jesus and His words are equated to the "Spirit" and "life." The same author also wrote, "For the one whom God has sent, speaks the words of God. For *God gives the spirit* without limit. The Father loves the Son and has placed *everything in his hands*" (3:34, 35, emphasis supplied).

Christ Himself further testifies:

> But when he, the Spirit of truth, comes ... He will not speak on his own; he will speak only what he hears, and he will tell you *what is yet to come.* He will bring glory to me by taking *what is mine* and making it known to you. *All that belongs to the Father is mine.* That is why I said the spirit will take from what is mine and make is known to you. (John 16:13–15, emphasis supplied)

The text states, "All that belongs to the Father is mine." Among other things, "all" could include both the sealed scroll and seven spirits, both of which Jesus received from the Father (see Rev. 4, 5) and then gave to the saints of God.[132]

---

[132] E.G. White stated, "The whole treasury of heaven is open to those He seeks to save. Having collected the riches of the universe, and laid open the resources of infinite power, He gives them all into the hands of Christ, and says, All these are for man" (Desire of Ages, p. 57).

THE SPIRITS OF GOD AND CONTEXTUAL ISSUES

Many scholars have used the passages of Revelation 1:1 and 19 and 4:1 to divide the text into two parts. In that context, the messages of chapters 1–3 were intended for the early church, whereas the predictive messages of 4–22 were to be reserved for the churches in later times.[133] Although 1–3 primarily consists of "what is now [current events from John's perspective]," and 4–22 reveals "what will take place soon [future events]," that does not mean that the author and his readers were mere custodians of a body of information that had no relevance to their time and context.[134] John and his audience encountered real problems, and Revelation in its entirety was a divine response to their immediate situations.[135] Therefore, from John being "in the Spirit" to the Lamb with "seven eyes" before the throne must be read in light of both the immediate (Revelation) and wider NT contexts.

"The Spirits of God" and the "spirit of demons" in the Early Church

The "spirits of God" must be read within the context of the "spirits of demons" of Revelation 13–18 and their related activities. The emphasis on the spirits of God in Revelation is intended to counter the role of the spirits of demons in and during John's time. The "seven churches in the province of Asia" could relate to these issues. An objection to such an approach could be that the activities of the spirits of demons in 13–18 are reserved for the end times. While this is true, it is also true that John and his audience never saw the world existing past 2,000 years because

---

[133] For a thorough discussion on this, refer to chapter 4 of this volume.

[134] For further discussion on the concept of "what is now" and "what will take place soon," refer to chapter 4 of this volume.

[135] At least the author and his community of believers thought the message was for them, but only God in His wisdom saw otherwise—That the same messages could speak to both the immediate and distant audiences.

they thought that they were living in the last hour. "Dear children, this is the *last hour*; and as you have heard that the antichrist is coming, even now many antichrists have come. This is how we know it is the *last hour*" (1 John 2:18, emphasis supplied).

Note two aspects of this text: 1) The emphatic use of the phrase "last hour" suggests John had a specific hour in mind; 2) The phrase "as you have heard" implies that John was reinforcing something his audience already knew, which was related to antichrists or false prophets coming in the last hour. He was probably referring to those in the Pauline epistles or Synoptic Gospels. However, the closest link is found in Revelation 17. Consider the following similarities:

"Antichrists" (1 John 2:18–19)	"Babylon" (Revelation 13–18)
"last hour"	"And the ten horns which you saw are ten kings, who have not yet received a kingdom, but they receive authority as kings with the beast for *one hour*" (17:12); "In *one hour* your doom has come," "In *one hour* such great wealth has been brought to ruin!" and "in *one hour* she has been brought to ruin!" (18:10, 17, 19) (emphases supplied)
"antichrists," "false prophets," "deceivers" (2:18–22; 4:1–6; 2 John 7)	"And the beast was seized, and with him the *false prophet* who performed the signs in his presence, by which he *deceived* those who had received the mark of the beast and those who worshiped his image" (19:20; 13:14; 16:14, emphasis supplied)
"you have heard that the antichrist is coming, many antichrists have come" (2:18)	"they are spirits of demons, performing signs, which *go out to the kings of the whole world*, to gather them together for the war of the great day of God, the Almighty" (16:14, emphasis supplied)

Considering the number of similarities between these passages, it is possible that John may have thought he was living within or before that awful "one-hour" period. Given such a scenario, he could have seen the false prophets of Revelation 13–18 as the antichrists in his own days (see 1 John 2:18, 19). Therefore, reading the "spirits of Christ" (Rev. 1–5) in the light of the "spirits of demons" (13–18) seems reasonable.

The Spirits of God, Spirits of Demons, and Their Activities

In the Apocalypse, the spirits of God stand diametrically opposed to the spirits of demons, just as the true prophets of God are opposed to the false prophets. The following table attempts to document, describe, and differentiate between the two spirits, their agents, activities, and relationship to Jesus:

Features	"Spirit of God"	"Spirit of demons"
Name	"spirit," "spirits of God" (1:10, 4; 4:5)	"spirits of demons" or "evil spirits" (16:13–14)
Source	God: "before the throne" (4:5; 5:6; 22:6)	Satan: "mouth of the dragon" and "spoke like the dragon" (13:13; 16:13)
Number of Spirits	"seven spirits" (1:4; 3:1; 4:5; 5:6)	"three frog-like spirits" (16:13, 14)
Looks or Identity	"seven blazing lamps before the throne" or "seven eyes" of the Lamb (4:5; 5:6)	"looked like frogs" (16:13)
Agents	Sent out from "before the throne," "eyes of the Lamb," and the "hand" of Jesus (1:4; 4:5; 3:1)	"came out from the mouth of the dragon, mouth of the beast and mouth of the false prophets" (16:13)
Scope of influence	"sent out into all the earth" (5:6)	"go out to the kings of the whole world" (16:14)
Relationship to the Lamb	"seven Spirits" are "seven eyes of the Lamb," and the "seven Spirits" are in the "hand" of Jesus (5:6; 1:4; 4:5)	"land beast with two-lamb-like horns," but later it "spoke like the dragon" (13:11)
Prophets/ Servants	i) John and "prophets" (1:10; 22:6) ii) churches and "all the earth" (chs. 2, 3; 5:6)	i) "land beast" and/or the "false prophets" (13:11–16; 16:13, 14) ii) "they go to the kings of the whole world" (16:13, 14)
Activities	Authentic "signs and wonders," "speaks," inspires, enables, empowers, "breath of life" (11:11)	"signs and wonders," "deception" (13:13, 14), 16:13, 14; 20:20), "allowed to give breath/life to the image" (13:15).

Although the above table is self-explanatory, two points require mentioning:

The Land Beast as the False Prophet. First, Revelation 13 introduces two beasts: the beast that comes "out of the sea" and the other one that comes "out of the earth." In chapters 14–20, the beast out of the sea consistently retains its name as "the beast," but the identity of the second beast as the "land" or "lamb-like" beast no longer receives a mention after chapter 13. However, the counterfeit, miraculous signs of the lamb-like beast and false prophets of 16:13–14 are similar, if not same. Scholars, therefore, rightly see the lamb-like beast of Revelation 13 and the false prophets of 16:13–14 (as well as 19:20 and 20:10) as one and the same.[136]

In other words, the name of this character changes from lamb-like beast to false prophets, but its characteristics and core functions remain unchanged. Concerning the same, Matthew wrote, "Watch out for false prophets. They come to you in sheep's clothing, but inwardly they are ferocious wolves" (7:15). This passage clearly teaches that false prophets are lamb-like beasts. Having the same people in mind, Paul warned the saints in Ephesus, "savage wolves will come in among you ... Even from your own number ... So be on your guard!" (Acts 20:29–31). Savage wolves and sheep cannot co-exist unless the wolves are dressed in sheep's clothing.

False Prophets, True Prophets, and the Lamb. Second, the false prophets are in turn contrasted with the true prophets who have the "Spirit of God" (Rev. 19:10; 22:6). Note especially the relationship of the Lamb with the two types of spirits and the two types of prophets.

True Prophets and the Lamb. The Lamb receives the "spirits of God" from "before the throne" and sends them "into all the earth," especially to the saints who "hold to the testimony of Jesus" (see Rev. 19:10). These spirits (and Christ), in turn, address the seven churches (see 2:1–3:22). When John stated that he was in the Spirit on the Island of Patmos, he was referring to these divine spirits because they are the "spirits of the prophets" (22:6). Thus, the true spirits of God are inseparably linked to and exclusively administered by Jesus Christ.

---

[136] Stefanovic, *Revelation of Jesus Christ*, p. 428. See also C. M. Maxwell, *The Message of Revelation*, volume 2, p. 330.

False Prophets and the Lamb. When the land beast of Revelation 13:11–18 "came out of the earth," it had "two horns like a lamb" but later "spoke like a dragon." Note the transformation of this beast. Initially, the land beast, similar to the saints and prophets of God, was also associated with the Lamb, but later spoke and acted like a dragon. The land beast may have believed in Jesus Christ during its initial stages, but later ceased "follow[ing] the Lamb wherever he goes." Concerning the antichrists or false prophets of 1 John, the author wrote, "They [antichrists or false prophets] *went out from us*, but they did not really belong to us. For if they had belonged to us, they would have remained with us; but their going showed that none of them belonged to us" (2:19, emphasis supplied).

By virtue of their (initial) faith in Jesus Christ, they may have also received the "spirits of God." However, when they went out from the faith in Christ, the spirits of God may have been replaced with another spirit. Without realizing this fact, the false prophets are still seen boasting about a superior anointing (see 1 John 2: 20–27). This "spirit" with its "anointing" is heavily involved in performing counterfeit "great miraculous signs" (Rev. 13:11–15; 16:13–14; 19:20), but "does not [acknowledge that] Jesus is from" God (1 John 4:3). Therefore, the false prophets neither know God nor possess His true Spirits because "no one who denies the Son has the Father" or His "Spirit" (2:23).

The 144,000 and the Land Beast

We have pointed out the Lamb's relationship to the two types of spirits and prophets. Furthermore, the immediate context shows another dimension of the relationship, especially between the false prophets (see Rev. 13:11–18) and the 144,000 (see 14:1–5). A few of the main features are discussed as follows:

<u>Lamb's Name on Foreheads Versus Two Lamb-like Horns on the Head</u>. Both the 144,000 and the land beast have something on their heads. Concerning the 144,000, John wrote, "there before me was the Lamb, standing on Mount Zion, and with him 144,000 who had his name and his Father's name written on their foreheads" (14:1). These saints have the

Lamb's name written on their foreheads and "follow the Lamb wherever he goes," whereas the land beast or the false prophets have "two horns like a lamb" on their heads and do not follow the Lamb at all (13:11).

The Mouths or Speeches of the False Prophets and the Saints. The second difference concerns the mouths of the false prophets and the 144,000 saints. The land beast "spoke like a dragon." The question is, How does a dragon really speak? The account in Revelation generally characterizes the false prophets and dragon as being involved in some kind of deception but offers no specific information regarding the nature and mechanics of their speech (see 12:9; 13:14; 20:3). However, in another book, John wrote, "You belong to your father, the devil, and you want to carry your father's desire. He was a murderer from the beginning, not holding to the truth, for there is no truth in him. When he lies, he speaks his *native language*, for he is a liar and the father of lies" (John 8:44, emphasis supplied).

> *While destructive lies proceed from the mouths of the false prophets, the true words of testimony that come from the saints help them overcome the dragon.*

A couple of things can be deduced from this passage. First, according to Revelation 20:3, the dragon is the same devil of John 8:44. Second, if the dragon's native language involves lying, then that is exactly what the false prophets of Revelation 13 and 16 are doing.[137]

By contrast, the 144,000 are described this way: "No lie was found in their mouth" (14:5; see also John 7:18).[138] Not only does the absence of lies characterize the saints of God, but also that which was found in their mouths enabled them to overcome the dragon. "They overcame him [the dragon] ... by the word of their testimony" (Rev. 12:11). While

---

[137] The manner or nature of the "lying" from the "dragon" and "false prophets" can be described as "deception." Lying, in its crude form, can be easily discerned by the subjects, whereas deception involves a mixture of falsehood and truth. In Revelation, deception is featured (see 13:11–18; 16:13, 14).

[138] Note that Satan's "native language" is contrasted with Christ's "language": "Why is my language not clear to you?" (John 8:43).

destructive lies proceed from the mouths of the false prophets, the true words of testimony that come from the saints help them overcome the dragon.[139]

Other related questions arise at this stage concerning the exact details of those lies, truths, and the identities of those engaged in them. However, these issues will be discussed a little later.[140]

"They follow the Lamb wherever He goes"

The 144,000 are further described as those who "follow the Lamb wherever He goes" (14:4). The logical implication here is that the false prophets had either ceased following or do not follow the Lamb at all. The transformation of the land beast in Revelation 13:11 shows that the false prophets may have begun by following the Lamb, but have now ceased to do so. If this is true, then it opens doors to other antichristological activities by the false prophets. The following table illustrates these activities:

Genuine Prophets and the Saints of God	False Prophets and the Deceived
"stand on Mount Zion"	The "beast" came "out of the sea," the land beast "came out of the earth"
"Lamb's name on their foreheads" (14:1)	"two-lamb-like horns" and "mark of the beast" (13:11)
"No lies found in their mouth" (14:5; 12:11)	"spoke like a dragon [they lie]" (13:11)
"stand with the Lamb" (14:1)	Stand with sea and land beasts and the dragon
"they follow the Lamb wherever He goes" (14:4)	They follow the land and sea beasts and the dragon ["whole world follows the beast"]

---

[139] This brings to mind the "two-edged sword" from Christ's mouth that slays the nations, beast, and false prophets (see Rev. 1:16; 2:12, 16; 19:15, 21). Christ is not only designated as "True" or "Truth" (Rev. 19:11, John 14:6), but that which proceeds from His mouth is also "truth." Therefore, Christ and His followers are known for holding, keeping, believing, telling, and living the truth, whereas the devil and his agents are associated with error, deceit, falsehood, and lies.

[140] The main discussion in part 3 of this volume deals with these questions.

Genuine Prophets and the Saints of God	False Prophets and the Deceived
"the Lamb is their shepherd [leader]" (7:17)	The Lamb is not their shepherd/leader, by implication, the dragon and his agents (sea and land beasts)
"washed their robes and made them white in the blood of the lamb" (7:14)	If they rejected Jesus as the Christ/Lamb, then they remain in sin. They either are naked or defiled their robes
"names written in the Lamb's book of life" (13:8; 17:8)	Their names are not written in the book of life (see 13:8; 17:8)
"called, chosen and faithful followers" of the Lamb (17:14)	Were once called and chosen, but they are not faithful (Rev. 13:11)
They are characterized as having "patient endurance" (1:9; 6:9–11; 14:12)	Their "fall away" shows that lack "patient endurance"

Our analysis of this table is as follows: The saints of God who possess the Spirit of God are those who love and follow the Lamb wherever He goes. They "have [also] washed their robes and made them white in the Lamb's blood." Their names are not only written in the Lamb's book of life, but the Lamb's (and Father's) name is also written on their foreheads. If following the Lamb means believing in Him, then the 144,000 saints are those who believe in Jesus Christ and His sacrificial death.

The false prophets, however, may have accepted Jesus Christ sometime in the past, but they no longer follow Him now. Similarly, when they first believed in Jesus, they may have received the Spirit of God. However, because they do not follow the Lamb, the spirit and miraculous signs manifested in their camp is not of God, but of the spirit of demons. "As those disaffected disciples turned away from Christ, a different spirit took control of them. They could see nothing attractive in Him [Jesus] whom they had once found so interesting."[141] Other Johannine works provide crucial insights regarding this thesis.

---

[141] White, Desire of Ages, p. 392.

THE "SPIRITS" AND "JESUS" IN JOHANNINE LITERATURE

The Father, Spirit, and Jesus in the Early Church

Immediate Context: 1 John. The false prophets and their related activities are manifestly countered in the NT literature. The immediate context, particularly the biblical data in Revelation 1–3, 1 and 2 John, and the Gospel of John, are crucial to the current study. Consider the following passages, for instance:

> Dear children, this is the last hour; and as *you have heard that the antichrist is coming*, even now *many antichrists have come*. This is how we know it is the last hour. *They went out from us* but they did not really belong to us. For if they had belonged to us, they would have remained with us; but their going showed that none of them belonged to us … Who is the liar? It is the man who denies that *Jesus is the Christ*. Such a man is the *antichrist*—he denies the Father and the Son. *No one who denies the Son has the Father*; whoever acknowledges the Son has the Father also. (1 John 2:18–23, emphasis supplied).

> Dear friends, do not believe *every spirit, but test* the spirits to see whether they are *from God*, because *many false prophets* have gone out into the world. This is how you can recognize the *Spirit of God*: Every spirit that acknowledges that *Jesus Christ has come in the flesh is from God*, but every spirit that *does not acknowledge Jesus is not from God*. This is the *spirit of the antichrist*, which you have heard is coming and *even now is already in the world*. … This is how we recognize the *Spirit of truth and the spirit of falsehood*. (1 John 4:1–3, 6, emphasis supplied).

We will return to these passages when we study Revelation 12–14, but for now we will make several observations. These passages elucidate the relationship between the Lamb, spirits, and prophets in numerous ways. The first concerns the existence of two types of spirits: the Spirit of God and the spirit of antichrist (falsehood or demons). The second comprises two groups of prophets: true and false. The false prophets are also called liars or antichrists and described as having a counterfeit anointing. Third, it is apparent that both groups may have claimed to have the approval, anointing, and Spirit of God.

Therefore, as if to distinguish the true from the false, the author presented God's anointing and Spirit contingent upon acknowledging Jesus as the Christ or coming from God. Thus, Jesus is presented as the exclusive "test" for both receiving the Spirit of God and having a genuine fellowship with the Father. In this case, those labeled as "false prophets" may have denied Jesus' Christology, provenance, authority, and relationship to and with the Father and Holy Spirit. These discussions are summarized in the following tables:

Trinity	Antichrists/False Prophets	Saints/True Prophets
God	Believe in God as Creator, Father. Claim to have access to, fellowship with God, but apart from or outside of Jesus. Maybe through Abraham, Jacob, Moses, or Baptist.	Believe in God as the Creator, Father. Had access to the throne through Jesus. Can know the Father through Christ, have fellowship with the Father through Jesus.
Spirits of God	That the spirits and anointing are from God. The spirits came in fulfillment of God's OT promises. Jesus has no role in the reception of the Spirits. If any, John the Baptist may have had something to do with it.	The Spirits are "of" and "from God," but they are in the hand of Jesus, form the "seven eyes of the lamb." Jesus promised during his ministry and later "sent it to all the world."
Jesus	Do not believe Jesus is the Christ, the coming One, as coming from God, much less from the beginning or eternal.	Believe Jesus to be from God, the Lamb of God, the coming Messiah, from the beginning, eternal, even God Himself.

Immediate Context: Revelation, 1 John, Gospel of John. If John, who wrote the Apocalypse, also wrote the epistles and Gospel, then a comparative study of the Christological issues may further aid our understanding of the contextual issues of Revelation. The following tables show the similarities between these false prophets and their related activities in the Johannine writings:

Features	Revelation 4–22	Revelation 1–3	1 and 2 John
Spirit of God	"seven spirits of God," "spirit" (1:4; 4:5; 5:6; 22:6)	"spirit" (2:7, 11, 17, 29; 3:6, 13, 22)	"Spirit of truth," "Holy Spirit" (4:1–3)
Spirit of Satan	"evil spirit," "spirits of demons" (13:11–18; 16:13–14; 19:20; 20:12)		"counterfeit" (2:27), "spirit of error," "test the spirits," "not all spirit are of God" (4:1–3)
False Prophets	"false prophets" (13:11–18; 16:13–14; 19:20; 20:12)	"false apostles," "not Jews," "Jezebel, prophetess"	"false prophets," "deceivers," "antichrists," "liars," "wicked works" (2:18–23; 4:1–3; 2 John 7–11)
Activities of the False Prophets	"performing signs and wonders," "go to all the kings of the whole world" for deception (13:11–18; 16:13–14; 19:20)	The activities of the "false apostles," "false Jews," and "Jezebel, prophetess"	"you heard that the antichrists were coming, many have come out now" to deceive, lie, lead you astray (2:18–23; 4:1–3; 2 John 7–11)
Claims of the False Prophets		"Satan's deep secrets"	claiming to have an anointing from God (see 2:18–23; 4:1–3; 2 John 7–11), claims to have fellowship with the Father (see 1:5–2:6)

THE "SPIRITS," "JESUS," AND OLD TESTAMENT PROPHETS

Two Conduits Through Which the Spirit of God Came

Before we summarize the discussion, one more aspect needs to be inserted at this stage: a comparative analysis of the nature and role of the Holy Spirit in the lives of the OT prophets and Jesus Christ. In other words, if Jesus was the One about whom Moses and the prophets wrote, then how does the role of the Holy Spirit validate this? The following table compares and contrasts the role of the Holy Spirit in the lives of

Moses, Elijah, Elisha, John the Baptist, and Jesus Christ (Also compare this with the two conduits of the Word of God in chapter 10 of this study):

Jesus and the Holy Spirit	Moses, Prophets, and the Holy Spirit		
Jesus	*Moses*	*Elijah and Elisha*	*Other Prophets and Saints*
Jesus is the Son: "All that belongs to the Father is mine" (John 16:15; see also Heb. 3:6)	Moses was a servant. "there was never a prophet like Moses" (Heb. 3:5)	Elijah, Elisha, and others as prophets of God	John the Baptist: of all born of women, John ranks as the greatest (see Luke 7:26, 28)
Promised spirit: "I will ask the Father to send," "Father will send in my name," "I will send" (John 14:16, 26; 15:26)	Moses merely wished all would be anointed with the Spirit, but only 70 received the Spirit (see Num. 11:29)	Conditional promise: "If you see me go …" Request is beyond Elijah's control (1 Kings 2:10)	Joel: God promised the spirit on all through the prophet Joel (see Acts 2:16–21)
"Unless I go away, the Counselor will not come" (John 16:7)		Elisha received a double portion during Elijah's departure (see 2 Kings 2:10)	All saints: Spirit came on all only after His ascension (see Acts 2:3, 4, 38, 39)
"whatever you ask in my name" I will give, "ask me for anything in my name, and I will do it" (John 14:13, 14)		Elisha asked for a double portion— "a difficult thing" for Elijah to grant (2 Kings 2:9, 10)	
"seven spirits in Christ's hand," "seven spirits as seven eyes of the lamb" (Rev. 3:1; 5:6; John 3:35).	God "took … of the Spirit that was on him [Moses] and put it on the seventy elders" (Num. 11:25)		The seven spirits in Christ's hand, or the Lamb's eyes are given to "all the earth world" (Rev. 3:1; 5:6)
"gives the spirit without limit" (John 1:34)	Spirit from Moses to only seventy. Also, the seventy prophesied once and did not continue (see Num. 11:25)	Elisha received only a double portion of the spirit Elijah had (see 2 Kings 2:10, 12–14)	Beginning with the 120, then the *whole world* thereafter received the spirit without limit (see Acts 2:3, 4; Rev. 5:6)

Jesus and the Holy Spirit	Moses, Prophets, and the Holy Spirit		
Jesus	Moses	Elijah and Elisha	Other Prophets and Saints
When the spirit comes, "you will do greater things than this" (John 14:12)	However, like Moses, Christ actually did more too (see John 20:30)	Elisha did more miracles than Elijah (see 2 Kings 2–7)	God did more "extraordinary miracles through" Paul and the twelve (see Acts 19:11, 12)
He baptizes with the Holy Spirit and fire (John 1:33)		Elijah is the prophet of "fire" (1 Kings 18:38; 2 Kings 2:11)	John the Baptist: "baptism of repentance," "I baptize with water" (John 1:26)
Born by the will of God; "born of water and spirit" (John 1:13; 3:5)			Abraham: "Abraham's descendants," "natural descent" (John 8:33; 1:13)

As shown here, each of the prominent statement Christ makes concerning His relationship to the Holy Spirit is intended to demonstrate two things: 1) that the manifestation of the Spirit of God through Christ is more abundant, complete, and superior than the manifestation done through various prophets in ancient times; 2) that Christ is either equal to or greater than any one or all of the OT prophets put together. These two points are further discussed in the following paragraphs.

Christ Superior to Elijah and Elisha. First, Christ is quoted as saying, "unless I go away, the Counselor will not come" (John 16:7). He also assured His disciples that "you will do greater things than this" because He goes away to the Father (14:12). Both of these statements echo the role of the Spirit in the lives of the prophets Elijah and Elisha. Elijah had to "go away" in order for Elisha to receive the Spirit of God, after which he did more miraculous signs than his master.

Christ Gives More Spirit than Moses and Elijah. Second, John the Baptist declared that Christ "gives the Spirit without limit" (John 1:34). This is to show that in matters concerning the Spirit, Christ is superior to

Moses, Elijah, and Elisha. This is because through Moses, God anointed only seventy elders, while Elijah acknowledged Elisha's request for a double portion as being a difficult thing. These references concerning the Spirit show two things: 1) that the Spirit that came from and through Christ is superior to the ones that came through other prophets; 2) that Jesus Christ is either One like or greater than Moses and all the prophets.[142]

<u>Christ Has More Authority than Moses and Elijah</u>. Third, when God anointed seventy elders in the wilderness, Moses wished that all Israelites had the same Spirit and were prophets. By merely wishing, he recognized his limitations and lack of authority. When Elisha asked for a double portion of the Spirit, Elijah acknowledged the request as a difficult thing. Like Moses, Elijah also saw his limitations. Now in contrast to these, Christ promised His disciples that He will either "ask the Father to send the Holy Spirit" in His name, or He Himself "will send another Comforter." No wonder why people marveled, saying, "He speaks as one having authority."

<u>Christ Has More Spirit than Moses and Elisha</u>. Finally, the seventy elders were not anointed with fresh anointing, but God took the Spirit that was already on Moses and gave it to them (see Num. 11:25). The same is implied in Revelation. We see Christ standing with either "seven spirits in his hand" or "seven eyes on the Lamb." And John wrote that the "seven eyes are the seven spirits which He sent into the whole world" (Rev. 5:6). Therefore, when God sent the Holy Spirit at Pentecost to anoint the disciples (and us today), He takes the Spirit that is on Christ and gives it to the world.

Again if "seven" signifies perfection and completeness, then unlike Moses, Christ undoubtedly gives the Spirit without limit. The same is also true with Elisha and Elijah. Elisha received only a double portion of what Elijah had. Now if Christ has the "seven spirits," then He has the capacity to give us more than what Elijah gave to Elisha. That is why the Bible says Christ "gives the Spirit without limit." Perhaps this was the reason why He

---

[142] Here, the author used the nature and function of the Spirit of God to testify of Jesus' superiority over other prophets. He does the same with the concept of the "word of God." For a discussion on the "word of God" that came through Christ being superior to those who came through other prophets, see chapter 10 of this volume.

said that when we ask for the Holy Spirit, we should ask in His name. This analysis is not exhaustive. Similar lessons can be drawn from the rest of the features in the table.

ANALYSIS AND SUMMARY

If, as discussed, the prologue (Rev. 1:1–3), introductory remarks (vv. 4–8), and epilogue (22:7–21) were not part of the actual vision, then these thoughts convey the author's own insights and reflections on the main messages.[143] In other words, the materials in these sections (1:1–9; 22:7–21) should serve as a guide to a proper understanding of John, his audience, the problems they encountered, and how Revelation spoke to them in their times and context. Given the 2,000 years of history between the Johannine world and us, our views may not exactly fit that of John's. However, to gain an accurate assessment of what these prophecies may mean to us, we must first seek to understand what they meant to the early church. Therefore, we have gleaned the following from our discussion on this section:

<u>Jesus and God</u>. The author used literary crescendo to demonstrate Jesus' divinity. He particularly used this literary style when arguing from that which is *agreed* or *accepted* to those things that are *disputed*. Because

---

[143] E. Mueller appropriately sees the introductory passage as the "summary statement of the entire Apocalypse. It is Revelation in a nutshell." See "Jesus and His Second Coming in the Apocalypse," *Journal of the Adventist Theological Society* 11/12 (2000): p. 208.

the false prophets denied Jesus' Christology, divinity, and authority, John used various arguments to counter these teachings. He first designated God as the "Alpha-Omega," "coming One," and "eternal life," then gradually transferred these designations to Jesus, thus making Him almost identical to God. However, with Jesus' relational title of "the Son," the author first presented Him as someone separate and somewhat inferior to the Father. However, toward the end, he identified Christ as the "true God." Therefore, the literary style and distorted language are indicative of serious Christological issues in the early church.

<u>Jesus and the Holy Spirit</u>. The second issue concerns Jesus' relationship with the Holy Spirit. The manner in which the author of Revelation combined the spirits of God and the Lamb is intriguing. First, the spirits of God move from before the throne to the hand of Jesus. Then the seven spirits transform into seven eyes of the Lamb. The way in which the seven spirits of God shift from one place to another speaks volumes regarding certain issues the early church experienced. The false prophets may have claimed to have the anointing of God and fellowship with the Father—all apart from and outside of Jesus Christ. For this reason, the text attempts to link Jesus as closely as possible to both the Father and the Spirit of God, even making Him the only way to the Father. Thus, anyone claiming to know the Father or having the Spirit of God outside of Jesus Christ would find his or her claims invalidated.

<u>Testing the Spirits</u>. John wrote, "test the spirits to see if they are of God." This is because apart from the spirits of God, there are also the spirits of demons. These spirits are also presented as the "Spirit of Christ" and the "spirit of antichrist" or the "Spirit of truth" and the "spirit of falsehood." They are also described as the "real" and "counterfeit" anointing. To distinguish between these two types of spirits, the author presented "acknowledging Jesus as Christ" and the same as coming "from God" as the ultimate test for having God's true Spirit. If these discussions and conclusions are valid, then the issues discussed here are not unique to Revelation. They are the same as those discussed in the other NT traditions. Therefore, such conclusions could serve to increase the early church's comprehensibility of the prophecies of Revelation.

9.
JESUS CHRIST

And from Jesus Christ, who is the faithful witness, the firstborn from the dead, and the ruler of the kings of the earth. To him who loves us and has freed us from our sins by his blood, and has made us to be a kingdom and priests to serve his God and Father—to him be glory and power for ever and ever! Amen. "Look, he is coming with the clouds," and "every eye will see him, even those who pierced him"; and all peoples on earth "will mourn because of him." So shall it be! Amen. (Revelation 1:5–7)

INTRODUCTION

Thus far, we have noted the following: 1) how a literary crescendo is used to show that Jesus is identical with God in status and authority. The argument advanced here is that Christ is essentially God Himself. 2) the Lamb's relationship with the Spirit of God. Because of many types of spirits, the Spirit that acknowledges Jesus as Christ or from God is the true Spirit of God. Therefore, those advancing a *Christ-less* relationship to God or claiming to have a *Christ-less* access to God's Spirit are false prophets and antichrists. The previous discussions have led us to conclude that Jesus Christ is like God and the spirits of God belong to Jesus Christ. Now we turn to the passage that heavily discusses Jesus Christ Himself (Rev. 1:5–7).

JESUS' NAMES AND TITLES

Jesus Christ: His Name, Titles, Designations, and Deeds, Part I

The Designations of Christ. This passage combines nearly a dozen phrases that reveal Jesus' names, titles, designations, or deeds and accomplishments, which is about four per verse. These designations include "Jesus," "Christ [Messiah or the Anointed One]," "Faithful Witness," "Firstborn from the dead," "Ruler of the kings of the world," "Him who freed us [a liberator like Moses]," "by His own blood [the Lamb]," "Him who made us to be a kingdom [Jesus as the Prince or the King]," "Him who made us to be priests [Jesus as the High Priest]," "His Father [implying Jesus as the Son]," "to Him be glory and power [He who is like God]," "He is coming with clouds [or "He who is to come"]," "all eyes will see Him, even those who pierced Him [the suffering servant]," and "Amen."

The Sources of the Designations. The meaning, nature, functions, and other nuances of some of these designations will be discussed later.[144] At this stage, however, it is important to recognize that these designations of Christ are drawn from other parts of Revelation. Therefore, we first identify the locations where these titles are featured in the main text, as indicated in the following table:

Descriptions of Jesus	Texts alluded to in Revelation
Jesus "Christ" (Jesus/name, Christ/title)	1:9–20; chs. 4, 5, 12, 17, 19–22
"Faithful witness"	1:9–3:20; 19:11–16
"Firstborn from dead"	chs. 1–5, 17, 19–22
"Ruler of the kings of the world"	chs. 8–12, 17–21
"Freed us from our sins by His own blood"	chs. 4, 5, 7, 12, 17, 19
"made us to be a kingdom"	chs. 7, 19–22
"made us to be priests"	chs. 7, 19; 20:6
"His God" (implying Christology)	chs. 7, 19–22

---

[144] These and other designations of Jesus are discussed in the "seven addresses" (Rev. 2–3) in Part 3 of this volume.

Descriptions of Jesus	Texts alluded to in Revelation
"His Father" (implying Sonship)	chs. 7, 19–22
"to Him be glory, power ..."	chs. 4, 5, 11, 17, 19–22
"He is coming with the clouds"	chs. 6, 11, 14, 16, 19, 20
All "eyes will see Him, even those who pierced Him"	chs. 7, 14, 19
"all the people on earth 'will mourn because of Him'"	chs. 7, 19
"so shall it be! Amen."	3:14; 22:20, 21

The above assessment shows that the names are drawn from twenty of the twenty-two chapters (13 and 15 are the exceptions). This is not only indicative of the pervasiveness of Jesus in the text, but it also speaks volumes about John's comprehension of the text. In other words, the messages of Revelation first and foremost spoke to John's time as much as they speak to our time. As discussed in chapter 1, the historical method claims that only the messages of Revelation 1–3 were relevant to the early church. That would make them mere custodians of most of chapters 4–22 because they would have had limited understanding. Even if they had understood the language, they would not have fully comprehended the messages, for the prophecies were for a later time. However, the manner in which John bookended Revelation suggests that it spoke to his time and he fully understood the entire messages.

Other Similarities in Revelation. In this single passage, the author combined most of Jesus' designations that are featured throughout the text. As indicated earlier, we believe that Revelation 1:9–22:6 consists of the *actual* visions revealed to John at Patmos. However, 1:1–8 and 22:7–21 comprise the author's own insights, reflections, and summation. Therefore, the passage under study falls under the "author's reflection" section. This is important because in this passage, the author attempted to emulate Revelation 19:11–16, to which we will now turn.

Jesus Christ: His Names, Titles, Designations, and Deeds, Part II

Revelation 19:11–16. At least fifteen designations for Jesus are lumped together in these six verses, which is nearly three designations in every verse. Before we discuss the details of these designations, this passage is quoted here for comparative purposes:

> I saw heaven standing open and there before me was a white horse, whose *rider* is called *Faithful* and *True*. With justice *he judges* and *wages war*. His *eyes are like blazing fire*, and on his head are many *crowns*. He has a *name* written on him that no one knows but he himself. He is dressed in a robe dipped in *blood*, and his name is the *Word of God*. The armies of heaven were *following him*, riding on white horses and dressed in fine linen, white and clean. Coming out of his mouth is a *sharp sword* with which to strike down the nations. "He will *rule them with an iron scepter.*" *He treads the winepress* of the fury of the wrath of God Almighty. On his robe and on his thigh he has this name written: *King of kings* and *Lord of lords*. (emphasis supplied)

Comparative analysis of Revelation 1:5–7 and 19:11–16. Similar to the passage under study, Jesus' designations are also pervasive, being pulled together from nearly every chapter of Revelation. Note the similarities between the two lists of names and designations:

Revelation 1:5–7	Revelation 19:11–16
"He is coming with the clouds"	the rider on the "white horse"
"Ruler of the kings of the world"	"rule with an iron scepter"
"Freed us from our sins by His own blood"	"robe dipped in blood"
"made us to be a kingdom"	"King of kings"
"Faithful witness"	"Faithful"
"made us to be priests"	"name … no one knows"
"His God" (implying Christology)	"True"
"His Father" (implying Sonship)	"He treads the winepress"

Revelation 1:5–7	Revelation 19:11–16
"to Him be glory, power …"	"Lord of lords"
Jesus "Christ" (Jesus/name, Christ/title)	"He judges"
"Firstborn from the dead"	"His eyes are like blazing fire"
All "eyes will see Him, even those who pierced Him"	"He wages war … many crowns"
"all the people on earth 'will mourn because of Him'"	"an army of heaven was following Him" (commander)
"so shall it be! Amen."	"Word of God"
	"sharp sword"

<u>Similarity in Method, but Not in Content</u>. Only the first five designations share some similarities, and even those similarities are more nuanced than expressly stated. Four of these five are not taken from the same place in Revelation. For instance, Jesus coming with the clouds shares resemblance with chapter 14, whereas Him riding on the white horse alludes to chapter 6. Similarly, Jesus as the Ruler of the kings of the world appears to have a strong relationship with Revelation 17 where the Lamb defeats all the kings of the world. However, Jesus as a ruler with an iron scepter is referred to in chapter 12. Then Jesus liberating his subjects with His own blood is taken from Revelation 5, whereas the language of Jesus being clothed in a bloody robe resembles the saints of chapter 7.

The only designation that shares some similarities is Jesus as the Faithful One. Both of these designations have their origins in 3:14. Therefore, the similarities between these passages are limited in their methodology (i.e., the process of clustering Jesus' designations), but the actual designations in these two passages are widely dissimilar. This again speaks of Jesus' pervasiveness in the text.

The Composite Character of Jesus in Revelation

The clustering of Jesus' deeds and designations so eloquently speaks of His composite nature in Revelation. In the Apocalypse, Jesus is never presented as a single character. He is always revealed as having several characters, offices, institutions, and rituals all fused together. This composite nature of Jesus is typically represented in one of two ways: verbal or graphical representations.

Verbal and Graphical Representation of Jesus. In the verbal representation, Jesus is described or painted in words. A classic example is Revelation 1:5–7. In this passage, the author described Jesus using multiple imageries. However, the graphic and pictorial representations are numerous. The main ones among these include the "One like the Son of Man" (see 1:9–20), the "Lion-Lamb" (see 5:5, 6), the "Michael-Male Child" (see 12:7), and the Rider on the white horse (see 19:11–16).

> *The clustering of Jesus' deeds and designations so eloquently speaks of His composite nature in Revelation.*

Jesus Christ: His Names, Titles, Designations, and Deeds, Part III

Jesus' composite identity is not limited to the book of Revelation. In the Gospel of John and the Synoptic Gospels, Jesus is also presented as having multiple identities. In John 1:36–51, the author wove thirteen designations of Jesus into the narrative, which is nearly one title per verse. Similar to Revelation 1:5–7 and 19:11–16, this passage is also laden with Jesus' names, deeds, and titles.

John 1:36–51
"Jesus" (v. 36)
"Lamb of God" (v. 36)
"Rabbi" (vv. 38, 49)
"Messiah" (v. 41)
"Christ" (v. 41)
"the one Moses wrote about" (v. 45)
"the one … whom prophets also wrote" (v. 45)
"Jesus of Nazareth" (v. 45)
"the son of Joseph" (v. 45)

John 1:36–51
"Son of God" (v. 49)
"king of Israel" (v. 49)
Jacob's Ladder (v. 51)
"Son of Man" (v. 51)

THEOLOGICAL IMPLICATIONS

In the discussion on the title of the book ("Revelation of Jesus"), we concluded that Jesus serves both as the "medium" and the "message" of the Apocalypse because the messages were not only *about* Jesus but also communicated *by* and *through* Him. In our discussion on 1:4–8, particularly on God and the Holy Spirit, Jesus plays a pivotal role. First, He is revealed not only as Someone coming from God, but is also likened to God. We noted how each of God's names, titles, and designations were meticulously transferred to Jesus. Thus, Jesus is referred to as "the true God." Second, although the spirits are of God, only Jesus has the exclusive right to access and disperse them into the world.

Because of the nature of Jesus' relationship with His Father and the Holy Spirit, the false prophets, who deny Jesus as the Christ and coming from the Father and claim to know God or have his anointing (outside of Jesus), are branded as deceivers and liars. John described those opponents this way: "Who is the liar? It is whoever *denies that Jesus is the Christ*. ... No one who denies the Son has the Father; whoever acknowledges the Son has the Father also." "This is how you can recognize the Spirit of God: Every spirit that does not *acknowledge Jesus* is not from God. This is the spirit of the antichrists, which you have heard is coming and even now is already in the world" (1 John 2:22, 23; 4:3, emphasis supplied).

Having set the stage, the author enlisted certain designations of Jesus that he considered to be important—designations that are not mere names or titles, but encapsulate 1) Jesus' core accomplishments as they relate to mankind's redemption. Some of these works were accomplished in the past, but their effects are ongoing; 2) what Jesus is doing now or will do soon, including His glorious return; and 3) Jesus' relationship to and with His Father. The table below attempts to capture these. Note that some of these may overlap.

Accomplishments	Doing and Will Do	Relate to Father
"His God" [Christ]	"His God" [Christ]	"His God" [Christ]
"His Father" [Son]	"His Father" [Son]	"His Father" [Son]
Jesus "Christ" [Christ]	Jesus "Christ" [Christ]	Jesus "Christ" [Christ]
"to Him be glory, power …" [God]	"to Him be glory, power …" [God]	"to Him be glory, power …" [God]
"Freed us from our sins by His own blood" [Liberator, Savior/Lamb]	"Ruler of the kings of the world" [King of kings]	
"made us to be priests" [High Priest]	"made us to be priests" [High Priest]	
"made us to be a kingdom" [King]	"all the people on earth 'will mourn because of Him'" [Lamb]	
All "eyes will see Him, even those who pierced Him" [Jesus Christ]	"He is coming with the clouds" [King]	
"Firstborn from dead" [Resurrection and Life]	"Faithful witness" [Advocate, Judge]	

To avoid repetition, these designations of Christ will not be discussed at this stage, but we shall do that when we come to the main text where they are found.

SUMMARY STATEMENT: CHAPTERS 1–9

Before proceeding to the first part of the actual prophetic vision (Rev. 1:9–20), we summarize the discussion on the prologue (1:1–8).

1. <u>Literary Features</u>: Certain literary features enabled the author of Revelation to communicate its message more effectively. One such feature is Jesus' composite identity. In certain passages, Jesus assumes

a multifaceted identity. Some are pictorial, whereas others are linguistic in nature. Although the reasons for such representations have not yet been identified, it appears that these imageries may have influenced John to describe the book as the "Revelation of Jesus." The second literary device John used is the "literary crescendo." This style is heavily used in addressing certain, delicate, theological, Christological, and ecclesiastical issues in the early church. Particularly in areas where Jesus' provenance, identity, and authority were questioned, the author used the literary crescendo to build the argument, moving from the agreed to the disputed.

2. Trinity: The general emphasis on the Trinity in the NT, particularly in Revelation, is indicative of some serious theological or Christological issues during John's time. All three members of the triune God are stressed in the prologue, Revelation 4 and 5, and throughout the text.

3. Christology: Jesus, His deeds, names, titles, and designations are infused in the text. In most cases, He assumes certain intriguing composite characters. For instance, only in Revelation is Jesus depicted as the "Lamb-Shepherd," the "Lion-Lamb," "wrath of the Lamb" (or "warrior-Lamb"), and the "Michael-Male Child." These distorted imageries and languages could either reflect the author's literary craftsmanship or certain serious charges against Jesus during John's time. These and other areas remain to be explored.

4. Nearness of Time: As seen earlier, nearly every chapter in Revelation communicates the urgency and nearness of Jesus' return. How did the Johannine communities read declarations such as "the time is short" and "Behold! I am coming soon"? What would have been the impact of these statements in the lives of the readers, particularly if they understood the prophecies as being applicable to their own times and context?

5. Comprehensibility: The author described the book as the "Revelation of Jesus." Its content—the composite characters, clustering of multiple designations, and Jesus as both the Message and the Messenger—all seem to justify that title. These, coupled with the manner in which

John prefaced (1:1–8) and post-scripted (22:7–21) the main text (1:9–22:6) suggests John's comprehension of the entire text.

6. Dual Focus: The dual-focused method (as opposed to historicism, idealism, preterism, and futurism) assumes the messages of Revelation (both 1–3 and 4:1–22:6) were clear and applicable to the churches that first received them. John and his audience may have identified the issues, events, dates, institutions, and main characters involved. It also assumes that the same prophecies had a much larger or grander fulfillment at a later time. As much as applicable, we first establish what the messages meant to John and his contemporaries and then identify what they mean to us today.

   Dual-intentionalism in Revelation functions in three ways: 1) The prophecies that spoke to John's time also speak to us; 2) The specific details (historical fulfillment, dates, characters, etc.) may not be totally identical, but both should still harmonize; and 3) Some details applied to John's time, while others apply to our time. However, whether they had immediate, distant, or dual fulfillment, these parts of the prophecies may be lumped together, similar to Matthew 24. Therefore, determining the "immediate" from the "distant" and "dual" helps us fully understand and appreciate the prophecies.

7. Contextual implications. If John and his audience understood the prophecies of Revelation, then we need to determine where they saw themselves. For example, when they read the seven seals or seven trumpets for the first time, which seals/trumpets constituted their past, present, and future? The last 2,000 years of history provide us with clues as to where we stand in the prophetic stream of time. Similarly, John and his audience may have also sensed where they were. Therefore, determining where he and his audience saw themselves is necessary. Which of the seven seals or seven trumpets did they identify as describing their time, situation, and context? Which part of the prophecies constituted their past, and which were still in their future?

Similarly, their view on the remainder of Revelation (12–22) must also be shown. Historicism basically equates the events of the first of the seven seals and seven trumpets as occurring in the first 100 years. However, if John and his audience understood the prophecies as applying to their time, then we need to establish where they saw themselves in their prophetic time.

CONCLUSION

The prologue (Rev. 1:1–8) serves as a prelude to the "what will take place later" section (4:1–22:6). Contrary to popular notion, our preliminary studies thus far reflect a high degree of comprehension on the part of John. This is based on the fact that John was not only an inspired author but also he understood the message in his time and context. The next two chapters will discuss "the word of God and the testimony of Jesus" (1:9).

10.

DUAL FOCUS OF THE WORD OF GOD

> **I, John, your brother and companion in the suffering and kingdom and patient endurance that are ours in Jesus, was on the island of Patmos because of the word of God and the testimony of Jesus (Revelation 1:9)**

JOHN AND HIS BROTHERS

John and the Churches

In Revelation 1:1–3, John, the angel, and the seven churches are addressed as servants. As far as God is concerned, these three are indeed His servants. However, John affectionately called his readers brothers and then proceeded to qualify their brotherhood by enlisting common ingredients that serve to bind their brotherhood. These ingredients include "suffering," "kingdom," "patient endurance," and "Jesus." This list is not exhaustive. As discussed earlier, the brothers here also share the spirits of God, the word of God, and the testimony of Jesus.

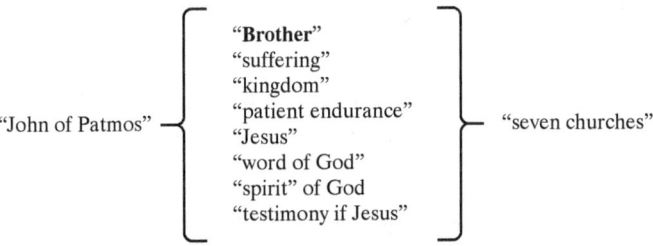

"Brothers" and "Servants"

The terms "servants" and "brothers" are also used in Revelation 6:9–11 and 19:10. However, in those contexts, they assume a slightly different meaning. The nuances of these terms will be discussed in the next chapter. In this instance, their brotherhood mingles the reality of the present suffering with the hopes of a future kingdom. To John, Patmos constituted the epitome of his suffering, while each of the seven churches was urged to overcome various forms of internal and external challenges.

THE WORD OF GOD AND THE TESTIMONY OF JESUS

The Occurrences and Uses of the Terms

The primary reason for their suffering is described as "the word of God and the testimony of Jesus."[145] As indicated earlier, these phrases appear in several key places as captured in the table that follows.[146] At the beginning of the prologue (Rev. 1:1–3), John summarized "everything he saw" as "the word of God and the testimony of Jesus." Those who had suffered martyrdom in 6:9 did so "because of the word of God and the testimony they had maintained."

The "word of God" and the "testimony of Jesus" are also the reasons for those who are currently suffering (see 1:9). Those who will suffer "soon" will do so also because of the "word of God and the testimony of Jesus" (6:11; see also 12:17; 14:12–13). Finally, the souls who have suffered, are suffering, and will suffer for the word of God and the testimony of Jesus will come back to life during the first resurrection (see 20:4). If the elements "word of God" and "testimony of Jesus" are that crucial, then determining what they meant to John (and his audience) and what they mean to us now is necessary.

---

[145] For further reading, especially on the current Adventist position on these two concepts, see an article by Gerhard Pfandl, "The Remnant Church and the Spirit of Prophecy," in Symposium on Revelation—Book II, pp. 295–333.

[146] See the discussion of these words in the prologue (Rev. 1:1–3).

"word of God and testimony of Jesus"	Reasons, Results, Causes, and Other Details
"word [*ton logon*] of God and the testimony [*tēn marturian*] of Jesus" (1:2)	John summarized Revelation as the "word of God" and the "testimony of Jesus."
"word [*ton logon*] of God and the testimony of [*tēn marturian*] Jesus" (1:9)	John saw himself and his readers as "brothers" because they had in common the "word of God" and the "testimony of Jesus."
"word of God and the testimony [*tēn marturian*] they had maintained" (6:9)	The cause of those who had died was the "word of God" and the "testimony" of Jesus. The passage also signals that those who "will die" will do so for the same reasons.
"God's commandments [*tas entolas*] and hold to the testimony of [*tēn marturian*] Jesus" (12:17)	Satan is angry with the saints who possess the "commandments of God" and the "testimony of Jesus." These two commodities are identifying marks of God's true worshipers.
"God's commandments [*tas entolas*] and remain faithful [*tēn pistin*] to Jesus" (14:12)	Those who keep the "commandments of God" and "remain faithful to Jesus" will be persecuted soon.
"testimony of [*tēn marturian*] Jesus and … word of [*ton logon*] God" (20:4)	Those who have the "testimony of Jesus" and are loyal to the "word of God" will be raised in the first resurrection.

Literary Analysis of the Statements

John consistently used these two elements—"word of God and the testimony of Jesus"—in this order—in three of six places (see 1:2, 9; 12:17). In 20:4, however, the phrases appear in reverse order—the "testimony of Jesus" precedes the "word of God." In 6:9, the word "testimony" appears alone; its accompanying phrase "of Jesus" is omitted. Because John had written them earlier, he probably assumed their familiarity with his audience. In 12:17, the term "commandments of God" replaces the phrase "word of God." In 14:12, John repeated the word "commandments," but then replaced the phrase "testimony of Jesus" with either "faith of Jesus" or "being faithful [*tēn pistin*]" to Jesus.

The variations in word order, partial omissions, and use of entirely different words do not reflect a significant change. If John felt his audience knew what these phrases meant, he may have expressed the same concepts by using different words to reduce monotony. Such is possible because throughout the Johannine literature, the designations "word of God" and the "commandments of God" are used interchangeably (see 1 John 2:3–5). The same could also be true for the terms "testimony of Jesus" and "faith of Jesus."

Early Church's Comprehension of Revelation 4:1–22:6

If John and his readers saw their own suffering in light of these two elements, then it is possible that they saw both messages (Rev. 1–3 and 4–22) as applying to their time. This suffering was not something that only those living centuries later would experience,[147] but something through which John and his brothers were living. Therefore, a proper method of interpretation is necessary to determine exactly what constituted the "word of God" and the "testimony of Jesus" in John's world and ours.

Dual Focus: the "word of God" and the "testimony of Jesus"

Because this study attempts to argue for a dualistic approach to the prophecies of Revelation—a method in which the same prophecies that spoke to John in his immediate and local context also have a broader and ultimate application to a later time, such slight and seemingly insignificant variations (like "word of God" or "commandment of God" and "testimony" or "faith" of Jesus) play an extremely important role in facilitating this process. For example, similar to modern historicists who consider these two criteria as important distinguishing marks for a true end-time church, John and his audience also saw the same two elements as having a similar role in their own time. These two criteria set them apart as God's true church from other competing religious movements in their era (see also Isa. 8:20).

---

[147] This does not mean that the prophecies do not apply to our time. In every way it does. However, it would be advisable to properly exegete the text to discover what it meant to John and his readers before one can apply it to our times.

In the following sections, we discuss only the "word of God" and the "commandments of God." The "testimony of Jesus" will be discussed in chapter 11. We address two particular questions: 1) What did these two elements mean to John and his audience? and 2) What do they mean to us?

THE WORD OF GOD

Review of Views on the "word of God"

The "word of God." In the OT, a prophetic message received and delivered by the prophets was typically referred to as the "word of the Lord." In Revelation, however, one must decide whether the "word of God" refers specifically to the messages in the book of Revelation or something else. While commenting on Revelation 1:2, Ranko Stefanovic suggests that the designation refers only to the "symbolic visionary presentations" Jesus gave to John.[148] As far as this verse is concerned, Stefanovic is correct, since the "word of God and the testimony of Jesus" does seem to summarize the content of everything John saw. However, the same cannot be said of 1:9, 6:9–11, 12:17, or 20:4. Revelation 1:9 seems to suggest that the "word of God and the testimony of Jesus" is something John and his audience already possessed (i.e., before the prophecies of Revelation were given).

> *John received the visionary messages of Revelation in the midst of his suffering, and that suffering came about as a result of the "word of God and the testimony of Jesus" that he already had.*

John received the visionary messages of Revelation in the midst of his suffering, and that suffering came about as a result of the "word of God and the testimony of Jesus" that he already had. Similarly, if the martyrs

---

[148] Stefanovic, p. 61. However, C. Mervin Maxwell suggests that the "word of God is the Bible, the sacred Scriptures" (The Message of Revelation: God Cares, Vol. 2), p. 78.

of Revelation 6:9 had already been killed (from John's perspective), and their fate resulted from the "word of God" and the "testimony" that they had, then what they had possessed obviously did not include the messages of Revelation. A similar case could be made for the other passages as well (e.g., 12:17, 20:4).[149]

Mervin Maxwell, however, suggested that the "word of God is the Bible, the [entire] sacred Scriptures."[150] He is generally correct, but his views do not seriously take into consideration the nuances in Revelation. In other words, the immediate context must help define this and other related terms. What does the phrase "word of God" mean in Revelation and the NT?

The "word of God" in Revelation and NT Literature

<u>Two Definitions of "word of God" in Revelation</u>. The book of Revelation offers two specific definitions for the phrase "word of God." First, any direct messages from God, either quoted by someone else or faithfully relayed by a messenger, are referred to as the "word of God." "[W]rite," the angel says to John, "'Blessed are those who are invited to the wedding supper of the Lord!' And then he added, 'these are the true words of God'" (Rev. 19:9; 21:5). "For the one whom God has sent [Jesus Christ] speaks the words of God …" (John 3:34). Second, the name of the rider on the white horse of Revelation 19:13 is called the "Word of God." In other Johannine literature, these two meanings are further elaborated.

---

[149] Revelation: "word of God" or "words of the prophecy in this book" (22:7). While it is true that the contents of Revelation are summarized as the "word of God" in 1:2, it is also true that the same is referred to as "the words of prophecy in this book" (1:3; 22:7, 10, 18, 19). Although the messages of Revelation originate with God (thus, "word of God"), the entire content of Revelation is repeatedly referred to as "the words of prophecy in *this* book." The phrase "in this book" seems to imply the existence of other books that could have also contained the "word of God." If so, then the contents of Revelation alone cannot be equated to the "word of God." In that case, the messages of Revelation could be seen as part of the entire "word of God."

[150] When he said the "Bible" or "Sacred Scriptures," he referred to the Old Testament. Mervin Maxwell, The Message of Revelation: God Cares, Vol. 2, p. 78.

Two Ways in Which the "Word of God" Came to Mankind. "In the past [OT] God spoke to our forefathers through the prophets at many times and in various ways, but in the last days God has spoken to us by His Son" (Heb. 1:1). This passage presents two conduits through which the Word of God came to mankind. In the past, God used various human agents like the prophets and prophetesses. Among these prophets, Moses alone came nearest to God. It is written of him, "no prophet has risen in Israel like Moses, whom the Lord knew face to face" (Deut. 34:10). However, Moses did not "see God," for "no one has ever seen God" (John 1:18; 1 John 4:20). Perhaps that is why Paul stated that what was shown to humanity was only in "part" as if in a "mirror" (1 Cor. 13:12, NKJV).

In the NT, however, the "word of God" came through John the Baptist, who was spoken of as the greatest. "During the high priesthood of Annas and Caiaphas, the *word of God* came to John son of Zechariah in the desert" (Luke 3:3, emphasis supplied). Jesus described John as being "more than a prophet" and further exclaimed that "among those born of women there is no one greater than John" (7:26, 28). However, like Moses, John also had limitations. He was merely the voice in the wilderness, whereas Christ Himself was both "the word" and the "Word [that] became flesh" (John 1:23, 14). Comparing his own testimony with that of Jesus', John said, "The one who comes from heaven is above all," and "He testifies to what he has seen and heard," whereas the "one who is from the earth belongs to the earth and speaks as one from the earth" (John 3:31, 32).

The "Word of God" That Came Through Jesus Is Superior. The "word of God" that came through Jesus is superior. In "these last days," the word of God came to us "by His Son." John said of the Son, "No one has seen God at any time. The only begotten Son who is at the bosom of the Father, he has declared Him" (John 1:18, NKJV). A related passage in Hebrews reads, "The Son is the radiance of God's glory and the exact representation of His being" (Heb. 1:2). Because the Son has "seen God," stands "at the bosom of the Father," and is the "exact representation of His being," the "Father has placed his seal of approval" on Him to make "Him [God] known" to mankind (John 6:27; 1:18). This makes the Son's testimony—that is, the "Word of God" that came through the Son—superior to that of previous human agents.

Not only is the word of God that came through Jesus superior, but also complete, truthful, and faithfully discharged. The table below shows a brief comparison of the two conduits through which the word of God came (also compare this table with the two conduits of the "Spirit of God" in chapter 8).

Prophets	Prophets: "many times and in various ways"	Jesus: "last Days … by his Son"
Many Ways	"many times and in various ways" (Heb. 1:1)	"I am the [only] Way" (John 14:6)
All Prophets	Through many "prophets" (Heb. 1:1)	"by his Son" (Heb. 1:2)
Moses	"No one [including Moses] has ever seen God" (John 1:18)	"One and Only at the Father's side, has [seen and] made him known [to us]" (John 1:18)
	"Moses was faithful as a servant" (Heb. 3:5; John 8:31–36)	"Christ is faithful as a son" (Heb. 3:6; John 8:31–36), "Jesus [is] worthy of greater honor than Moses" (Heb. 3:3)
	"law was given through Moses" (John 1:17a)	"grace and truth came through Jesus Christ" (John 1:17b)
David	"patriarch David" (Acts 2:29)	Jesus is David's Lord (Acts 2:34–36)
	David died and his grave is here with us (Acts 2:29)	Jesus died, rose, lives, and has the keys of David and the grave (Rev. 3:7; 1:18; Acts 2:31–32)
Paul	"like a mirror, dimly" (1 Cor. 13:12)	"exact representation of his [God's] being" (Heb. 1:3)
John the Baptist	"John was a lamp" (John 5:35)	"I am the light of the world" (John 8:12)
	"his [Baptist's] testimony about me is valid" (John 5:32)	"I have testimony weightier than that of John" (John 5:36)
Abraham	Father Abraham (John 8:33, 37, 39, 53)	"'Are you greater than our Father Abraham? … I tell you the truth,' Jesus answered, 'before Abraham was born, I am!'" (John 8:53, 58)

Prophets	Prophets: "many times and in various ways"	Jesus: "last Days ... by his Son"
Jacob	Jacob "gave us the well and drank from it himself ..." (John 4:12)	"Are you greater than our father Jacob ...?" "Everyone who drinks this water will be thirsty again, but whoever drinks the water I give him will never thirst" (John 4:12–14)

The "word of God" Through Jesus: More Complete, Accurate, Weightier, and Clearer. This table contrasts the two agents through whom the word of God came. The following are noteworthy: The NT account cites two of the greatest and most revered of prophets—Moses in the OT and John the Baptist in the NT. The testimony they bore is contrasted with the word of God that came through Jesus Christ.

a. In this, Moses' testimony is presented as somewhat incomplete, whereas Christ's is more complete. As a result, Jesus is "worthy of greater honor than Moses" (Heb. 3:3). Also note the emphasis on Moses' status as a servant who has no permanence in the house, whereas the Son has permanence.
b. A similar difference is stressed with that of John the Baptist's testimony. Jesus had previously stated that of all born of woman, John ranked as the greatest (see Luke 7:26–28). However, concerning being the "sent of God," John was merely a "lamp," whereas the Son was "the light." Hence, the testimony Jesus bore was weightier than that of John.
c. Paul considered all testimonies that came "through the prophets at many times in various ways" as a poor reflection as in a mirror, but the word of God that came through Jesus Christ is superior, weightier, clearer, and more complete and truthful because He is the "radiance of God's glory and the exact representation of His being" (1 Cor. 13:12; Heb. 1:1, 2).

Jesus is "Faithful." When addressing the last of the seven churches in Revelation, Jesus describes Himself as the "Faithful and true Witness" (3:14). The context here concerns His intimate knowledge and faithful assessment of the Laodicean condition. A similar usage is implied in 19:11. However, Jesus, as an emissary of God, is also "Faithful" in revealing God and God's word to humanity.

The Law and the Prophets "wrote about me." Moses and other prophets not only wrote about Christ, but their very own lives also prefigured Him. Prophets, priests, kings, institutions, and rituals were a type, and Jesus was and is the antitype. The NT is also about Jesus Christ. Thus, He is the embodiment of the entire Scriptures. In other words, Jesus is the "word of God" made audible, visible, and touchable!

Three Ways in Which the "Word of God" Came Through Jesus Christ

The word of God came through Jesus in three distinct ways. First, Jesus' own words were God's words. "These words," He said, "you hear are not my own; they belong to the Father who sent me" (John 14:24). Second, He showed that even His deeds were not His own, but God's. "I tell you the truth, the Son can do nothing by Himself; He can do only what He sees His Father doing, because whatever the Father does, the Son does also" (John 5:19). Jesus stated, "the world must learn that I love the Father and that I do *exactly* what my Father has commanded me" (John 14:31, emphasis supplied). He was the "Faithful and True Witness," did "exactly" what His Father did or commanded Him to do. Jesus, therefore, "did the works and spoke the words of God."[151] Third, because Jesus is the exact representation of God and does exactly what God commands Him to do, He is, in essence, the Word of God (see Heb. 1:3; John 14:31;

---

[151] E. G. White, The Desire of Ages, p. 407.

Rev. 19:13). No wonder why even His very name is called "the Word" (John 1:1, 2, 14) or "Word of God" (Rev. 19:13).

Jesus was with God during creation. He is the Word who "became flesh and made his dwelling among us" (John 1:1–4, 14). In this case, the "word of God" is not limited to the words Jesus spoke or the deeds He performed, but He embodies the "Word of God." E. G. White, therefore, could write, "He [Jesus] was the embodiment of the truths He taught."[152] Thus, Jesus likened His own words and deeds to "flesh and blood." He also stated, "the words that I have spoken to you are spirit, and they are life" (John 6:63). Additionally, the "Word of God is living and active" (Heb. 4:12–13). Therefore, when John reminded the believers that the "word of God lives in you," he meant Jesus being in them (1 John 2:14).

"Word of God," "Son of Man," The Rider on the "white horse." Finally, a relationship between the "Son of Man" (Rev. 1:12–16), the "Rider on the white horse" (19:11–16), and Hebrews 4:12–13 seems to suggest those three characters to be the word of God. Consider the passage in Hebrews and the comparative analysis of the three as follows:

> For the word of God is living and active. Sharper than any double-edged sword, it penetrates even to dividing soul and spirit, joints and marrow; it judges the thoughts and attitudes of the heart. Nothing in all creation is hidden from God's sight. Everything is uncovered and laid bare before the eye of him to whom we must give account. (Hebrews 4:12, 13)

This passage shares a lot of similarities with the other two passages in Revelation (1:12–16 and 19:11–16).[153] Consider the following examples:

---

[152] E. G. White, The Desire of Ages, p. 465.
[153] Perhaps this is one reason why we have proposed the Johannine authorship of Hebrews.

"Word of God" (Heb. 4:12–13)	"The Rider" (Rev. 19:11–16)	"Son of Man" (Rev. 1:12–16)
"word of God" (12)	"word of God" (13)	"son of Man" (13)
"sharper … doubled-edged sword"	"double-edged sword" (15)	"double-edged sword" (16; 2:12)
his eyes see everything	"eyes like blazing fire" (12)	"eyes like blazing fire" (14; 2:18)
"living and active"	"sword that came out of the mouth of the rider" kills beast/kings (19:19–20)	"strike her children dead" (2:23)
divides soul/spirit, joints/marrow, judges thoughts/attitudes"		"judges thoughts and attitudes" (2:23)

Observe the volume and quality of similarities these three passages share. First, note that the two passages in Revelation discuss living characters, while the one in Hebrews is not a person but a concept. Second, the two characters in Revelation have a "sharp, double-edged sword" coming out from their mouth, while in Hebrews, the concept of the Word of God is likened to a doubled-edged sword. Third, in all cases, that weapon is used for executing judgments. Fourth, the same character also has eyes that see everything, though in Hebrews, it is God who sees. The volume of similarities shows that the "word of God" is the "Rider on the white horse," the "Son of Man," and "Jesus Christ." After all, Jesus is indeed the "word [that] became flesh and made his dwelling among us" (John 1:14).

DUAL FOCUS OF THE WORD AND COMMANDMENTS OF GOD

What the "word of God" and "commandments of God" Meant to John and His Audience

What the "word of God" Meant to John and His Audience. In Revelation, those who are currently suffering (including John), those who have already been killed, those who would be killed in the future, and those who would come back to life in the first resurrection are the ones who "keep the word of God" and "have the testimony of Jesus." Therefore, when John talked about the "word of God," he was referring specifically to the words, deeds, and person of Jesus Christ.[154] The following reasons support this argument:

> *Therefore, when John talked about the "word of God," he was referring specifically to the words, deeds, and person of Jesus Christ.*

1. First, the OT, as the "word of God," "testif[ied] about me [Jesus]" (John 5:39). Therefore, Philip said, "Moses ... [and the] prophets" wrote about Jesus (1:45).
2. Second, the "word of God" that "came through the prophets" (i.e., the OT) was incomplete and lacked clarity than that which came through Jesus Christ (Heb. 1:1, 2). In other words, the superiority of the word of God that came through Jesus Christ outweighs the entire OT.
3. Third, the words Jesus spoke, the deeds He performed, and the life He lived was the exact representation of God's being. Therefore, Jesus was "Immanuel...God with us" (Matt. 1:23).
4. Finally, it is because of this that Jesus Christ is called the "Word of God" (Rev. 19:13).

<u>What the "commandment of God" Meant to John and His Audience</u>. However, in Revelation 12:17 and 14:12, the term "word" is replaced with the term "commandment." Thus, the phrase reads "commandment of God" rather than "word of God." Because Revelation so prominently features variation, the early church could have seen these two terms as

---

[154] This includes the OT because Jesus essentially said Moses and the prophets "wrote about me" (John 5:46).

referring to nearly the same thing.[155] This is because during that time, the "word of God" was considered as the "commandment of God."

Additionally, John defined the term "commandments" (or "commandments of God") this way: "And this is His commandment; to believe in the name of His Son, Jesus Christ ... as He has commanded us" (1 John 3:23). The commandment referred to here is what God spoke through Moses:

> The Lord your God will raise up for you a prophet like me from among your own brothers. You must listen to him. ... I will raise up for them a prophet like you from among their brothers; I will put my words in his mouth, and he will tell them everything I command him. If anyone does no listen to my words that the prophet speaks in my name, I myself will call him to account. (Deuteronomy 18:15, 18, 19)

This command is reiterated in Matthew 17:5: "This is my Son, whom I love; with him I am well pleased. Listen to him!" In Acts, Peter pleaded with the people, "For Moses said, 'the Lord your God will raise up for you a prophet like me from among your own people; you must listen to everything he tells you. Anyone who does not listen to him will be completely cut off from among his people'" (Acts 3:22, 23; see also Luke 9:35).

In a nutshell, the commandment of God is to hear, obey, believe, follow, love, and accept Jesus as being the *Christ* and *sent* of God. Any refusal or denial of Jesus Christ, therefore, is tantamount to "lawlessness," "disobedience," faithlessness, condemnation, and "sin" (1 John 3:4–6; John 3:18; 16:9).[156] Given such a scenario, John and his audience undoubtedly

---

[155] As seen earlier, and as we shall see later, Revelation is saturated with a single character or concept having multiple names, titles, and designations. We call these "variations." John probably employed this method for clarity and emphasis, but the same could also serve as a clue to the concept of "dualism."

[156] John continued, "Everyone who sins breaks the law; in fact, sin is lawlessness. But you know that He appeared so that He might take away our sins... No one who lives in Him keeps on sinning.

saw themselves as those who obeyed "the commandments of God" and kept the "word of God," both of which concerned believing in Jesus Christ. As the entire NT testifies, the person, identity, and deeds of Jesus Christ constituted the core issue in the early church.

What Do the "word of God" and "commandments of God" Mean to Us Today?

The end-time saints are persecuted because they "keep the commandments of God" (Rev. 12:17). To John and his audience, this commandment meant to "believe" in Jesus as the Christ in accordance with Deuteronomy 18. They did not see this as referring to the Ten Commandments in anyway. Moreover, the Ten Commandments were not an issue in the early church. Today, however, the word "commandment" seems to have a slightly different meaning than it did in the first century. Therefore, this discussion will attempt to establish its secondary meaning. If the textual evidences supports this, then that will serve to further reinforce the concept of dual-intentionalism in the prophecies of Revelation. We will discuss Revelation 4, 5 and 14.

The Three Angels' Messages. The first of the three end-time messages of Revelation 14 reads; "Then I saw another angel flying in midair, and he had the eternal gospel to proclaim to those who live on the earth—to every nation, tribe, language and people. He said in a loud voice, 'Fear God and give him glory, because the hour of his judgment has come.' Worship him who made the heavens, the earth, the see and the springs of water'" (vv. 6–7). The following observations can be made concerning this passage.

The Messenger. First, notice that the messenger is described as "another angel." The term "another" implies that the current angel is similar to an earlier one. The only other angel that had come proclaiming in a "loud

---

No one who continues to sin has either seen Him or known Him" (1 John 3:4–6). In 1 John, there is a heavy use of the word "sin." It is generically defined as "lawlessness," but the author does not say if he had a specific "sin" in mind. However, what he did say in this passage is that not following Jesus, not living in Jesus, not seeing or knowing Jesus, or not believing in Jesus is "sin," "lawlessness," and not keeping "God's commandment."

voice," was the "mighty angel" of Rev. 5: 2. Since that first angel was a "mighty" one, the second must be "mighty" as well. Second, the angel speaks in "a loud voice." The loudness of the voice does not necessarily indicate the volume, but clarity of the message. Further, the angel comes flying "in mid-air." This indicates the swiftness of the message.

The Solemnity of the Message. Apart from the volume, clarity, and the speed; notice the urgency, solemnity and the finality of this message. That which the mighty angel proclaims in a loud voice is in fact the end-time message. For after this message, the entire earth is then divided into two camps—the righteous gathered into the "harvest of the earth," while the wicked into the "clusters of grape" (Rev. 14:15, 18). This is why the message is addressed to every living person on the planet—'every nation, tribe, language and people." After the angel has done his job, all inhabitants of the earth will stand without an excuse, for all would have heard the wonders of God in their own language. The table below compares these two messengers.

Features	"mighty angel" of Rev. 5: 2	"another angel" of Rev. 14
The Messenger	"a mighty angel"	"another angel"
Nature of the voice	"proclaiming in a loud voice"	Proclaim the eternal gospel "in a loud voice"
The addressees	To those in "heaven or on earth or under the earth" (v. 3)	"To only those who live on the earth—to every nation, tribe, language and people" (v. 6)
Implication	If a "mighty angel"	then a mighty angel too

The Content of the Message. The content of the message is described as "eternal gospel." First of all, the events surrounding the birth, life, and the sacrificial death of Christ are consistently referred to as "the gospel" in the entire New Testament (Matt. 24:14). But these events are never called an *eternal* gospel. Secondly, the "eternal gospel" in Revelation 14 is closely associated with the Creation account, rather than the salvific work of the Cross. Finally, the text especially defines the "eternal gospel" as worshiping God "who made the heavens, the earth, the sea and the springs of water" (Rev. 14:7). Therefore, the "eternal gospel" that the first angel proclaims in Revelation 14 points us to God's creative works in Genesis.

The Creation and the Cross. This distinction between the "eternal gospel" and "gospel" is referenced elsewhere in Revelation too. The "eternal" gospel is gospel for all people in all time. In that case, the "gospel of Christ" can never be called an "eternal" gospel. This is because it is an emergency plan that God executed after the fall of man (Rev. 13:8; 17:8). Perhaps this is why, there is a distinction made in Rev 4 and 5. For example, Christ is worshipped as "worthy" because He "purchase men by his blood" (Rev. 5:9); while God is described as "worthy" because "he created all things" (Rev. 4:11). Here, both Christ and God are worshipped as "worthy" candidates, but for totally different reasons. God is worshipped for creation, while Christ for redemption. Or to put it differently, God for the "eternal gospel," while Christ for "the gospel."

The Nature of the Songs: The song that the four living creatures sing to God begins this way; "Day and night they never stop saying: 'Holy, Holy, Holy is the Lord God Almighty...'" (Rev. 4:8). Note that there is no time reference in the song that is being rendered to God. All it says is that "Day and night they do not stop" singing. Implied here is the continuous, unceasing, a timeless 'day and night' rendering of the worship to God ever since the creation. And as long as He remains the Creator, the song will never stop.

However, the song that the same characters sing to Christ is described merely as "a new song" (5:9). Those who have been singing "Holy, Holy, Holy" to God are now singing a "new song" to the Lamb. The context shows that this "new song" was added after Christ had "purchased men for God by His blood" at Calvary. So there is a direct relation between the concept of "eternal gospel" and the worship of God as the Creator. And a similar relationship exists between the "gospel of Jesus" and the singing of the "new song." The table below summarises these discussions:

Features	God (Rev. 4)	Christ (Rev. 5)
Text	"You are worthy, our Lord and God...for your created all things" (v. 11)	"You are worthy to take the scroll and to open its seals, because you were slain, and with your blood you purchased men for God" (v. 9)
Worthy Candidate	God is "worthy" (v. 11)	Christ is "worthy" (v. 9)
Reasons for Worship	"created all things" [Creation]	"you were slain" [Redemption]
Worshippers	"twenty-four elders" (v. 10)	"four living creatures and the twenty-four elders" (v. 8)
Type of Songs	"Day and night they never stop saying" (v. 8)	"And they sang a new song..." (v. 9).
Type of Gospel	"eternal gospel"	"gospel of Christ"

The commandment: Gospel versus Eternal Gospel. As discussed, if the term commandment initially meant to believe, accept, obey and follow Jesus Christ; then notice that that has something to do with the "gospel of Christ." However, if the same term has a secondary meaning, then it must have something to do the "eternal gospel" which concerns God's creative works. Therefore, it is necessary for us to revisit the creation account at this stage.

The Commandment and Revelation. The final message in Revelation 14 reads; "worship him who made the heavens, earth, sea and springs of water." There are two questions that must be answered. The first is: Why? Why a call to worship the creator God in the end of time? Is this an indication that man has forgotten to worship God as the "creator God"? If mankind is claiming to worship the creator God, then why do the heavens summon the earth to worship the same at such a critical time? Someone is making a fatal mistake at this critical hour—whether man has indeed forgotten to worship the creator God or that mighty angel's loud cry is irrelevant and should be dismissed forthwith. This leads us to our second question.

The Commandment and Creation. How do we know that the God we are worshipping is actually the creator God, and not just another god? This is an important question. For, if we answer this question correctly, then that answer will help shed light on the actual identity of the God we claim to worship. Now, as we revisit the creation account, observe the stunning similarities between the message of Revelation 14:7 and Genesis 2:1–2. The table below compares these two passages:

Revelation	Creation
"Worship him who made the heavens, the earth, the see and the springs of water" (Rev. 14:6–7)	"Thus the heavens and the earth were completed in all their vast array. By the seventh day God had finished the work he had been doing, so on the seventh day, he rested from all his work. And God blessed the seventh day and made it holy, because on it he rested from all the works of creation that he had done" (Gen. 2:1–2)
"eternal gospel"	"the seventh day"

The language used by John in Revelation 14 is taken from Genesis 2:1–2. The heavens, the earth, the seas and those who dwell in them were all created in six days, not in seven days. Actually, God did not create anything on the "seventh day." He instead blessed, sanctified, and rested on the "seventh day." In other words, God having completed the creation in six days, He added the seventh day Sabbath as a memorial of His creative powers. Therefore, the "eternal gospel" of Revelation 14 is tied in with the "seventh day" of the creation week in Genesis.

The Commandment and the Ten Commandments. Then notice how the same "seventh day" Sabbath is found in the heart of the Ten Commandments. The text reads;

> "Remember the Sabbath day to keep it holy... For in six days the Lord made the *heavens and the earth, the sea and all that is in them*, but he rested on the seventh day. Therefore the Lord blessed the seventh day and made it holy" (Exod. 20:8–11. Emphasis supplied).

Carefully observe the significance of the "seventh day" as far as God's creative work and power is concerned. First, if the entire creation was completed in "six days," then the "seventh day" was added to the creation week to serve a totally different purpose. Second, God blessed, rested, and sanctified the Sabbath day for holy use. Third, only in the fourth commandment, man is commanded to both remember and keep the Sabbath holy because God "made it holy." Fourth, the Sabbath commandment is the only commandment that identifies who the Creator and the Law-giver is. Finally, the fourth commandment also shows us *who* to worship, *when* to worship, and *how* to worship.

When Revelation 14, Genesis 2, and Exodus 20 are compared, it becomes more apparent that the language used in Revelation 14 is taken straight from both the creation account and the fourth commandment. This shows that the end-time angelic call to "worship the creator God" is a call to keep the Ten Commandments, especially the fourth one. The following table shows these similarities.

Features	Revelation	Creation	Commandment
Texts	"Worship him who made the *heavens, the earth, the see and the springs of water*" (Rev. 14:6–7)	"Thus the *heavens and the earth* were completed in all their vast array. By the seventh day God had finished the work he had been doing, so on the seventh day, he rested from all his work. And God blessed the seventh day and made it holy, because on it he rested from all the *works of creation* that he had done" (Gen. 2:1–2)	"Remember the Sabbath day to keep it holy... For in six days the Lord made the *heavens and the earth, the sea and all that is in them*, but he rested on the seventh day. Therefore the Lord blessed the seventh day and made it holy" (Exod. 20:8–11)
Gospels & Commandments	"eternal gospel"	"the seventh day"	The fourth commandment

The Prophet Ezekiel understood the significance of the Sabbath commandment when he wrote this:

> "Also I have given them my Sabbaths as a sign between us, so they would know that I the Lord made them holy... I am the Lord your God; keep my decrees and be careful to keep my laws. Keep my Sabbaths holy, that they may be a sign between

us. Then you will know that I am the Lord your God" (Ezek. 20:12, 19–20).

The author of Hebrews writing after the Cross of Calvary, indicated that the Sabbath Commandment was still binding. God;

> "has spoken about the seventh day in this words, 'And on the seventh day God rested from all his works…There remains, then a Sabbath-rest for the people of God, for anyone who enters God's rests also rests from his own works, just as God did from his" (Heb. 4:9).

As shown above, when man begins to keep the Sabbath holy, refrains from all secular activities, and worships God on it—that worship is considered as being rendered to the Creator God! However, when man shifts his focus and calls the name of the Lord on another day, Heaven considers that worship as being rendered to *another* god.[157] By choosing to keep Friday, Sunday or another day sacred, man has indeed forgotten to worship the creator God. It is no wonder that the mighty angel calls in a loud voice to everyone that dwells on the earth to worship the *Creator* God!

Analysis of the term Commandments. The prophecies of Revelation identifies the saints of God as those who "keep the commandments of God." To John and his audience, the term had a christologically nuanced meaning, but to those living in the end of time it means the fourth of the Ten Commandments. And as demonstrated here, the text supports both interpretations. The passage of time, events of the history, and activities of the "lawless man" over the last 2,000 years have morphed the same terms and concepts to adopt a slightly different meaning now. In other words, although the term "commandments" remain unchanged,

---

[157] Almost a thousand years before this change was effected, Prophet Daniel prophesied about it. He wrote that the "Little Horn" power would "speak against the Most High and oppress his saints and try to change the set times and the laws…" (Dan 7:25). And surely such a power did (and continues) to claim responsibility for this change. See Reverend. Peter Geiermann, *Convert's Catechism of Catholic*, p. 50.).

its contents, definitions, details, nuances, and characteristics are different. This indicates that God used the same terms, but with a double meaning to communicate to two completely diverse audiences living in different times.[158] Paulien describes the same concept this way: "God's explanations have extended meanings beyond what the original prophet could understand, but those extended meanings will never contradict the original revelation. They will be natural extensions of what the prophet received and understood."[159] As shown in the following table, the "commandments of God" (Rev. 12:17) could refer to the Ten Commandments today. Although the early church's issues are no longer ours, the same prophecies that spoke to them, speak also to us.

The following table captures these nuances and summarizes the above discussion:

Concepts	What They Meant to John and His Audience Then	What They Mean to Us Now
"word of God" (Rev. 1:2, 9; 6:9; 19:13)	"Jesus" (Rev. 19:13; John 1:1–5, 14), or words Jesus spoke, for Jesus "speaks the word of God, for God" (John 3:34; 8:37–40; 1 John 2:13–14). Jesus' words "spirit and life" (John 6:63), "if you keep my word, you will never see death" (John 8:51), Jesus "keeps his [God's] word" (John 8:55), "gods, to whom the word of God came" (John 10:35)	Generally, the Bible and specifically, the words, deeds, and person of Jesus.
"Commandments of God" (Rev. 12:17; 14:12).	"This is his [God's] commandment: to believe in the name of his son, Jesus Christ… [just] as he commanded us" (1 John 3:23; 2:3–4; John 5:45–47). God "commanded" Israel to obey the prophet like Moses whom He will raise up (Deut. 18:15–18). Obeying or believing in that prophet is akin to "obeying the commandments of God" (Matt. 17:5; Acts 3:22; Luke 9:35).	"the ten [4th in particular] commandments" (Dan. 7:25; Rev. 11:19; 12:17; 14:7, 12)

---

[158] This concept is richly illustrated in Revelation and other Johannine writings. Some of the examples we have seen thus far include the character and person of Jesus in chapter 9. More examples are sighted in chapters 11 and 12, and the discussion on the "angel" of Revelation 10 is in chapter 20.

[159] Paulien, "The Seven Heads of Revelation 17," p. 24. Copy of original manuscript is used here.

SUMMARY

In the NT, particularly in Revelation and other Johannine writings, the word of God denotes Jesus Christ. This is because the words He spoke and the deeds He performed cannot be separated from His being. Therefore, when John and his audience read about the word of God as the reason for i) those who had been killed (see Rev. 6:9–12), ii) those who would be killed soon (see 12:17; 14:12), iii) those who would be resurrected to life (see 19:4), and iv) those involved in current afflictions [John and his brothers (see 1:9)], they understood this as referring to Jesus Christ. If keeping the word of God meant possessing, imitating, and living in harmony with the words, deeds, and person of Jesus Christ, then keeping the commandments of God meant accepting and believing in Jesus as the long-awaited Messiah or Christ.

> *To those living at the end of time, the ancient definition of the term "commandment" (believing in Jesus as the Messiah) has less relevance than it once did. Thousands of years of history has transformed this phrase to mean something slightly different now.*

However, to those living at the end of time, the ancient definition of the term "commandment" has less relevance than it once did. Thousands of years of history has transformed this phrase to mean something slightly different now. Therefore, the phrase "commandments of God," which meant "to believe in Jesus," now refers to the fourth of the Ten Commandments. E. G. White agrees; "The great sin of the Jews was their rejection of Christ; the great sin of the Christian world would be their rejection of the law of God, the foundation of His government in heaven and earth."[160] This is not a coincidence. It reflects God's deep purposes, foreknowledge, and also the dual-intentionality of the prophecies of Revelation.

---

[160] E. G. White, *The Great Controversy*, p. 22.

11.

THE DUAL FOCUS OF THE TESTIMONY OF JESUS

INTRODUCTION

In the previous chapter, we demonstrated that the phrase "word of God" (or "commandment of God") has a double meaning. In the current study, we analyze the phrase "testimony of Jesus." We especially seek to determine what this phrase meant to the early church and what it means to us today.

USAGE OF THE PHRASE "TESTIMONY OF JESUS"

The "testimony of Jesus" has three uses: 1) The "testimony of Jesus" is similar to the "Revelation of Jesus," 2) The meaning and the significance of the "testimony of Jesus" and the "faith of Jesus" and 3) The "testimony of Jesus is the spirit of prophecy." We will now discuss these uses.

Literary Significance

The phrase "testimony of Jesus" has a similar usage and significance as does the "Revelation of Jesus" as discussed in Revelation 1:1–3. In our study of the phrase "the Revelation of Jesus," we indicated that the term could be interpreted both as an objective or subjective genitive. That is, this revelation is not only given by Jesus (medium), but He is also the content of these prophecies (message). A similar usage is implied here. This means that the "testimony of Jesus" involves "testimonies" or "evidences" concerning Jesus' Messiahship according to i) Jesus' own words, deeds, and life (see John 3:11) and ii) the testimonies according to the words, deeds, and lives of others, especially the eyewitnesses.[161] The Johannine writings are replete with examples endorsing both of these usages. Before we see some of these examples, it is important to point out that the phrases "testimony of Jesus" and "faith of Jesus" are interchangeably used.

"Testimony of Jesus" and "faith of Jesus"

In the initial part of Revelation, the author assumed that the meaning of the phrase "testimony of Jesus" was clear to his audience. However, in the middle and towards the end, two notable changes occur in how this phrase is used. First, the phrases "testimony of Jesus" and "faith of Jesus" are used as having a similar meaning (Rev 12:17; 14:12). This usage is similar to the terms "the word of God" and "commandments of God." Second, in Revelation 19:10, the author (for the first time) defined the phrase "testimony of Jesus" as the "spirit of prophecy." The occurrence in this verse seems like an afterthought effort, but one that is critically important to our current study. Therefore, we proceed to explore this third usage.

"Testimony of Jesus is the spirit of prophecy"

The Issue. As previously noted, this definition is supplied near the end of the book. The author used the term more than five times earlier in the text, but without defining it (see 1:2, 9; 6:9; 12:11, 17). These five usages assume the author and his audience were familiar with the meaning and significance of the phrase. However, why define a term at the end

---

[161] "The phrase 'testimony of Jesus' can be read in two ways in the Greek, subjective and objective. As subjective, it would be the testimony that Jesus Himself gives. As objective, it would be our testimony about Jesus. Fairly consistently in the New Testament, a phrase like this would be understood as subjective. In other words, this is a testimony from Jesus rather than a testimony about Jesus. Having said that, in both the Gospel of John and in Revelation one can make the case that this particular author often works from a 'both/and' perspective." Jon Paulien, *Facebook Commentary*.

of a document? Does this mean the reader must re-read Revelation in the light of this *new* definition? By no means. We shall proceed to discuss in detail the usages, significance, and nuances of the phrase "testimonies of Jesus."

NATURE AND TYPE OF TESTIMONIES

Evidentiary Testimonies

John's later works make it abundantly clear that the "testimonies" or the "testimonies of Jesus" concern signs, confessions, or evidences that help establish Jesus' Messiahship and divinity. As discussed earlier, these evidences include the testimonies of both ancient and contemporaneous witnesses that may be both human and divine. They also include Jesus' own words, works, and life. We categorize these testimonies as *evidentiary testimonies*.

If the false prophets or opponents had denied Jesus' Messiahship and divinity, then the apostle John enlisted a cloud of witnesses to testify that Jesus is indeed the "Coming One," "Messiah," "Christ," "from God," "from above," "the Eternal One," and the One from the beginning. Those testimonies can be further divided into ancient witnesses or testimonies and those who testified during Jesus' time.

Ancient Testimonies. The ancient witnesses can be summarized as "Moses and the Prophets" (Luke 16:29, 31), which include Moses' testimony (see John 1:44, 45; 5:45–47), Daniel's testimony (see John 5:22–27), Abraham's testimony (see John 8:56–58), Elijah and Elisha's testimonies (see John 2:1–11, 12–25; 4:7, 43–45), among others. Note that OT prophecies concerning the Coming One can also be included in this category.

Testimonies During Jesus' Time. Those who testified before, during, and after Jesus' ministry include John the Baptist (see John 1:19, 34; 3:22–36; 5:34), the disciples (see John 1:35–2:11), Jewish crowd (see 2:23–25; 12:17–19; 10:40–42), Samaritan woman (see 4:19–22), Greeks (see

12:20–28), Gentile official (see 4:43–54), Jewish leaders (see 3:1–3; 7:47–52; 12:42–43), Holy Spirit (see 15:26), God (see 5:37; 12:28–29), Jesus Himself (see 5:36), the author (see 19:35; 20:30–31; 20:24–25), crowd (see 3:22–26), and even the demon (see Mark 1:24), not to mention the testimonies of the miraculous signs Jesus performed. All of these testified that He was indeed the anticipated Coming One, the Christ whom "Moses wrote about in the Law, and whom the Prophets also wrote" (John 1:45).

Summary. In this case, the "testimony of Jesus" to John and his audience consisted of testimonies, statements, and miraculous signs or evidences establishing Jesus' Messiahship. The volume of evidences presented here far exceeds the legally required "two or three witnesses" accepted by the Jewish court of law. Therefore, considering the intense opposition by the opponents (the Jews, antichrist, and false prophets) to Jesus' Messiahship, those who believed in Him saw themselves as being in possession of the body of the "testimonies of Jesus" (Rev. 12:17; 19:10).

Prophetic Testimonies

As stated earlier, the definition in Revelation 19:10 injects fresh information into this discussion. The text reads, "the testimony of Jesus is the spirit of prophecy." We will briefly explore what that may have meant to John and his audience and further highlight any implications it may have for us today.

The Contents of Revelation as the Testimony of Jesus. Consider the following aspects: First, the terms "testimonies" and "testimonies of Jesus" are associated with the prophecies of Revelation. In the prologue, John described the contents of Revelation as the "word of God and the testimony of Jesus." He also described the same as "the words of this prophecy" (1:2, 3). The same is repeated in the epilogue (22:7), but this time he added, "the words of the prophecy in *this book*" (Emphasis added), as if to differentiate Revelation from other available books at that time. John then quoted, "I, Jesus, have sent my angel to give you *this testimony* to you for the churches" (v. 16). This suggests that the "words of the prophecy in this book" and "this testimony" refer to the same thing—i.e., the prophetic messages of Revelation. Therefore, we shall refer to Revelation as "prophetic testimonies," as opposed to evidentiary testimonies.

Revelation and Historical/Evidentiary Testimonies. Further, the terms "this testimony" and the "words of prophecy in this book" seem to imply that the prophetic testimonies of Revelation were given in *addition* to other testimonies already in existence. If those existing testimonies consisted of the ancient (Old Testament) and contemporaneous testimonies (New Testament)[162] as discussed earlier, then we refer to them, especially the eyewitness accounts of the NT, as *historical* or *evidentiary testimonies*.[163]

Prophetic and Historical Testimonies in the Early Church. Prior to the writing of Revelation, the body of testimonies the early church already had may have consisted primarily of historical and evidentiary testimonies. However, with the inclusion of Revelation, new testimonies called "prophecies" or "prophetic testimonies" were added to the church.[164] Both of these testimonies served essentially the same purpose of revealing Jesus Christ as being from God. Therefore, Ranko Stefanovic writes, "The book of Revelation is a gospel as much as the four Gospels are. The four Gospels and Revelation talk about the same Jesus; however, they focus on different aspects of His roles and existence."[165]

The four Gospels focus on Jesus' birth, ministry, death, resurrection, and ascension—all adding up to a period of fewer than four of His

---

[162] This author is of the opinion that the Gospel of John was written after Revelation, but a popular opinion is stated here.

[163] According to Paul, these testimonies were communicated to the saints "by word of mouth or by letter" (2 Thess. 2:15).

[164] Although he does not discuss this in detail, Mueller does point out the two definitions for the phrase "testimony of Jesus" in an article entitled "The End-time Remnant and the Gift of Prophecy." The first definition, according to Mueller, is "the content of the Book of Revelation and the gospel" (Rev. 1:2, 9). The second is "the Spirit of prophecy" (Rev. 19:10), which Mueller identifies as the manifestation of a prophetic voice in the church (Biblical Research Institute, General Conference of the Seventh-day Adventist Church, p. 1).

[165] Ranko Stefanovic, Plain Revelation, p. 11.

thirty-plus years on earth. Considering the preexistent nature and post-ascension role of Christ, a limited thirty-year stint on earth does seem like the tip of the iceberg. Even His closest friends were not aware of the full extent of His identity and mission.

The Role of Prophetic Testimonies. This is where Revelation emerges, propelling the discussion into a totally new realm. It removes the curtain and allows John (and us) to see Jesus "as He [really] is" (1 John 3:2)—that is, Jesus before, during, and after creation; Jesus before, during, and after the great Exodus; before, during, and after the Babylonian captivity; and Jesus before, during, and after Calvary. John was also allowed a glimpse of the ascended Jesus—what He is doing now and about to do soon. In this sense, the prophecies of Revelation now become additional "testimonies" for the church that, up to that time, only had ancient prophecies foretelling Jesus' first advent and their fulfillment as recorded by eyewitnesses in the Synoptic Gospels.

Each of the christological scenes in Revelation serves to illustrate or testify Jesus as the Christ in various settings. We will use one of them to illustrate this.

In Revelation 4 and 5, Jesus's identity, authority and christology is on trial, and several heavenly witnesses are brought in to testify on His behalf. Revelation 4 establishes "him who sits on the throne" as the only "worthy" One (v. 11). Revelation 5 begins with a search for Someone "worthy" to "break the seals and open the scroll" (v. 2). The "Lamb" is introduced as the only "worthy" candidate in the entire universe. He then walks over and takes the scroll (vv. 4–7). Following this event, a number of characters pay homage to Jesus in a more coordinated way. Notice especially the manner in which this is done: 1). First, the four living creatures and the twenty-four elders "fall down before the lamb," singing "You are worthy" (vv. 8–10); 2) Then "many angels numbering

> *Considering the preexistent nature and post-ascension role of Christ, a limited thirty-year stint on earth does seem like the tip of the iceberg.*

thousands upon thousands" sing; "Worthy is the Lamb" (vv. 11, 12); 3) The third set of testimonies comes from "every creature in heaven and on earth and under the earth and on the sea" who worship both "him who sits on the throne and ... the Lamb" (v. 13). What was implicit in the acts of the four creatures, twenty-four elders, and "many angels" is now clearly expressed in this single act—that Jesus is divine and equal to God; 4) After Jesus' equality with God has been established, the four living creatures agree, saying, "Amen" (v. 14a); 5) As if in agreement to these testimonies, the elders "fell down and worshiped" (v. 14b). Interestingly, the subject of their worship is not explicitly stated. The implication is that the same people who worshiped God in Revelation 4 are now worshiping *both* God and Christ, thus making Jesus Christ identical to God. Here is the point: many witnesses (in this order: the four living creatures, twenty-four elders, all angels, all creatures, four living creatures, twenty-four elders) testify and make the case for Jesus' christology and divinity in Revelation 5. Thus, the scene in Revelation 4 and 5 are intended to reinforce Jesus' christology—the very same issue discussed extensively in the rest of the NT texts. In this way, the prophecies of Revelation do serve as the additional 'testimonies of Jesus.'

Therefore, when the early church read about the saints being in possession of the "testimonies of Jesus" (Rev. 12:17; 6:9–11), they saw those testimonies as having two components: the historical or evidentiary testimonies and the prophetic testimonies that came from Patmos. What then is the "spirit of prophecy"?

TESTIMONY OF JESUS AS THE SPIRIT OF PROPHECY

What is the Spirit of Prophecy?

"Testimonies of Jesus as the Spirit of Prophecy." The Scripture clearly teaches that John, his audience, and the early church were being persecuted for being in possession of the historical or evidentiary testimonies (see Rev. 1:9; 6:9–11; 12:17). Now to that persecuted church, the prophetic testimonies were given. However, how do we understand Revelation

19:10? What does the phrase "testimonies of Jesus is the spirit of prophecy" mean? There is no direct answer to this question. There are few aspects about this passage that may serve as clues. We will turn to them.

Testimonies of Jesus as the Spirit of Prophecy. First, in this usage, the "testimony of Jesus" is equated with the "spirit of prophecy." As pointed out earlier, this definition is provided almost at the end of the document. Although it is not clear to us, this definition is neither general nor vague. It is specific, definite, crisp, and clear. These indications give the impression that the spirit of prophecy may be something totally different from historical or prophetic testimonies.

Spirit of Prophecy Focuses on the Process. Second, in historical and prophetic testimonies, the focus is on the testimonies or finished products, which the saints either had in possession or were being given. However, in the "spirit of prophecy," the focus is on the process that produces the prophecies or prophetic testimonies.

Spirit of Prophecy Focuses on the Agents. Third, the focus of Revelation 19:10 is not only on the process of prophecy, but also on the agents that prophesy or produce prophecies. As stated earlier, in this verse, the stress is not on the "testimonies," but on the spirit that facilitates, enables, or produces those prophecies. Revelation 22:6 further sheds light on this: "God of the spirits of the prophets, sent his angel to show his servants the things that must soon take place." When these two passages are analyzed, we learn the following:

1) Revelation 19:10 and 22:6 describe exactly the same event. Therefore, it is important that both passages be assessed together.
2) Apart from the "spirit," "the spirits of God," or the "spirits of the prophets," we also have the "prophets of God" as the second agent involved in the prophesying process.
3) The prophecies or prophetic testimonies are the product of the process that involves God, the Spirit of God, and the prophets of God. For example, God + Spirit of God + prophets of God = "things that must soon take place," i.e., the prophetic testimonies.

4) The "spirits of the prophets" are special "spirits of God" that are given only to the "prophets of God. These spirits are not the same as those given to all the saints (see 5:6; for further study on this, refer to the discussion on the two types of spirits in chapter 12).
5) Finally, although the prophet John and his prophetic testimony serve as classic examples of this prophesying process, the focus of Revelation 19:10 and 22:6 is more on God's ability to bless His church with further manifestations of prophecy or prophetic testimonies in the future. This means that as long as His church is here on earth, "God of the spirits of the prophets" can still give the Spirit that prophesies to other prophets in the future—if and when necessary.

Analysis of the "Spirit of Prophecies"

<u>Three Meanings of the Phrase "testimonies of Jesus."</u> Based on the above assessment, a couple of observations can be made. First, it is possible that the phrase "testimonies" (or "testimonies of Jesus") could have three layers of meanings: the evidentiary testimonies, prophetic testimonies, and spirit of prophesies. The discussions on these three are summarized in the following table:

Types of Testimonies	Significance	Notes
Evidentiary or historical testimonies	Ancient and historical events confirming Jesus' Christology and authority	John and His church already possessed these testimonies before the prophecies of Revelation were added to them
Prophecies of Revelation or prophetic testimonies	"Testimonies" or "prophecies in this book"	The contents of Revelation were additional testimonies that were given to the NT church
"Spirit of Prophecy"	The focus is on the "spirit" and the prophets that prophesy or produce prophecies	In the "historical" and "prophetic" testimonies, the focus is on the product, or the testimonies, but here the focus is on the agent of the spirit that produces prophecies or prophetic testimonies

<u>Testimonies of Jesus and Dualism</u>. Although a relationship does exist among all usages of the term "testimonies of Jesus", a secondary or dual meaning must exist. In all his writings, John had a tendency of using a single word, concept, or character, but with two or more different definitions or descriptions. If this literary style can be established, then that may help us understand the dual nature of the prophecies of Revelation better. Like the terms "commandments" and "testimony," John also used a host of other words and characters with a dual intent. These terms are fully discussed in chapters 12 and 19, but to help us appreciate this concept, let us explore the dual nature of the "testimonies of Jesus" further.

TESTIMONIES OF JESUS THEN AND NOW

Finally, we shall seek to answer two questions: What did the phrase "testimonies of Jesus" mean to the early church? and what do they mean to us now?

Testimonies of Jesus in the Early Church

By the time Revelation was written, the early church already possessed a body of testimonies. These testimonies primarily consisted of historical accounts written by eyewitnesses. However, what they did not possess was the prophetic testimonies, which came with, in, and through Revelation. Therefore, the concept of the testimonies of Jesus could have had dual significance to the early church. If these are what the testimonies of Jesus meant to the early church, then what does it mean to us today?

Testimonies of Jesus Today

To those of us living in the end of time, the meaning and significance of the testimonies of Jesus has not changed. This is because the historical and prophetic testimonies of Revelation still remain in force. However, such an interpretation also allows for further manifestations of the spirits of prophecy, either through a living prophetic voice or a prophet's body of works. Just as the prophetic voice and pen of John spoke to and guided the early church during a difficult time, a prophetic voice can also play a similar role in our times. Thus, the claim of the Seventh-day Adventist church that Ellen G. White and her testimonies played a pivotal role during the inception of this movement and continues to do so now is perfectly legitimate and supported by the text (see Rev. 19:10 and 22:6).[166] However, notice that the true saints of God must have all three testimonies. She must treasure the historical testimonies of Jesus, correctly interpret the prophetic testimonies of Revelation, and have further prophetic voices or testimonies in the end of time.

Summary. The following table shows the dual meanings of the terms "word of God," "commandments of God," and the "testimony of Jesus":

---

[166] **Patient Endurance**. Before we wrap up this discussion, we will consider two more aspects concerning Revelation 1:9. The Greek term translated "patient endurance" (*hupomonē*) is the dative feminine singular form of the word *hupamonē*, which also means "steadfastness, perseverance, or fortitude." The same term is also used in a similar context in 14:12: "This calls for patient endurance [*hupomonē*] on the part of the saints who obey God's commandments and remain faithful to Jesus." John must have had this verse in mind when he described his relationship with his readers as "brothers" in *hupomonē* in 1:9. If so, what does this mean for John and his readers? To them, the issues and messages of Revelation were something with which they could identify. Therefore, assuming that only the seven messages of chapters 1–3 addressed their (John and his audiences) issues and chapters 4–22 consisted of predictive messages for future generations constitutes a questionable approach to the prophecies of Revelation.

11. The Dual Focus of the Testimony of Jesus

Concepts	What They Meant to John Then	... to Us Now
"word of God" (Rev. 1:2, 9; 6:9; 19:13)	Jesus (Rev. 19:13; John 1:1–5,14), or words Jesus spoke, for Jesus "speaks the word of God, for God" (1 John 2:13, 14; John 3:34; 8:37–40); Jesus' words "spirit and life" (John 6:63); if you keep my word, you will never see death" (8:51); Jesus "keeps his [God's] word" (v. 55); "gods, to whom the word of God came" (10:35)	Generally, the Bible, and specifically, Jesus.
"Commandments of God" (Rev. 12:17; 14:12).	"This is his [God's] commandment: to believe in the name of his son, Jesus Christ ... [just] as he commanded us" (1 John 3:23; 2:3, 4; John 5:45–47); God "commanded" Israel to obey the prophet like Moses whom He will raise up; obeying or believing in that prophet is akin to "obeying the commandments of God" (Deut. 18:15–18; Matt. 17:5; Acts 3:22)	The Ten Commandments (fourth in particular—Dan. 7:25)
"testimony of Jesus" (Rev. 1:2, 9; 6:9–11; 12:17; 19:10; 20:4)	1. *Historical or Evidentiary Testimonies*: that Jesus is the "Christ" (John 1:41), "from God" (John 3:31; 6:41, 42), "from the beginning" (1 John 1:1; 2:13, 14); Jesus' testimony by Himself (John 8:14–18), by His own works (5:36; 10:25, 37–39), by God (5:37, 38; 8:16–18; 12:28–31; 1 John 5:9–11), by the Spirit (John 15:26; 1 John 5:6–8), by Moses (John 5:45–47), by the OT (John 5:39; 20:30, 31; 21:24, 25), by John the Baptist (John 1:6–9, 15, 19–35; 3:27–30; 5:31–36), by the disciples (John 1:49; 2:11; 19:35; 21:24; 15:27), by the crowd (John 3:22–26), by Jesus' opponents (John 3:1, 2), by Samaritans (John 4:42), and by demons (Mark 1:24). 2. *Prophetic Testimonies*. Contents of the prophecies of Revelation (Rev. 1:2, 3; 22:7, 16).	1. Historical or evidentiary testimonies 2. Correct interpretation and appreciation of Revelation (and Daniel) 3. The testimonies of E. G. White (Rev. 19:10; 6:9–11; 22:6)

CONCLUSION

Double Significance of the Spirit of Prophecy

Testimonies of Jesus have layers of meanings. First, the early church already possessed the "testimonies of Jesus." For example, John was banished to the Island of Patmos because of the testimonies he possessed; the saints were martyred because of the testimonies of Jesus; those who would be persecuted in the future, as well as those who would come to life in the end, will do so because of the testimony of Jesus. These testimonies were both historical and evidentiary in nature. The prophetic testimonies were added later. The prophetic testimonies of Revelation, which spoke to the early church, must also speak to us. However, when John offered a secondary definition of the "testimony of Jesus [as] the spirit of prophecy," it allows for future manifestations of prophetic testimonies as well.

Prophetic Testimonies: for Both Them and Us

The prophecies of Revelation, therefore, carry a dual meaning. They had an immediate and an ultimate application. The messages of Revelation (both 1–3 and 4–22) first addressed issues and spoke to John and his readers in their time and context. Then it has and continues to speak to our times. Therefore, it is important to get a clearer picture of what it meant to the initial readers before we seek to understand what it means to us.

12.

DUAL FOCUS IN REVELATION, 1 JOHN, AND THE GOSPEL OF JOHN

DUAL MEANINGS IN REVELATION

Dual Meanings and Applications of Servants, Brothers, and Spirits

Thus far, we have discussed the double meanings of the terms "commandments of God" and "testimonies of Jesus."[167] A single word, concept, or phrase having a double meaning or application is not limited to these two words.[168] What follows next is a discussion on other key words, concepts, and characters that also have a dual significance.

The "servants." The following table presents three terms that have dual meanings: "servants," "brothers," and "spirits" (the testimony of Jesus and the commandments of God are restated for emphasis).

Features	John and Prophets only	All Saints
"servant"	"His servant John" (1:1b), "his servants the prophets" (10:7), "fellow servant" (19:10), "I am your *fellow servant* and with your brothers the prophets" (22:9, emphasis supplied).	"His servants" (1:1a)

---

[167] Refer to the discussions in chapters 10 and 11.

[168] We also saw other words that are linguistically different but carry the same meaning. For instance, the terms "word of God" and "commandment of God" are used interchangeably; "testimonies of Jesus" and "faith of Jesus" are used in a similar way too. Earlier we saw the lamb-like beast that came up out of the earth (see Rev 13:11–18) and the false prophets (see 16:13, 14) used in a similar way.

Features	John and Prophets only	All Saints
"brothers"	"until the number of their *fellow servants and brothers* who were to be killed as they had been was completed" (6:11, emphasis supplied); "I am a *fellow servant with you and your brothers* who hold to the testimony of Jesus/spirit of prophecy" (19:10, emphasis supplied); "I am your fellow servant with you, and your *brothers the prophets* and with those who keep the words of this book" (22:9, emphasis supplied)	"*brother* and companion in suffering, kingdom and patient endurance ... word of God and testimony of Jesus" (1:9, 2, emphasis supplied). "I am a fellow servant with you and with your brothers the prophets *and of all who keep* the words of this book" (22:9, emphasis supplied)
"spirit"	"spirit of the prophets" (22:6). The holy spirit "will tell you what is yet to come" (John 16:13)	"seven spirits" or "seven spirits of God sent out into all the earth" (2:7, 11, 17; 5:6)
"hold to the testimony of Jesus"	"testimony of Jesus" and the "testimony of Jesus is the *spirit of prophecy*" (19:10, emphasis supplied)	"testimony of Jesus" (1:9; 12:17)
"commandments of God"	"believing in Jesus Christ" (1 John 3:23)	The Ten Commandments (Rev. 12:17)

The Servants. The term "servant" and its derivatives are used in three different ways in Revelation. First, when the term is used in reference to the general saints, it usually appears in the plural (see 1:1a). Second, the same is also used extensively to describe the author, which mostly occurs in the singular (see v. 1b). Then, finally, the word is coined with other terms like "fellow" or "prophets" to describe the author's relationship with other prophets and angels (see 10:7; 19:10; 22:9).

"Fellow-servants" and "servants the prophets." The general believers and saints are not addressed as "fellow servants" in Revelation. In three places, this phrase is reserved for either an "angel" or those with prophetic ministries (see 6:11; 19:10; 22:9). This distinction and the dual intent of the term "servants" become more pronounced in Revelation 11:18 where the term "the prophets" is used in apposition to "servant."[169]

---

[169] In Greek, the subject of a sentence is called "nominative," but it comes in numerous, different constructions. One such construction is "apposition." That is when two or more different nominatives

For instance, John wrote, "the time has come for judging the dead, and for rewarding your servants the prophets" (11:18; see also 10:7). In this construction, the word "the prophets" is used to either define, narrow, or further describe "your servants." In this case, the clause can be rendered as "your servants, who are the prophets." This becomes even clearer in Revelation 22:9, where the angel said to John, "I am your fellow servant with you, and your brothers the prophets and with those who keep the words of this book."

The Dual Intent of the Word "servants." Therefore, the term "servant" assumes a dual role in Revelation. First, all saints or believers are described as "servants" (Rev. 1:1a). Then in 19:10 and 22:9, the term is used to describe John's relationship with either an angel or other prophets, respectively.

<u>Brothers and Your Brothers the Prophets</u>. Two definitions and usages apply to the term "brothers" also. It first describes John's relationship to and with *all* the saints (see 1:2, 9). Then it describes John's relationship to those with prophetic ministries (see 19:10). For example, the author carefully defined and stressed the basis of his brotherhood with all saints as "suffering, kingdom and patient endurance," but not in calling and ministry (see 1:9). He then described his brotherhood to those with prophetic ministry as "fellow servants and brothers" (see 6:9; 19:10).

The conjunction "and" in Revelation 6:9 "functions epexegetically as 'that is' or 'namely.' Thus the text presents two perspectives on a single group" of people.[170] Perhaps that was intended to differentiate the "all saints–brothers" of 1:9 from the "fellow servant–brothers" of 6:9 and 19:10. Furthermore, 22:9 explicitly states that John's fellow servants and brothers are "prophets": "But he said to me, 'Do not do it! I am a fellow servant with you and with your brothers the prophets *and* of all who keep the words of this book'" (emphasis supplied). While this passage serves to identify John's fellow servants and brothers as the prophets, it

---

are used to describe, clarify, or identify a substantive. For more on this, see Daniel B. Wallace, *The Basics of New Testament Syntax*, p. 33.

[170] Aune, as quoted by Stefanovic, p. 245. See Aune, *Revelation 6–16*, p. 411.

also identifies the general saints as "all who keep the words of this book." Therefore, as in the use of the term "servant," the word "brother" also has a dual role.[171]

<u>Spirits of God and the Spirits of the Prophets</u>. The text seems to suggest two different types of Holy Spirit. Concerning the Holy Spirit given to all the saints, the text reads; the "seven spirits of God sent out into all the earth" (Rev. 5:6. See also Rev. 2:7, 11; 17). This is the Spirit of God poured out on "all people" at Pentecost (Acts 2:17a, 4). Then there is another Spirit which John describes as the "spirit of the prophets" (Rev. 22: 6). This is the "spirit of prophecy" which is poured out on those with prophetic gifts (Rev. 19:10). In this sense, it seems possible that only John and his "brothers the prophets" have the "spirit of the prophets," while all the saints received the "seven spirits." For more discussion on this, refer to the comparative analysis of Rev. 19:10 and 22:6 in chapter 11 of this study.

Further, apart from Revelation, the books of Hebrews and Acts also supports the existence of two types of spirits. The table below captures these distinctions.

Books	The Holy Spirit distributed to all saints (emphasis supplied)	"Spirit of the Prophets"
Revelation	"seven spirits sent into *all* the earth,"	"The Lord, the God of the spirits of the prophets" (22:6); "spirit of prophecy" (19:10)
Hebrews	"gift of the spirit distributed according to His will" (2:4), "submit to the Father of *our* spirits" (12:9), "You have come to God, the judge of *all* men, to the spirit of righteous men" (12:23)	

---

[171] Note the existence of two groups of people as demonstrated in this text. Here you have John the prophet and his "fellow servants" and "brothers the prophets" and all the saints who "keep the words of this prophecy." Therefore, Revelation keeps these two groups of people distinct and separate as much as possible.

Books	The Holy Spirit distributed to all saints (emphasis supplied)	"Spirit of the Prophets"
Acts	"I will pour out my Spirit on *all* people" (Acts 2:17a), "*All* of them were filled with the Holy Spirit" (2:4)	"your sons and daughters will prophesy, your young men will see visions, your old men will dream dreams. Even on my servants, both men and women, I will pour out my spirit in those days, and they will prophesy" (2:17b–18)

A cursory glance at the above table reveals the following: (i). that Revelation teaches about two types of Spirits. The "seven spirits" are sent into all the earth, while the "spirit of the prophets" are given only to the prophets. (ii). that the teaching in Revelation and Hebrews on the Holy Spirit complement each other. While Revelation 22:6 presents the Lord as the "God of the spirit of the prophets" (22:6), Hebrews adds that the Lord God is also the "Father of *our* spirits" (Heb. 12:9). The "our spirits" here is further explained as "the spirit of righteous men," signifying *all* righteous saints (Heb. 12:23). So from the same source comes two types of spirits—the "spirits of the prophets" and the "spirits of [all] righteous men." (iii). that the same distinction between these two types of spirit is stressed in Acts 2:17–18. Note that God pours out "his Spirit on all people" (v. 17a) and He also pours out "his Spirit" on a select few—"sons and daughters," "young men" and "old men" and "servants" (vv. 2:17b–18). The texts makes is clear that the Spirit given to the select few is used primarily for "see[ing] visions," "dream[ing] dreams," and "prophesy[ing]." Therefore, the teaching on two different types of Holy Spirit in Revelation is reinforced by Hebrews and Acts.

Testimony of Jesus and the Spirit of Prophecy. In the same vein, note that the "testimony of Jesus" refers to the body of teachings held by all believers, including the prophets. However, "the spirit of prophecy" refers to something that is held or administered by the prophets only.

Similar to the "word of God," the "testimonies of Jesus," and the "commandments of God," the terms "servants," "brothers," and "spirits of God" also assume a dual meaning in Revelation. The same terms that describe John's relationship with all the saints are redefined when used in conjunction with his relationship to the prophets. To ensure that such literary constructions are not coincidental but intentional, we shall explore some more examples.

Other Words, Concepts, and Characters with Dual Meanings in Revelation

There are many concepts and characters that have dual significance as well. In the following table, we list eight of the main ones:

Concepts or Characters	Meaning 1	Meaning 2
144,000	Sealed "144,000 **from all the tribes of Israel**" (Rev. 7:4).	"who had been redeemed **from the earth**," "these are those who did not defile themselves with the women," "they were purchased **from among men** and offered as first fruits to God and the Lamb" (Rev. 14:3, 4)
"two witnesses" of Revelation 11	"These are the **two olive trees** … that stand before the Lord of the earth" (v. 4).	"These are the…**two lampstands** that stand before the Lord of the earth" (v. 4)
"the great city" of Revelation 11	Literally, "where the Lord was crucified [**Jerusalem**]" (11:8)	Figuratively called "**Egypt and Sodom**." An adulterous woman-city during sixth trumpet. Earthquake destroys only a "**tenth of the city**" but continues to live (v. 13). First beast (ch. 13)
"the great city" of Revelation 17	"**Why are you astonished?** I will explain to you the mystery of the woman and the beast she rides" (vv. 6, 7)	Figuratively call "**Babylon**." Final adulterous woman-city. Rules with the beast, and 10 horns for **"one hour"** before total **"destruction"** (vv. 8, 11)
"the seven heads"	"**seven hills** on which the woman sits"	"they are also **seven kings**" (17:9, 10)
"ten horns" of Revelation 13 and 17	Rev. 13: Not same as the ten kings of Rev. 17. Their reigns coincide with the sea beast for they have "ten crowns."	Rev. 17: final ten kings who reign for "one hour" with the beast and Babylon. At the time John saw, no crowns yet.

Concepts or Characters	Meaning 1	Meaning 2
First beast of Revelation 13	The sea beast	Adulterous woman (14:8; 17:5)
Second beast of Revelation 13	Lamb-like beast	"false prophets" (16:13, 14; 19:20; Matt. 7:15)

Notice the volume and the quality of the characters with double meanings. Below is a brief discussion on each of these characters.

The 144,000. The 144,000 is prominently featured in two places in Revelation. In chapter 7, the 144,000 are identified as being "from all the tribes of Israel," while in chapter 14, the same characters are identified as the "first fruit ... from the earth," *not* from Israel. Who are they? Are they from the tribes of Israel or the earth? Scholars have postulated numerous theories trying to harmonize the two, but the issue remains elusive.[172] However, the simple fact is that the text supports both answers: The 144,000 of Revelation 7 are Israelites, while those of chapter 14 are from the earth. The identity of this group will remain a contentious issue, unless we agree to reconsider our own methodology and assumptions about the text. At this stage, in the light of dualism, the questions that remain to be asked are, What did the 144,000 mean to John and his audience? and what do they

> *In chapter 7, the 144,000 are identified as being "from all the tribes of Israel," while in chapter 14, the same characters are identified as the "first fruit ... from the earth," not from Israel. Who are they? Are they from the tribes of Israel or the earth?*

---

[172] Stefanovic, *The Revelation of Jesus Christ*, p. 262–268., See also, Stefanovic, *Plain Revelation*, p. 92–97. Aune, *Revelation 6–16*, p. 440–450. C. Mervyn Maxwell, *God Cares, Vol. 2*, p. 212–214.

mean to us today? Like the rest of the terms and concepts, there is a dual intent embedded in this as well.[173]

What Did the 144,000 of Revelation 7 Mean for John and His Audience? For John and his audience, the 144,000 consisted of 12,000 from each of the "tribes of Israel." As far as John and his audience were concerned, the "hour of judgment has [already] come" (14:7), and that judgment began "with the family of God [Israel]" (1 Peter 4:17). The result of this is that 144,000 Israelites were already sealed with the "seal of the living God." However, if the document was written primarily to a Gentile church, then how was this intended to encourage them? Without skipping a beat, John continued, "After this I looked and there before me was a great multitude that no one could count, from *every nation, tribe, people and language*, standing before the throne and in front of the Lamb. They were wearing white robes and holding palm branches in their hands" (Rev. 7:9, emphasis supplied).

Since the Gentile believers, especially the seven churches, were not part of the sealed "144,000," they may have been greatly encouraged when they realized that apart from the 144,000 from the house of Jacob, an innumerable "great multitude" "from every nation [including their own nations]" was also sealed and saved. And as if to drive the point home even further, an elder asked John, "These in white robes—who are they and where did they come from?" (v. 13). There is no doubt that every saint

---

[173] If the early church was plagued with questions like "Have any of the rulers or of the Pharisees believed in him?" (John 7:48) and the response was essentially a resounding "No," and for the "mob that [knew] nothing of the law" to believe in Jesus was considered a curse (v. 49), then for the Gentile pagans (who did not even have access to the law) to believe in Christ may have been seen as insanity. If Revelation was written in such a context, then 12,000 from each tribe "of Israel" to believe in Jesus does seem like a huge endorsement of His Christology. Moreover, this number does not consist of mobs only, but according to John, many members of the Sanhedrin joined also. For instance, "Nicodemus ... who was one of their own number" (v. 50) responded to the above question with a rhetorical question: "Does our law condemn a man without first hearing him ...?" (v. 51). Therefore, if the Jews were denying Jesus' Christology based on the number of Jewish followers, then "144,000 from all the tribes of Israel" appears to put that issue to rest.

in those seven churches could answer these questions, for they saw themselves in that group. However, notice the elder's own answer: "These are they who have come out of the great tribulation: they have washed their robes and made them white in the blood of the Lamb" (v. 14).

What Did the 144,000 of Revelation 14 Mean to the Early Church? "They were purchased from among men and offered as firstfruits to God and the Lamb" (Rev. 14:4). If the 144,000 of Revelation 7 consisted of sealed Israelites, then *this* 144,000 consists only of the first-fruits "from among men [Gentiles]." This means, at least to the early church, that the total number of Gentile first-fruits sealed so far is the same as those sealed from Israel. It also means that the sealing among the Gentiles has not been completed. It is still in progress. Therefore, the final "great multitude that no one could count, from *every nation, tribe, people and language*" in Revelation 7:9 is made of the sealed Israelites (144,000) + the Gentile first-fruits (144,000) + the final harvest from all nations (see 14:14–16).

> *The number 144,000 in Revelation 7 and 14 is the same, but the actual identity of the people who made up that number varies significantly. In the first instance, it was the Israelites who were already judged, sealed, and found worthy in the early church. In the second, it is the first-fruits "from the earth."*

What Does the 144,000 Mean to us Today? "They were purchased from among men and offered as firstfruits to God and the Lamb" (Rev. 14:4). The number 144,000 in Revelation 7 and 14 is the same, but the actual identity of the people who made up that number varies significantly. In the first instance, it was the Israelites who were already judged, sealed, and found worthy in the early church. In the second, it is the first-fruits "from the earth." The early church, especially the seven churches, may have rightly thought the first-fruits included some of the faithful members from among their own brethren in their own time.[174] However, Christ has not come as they thought He would, and the anticipated harvest has not taken place.

Therefore, apart from 144,000 Israelites and 144,000 Gentile first-fruits in the early church, there still remains the 144,000 from the earth who shall stand for God in the "final hour." In Revelation 14, another 144,000 is represented by the three *angels* that are involved in the proclamation of the eternal gospel (vv. 6–9).[175] In chapter 17, it is the team that is described as the "called, chosen and faithful followers" of Christ in the final showdown (v. 14). Then in 19, it is the "armies of heaven" that come riding on "white horses" as "conquerors bent on conquest" (v. 14; see also 6:2). Finally, the 144,000 is the team that produces the final harvest (see 14:15–18) that "no one could count" (7:9).

Interpretation	144,000 of Revelation 7	144,000 of Revelation 14
Early Church	Judged and sealed Israelites	First-fruits from among men (Gentiles), which included some of the "seven churches"
Today	Judged and sealed Israelites	End-time militant saints who, in total obedience, proclaim the eternal gospel; number which may include some from among our own selves

<u>The Two Witnesses</u>. The second issue concerns the identity of the two witnesses of Revelation 11:3. These two are variously described as two "witnesses," and the text also identifies them as "two olive trees and the

---

[174] That means that the innumerable "great multitude" before the throne in heaven must include 144,000 Israelites who believed in Christ in the first century, plus the 144,000 first fruits from among humanity who must stand for God in the end of time, plus the results of the final harvest (see Rev. 14:15–18), plus the believers who died before Calvary.

[175] See the discussions on "angels as human messengers" in chapter 19 of this study. In the light of that discussion, what Daniel wrote in 12:3 serves as an important clue in connecting the 144,000 to the "three angels": "Those who are wise will shine like the brightness of the heavens, and those who lead many to righteousness, like the stars forever and ever."

two lampstands" (v. 4). They are also referred to as "two prophets" in the likeness of Elijah and Moses (v. 10). Who are they really? Are they two witnesses, two olive trees, two lampstands, or two prophets? Scholars have theorized these two as the "Law and the Prophets, the Law and the Gospel, Moses and Elijah," the Old and the New Testaments, or two other prophets who shall live in the end of time.[176] Unless we seriously reconsider other methods of interpretation, we will continue to multiply unsatisfactory and conflicting theories. As we have done previously, we must ask two fundamental questions when approaching such difficult passages: What did the two prophets or witnesses mean to John and his audience? What do they mean to us today? These questions imply that the prophecies of Revelation were applicable and relevant to both the early church and us today. Further, there is sufficient information in the text that seems to adequately answer both of these questions.[177]

Revelation 11: Sodom and Egypt as Jerusalem. Four designations are used to describe the city of Revelation 11—"great city," "Sodom and Egypt," and the "city where the Lord was crucified." To John and his audience, the only adversarial character that had crucified the Lord and now threatened their existence was literal Jerusalem (11:8).

Sodom and Egypt Stand for Jerusalem. Also, the "great city" of Revelation 11 is symbolically called "Sodom and Egypt." In Isaiah, the daughter of Zion (i.e., Jerusalem) is also called Sodom and Egypt (see Isa. 1:8–11). Therefore, to John, these symbolic and literal designations referred to Jerusalem.

Why four designations? However, the fact that the author gives four different designations raises the question: Why? If this city was literal Jerusalem, then just saying "the city where the Lord was crucified" would have adequately identified this character. But why does the author

---

[176] Stefanovic, *The Revelation of Jesus Christ*, p. 352–356., See also, Stefanovic, *Plain Revelation*, p. 129–133. Aune, *Revelation 6–16*, p. 598–603. C. Mervyn Maxwell, *God Cares, Vol. 2*, p. 284–287. See also Kayle B. de Waal, "The Two Witnesses and the Land Beast in the Book of Revelation," *Andrews University Seminary Studies* 53, no 1 (Spr 2015).

[177] These two witnesses are briefly discussed here for illustrative purposes.

provide four different designations for a single character? Like the "two witnesses" of Revelation 11, the multiplicity of designations is intended to provide clarity, on one hand, while at the same time to accommodate the dual nature of the text. And especially when one considers the relationship between this character and the adversarial characters of Revelation 13 and 17, its dual meaning becomes even more apparent.

<u>Sodom, Egypt, Babylon, and the Beast of Revelation 11, 13, and 17</u>. If John and his audience thought the opponent of Revelation 11 was Jerusalem, then it is possible that they may have read Revelation 13 and 17 in the light of this. Since the relationship among these three characters is so close, a comparative analysis of the same will attempt to do justice to the text and enhance our understanding on the dual nature of these characters. The table below compares these three characters.[178]

"Great City" (Rev. 11)	"The Sea Beast" (Rev. 13)	"Great City" (Rev. 17)
"*great* city" (v. 8)	has "*great* authority" (v. 2)	"*great* city" (v. 18)
"*Sodom* and *Egypt*" (v. 8)	Resembled "lion", "bear," "leopard" (v. 2). According to Dan 2 & 7, the "lion" is analogous to *Babylon*	"*Babylon* the Great" (v. 5)
City where the "Lord was crucified" (v. 8)	"exercises authority for forty-two months" (v. 5)	"city that rules over the *kings of the earth*" (v. 18)
Sixth trumpet destroyed only a "tenth of the city" (v. 13)	Fatally wounded after forty-two months (1, 200 days), but was healed and continued to live again (vv. 3, 5, 12)	Total destruction by Christ's Second Coming (vv. 11, 16)
Persecutes two prophets for "*1260 days*" (v. 3)	Persecutes the saints for "forty-two months [*1,260 days*]"	"woman drunk with the blood of the saints" (v. 6)
	All whose names not written in the Lamb's "*book of life*" will worship the beast (v. 8)	All whose names not written in Lamb's "*book of life*" will worship the beast (v. 8)
"beast that comes up from the *Abyss*" (v. 7)		Beast will come "out of the *Abyss*" (v. 8)

---

[178] In Rev. 17, the "woman" on the beast is called "great city." So strictly speaking, this should be a comparison between Rev. 11, 13 and the "woman" of Revelation 17 (and not the beast). But because of the closeness of the woman and the beast she rides on, we are treating them as one in this assessment.

"Great City" (Rev. 11)	"The Sea Beast" (Rev. 13)	"Great City" (Rev. 17)
	World "astonished," "followed" and *"worshiped"* the beast (vv. 3, 4, 8)	World will be "astonished" and *worship* the beast (v. 8)
	"ten horns, seven heads, each head with *blasphemous names"*	Beast has *seven heads and ten horns*. Each head with *blasphemous names* (v. 3)

Relationship between Rev 11 and 13. The "great city" of Revelation 11 and the sea beast of Revelation 13 have four characteristics in common. Both cities possess and exercise great power and authority; have symbolic names (though they differ in specifics); are sworn enemies of God; and persecute saints for exactly the same period of time—for 1,260 days in Revelation 11 and forty-two months in Revelation 13.[179]

Relationship between Revelation 11 and 17. The two city-prostitutes of Revelation 11 and 17 are similar in many ways. First, they both are called "great city" (Rev. 11:8; 17:18). Second, they both originate or come out from the same place (Abyss). Third, they both have figurative names. The one in Revelation 11 is called "Sodom and Egypt," while the one in Revelation 17 is called "Babylon the Great." Fourth, they both are sworn enemies of God, and they actively persecute His saints. Finally, without naming names, the cities are given literal identities. One character is described as the "city where the Lord was crucified," whereas the other is described as "city that rules over the kings of the earth." The table below summaries these similarities.

Features	"Great City" (Rev. 11)	"Great City" (Rev. 17)
Description of cities	"great city" (v. 8)	"great city" (v. 18)
Figurative names	"Sodom and Egypt"	"Babylon the Great" (v. 5)
Literal names	"city where the Lord was crucified"	"great city that rules over the kings of the earth" (v. 18)
Place of Origin	"Abyss" (v. 7)	"Abyss" (v. 8)

---

[179] Kayle de Waal, on the other hand, demonstrates the relationship that exists between the two witnesses of Revelation 11 and the land beast/false prophets of Revelation 13. See, "The Two Witnesses and the Land Beast," p. 171–173.

Features	"Great City" (Rev. 11)	"Great City" (Rev. 17)
Their Activities	"city where the Lord was crucified," and then she proceeds to persecute the two witnesses	"the woman was drunk with the blood of the saints, the blood of those who bore testimony to Jesus" (vv. 6, 14)

Relationship between Revelation 13 and 17. Revelation 13 is similar to Revelation 17 on six points. Both have and exercise great authority over the whole world; are symbolically likened to Babylon; are sworn enemies of God; all whose names are not written in the Lamb's book of life worship them; have seven heads and ten horns which are covered in blasphemous names.

So there is a triangular relationship emerging among these three characters. Revelation 11 is related to Revelation 13 on four areas, while the same is related to Revelation 17 on five. And then Revelation 13 is similar to Revelation 17 on six areas. What did these overlapping similarities mean for John and his initial readers? To John and his audience, these three characters were one and the same—Jerusalem. And there is no reason to think otherwise. The following diagram summarizes these discussions. Further literary, thematic, and exegetical evidences will be discussed next.

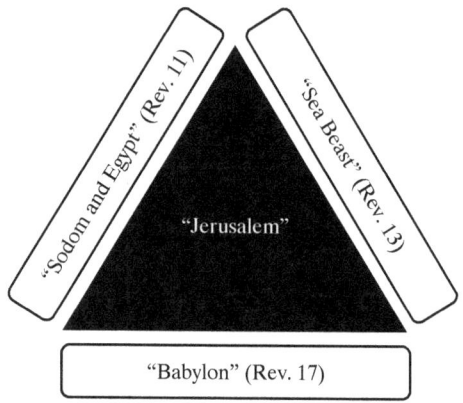

Literary style. When one considers the number and the quality of similarities shared among these characters, it is reasonable to conclude that for John and his audience, they were looking at a single entity. They saw the same character described variously in three different places (Rev. 11, 13, 17). Actually, this literary construction is common in Revelation. In chapter 13 of this study, we shall see that the "one like the son of man" (see Rev. 1), "Michael" (see Rev. 12), and the Rider on the white horse (see Rev. 19) are one and the same character. Certain details and description of the Rider are similar to the "one like the son of man," and others are similar to Michael. Thus, the Rider serves as the linking character that holds the other two together. The table demonstrating these in chapter 13 is reproduced here for illustrative purposes.[180]

Further, as these imageries show, certain descriptions of the same character is repeated throughout the text, and each time they are repeated, new information and details are added for clarity and emphasis. And if John and his audience saw this to be true for the Christological passages of Revelation 1, 12, and 19; then it would be unreasonable for anyone to see the antagonistic characters of Revelation 11, 13, and 17 differently.

---

[180]

Rev. 1:12–16	Rev. 19:11–16	Rev. 12:7–10
"Faithful and True Witness" (3:14)	"Faithful and True" (v. 11)	—
—	"With justice he... makes war" (v. 11)	Michael makes war with the dragon (see v. 7)
"His eyes were like blazing fire" (v. 14)	"His eyes are like blazing fire" (v. 12)	—
—	"The armies of heaven were following him" (v. 14)	"Michael and his angels fought against the dragon" and his angels (v. 7)
"Dressed in a robe" (v. 13)	"dressed in a robe dipped in blood" (v. 13)	—
	—	
—	"He will rule them with an iron scepter" (v. 15)	"a male child, who will rule all the nations with an iron scepter" (v. 5)
"out of his mouth came a sharp double-edged sword" (v. 16)	"Out of his mouth comes a sharp sword" (v. 15)	—
—	With the sword of his mouth he kills the kings of the earth and their armies, captures the beast, and its image, and throws them into the fire (vv. 19–21)	Satan was not strong enough. He lost his place in heaven. He and his angels were cast out (vv. 8–9)

To avoid repetition, additional exegetical evidences on this are provided under the discussion on "Babylon as Jerusalem" below.

<u>What did Revelation 11 (13, 17) mean to John and his audience?</u> At this stage, this study asserts that to John and his audience—the characters of Revelation 11, 13 and 17 are one and the same, and that is the literal city of Jerusalem. The following additional evidences reinforce this position.

Paul Saw Jerusalem as the Main Enemy. Writing to the Galatian believers, the apostle Paul described the "present city of Jerusalem" as the antagonistic figure (Gal. 4:24–30). Therefore, to both Paul and John, their issue was not with pagan or papal Rome, but with the literal city that crucified the Lord.

Peter Saw Jerusalem as Babylon. The early church may have used various symbolic names to describe Jerusalem, of which Sodom, Egypt, and Babylon are some. We have seen how the Scriptures refer to Jerusalem as "Sodom and Egypt." Now observe how the apostle Peter likened the same city to Babylon. Writing to "God's elect" scattered throughout the world (1 Pet. 1:1), he said, "She who is in Babylon, chosen together with you, sends her greetings" (1 Pet. 5:13). If Peter—the apostle who was revered as the "apostle to the Jews" (Gal. 2:8)—wrote his letter from Jerusalem, then Babylon could be an additional name for Jerusalem. Further, Paul even equates the "present city of Jerusalem" to Hagar, Sinai, or some other hostile characters (see Gal. 4:24–25).

Matthew Describes Jerusalem as the Babylon of Revelation 17. Finally, Matthew quoted Jesus as saying; "O Jerusalem, Jerusalem, you who kill the prophets and stone those sent to you… Look, your house is left to you desolate. For I tell you, you will not see me again…[then] Jesus left the temple and was walking away with his disciples" (23:37–24:1). According to Mathew, Babylon is not only responsible for the blood of those sent to her in ancient times, but at the time when John saw her, she was "drunk with the blood…of those who bore testimony to Jesus" (Rev. 17:6).

Notice that all leading NT characters like Paul, Peter, Mathew, Luke, and John saw Jerusalem as their primary institutional enemy.

If the pillars of the early church are speaking with one voice, then it is imperative for the modern scholar to at least acknowledge this.

Whether or not the early church interpreted the prophecies correctly is an entirely different issue. Further, if Revelation was one of those early books written, then it is possible that these men must have read the prophecies of Revelation 11, 13, and 17 in this context.[181] But there are sufficient evidences to claim that the prophecies did speak to John and his audience in their time, and context. We cannot use what we know now—the evils of the Dark Ages that eclipse any sins literal Jerusalem may have committed in the first century—to ignore, undermine, or trivialize John's interpretation of the text.

<u>Further Exegetical Evidences: Babylon as Jerusalem</u>. In our study of Revelation 11, we concluded that to John, the "city where the Lord was crucified" was "Jerusalem." Now what was his view on the Babylon of Revelation 17? There are several indications that show that John did not see any differences between these two characters. John assumed that both "great cities" are one and the same, i.e., Jerusalem.[182] The reasons for this assertion are discussed as follows.

John's reaction showed understanding. First, when John saw the "woman" he was "greatly astonished" (Rev. 17:6). This reaction does not imply confusion, lack of clarity, or misunderstanding. Whenever the Greek word for being "astonished" or "amazed [*ethaumasa*]" is used elsewhere in the NT, it usually indicates awe, surprise, and wonder that exudes from understanding (Mark 5:2; Luke 2:18; Acts 2:7). In other words, John's reaction indicates that he *thought* he knew the identity of this woman.

---

[181] This position is similar to the views espoused by presterism. Preterists argue for an earlier dating of Revelation (66–68 AD); and they see the antagonistic characters of Revelation 11, 13 and 17 as literal Jerusalem in John's time. For more details on the preteristic view, read; DeBruyn, Lawrence A. "Preterism and 'This Generation.'" *Bibliotheca Sacra* 167, no. 666 (April 2010): 180–200. Swanson, Dennis M. "International Preterist Association: Reformation or Regression?" *The Master's Seminary Journal* 15, no. 1 (2004): 39–58. Noe, John. "An Exegetical Basis for a Preterist-Idealist Understanding of the Book of Revelation." *Journal of the Evangelical Theological Society* 49, no. 4 (December 2006): 767–96. However, the difference between preterism and dual-intentionalism is that the latter also views these characters as symbols of the end-time opponents of God.

[182] Apostle Paul also treated "the present city of Jerusalem" as the persecutor (Gal. 4:21–31).

Perhaps that is why the angel rebukes John for being astonished and offers to "explain to [him] the mystery of the woman" (Rev. 17:6–7).

John's understanding on the "one hour." As discussed in chapter 3 of this study, John believed and wrote in 1 John 2:18–19 that he was living in the "last hour." This "last hour" reference is taken from Revelation 17:12.[183] In other words, he did not think the world would last another 2,000 years! Therefore, to him, his Babylon was Jerusalem.[184]

John's use of Revelation 17 in John 4. Third, we have also seen (in chapter 3) the blending of historical material with a symbolic or prophetic twist in the Samaritan woman's account (see John 4). In this account, Jerusalem is likened to the unfaithful Samaritan woman. Jerusalem, who had known "five men," and her current (sixth) one is not her husband, too. This is similar to the seven-headed beast on which "Babylon" rides (Rev. 17). Concerning the seven heads, the angel says to John, "five have fallen," the sixth is reigning now, and the seventh one is yet to come.[185] It could be just a coincidence, but there are noticeable similarities between these accounts.

Jesus returns after "a little while" and "one hour." According to Revelation 17, John was told that he was living during the reign of the sixth-head period. Therefore, whatever was left before Jesus returned boiled down to just two short time periods. 1). When the seventh head came, he would reign only for "a little while" (Rev. 17:10; 2). Then the eighth king—which was also the beast on which the woman sat—would rule for only "one hour" (Rev. 17:12). So as far as John was concerned, the time left for Jesus' return was "a little while" plus "one hour." By any calculation, "a little while" and an "hour" is not a lot of time! John indeed thought he was living in the "last hour."[186] So, again, to him, the woman was Jerusalem.

---

[183] For more discussion on this, read the section "Gospel of John and Revelation 4–22" in chapter 3.

[184] This appears to be the common understanding in the early church. See for instance 1 Pet. 5:23; Gal. 4:24–26. See Jon Paulien, "The End of Historicism? Reflections on the Adventist Approach to Biblical Apocalyptic—Part One" in *Journal of the Adventist Theological Society* 11 (Fall, 2003): 15–43.

[185] For further discussion on this, refer to the same section in chapter 3.

[186] Other NT writers made attempts to resolve issues arising from such misunderstandings. Concerning the 'day of the Lord,' Luke wrote; "Once having been asked by the Pharisees when the kingdom of God would come, Jesus replied, 'The kingdom of God does not come with your careful

That is why he reacted the way he did. But the angel seeing otherwise, sought to correct him.

The author addresses the "little while" issue in the Gospel of John. Additionally, note that the "little while" is the same period God gave to John in Revelation 6:9–11 and 17:10. This time period later became a contentious issue, which John attempted to address in John 16:16–33.[187]

Therefore, John's use of Revelation 17 in his other works shows that he understood the prophecies of Revelation 17. To him, "Babylon" was Jerusalem also. Since all key characters in Revelation had multiple designations, names, and titles, Jerusalem being variously described as "Egypt," "Sodom," and "Babylon" could have been considered acceptable.

What Do the Characters of Revelation 11, 13, and 17 Mean to Us Today? Although there are considerable similarities between the two 'great cities' (Rev. 11 and 17) and the sea beast of Revelation 13, the differences among them are equally profound (as shown below). In other words, the nuances in the text show that these characters have layers of meanings.

Features	Rev. 11	Rev. 13	Rev. 17
Figurative Names	Sodom and Egypt	Sea Beast: seven heads, ten horns	Babylon: rides on beast with seven heads, ten horns
Literal name	"Lord was crucified"	Little horn of Dan 7	Rules over all earthly kings
Date of rulership	During sixth trumpet		End of time
Duration of rulership	For 1,260 days	42 months	For "one hour"

---

observation...'" (Luke 17:20). It is possible that issues concerning surrounding these "careful observations," revolved around temporal references in Revelation. Notice that all temporal references in Revelation are either in "minutes," "hours," "days," or "months." It is possible that there may have been issues concerning the significance of these time references. Apostle Peter, sensing the same problem (as did Luke), writes; "With the Lord, a day is like a thousand years, and a thousand years like a day" (2 Peter 3:8). So apart from the regular—"no one knows that day or the hour"—response, Luke and Peter tried other methods to address the same issues.

[187] For more discussion on this, see a section entitled "Gospel of John and Revelation 4–22" in chapter 3. These are some of the reasons why we stated that Revelation was written before the Gospel and the Epistles of John. See the discussions on chapters 2 and 3.

Features	Rev. 11	Rev. 13	Rev. 17
Domain of rulership	City Lord was crucified	"whole world"	The entire earth
Time of destruction	During sixth trumpet period	End of 42 months	During Second Coming
Result of destruction	Only a "tenth of the city" is destroyed"	One of seven heads is fatally wounded, but was healed	Total and final destruction
Saints of God	Two witnesses prophecies in sackcloth during the 1,260 days of persecution	Persecuted for 42 months	Three angels flying in midair/ or 144,000 faithful followers

As we have seen in this study, the use of multiple identities serves two purposes: 1) for clarity and emphasis as in the case of Christ in Revelation 1, 5, 12, and 19; 2) and to accommodate and facilitate dual interpretations. The fact is that the concept of dual-intentionalism actually flourishes on such literary constructions, as shown in Revelation 11, 13, and 17. These differences are briefly discussed as follows.

Figurative Names. There are two meanings for the great city of Revelation 17. This city's symbolic name is "Babylon." The use of the name "Babylon" signifies two things. First, as we have seen throughout this study, "Babylon" can be an additional designation for other entities as studied earlier. Second, this designation immediately serves to distinguish "Babylon" from the earlier cities of Sodom and Egypt of Revelation 11.

Date of Rulership. These differences are further reinforced when one considers the time they came into power. Sodom-Egypt was to rule during the sixth trumpet period. Babylon, however, is the end-time city that reigns for only "one hour," and her destruction coincides with Christ's Second Coming.

Duration of Rulership. Sodom rules for a period of "1, 260 days," while the sea beast rules for "42 months." (Earlier we stated that these two periods are identical, but then again one wonders whether different modes of expression have any significance. For example, if the number "144,000" of

Revelation 7 and 14 are exactly the same but the actual identities of the people are wildly different, then there is a world of difference between "42 months" and "1, 260 days."). Babylon, however, is given authority for only "one hour." During each of these periods, Sodom-Egypt persecuted the "two witnesses" within the city walls, the sea beast and Babylon persecuted the "saints of God" in the whole world.

Destruction of the Characters. The time and the manner these characters are destroyed is also different. The sixth trumpet destroys only a "tenth of the city" of Sodom-Egypt, while one of the seven heads of the sea beast receives a deadly wound after forty-two months of global dominion. And as stated earlier, Babylon is captured and thrust into the "lake of fire" at Christ's return.

John Versus the Angel. Also as discussed, John thought he knew the identity of Babylon, but the angel begged to differ and proceeded to rebuke John for being astonished. "Why are you astonished? I will explain to you the mystery of the woman" (Rev. 17:6–7). Notice that John does not show in any way that the woman is a "mystery" to him. Nor did he ask for the vision's interpretation. He thought he had it wrapped up, but recognizing the mistake the angel volunteers the information.[188] While there may have been some similarities between Jerusalem and Babylon, the angel knew that there were deeper purposes for which John was clueless, so he sought to correct him. Therefore, to a modern reader, "Babylon" is the final power that "rules over the kings of the earth"—especially the "beast," the "seventh" head, and the "ten horns"—for "one hour."

With the information he had, John probably thought he understood the prophecies of Revelation. Regardless of what he assumed, it would be wrong for us to assume as he did because we have the benefit of the historical events of the last 2,000 years. It is for this reason that we suggest a secondary application for each of these characters as shown below.

---

[188] Also notice that like the definition of the "testimony of Jesus" that is offered towards the end of the book, the explanation of this mysterious woman is offered towards the end of the book. The angelic guide does not provide such explanations to the characters of Revelation 11 and 13.

Characters	Names and titles	Primary meaning	Secondary Meaning
Great city of Rev. 11	"great city," "Egypt and Sodom," "city where the Lord was crucified"	*Jerusalem*: Persecutes two saints for literal three-and-half literal years	Saints of God persecuted for forty-two prophetic months by Sea beast/Little Horn of Daniel 7/*Papacy*
Sea Beast of Rev. 13	"sea beast," "beast"	*Jerusalem*: 1, 260 for literal days of persecution	Little Horn or *Papacy* persecuted saints for 1, 260 years
Great city of Rev. 17	"Woman," Prostitute, the Mother of harlots, "Great city"	*Jerusalem*: Refer to the above reasons as discussed	*Babylon* (a counterfeit trinity consisting of the dragon, false prophets and the beast) that rules the earth in the end (see also Rev. 16:17–21)

Jon Paulien perfectly captures our discussion in these lines: "The book of Revelation was definitely written to people in its time and place. It definitely meant something to them, and *the more we can understand what they understood, the better our understanding of the book will be.*"[189]

He repeats the same counsel in another place: "An Adventist approach…believes that God places in the apocalyptic visions accurate information about the far future, but that future is described in the language of the prophet's time and place. *If we want to understand what God was telling John about the future, we need to first understand what John understood.*"[190]

Although, he does not say dual or double meanings, he expresses the same concept this way: "God's explanations have extended meanings beyond what the original prophet could understand, but those extended meanings will never contradict the original revelation. They will be natural extensions of what the prophet received and understood."[191]

---

[189] Jon Paulien, *Simply Revelation—Part 1*, 2. (a copy of the original manuscript is used here. Copies of these published and unpublished articles and books were bought through his online store). Emphasis supplied.

[190] Jon Paulien, This is an "Appendix" to *The Seven Heads of Revelation 17*, 17. (a copy of his original manuscript is used here). Emphasis supplied.

[191] Jon Paulien, "Appendix" of *The Seven Heads of Revelation 17*, 24. See also *The Deep Things of God*, 33–38.

Conclusion. We have discussed sufficient terms, concepts, and characters at this stage to illustrate dual-intentionalism in Revelation. Thus far, the following characters, concepts, and numbers have a dual meaning: "word of God," "commandments of God," "testimonies of Jesus," "Spirits of God," the "servants" of God, the "brothers," "the two witnesses," the "144,000," "the great city" of Rev 11, the "great city" of Rev 17, and the two beasts of Rev 13. We do not have time to discuss the "seven heads" and the "ten horns" of Revelation 13 and 17. For a discussion on the "seven heads" of Revelation 17, refer to the *"Criteria for a Modified Historicism"* section in chapter 1 of this study.

Incidentally, the entire content of Revelation is summarized as "the word of God and the testimony of Jesus Christ" (Rev. 1:2). If both of these cardinal concepts have a dual meaning, then that should provide the reader with a sense of direction concerning the way the text can be approached.[192] Additionally, if the text consistently provides dual meanings and applications for *all* the dominant terms, themes, numbers, and characters, then such evidences should make one wonder if the prophecies of Revelation actually has dual focus.

DUAL MEANINGS IN 1 JOHN

The concept of dualism, or a single word or character assuming two or more meanings, is not limited to Revelation. The same literary style is evident in John's other writings too. To demonstrate this proposition further, we shall discuss a few more examples from the epistle and Gospel of John.

Dual Meanings in 1 John[193]

In 1 John, the terms "commandment," "liar," and "message" have a dual definition.[194] These terms are used to describe both the

---

[192] The list of words, concepts, and characters with dual meanings provided here is not exhaustive. There are many other examples discussed elsewhere in this volume.

[193] The discussion of 1 John is taken from some study notes on 1 John by this author.

[194] Compare with Georg Strecker, *The Johannine Letters: A Commentary on 1, 2, and 3 John* (Augsburg: Fortress Press, 1996), p. 46. See also Brown, *The Epistles of John*, pp. 49–55.

Christological and love-hate issues and their associated opponents. Below is a discussion on each of these terms:

Commandment. The term "commandment [*hē entolē*]" or one of its derivatives (*entolas, entolēn*) occurs fourteen times in 1 John (2:3, 4, 7, 8; 3:22–24; 4:21; 5:2–3). All occurrences are concentrated in only three places: six times in 2:3–8, four times in 3:22–24, and four times in 4:21–5:3. For various reasons, the scholars do not stress the differences in nuances between the commandments of 2:3–8 and 4:21–5:3, but they do debate the two definitions of the term as given in 3:23–24: "And this is His command: to believe in the name of His Son, Jesus Christ, and to love one another as He commanded us." For instance, the author described *hē entolē* as both "believe in the name of His Son" and "love one another." Although scholars see a relationship between these two commandments, the exact nature of their relationship is debated. We will briefly consider three of the main views.

> *The concept of dualism, or a single word or character assuming two or more meanings, is not limited to Revelation. The same literary style is evident in John's other writings too.*

Brown and Marshall argue for an equational relationship where "a belief in Jesus Christ" is the same as "loving one's brother." Since these two elements are brought "under the rubric of one commandment," Brown asserts a *logical* reason to suggest that the term links the two themes (belief and love) and their associated opponents together. The "logical" reason to which he refers is simply because the text "give[s] little reason to think of a variety of adversaries."[195] However, being aware of the lack of evidence to support his (or any) view for that matter, Brown

---

[195] Brown, *The Epistles of John*, pp. 49–50. Marshall also takes a similar position but suggests that a single commandment "as having two parts" (see *The Epistles of John*, pp. 200, 201).

hastens to admit that "none of this is firm proof."[196] As will be demonstrated, this view fails to consider the consistent distinction the author made in all three places where the term "commandment" occurs (2:3–8; 3:23–24; 4:21–5:3).[197]

Second, Burdick and Lenski view the commands to "believe in Jesus Christ" and "love one another" as complementary in nature. They consider the Johannine commands to "believe" and "love" as two sides of a coin, where one cannot do without the other.[198] This view sees the Johannine teaching on belief and love as analogous to either the two great commandments of the Synoptic Gospels (love to God and *all* neighbors) or the Pauline teaching on faith in God that finds its expression in love and service toward fellowman.[199] Although similarities exist between the Synoptic tradition/Pauline epistles and 1 John, this view fails to account for the intended definition, usage, and contexts of the text. The specific nature of 1 John seems to suggest a particular problem in this epistle. Therefore, rather than allowing the similarities in other writings (Pauline and the Synoptics) to overshadow the interpretation of 1 John, one must seek to understand what the author probably meant. Further, if *hē entolē* (see 3:23, 24) plays a complementary role, then that relationship must be reflected in the two discourses it connects (3:11–24 and 4:1–6). However, the proponents of the complementary view do not show how the love-hate discourse in 1 John 3:11–24 complements the ensuing Christological discourse in 1 John 4:1–6.

In his book *The Johannine Commandments*, Urband C. von Wahlde proposes a "familial" relationship between the two commandments of 1 John 5:1–3 in which those who claim to love the Father are also urged to love His Son and children as well. Thus, loving His Son is akin to "believing Jesus as the Christ," and loving His children is similar to loving one's

---

[196] Brown, *The Epistles of John*, p. 50.
[197] We shall discuss these distinctions a little later.
[198] Consciously or not, Marshall actually prefers both the "equationary" and "complementary" views, or perhaps he considers these methods as one and the same (pp. 200, 201).
[199] Burdick, pp. 278, 279; Lenski, p. 479.

brother.[200] This rendering is consistent with the text because it naturally lends itself to it. However, the familial relationship is limited to 5:1–3. The same cannot be said of 2:3–8 and 3:23–24 because the metaphor is not so apparent.

Wahlde's contribution, however, opens the door to another, greater reality. The dual definition/application of the term "commandment" in 1 John 3:23–24 is also applicable to the "commandments" of 1 John 4:21–5:3. In the three places where the *entolē* is employed (see 2:3–8; 3:23–24; 4:21–5:3), the author consistently drew either a dual definition or a dual application. As noted earlier, the dual definition of the term in 1 John 3:23–24 is clear. As Wahlde points out, the author described the *entolē* as "loving His Son" and "loving one's brother" in 1 John 4:21–5:3. Here, under the "familial love" rubric, the author pointed out the two "children" (the Son and brother) whom the professed God-lovers ought to love. The same is also apparent in 1 John 2:3–8, where the author used "His commandment" in conjunction with believing or imitating Christ (see 1:5–2:6) and loving "one another" (see 2:7–11).

In all cases (2:3–8; 3:23, 24; 4:21–5:3), the author used a single word (*entolē*, "commandments") but consistently offered two different definitions (3:23), two different applications (2:7, 8), and two different imageries (4:21–5:3) to describe it. Therefore, these similarities could be a mere semantic relationship rather than a thematic one. The fact that the author diversely described the same two themes in all three places could indicate his intention of clarity.

Therefore, the relationship could be limited to a linguistic or metaphoric one, but not a thematic one. The immediate context, definitions, and application of this term and the design of the structure consistently favor two parallel concepts (Christology and brotherly love).[201]

---

[200] Urban C. von Wahlde, *The Johannine Commandments: 1 John and the Struggle for the Johannine Tradition*, ed. Lawrence Boadt, Theological Inquiries (New York: Paulist Press, 1990), pp. 60–62.

[201] See von Wahlde, *The Johannine Commandments: 1 John and the Struggle for the Johannine Tradition* (New York: Paulist Press, 1990), pp. 4, 6, 49–70. Here he conclusively demonstrates the existence of the "two commandments" in the Johannine epistles. Also for a thorough discussion on the Johannine "commandment," see chapter 10 of this study.

Liar. The Greek term translated "liar" is *pseustēs*. The author labeled both the "brother-hater" (see 4:20) and antichrists (see 2:22) as liars, but offered different reasons why he did this. Because of scant evidence supporting two different groups of opponents, many scholars consider the designation as indicative of the antichrists being involved in two activities (denying Christ and hating brothers).[202] For example, Burdick and Hiebert treat all uses of "liar" as referring to the antichrists only.[203] However, Brown acknowledges that the occurrences in 1:6, 2:4, 21, and 22 are associated with the Christological issue, whereas the one in 4:20 is related to the brotherly-love issue. Yet he uses the semantic similarity as evidence to link the "secessionists" (2:21, 22) and "brother-haters" (4:20) into a single group of opponents.[204] However, he admits the evidence is insufficient to support his equational view. In his own words:

> The same language of lying and deceit is used of the Christological error (A5,6) and of the moral error (B1–4, 14) … This impression of two closely allied errors is strengthened when it can be shown that there is a logical connection between them (see pp. 54–55, 80–81 below). None of this is firm proof; but one can state that I and II John give little reason to think of a variety of adversaries and can quite logically be explained if one well-defined group of adversaries was being attacked. It seems an appropriate occasion to apply 'Ockham's razor': Postulated entities should not be multiplied without necessity.

However, if and when this term is seen through the dualism framework, some of these inherent inconsistencies can be minimized.

The word "liar [*pseustēs*]" (or related terms) appears nine times in 1 John (1:6, 10; 2:4, 21, 22, 27; 4:1, 20; 5:10). The author called the antichrists

---

[202] Brown, Burdick, Hiebert, and many others are of this opinion. See also Rensberger, *1 John, 2 John, 3 John*, pp. 34–38.

[203] Burdick, p. 340. See also Hiebert, pp. 220, 221.

[204] Brown, The Epistles of John, p. 50. This is the same approach he took with the term "commandment." He attempted to use the terms "commandment," "liar," and others to "connect" the two issues.

liars for two reasons: because of their failure to obey God's command (see 2:4) and for denying Jesus as being the Christ (see v. 22). He also described them as the "false prophets [*pseudoprophētai*]" because they are not used by the Spirit of God (see 4:1). In 2:1 and 2:27, the antichristological teaching is called a "lie" (*pseudos*), and in 1:10, their failure to admit their guilt, contrary to God's Word, makes God a "liar" (*pseustēn*). Finally, in 4:20, the author labeled the brother-hater as a "liar" (*pseustēs*). From the analysis of these usages, eight of the nine occurrences are used in association with the antichrists and their activities. However, the one in 4:20 is used to describe the adversary in the love-hate issue.[205]

The semantic similarities seem to support the theory that sees only one group of opponents. However, if the author intentionally offered two different descriptions, then it is also possible that he perhaps had two or more groups of opponents in mind. In support of this, we consider two crucial factors.

First, despite the semantic similarities ("liar"), the author disclosed specific details about the two types of liars. Second, the context also endorses this view. For example, the discussion in 1:5–2:6 and 2:18–3:9, where eight of the nine "liars" are found, are on Christology, whereas the discussion in 4:7–21 deals with the love-hate issue. If this contextual issue is seen in the light of how the book is arranged and structured, then seeing two different groups of opponents in 1 John becomes more likely.[206]

In such a situation, one is left with the choice of either embracing the linguistic similarities ("liars") and ignoring the differences in definitions, description, nuances, and contexts, or accepting the differences as stated in the text and then attempting to discover the reasons why the author may have used the same labeling. In other words, it is the articulated

---

[205] The author uses the designation *pseustēs* in only three places (see 2:4, 22; 4:20). Two of them refer to the opponents in the Christological issue (2:4, 22), while the other one is in reference to the brother-hater (4:20).

[206] Paki, George. *The Structural and Thematic Analysis of 1 John*, Study Notes. In this, the present author argues for a 'weaving structure' for 1 John. The structure, in so many ways, is similar to the one George Guthrie offered on the book of Hebrews.

definition, differences in nuances, and immediate context of these terms that must provide the clue to addressing the labeling issue, and not the other way around.[207]

Finally, if the author consistently offered two definitions for the terms "commandment" and "liar" to describe either two issues or two groups of opponents, it could indicate that he is addressing two issues/opponents in a single letter.[208] For instance, the antichrist is called a "liar" because of his claim to sinlessness and denial of Jesus Christ (see 1:6; 2:4, 22). Conversely, the brother-hater earns the title "liar" because of his verbal claim to love God while insistently persecuting or not loving his brothers (see 4:20).[209] Thus, this term being seen as having a dual meaning and application seems consistent with the text, context, and structure.

Message. To illustrate this concept further, we explore another word—"message." The Greek word translated "message" is *hē aggelia*, which is prominently featured in 1 John 1:5 and 3:11. In 1:5, the author described "God is light" as the "message." This disclosure introduces the first of several Christological units (see 1:5–2:6). Two chapters later, a similar statement appears: "And this is the message you have heard from the beginning. We should love one another" (3:11). Here, "message" is described as "we should love one another."

Although this does not prove anything, the similarities that exist between these terms ("commandments," "liars," and "messages") are noteworthy. When viewing them together, a particular pattern begins to emerge. Not only did the author use a single word to draw two different definitions, imageries, and applications, but also the two definitions, imageries, and applications in each of the cases are *parallelly* similar. Whenever these terms occur in the Christological units of the structure, they

---

[207] Brown, The Epistles of John, pp. 49, 50.

[208] The author does the same with the word "message." The term appears many times in 1 John, but it is prominently featured in 1:5 and 3:11. In 1:5, the "message" is expressed as "God is light," while in 3:11, it is described as "love one another."

[209] As we shall see later, the metaphor of light in 1 John 1:5–2:6 and 2:9–11 is used in a similar fashion.

assume a Christologically nuanced meaning. However, when the same terms appear in the love-hate passages of the text, they specifically discuss the love-hate issue. The following diagram summarizes the discussion on this section. Therefore, these terms having some sort of a dual meaning, application, and significance is more likely.

Concepts	Antichrists/Christology	Brother-hater/Brotherly-Love issue
"commandment"	2:3, 4, 7, 8; 3:22–24; 4:21; 5:2–3	2:3, 4, 7, 8; 3:23, 24; 4:21; 5:2–3
"message"	1:5	3:11
"liar"	1:6, 10; 2:4, 21, 22, 27; 4:1; 5:10	4:20

Analysis of 1 John

The nature, definition, usages, and context of the terms "commandment," "liar," and "message" allow for two possibilities. First, they support the possibility of a two-issue or two-opponent theory in 1 John—that is, the Christological and brotherly-love issue and their associated opponents. Second, the manner in which the terms are defined, stressed, illustrated, and applied heavily supports a dualistic approach. The author used a single word but consistently offered two different definitions (usages or illustrations).[210] If the same author was behind Revelation and 1 John, and if Revelation preceded the Epistles, then a literary or a methodological relationship exists between how the key terms of concepts are defined and used in Revelation and how the terms "commandments," "messages" and "liars" are used in 1 John.[211]

---

[210] As in Revelation and the epistles of John, the same is also true in the Gospel of John. Consider how the author intentionally used the following words with dual meaning: "temple/body" (2:19–22), "sleep/death" (11:4–15), "birth" (3:3–9), bread/bread of life (6:26–51), eating His body and blood (6:51–58), and the concept of blindness (9:35–41). All these and other terms or concepts have two layers of meanings.

[211] In Revelation 19:10, it was the "angel" who defined the term "testimony of Jesus." And if John attempted to imitate the same in his first epistle, then the probability of him learning from the angel is higher than that of the angel imitating John. That means that Revelation has to precede other

DUAL MEANINGS IN THE GOSPEL OF JOHN

Thus far, we have seen how John wrote with dual intent in 1 John and Revelation. One more evidence needs to be considered at this stage. The concept of dual-intentionalism or words, imageries, concepts, and characters having a double meaning is even more pronounced and widespread in the Gospel of John.[212] Consider for instance, the literal and symbolic temple of 2:19–22; the two layers of birth in 3:1–21; the two meanings of water in 4:1–42 and 7:37–39; and even the Samaritan woman has a dual significance (see chapter 3; John 4:1–26). Also, the length of time the invalid had been sick (thirty-eight years) in John 5:5 has a dual meaning. Undoubtedly, the invalid may have been on his mat for thirty-eight years, but this is the same period the Israelites wandered in the wilderness (see Deut. 2:14).

> *Perhaps "the older ones" in the crowd were the first to recognize that the very same fingers that wrote the commandment twice at Horeb has now stooped down to write grace and truth twice on the ground.*

Similarly, there are two types of bread in John 6: the one Moses gave and the "true bread" that came down from heaven. Further, the story of the adulterous woman, especially Jesus stooping down and writing twice on the ground with his finger, has a dual significance (see John 8:1–8). Perhaps "the older ones" in the crowd were the first to recognize that the very same fingers that wrote the commandment twice at Horeb has now stooped down to write grace and truth twice on the ground (see 1:17).

Johannine books. If Revelation was John's first book, this also explains why it was written in "poor" Greek, as opposed to his later books.

[212] To serve our current purpose, we are merely listing the terms and concepts that have dual meaning, but in a later project, we intend to fully develop these materials.

Finally, we do not have time to discuss the two meanings of blindness in John 9, the two shepherds, two sheep, and two sheepfolds in chapter 10, or the two meanings of sleep and the two types of resurrections in chapter 11. It is apparent that the entire Gospel of John is literally saturated with double, dual, or figurative meanings.

Features	Meaning 1 (Literal)	Meaning 2 (Figurative)
Temple	Literal temple (John 2:19, 20)	Christ's body (John 2:21)
Birth	Literal birth from woman's womb (3:4)	Of water and spirit (3:5–8)
Water	Literal water (4:10, 11)	Jesus Christ, Holy Spirit (4:13–15; 7:37–39)
Samaritan woman	Literal woman (4:17, 18)	Israel's faithlessness (Rev. 17:10)
Invalid being sick for thirty-eight years	Literal thirty-eight years of sickness (5:5)	Israelite's wondering in wilderness (Deut. 2:14)
Bread	Literal bread He gave (6:49)	Jesus as the True Bread (6:35)
Finger of God writing twice	Literal writing in John 8 (vv. 6–8)	God writing twice at Sanai (6:6–9)
Blindness	Literal blindness (9:1, 40)	Symbolic or spiritual blindness (9:39–41)
Two gates/doors	Literal gate/door (10:2)	Jesus as the Gate/Door (10:7, 9)
Jesus' removal of outer garment	Literal removing of outer clothes (13:4, 5, 12)	Jesus' putting on humanity (16:28)
Peter's removal of his outer garment	Literal removal of the garment (21:3, 7)	Spiritual backsliding, returning to fishing (21:3, 7)
Night and darkness	Literal night and darkness (13:2)	Symbolic spiritual darkness (13:30; 1 John 2:9–11)
Wine	Literal grape juice (2:3)	Jesus (2:10)
Others will lead you	Literally leading the elderly (21:18)	Showing how Peter would die (21:19)

CONCLUSION

Therefore, if John consistently used terms, concepts, and characters with dual focus in most (if not all) of his books, then that suggests three things: 1) Apart from understanding the contents and significance of the prophetic messages, John was fully immersed in the literary and linguistic features of Revelation as well; 2) This increases the probability of the prophecies of Revelation having a dual intent. Just like 1 John and the Gospel of John, the prophecies of Revelation could also have a dual significance; 3) These evidences also increase the probability that Revelation was written before the Epistles and Gospel of John.

PART 3:
JESUS, THE ONE LIKE THE SON OF MAN (REVELATION 1:10–3:22)

13.

THE SON OF MAN, PART I

On the Lord's Day I was in the Spirit, and I heard behind me a loud voice like a trumpet, which said: "Write on a scroll what you see and send it to the seven churches: to Ephesus, Smyrna, Pergamum, Thyatira, Sardis, Philadelphia and Laodicea. I turned around to see the voice that was speaking to me. And when I turned I saw seven golden lampstands, and among the lampstands was someone like a son of man, dressed in a robe reaching down to his feet and with a golden sash around his chest. His head and hair were white like wool, as white as snow, and his eyes were like blazing fire. His feet were like bronze glowing in a furnace, and his voice was like the sound of rushing waters. In his right hand he held seven stars, and out of his mouth came a sharp, double-edged sword. His face was like the sun shining in all its brilliance. When I saw him, I fell at his feet as though dead. Then he placed his right hand on me and said: "Do not be afraid. I am the First and the Last. I am the Living One; I was dead, and behold I am alive for ever and ever! And I hold the keys of death and Hades. "Write, therefore, what you have seen, what is now and what will take place later. The mystery of the seven stars that you saw in my right hand and of the seven golden lampstands is this: The seven stars are the angels of the seven churches, and the seven lampstands are the seven churches (Revelation 1:10–20).[213]

---

[213] Scriptures are taken from the *New International Version*. Copyright 1973, 1978, 1984 International Bible Society. Zondervan Bible Publishers.

INTRODUCTION

Our discussion on the "son of man" consists of two parts. Chapter 13 discusses the text and themes, whereas chapter 14 assesses the contextual and theological implications of this passage. This is done in order to accommodate the volume of material on this passage.

"Son of Man" in Daniel 7, 10, and Revelation 1

On the "Lord's Day" at Patmos, John heard a "loud voice" behind him. The voice commanded him to "write what you see and send it to the seven churches: to Ephesus, Smyrna, Pergamum, Thyatira, Sardis, Philadelphia, and Laodicea" (Rev. 1:10–11). John then turned to see the voice because the very words "write what you *see*" sort of invited him to see the One speaking. Upon turning, John saw "someone like a son of man."

The physical description of the divine being he saw is nearly identical to another divine character the prophet Daniel saw centuries earlier. The following table compares these two characters:

Revelation 1:12–16	Daniel 7 and 10:4–19
"I saw seven golden lampstands" (v. 12)	"on the banks of the great river, the Tigris" (10:4)
"someone, 'like a son of man'" (v. 13)	"like a son of man" (7:13)
"voice like trumpet," "sound of rushing waters" (vv. 10, 15)	"voice like the sound of a multitude" (10:6)
"dressed in a robe reaching down to his feet" (v. 13)	"dressed in linen" (10:5)
"a golden sash around his chest" (v. 13)	"belt ... around his waist" (10:5)
"His head and hair were white like wool, as white as snow" (v. 14)	—
"eyes were like blazing fire" (v. 14)	"his eyes like flaming torches" (10:6)
"feet were like bronze glowing in a furnace" (v. 15)	"legs like the gleam of burnished bronze" (10:6)
"In his right hand, he held seven stars" (v. 16)	—

Revelation 1:12–16	Daniel 7 and 10:4–19
"out of his mouth came a sharp, doubled-edged sword" (v. 16)	—
"His face was like the sun shining in all its brilliance" (v. 16)	"his face like lightning" (10:6).
—	"His body was like topaz" (10:6)
"fell as though dead" (v. 17)	"no strength ... my face turned deathly pale" (10:8)
"Then he placed his right hand on me" (v. 17)	"A hand touched me" (10:10)
"do not be afraid" (v. 17)	"do not be afraid" (10:12)

Revelation's "son of man" features a total of fourteen identifying characteristics, whereas the one in Daniel has twelve. The two characters share ten of these features. Revelation has four unique details, whereas Daniel has two. The unique features serve to contextualize these divine characters. Consider, for instance, the setting of these two accounts. Daniel's account took place "on the banks of the great river," whereas John saw the glorified Christ among the "seven golden lampstands." Jesus holding the seven stars or having wool-like hair is also intended to contextualize the message to communities that received these messages. These features will be discussed later.

Relationship Between Revelation 1:4–8 and the Vision

<u>Lexical Representation of Jesus</u>. We previously demonstrated how the Johannine text progressively builds the case for Jesus' divinity.[214] In Revelation (and 1 John), the author used certain literary and divine designations ("Alpha and Omega," "who was, who is, and who is to come," "eternal," and the "son") to elevate Jesus' identity as deriving from "above," "the Beginning," "God," as well as being "eternal," the "son of God," and eventually "God" Himself. A common aspect of these approaches is that the author used the OT titles and designations of God to describe Jesus

---

[214] See chapter 4 of this book.

in the NT text. How does that relate to the vision of the "son of man" in Revelation 1:12–16?

Pictorial Representation of Jesus. First, instead of using words to designate or describe Jesus' pre-incarnate and post-ascension identity, authority, and roles, John was shown a pictorial representation of the "son of man." Second, similar to the passages of Revelation 1:5–7 and 19:11–16 (which are impregnated with Jesus' names, titles, and designations), this vision of Jesus also combines numerous divine characters in both the Old and New Testaments. We will explore this composite character in detail.

PREINCARNATE CHRIST

In this discussion, three aspects of Jesus Christ will be explored: 1) certain OT divine characters as the pre-incarnate Christ, 2) Jesus Christ's post-ascension characters and roles, and 3) the significance and implications of this vision for its original readers.[215]

Jesus, the Son of Man

Jesus Is the "son of man." Is the "son of man" in Revelation 1:12–16 the same as the one who "looked like a man" in Daniel 10? Is "Prince Michael" of Daniel 10–12 the same as the Michael of Revelation 12? Is the man-like character in both books the same as the Michael figure? What is the relationship between these characters and God?

The number of similarities (as established earlier) between the "one like a son of man" (see Rev. 1:10–20) and the one who "looked like

---

[215] The vision concerning one "like a Son of Man" described here is replete with abundant Christological names, titles, designations, and roles. Thus far, we have seen two passages (Rev. 1:5–7; 19:11–16) equally laden with Jesus' names, titles, and functions. However, these designations consist of only "words." The vision here plays a similar role, except that it is a graphic representation. What this vision does (as do the visions of Rev. 5 and 12) is fuse together the "Son of Man" character, several Old Testament divine/messianic characters, and the post-ascension roles of Jesus Christ.

a man" (see Dan. 10) suggests that these two characters represent the same person. The appearance, clothing, belt, eyes, voice, feet, face, and mouth are similar. The reactions of the two prophets who saw this majestic being and how they were revived are exactly the same. Therefore, it is apparent that the characters in both books represent either the pre-incarnate or post-ascended Christ. However, as highlighted in the first table, the Revelation portrait contains a few notable omissions and/or additions. These differences serve to either reinforce certain truths about Jesus or contextualize them to the readers. Before examining these differences, we first discuss "Prince Michael" and His relationship to the "son of man."

"son of man" (Rev. 1:12–16)	Old Testament Divine Characters	Notes
"son of man"	"son of man" (Dan. 7:13, 14); "son of the gods" (3:25)	Distinct from the "Ancient of Days"
Divine character	"a man" (Dan. 10:5), or "looked like a man" (vv. 16, 18)	Does not say "son of man," but only that he "looked like a man"
"His head and hair were white like wool, as white as snow" (v. 14)	"Ancient of Days" (Dan. 7:9)	The descriptions in Revelation are similar to the man of Daniel 10, except that his head/hair is like the Ancient of Days
"Clothes"	"long robe," walks among "lampstand," denotes a "priest"	"made as priest," implied Jesus as high priest, a theme developed in Hebrews
"Michael" (implied here but mentioned in Rev. 12:7)	Prince Michael (Dan. 10:13; 12:1)	Michael mentioned (Dan. 10), inferred as one who does not lose a battle
Revealer of Mysteries (1:11)	Daniel wanted "understanding" of future events (10:1). One "like a man" came to reveal as well as to fight	Similar in both settings

Jesus, the Prince Michael

The "son of man" and "Michael." Similar to the "son of man" who appears in both books (see Dan. 7, 10; Rev. 1), "Michael" is also featured in both books (see Dan. 10–12; Rev. 12). However, the text does not indicate whether the "son of man" is the same as "Michael." Nevertheless, certain details concerning these characters serve to inform us that they are one and the same.

"Son of man" and "Michael" are equally powerful. In both Daniel and Revelation, the prophets "turned deathly pale" in the presence of one that "looked like a man," who also had power to supernaturally strengthen them (see Dan. 10:8–19; Rev. 1:17, 18).

Prince Michael in Daniel 10–12. In Daniel, Michael is described as "one of the chief princes" or the "great prince" (Dan. 12:1). He is also presented as Daniel's prince (see 10:21) and One who "protects his people" (12:1). Michael not only helps humans, but also supports the other divine being (see 10:13, 21). This is because the other divine being (possibly an angel) was either resisted or "detained" for "21 days" by the "prince of Persia," and Prince Michael came and helped him.

Prince Michael in Revelation 12. Even before the "war in Tigris," "Michael and his angels" fought against the "dragon and his angels" in heaven (Rev. 12:7). Similar to the results of the Tigris war (see Dan. 10–12), Michael defeats and casts out the dragon and his angels (see Rev. 12:9, 10). In both books, Michael is a great Prince who supports His people, fights against the enemies of His people, wins every battle He fights, and has an army of angels who help Him in this mortal combat. Whoever this character is, He obviously assumes the designation "Michael" and comes through as a "Great Prince" when engaged in war. Therefore, the question is, Is "Prince Michael" the same as the "son of man"? In Revelation (1 and 12), as in Daniel (10–12), such a relationship is implied, but the text does not explicitly state it. However, Revelation 19:11–16 serves as a link in connecting these two divine characters.

Jesus, "Prince Michael," and the "son of man"

Revelation 19:11–16 supplies the link, thus connecting the "Michael" of chapter 12 to the "son of man" in chapter 1 (as well as in Daniel

10 and 12). The following table comparatively analyzes the "son of man" (Rev. 1), "Michael" (Rev. 12), and the "Rider" (Rev. 19).

Revelation 1:12–16	Revelation 19:11–16	Revelation 12:7–10
"faithful and true witness" (3:14)	"Faithful and True" (v. 11)	—
—	"With justice he makes war" (v. 11)	"Michael makes war with the dragon" (v. 7).
"His eyes were like blazing fire" (1:14).	"His eyes are like blazing fire" (v. 12)	—
—	"The armies of heaven were following him" (v. 14)	"Michael and his angels fought against the dragon and his angels" (v. 7).
"Dressed in a robe" (v. 13)	"dressed in a robe dipped in blood" (v. 13)	—
	—	
—	"He will rule them with an iron scepter" (v. 15).	"a male child who will rule all the nations with an iron scepter" (v. 5)
"out of his mouth came a sharp two-edged sword" (v. 16)	"Out of his mouth comes a sharp sword that strikes down nations" (v. 15).	—
—	With the sword of his mouth he kills the kings of the earth and their armies, captures the beast and its image, and throws them into the fire (vv. 19–21).	Satan was not strong enough. He lost his place in heaven. He and his angels were cast out (vv. 8, 9).

<u>Son of Man and the Rider on the White Horse</u>. An analysis of these passages reveals a prima facie case emerging, linking the "son of man" to "Prince Michael." Note the particular relationship between the Son of Man in Revelation 1 and the Rider on the white horse in chapter 19: the "blazing eyes," "two-edged sword," "robe," and His designation as the "Faithful and True Witness" all show these two characters as one and the same.

<u>Michael and the Rider on the White Horse</u>. Now consider the relationship between the Rider on the white horse and Michael in Revelation 12. They have the following characteristics in common: both characters are

portrayed as fighting generals, have an army of angels following or fighting for and with them, and are victorious in their respective wars. Michael defeats the dragon and his angels, whereas the Rider slays the earthly kings and their armies. Both passages feature the male child and rider as the One who is to rule with an iron scepter.

Therefore, the volume of similarities between the "son of man" (Rev. 1) and the Rider on the white horse (ch. 19) shows that these two are identical. Then the relationship between the Rider and Michael (ch. 12) shows that these characters are one and the same also. In this case, one of the divine characters, the "son of man" in Revelation 1, alludes to "Prince Michael." The following diagram attempts to show a cyclical relationship between these three divine characters:

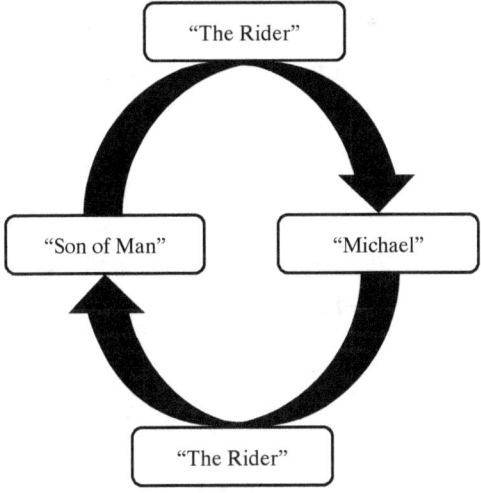

Jesus, the "son of man" and "son of God"

Jesus, the Son of Man. John described what he beheld as one like the "son of man" (Rev. 1:13). This is reminiscent of another divine character in Daniel. In a similar vision, Daniel was shown two authoritative divine characters: one was the "Ancient of Days," while the other looked like the "son of man" (ch. 7). Therefore, John's designation of Jesus as the "son of man" fits the second character.

Jesus, the Son of God. Years earlier, a pagan monarch first described the fourth character in the fiery furnace in an interesting way: "Look! I see four men walking around in the fire ... and the fourth [man] looks like a *son of the gods*" (Dan. 3:25, emphasis supplied). Note that it is the "fourth man" who looked "like a son of the gods" who now describes Himself as the "Son of God" in Revelation 2:18.

> Daniel's visions consistently present the pre-incarnate Christ as a separate and distinct character from the Ancient of Days. John's designations, however, blur this line and present Jesus as the Ancient of Days.

Daniel's visions consistently present the pre-incarnate Christ ("son of man," "son of the gods," and "Prince Michael") as a separate and distinct character from the Ancient of Days. John's designations, however, blur this line and present Jesus as the Ancient of Days. We shall discuss this next.

Daniel's "Ancient of Days—son of man" and Revelation's "the One on the throne—the Lamb"

The Ancient of Days and the Son of Man in Daniel 7. The distinction between the Ancient of Days and the Son of Man are maintained in both Daniel and Revelation. In Daniel, the Ancient of Days is presented as someone superior and seated on his throne (see Dan. 7:9). The fact that the "son of man" is ushered "into his presence" and bestowed "authority, glory and sovereign power" *by* the one seated on the throne (Dan. 7:13, 14) suggests that the Father is greater than the Son is (see John 14:28). However, the fact that the Son is worshiped by all peoples and nations puts the Son on equal footing with the Ancient of Days.

The Enthroned One and the Lamb Before the Throne. The events and characters of Revelation 4 and 5 are identical to those in Daniel 7:13–14. The "great white throne" and "him who sat on" it in the former is nearly identical to the "Ancient of Days" in the latter. The Lamb, similar to the "son of man, is escorted into the presence of the enthroned One (see Rev. 5:5–8) where He is bestowed "power and wealth and wisdom and strength and honor and glory and praise!" (v. 12; see also Matt. 28:18). Similar to Daniel 7:14, the Lamb of Revelation 5 is also worshiped by "every creature in heaven and on earth and under the earth" and all "angels" (vv. 11–13). The worship of the "son of man" in Daniel 7 and the "Lamb" in Revelation 5 makes Jesus nearly identical to God.

"Son of Man" Is like the "Ancient of Days"

We now return to the two man-like characters of Revelation 1:12–16 and Daniel 10:4–19. Note particularly the unique or additional characteristics presented as follows:

Revelation 1:12–16	Daniel 10:4–19
"I saw seven golden lampstands" (v. 12)	"on the banks of the great river, the Tigris" (v. 4)
"hair on his head was white like wool, as white as snow" (v. 14)	"body like topaz" (v. 6)
"In his right hand he held seven stars" (v. 16)	
"out of his mouth was a sharp, double-edged sword" (v. 16)	

As stated earlier, observe the four unique or additional characteristics of Revelation 1:12–16. These additional features play a crucial role in advancing Jesus' divinity and contextualizing Him to the seven churches that first received the book of Revelation. Consider especially the color of Jesus' hair: "The hair on his head was white like wool, as white as snow" (v. 14). John employed the imageries of wool and snow to describe Christ's hair. These descriptions, unfortunately, are not found in Daniel 10. However, in 7:10, the "wool" and "snow" imageries are used to describe the "Ancient of Days [God]." Even in that image, the phrase "white as snow" does not refer to God's hair, but His "clothes," whereas His hair was "white like wool" (v. 9). However, in Revelation 1, both of these descriptions are combined and used to describe Jesus Christ's hair. What then is the significance of this?

We have previously observed how John intentionally used words and titles to transfer attributes of God such as "Alpha-Omega," "who was, is, and is to come," "eternal," and "true God" to Jesus. The same is done here, but using graphics. In Revelation, John advanced the argument that the "son of man" of 1:12–16 is not only like the "son of man" or man-like character of Daniel 7:13–14 and 10, but also the "Ancient of Days" in 7:10. The following figure summarizes this rendering:

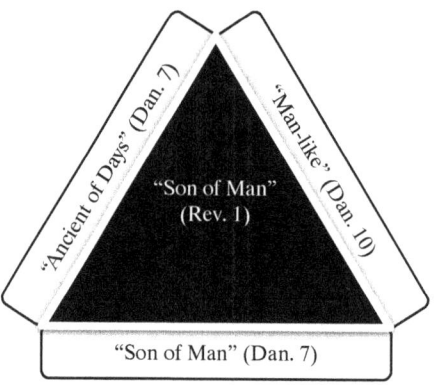

POST-ASCENSION AND FUTURE ROLES OF JESUS

Jesus, the High Priest-King like Melchizedek

Similar to the glorified Christ resembling Prince Michael, the Rider on the white horse, the Son of Man, the Son of God, and the Ancient One, Jesus also assumes several human characters, offices, and institutions. Stefanovic suggests that the long robe the Son of Man wears "emphasizes the priestly as well as the royal character of the glorified Christ."[216]

---

[216] Stefanovic, *Revelation of Jesus Christ*, p. 104 (see also pp. 100, 101). Observe that the Pharisees and teachers of the law also "walk[ed] around in flowing robes" during Jesus' time (Luke 20:46). In this way, Jesus's attire suggests that He was a type of priest, king, and a teacher of the law.

These conjoined themes of Christ as either the High Priest, King, or Priestly-King are discussed as follows, beginning with Jesus' priesthood.

<u>The Saints as Priests</u>. Jesus' priestly role is evident because i) He is "dressed in a robe reaching down to his feet" (Rev. 1:13) and ii) He is standing in the midst of the "seven golden lampstands" (v. 12). Viewing these symbols in the context of what is written in Revelation and other NT and OT books, the priestly representation of Jesus in this vision becomes more pronounced.

The priesthood theme is first mentioned in Revelation 1:5–6. John wrote that Jesus "has freed us from our sins by his blood," and "has made us to be a kingdom and priests to serve his God and Father." This text reveals two things. First, one of the roles of the saved is to serve God as priests. Second, Jesus enables both the salvation and priestly role of the saints. Having made His saints to serve as priests, He then clothes them with "white robes"—robes that are washed and "made white in the blood of the Lamb" (Rev. 6:11; 7:14). Arrayed in white, the saints "serve him [God] day and night in his temple," both here on earth (Rev. 7:15) and in heaven. These priestly roles of the saints do not materialize until after Revelation 20: "Blessed and holy are those who have part in the first resurrection ... [because] they will be priests of God and of Christ and will reign with him for a thousand years" (v. 6). If the saved are priests, then that makes Jesus the High Priest in both worlds.

<u>Jesus, the High Priest</u>. The long priestly robe, candlelight illumination, Aaronic sash (see Exod. 28:4), and other features portray Jesus as the High Priest. This post-ascension role is heavily discussed in Hebrews: "We do have such a high priest, who sat down at the right hand of the throne of the Majesty in heaven, and who serves in the sanctuary, the true tabernacle set up by the Lord, not by a mere human being" (Heb. 8:1, 2). The compassionate High Priest referred to here is Jesus, for the same author wrote, "we have a great high priest who has gone through the heavens, Jesus the Son of God" (Heb. 4:14).

The High Priestly King and His "kingdom of priesthood"

<u>Jesus, the High Priest in the Order of Melchizedek</u>. Concerning the nature of Jesus' priesthood, the same author wrote that He was "designated by God to be high priest in the order of Melchizedek" (5:10). In the OT, Melchizedek was both a king and high priest, therefore making him a type of Jesus Christ. Perhaps this is why Jesus is presented as a "high priest" sitting on the "throne of grace" (4:14–16). Hebrews 8:1–2 also presents Jesus as sitting "at the right hand of the throne," yet He also "serves [God] in the sanctuary, the true tabernacle."

Jesus, the King and His kingdom

Jesus is not only revealed as the High Priest or Priestly-King in the likeness of Melchizedek, but also as the King in the lineage of David. We shall explore this theme in Revelation and other Johannine writings.

<u>The King and His Subjects</u>. We have noted how the saints of God "serve him [God] day and night in his temple" as priests (Rev. 1:6). Many passages also present Christ as King and His saints as "a kingdom," respectively (5:6; 7:15). We are told of a "great white throne" and Jesus sitting on the "right hand" of "him who sits on that throne [God]." If a throne denotes a kingdom, then the one who sits on it is the monarch. This would therefore make the saints subjects of a kingdom that "serve[s] our God" (5:10).

<u>Jesus, the King of kings</u>. Jesus is first introduced as the "ruler of the kings of the earth" in Revelation 1:5. The title "ruler of the kings" is based on Rev. 17:14 and 19:6, where Jesus is hailed as "Lord of lords and King of kings." The Rider of the "white horse" in chapter 19 does indeed come through as a victorious King as He is followed by "armies of heaven."

<u>Jesus, the Lamb, Lion, and Root of David</u>. The title "King of kings" used to describe the Rider in Revelation 19 is first used in 17:14 to describe a lowly "Lamb." How could this Lamb possibly be a king, let alone the "King of kings"? The answer is found in Rev. 5:5–6, where we

see a composite image of a "Lion-Lamb-King." There, the conquering "Lamb" is described as the "Lion of the tribe of Judah, the Root of David," suggesting that Jesus is the "Son of David," or a King in the likeness and lineage of David. Therefore, one of the imageries contained in the vision of Revelation 1:12–16 is Jesus as *the* King. He is not only a King in the bloodline of David, but also more than a King; He is the King of all kings!

Jesus, the Better Teacher of the Law

And finally, Jesus' long flowing robes also suggest that He is greater than all Jewish teachers of the law. Concerning these Pharisees and the teachers of the law, Jesus taught, "Beware of the teachers of the law. They like to *walk around in flowing robes*" (Luke 20:46, emphasis supplied).

Both Nicodemus and the Samaritan woman's encounters with Christ testify to this fact. The Samaritan woman expressed the prevailing expectations of the people in her day: "I know that Messiah (called Christ) is coming. When he comes, he will explain everything to us." And to this, Jesus declared, "I who speak to you am he" (John 4:25, 26). Nicodemus confessed the same: "we know that you are a teacher who has come from God" (3:2).

> *Apart from the priests and kings, the Pharisees and teachers of the law did walk around in flowing robes. Therefore, Christ being dressed in a robe reaching down to His feet and walking among the seven candlesticks suggest that He was the true Teacher of the law.*

Apart from the priests and kings, the Pharisees and teachers of the law did walk around in flowing robes. Therefore, Christ being dressed in a robe reaching down to His feet and walking among the seven candlesticks suggest that He was the true Teacher of the law.

Summary

In the composite figure of the One like the "son of man" in Revelation 1:12–16, we find the following OT and NT characters fused together, culminating in the life of Jesus Christ as the "son of man" (Dan. 7; Rev. 1) having a man-like character (Dan. 10; Rev. 1), the "Son of God" (Dan. 3; Rev. 2:18), "Michael" (Dan. 10; Rev. 12), the "Ancient of Days" (Dan. 7), the true teacher of the law, the Jewish High Priest, the Priestly-King like Melchizedek, and a King in the lineage of David.

COMPOSITE DIVINE FIGURES IN NEW TESTAMENT WRITINGS

John 1:35–49

To appreciate these multifaceted portrayals of Jesus, we assess another example in John 1:35–49. In this passage, John the Baptist introduced Jesus to his disciples, saying, "Behold the Lamb of God," and he did this for two consecutive days (John 1:29, 35). "Andrew ... one of the [disciples] who heard what John had said," told his brother Simon, "We have found the messiah' (that is, the Christ)" (vv. 40, 41). A little later, Philip invited Nathaniel, saying, "We have found the one Moses wrote about in the Law, and about whom the prophets also wrote" (v. 45). After seeing Jesus, Nathaniel declared, "Rabbi, you are the Son of God; you are the king of Israel" (v. 49).

Two points are noteworthy here. According to the text, John the Baptist had introduced Jesus as the "Lamb of God" in the course of two days. However, *that* designation transforms into seven different titles within this short passage. Andrew, one of the disciples who heard John the Baptist introduce Jesus as the Lamb, went to invite his brother Peter to "come and see" the "Christ." Philip went and did the same. He invited Nathaniel to "come and see" the "one Moses" and the "prophets ... wrote about." However, upon seeing the One about whom Moses wrote, Nathaniel declared to Jesus, "Rabbi, you are the Son of God, you are the King of Israel."

In this passage, as in Revelation, Jesus assumes a multiplicity of designations. In fact, Andrew, Simon, and Nathaniel were invited to "come and see" a certain aspect of Jesus (i.e., "the Lamb"), but upon actually seeing, these individuals confessed another designation. What does this imply? The composite character John painted here is similar to the multi-layered figure of the "son of man" in Revelation 1:12–16. The obvious difference is that in the Gospel, those characters of Jesus are represented in words, whereas in Revelation, they are presented in graphics or pictorials.

Revelation 5:5–6

What John did in the Gospel underscores a basic literary feature that he heavily used in Revelation as well. In 5:5–6, John was invited to "See, the Lion of the tribe of Judah," but he actually saw a "Lamb." Also, when John was invited to "write what you see," he saw a composite divine figure in 1:12–16.

Luke's Use of Daniel 7 and 10

The composite depictions of Christ as presented by John in Revelation 1, 5, and John 1 are not limited to him. Luke did something similar in 1:28–35. First, his choice of words, names, titles, and imageries were also intended to evoke the divine being of Daniel 7 and 10. For instance, Luke referred to God as the "Most High" in two places in this short passage. That same designation is heavily used for God in Daniel. The remaining similarities are presented in the following table:

"Jesus" (Luke 1:13–35)	"Son of Man" (Dan. 7 and 10)
Gabriel to Mary: "You are highly favored!" (v. 28)	Gabriel to Daniel: "You are highly esteemed" (10:11)
Title "Most High" for God (vv. 32, 35)	The title "Most High" for God (7:18, 22, 25, 27)
"Son of the Most High" (v. 32)	"one like a Son of Man" (v. 13)

"Jesus" (Luke 1:13–35)	"Son of Man" (Dan. 7 and 10)
"the Lord God will give him the throne of his father David" (v. 32)	"He was given authority, glory and sovereign power. His dominion ... and his kingdom is" everlasting" (7:14).
"reign over Jacob's descendants forever" (v. 33)	"His kingdom will be an everlasting kingdom" (7:14, 18, 27)
"his kingdom will never end" (v. 33)	"His dominion is an everlasting dominion that will not pass away" (7:14, 18, 27).
"holy one" (v. 35)	"holy one" (4:23; 8:13)
"Son of God" (v. 35)	"one like a Son of Man" (7:13)

Second, Luke attempted to present Jesus as a composite character. In this scheme, He comes through as the "holy one," "one like the Son of Man," "Son of Man," and "Son of God." As noted earlier, these same titles are heavily featured in Daniel 7 and 10. Further, Jesus is also presented as the "Son of David," "the King," and the "Star of the house of Jacob."

CONCLUSION

The following diagram attempts to capture Jesus as projected in the passages we have previously discussed (i.e., Rev. 1:5–7; 12–16; 19:11–16; Dan. 7; 10; John 1:35–49; 1 John). This list is not exhaustive, as no attempt has been made to explore Jesus in the rest of Revelation, other Johannine books, and NT writings. Further discussions will require more "wheels" to add other designations of Jesus. To paraphrase John, "Jesus possesses other names, titles, and designations that are not written in this book. If every one of them were written down, I suppose that even the whole world would not have room for the [wheels] that would be [made]" (John 21:25).

Therefore, the vision of Revelation 1:12–16 fuses together several divine characters, human offices and institutions. The most notable include Jesus as the "son of man," the "Son of God," "Michael," "like God," "Ancient of Days," "High Priest," Priestly-King in the order of Melchizedek, "a King," "King of kings," "Lord of lords," the Rider on the white horse, "son of David," the "Lamb," and the "Lion." Perhaps

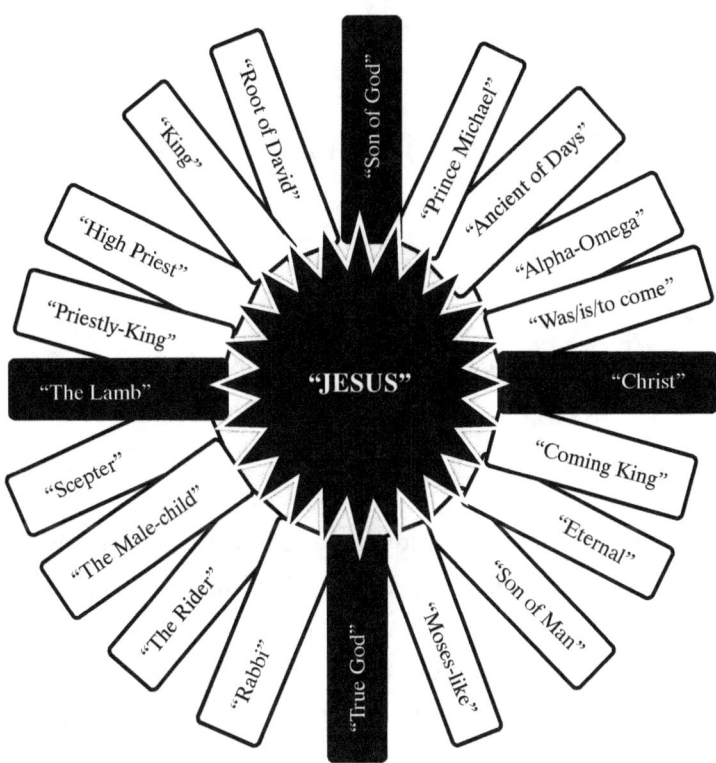

John was well aware of these characteristics when he entitled the book "The revelation of Jesus Christ" and wrote that if everything about Jesus was "written down ... even the whole world would not have rooms for the books that would be written" (John 21:25). Paul was obviously aware of the same when he said, "He [Christ] is before all things, and in him all things hold together." In another place, he also wrote, "but Christ is all, and is in all" (Col. 1:17; 3:11). These similarities suggest that the theological and ecclesiastical context of Revelation is not entirely different from that of Lukan, Pauline, or other NT writings.

However, why is Jesus presented in Revelation in such a manner? Why is the argument concerning His origin, authority, divinity, and roles subtly packaged in these visions? These questions lead us to the contextual and theological issues with which John and his audience may have grappled. These contextual and other related issues will be discussed in the next chapter.

14.

THE SON OF MAN, PART II

REVIEW: ASSUMPTIONS AND OBJECTIVES OF THIS STUDY

Aims and Objectives of This Study

The primary aims of this study are as follows: First, to show that the entire messages of Revelation (i.e., both 1–3 and 4–22) were comprehensible to John and his audience; second, to show that the issues, concerns, characters, and institutions as discussed (Rev. 4–22) were relevant and entirely applicable to their time; third, to make a case for a dual application of the prophecies of Revelation, conceding that the same prophecies that first spoke to John and his audience in their time and context also speak to us today; finally, to show that the contextual and theological issues discussed in Revelation (and other Johannine books) are similar to the ones discussed in the Synoptic, Lukan, and Pauline traditions. Given this situation, how does our study of the "son of man" shed light on these assertions?

General Assumptions of This Study

This study subscribes to two assumptions. The first concerns the order in which the Johannine books were written—that Revelation was the first of the Johannine books, followed by the three epistles, with the Gospel of John being written last of all.

The epistles and Gospel of John were written to the same audience, addressing the same issues, but at different times. The epistles were written in haste to address certain pressing issues. The manner, style, voice, and tone of these letters are patterned after Revelation 1–3. The approach of all these documents is direct, following an "I-am-writing-to-you" format.

John subsequently wrote an elaborate volume (the Gospel of John) to address essentially the same issues. However, the Gospel emulates Revelation 4–22 in numerous ways, particularly the approach is more indirect than in the epistles. In these two works (Rev. 4–22 and the Gospel of John), the addressees took a silent-observer status, watching as the divine response to their own struggles was presented in a series of enactments called "visions," "signs," and "miraculous signs."

The second assumption involves the authorship of the book of Hebrews. This writer is of the view that the Gospel of John was not John's final work. Sufficient evidence suggests that the book of Hebrews also bears the imprint of John. The language, imagery, literary style, theology, Christology, and structure all resemble the other Johannine books.[217] However, it is not the intention of this project to engage in these discussions at this time. These points are merely mentioned to inform the reader of this writer's working assumptions.

THEOLOGICAL IMPLICATIONS

Thus far, we have examined Revelation 1:1–20. Verses 1–8 consist of an elongated prologue in which the author attempted to not only introduce but also reflect on the main messages of 1:9–22:6. The materials in the prologue, epilogue, and the author's other works indicate i) whether John understood the messages of Revelation, ii) whether his audience understood the contents and the meanings of 4–22, iii) whether the prophetic messages of 4–22 were applicable to their time, and iv) if they were, then the text must be allowed to provide the nature, extent, and manner of those issues. Addressing these concerns will facilitate highlighting the contextual and theological milieu of John and his audience.

Given our assessment of the prologue and epilogue, the author undoubtedly had a far clearer grasp of the material in Revelation.

---

[217] For some preliminary discussions on this, please refer to chapter 2 of this study.

He understood those prophecies to be applicable to his own time (as much as we do ours), not only because he was an "inspired author,"[218] but also those prophetic messages spoke to him in his time and context. The emerging contextual story is briefly summarized as follows:

Jesus Surpasses Those Who Prefigured Him. John's title of the book ("Revelation of Jesus") essentially sums up the content. Jesus is the ground and central focus of the entire book. Although it is true that the Synoptic tradition presents the words and deeds of Jesus during His brief earthly ministry, Revelation presents them in a richer, fuller, and more complete manner. It removes the garb of humanity and allows John (and us) to "see him as he [really] is" (1 John 3:2). He is not only like those Old Testament *human* characters, institutions, offices, and rituals that prefigured Him, but also greater than all of them combined![219]

Jesus Is from the "Beginning" and "Above." The composite figure of Revelation 1:12–16 seems to suggest that unlike Moses, David, Melchizedek, and other prophets who prefigured Jesus,

> *Although it is true that the Synoptic tradition presents the words and deeds of Jesus during His brief earthly ministry, Revelation presents them in a richer, fuller, and more complete manner. It removes the garb of humanity and allows John (and us) to "see him as he [really] is" (1 John 3:2). He is not only like those Old Testament* human *characters, institutions, offices, and rituals that prefigured Him, but also greater than all of them combined!*

---

[218] As suggested by Ranko Stefanovic, *Revelation of Jesus*.

[219] Matthew made exactly the same point when he said things like Jesus "is greater than Jonah," "greater than Solomon," and "greater than the temple" (Matt. 12:41, 42, 6). Although Christ is heavily presented as the "Son of David" in the NT literature, Luke departed from this and presented Jesus as David's "Lord" (Luke 20:41–44; Acts 2:34, 35).

He predates them all because He was "from the beginning" (1 John 1:1; 2:13, 14; Micah 5:2). At the inception of this world, Jesus "was with God in the beginning" (John 1:2). He was also "from above," "from heaven," and "from God" (3:31; 8:23, 42), who "came down" to us in human form (6:33, 41, 42, 51, 58).[220]

Jesus Is Like God Who "came down." Further, Jesus is like God who "came down." To Abraham, Jesus was the "stranger" who came to the "great trees of Mamre" (Gen. 18:1; Heb. 13:2; John 1:50). To Jacob, He was the "ladder" upon which the "angels of God were ascending and descending" (Gen. 28:12, 13; John 1:51). To Moses at Horeb, He came down as the "Great I am" (Ex. 3:14; John 8:58). Then to him at the "top of mount Pisgah," the Lord came down as "the archangel Michael" (Deut. 34:1–6, Jude 9). To Joshua, He said, "as the commander of the army of the Lord I have now come" (Josh. 5:14; Rev. 19:11; 12:7; 6:2). Centuries later, that same nameless Commander appeared to Daniel and John as "Prince Michael" (Dan. 10:13, 21; 12:1; Rev. 12:7). Finally, Jesus came as a "male child" to be "God with us" (Rev. 12:5; Matt. 1:23). Yes, Jesus is indeed all of these and much more, but when He came the first time, He came as the "Lamb of God" (John 1:29, 36; Rev. 5:6), and when He comes the second time, He will come as the "King of kings and the Lord of lords" (John 14:3; Rev. 17:14; 19:16). However, until then, He now lives as our Great High Priest and King-in-waiting.

Jesus as the *Son of Man, Son of God,* and *God Himself*. From the vision of Revelation 1:12–16, the glorified Christ was the "son of the gods" whom a pagan monarch confessed (Dan. 3:25), who is also the "son of man" who comes before the "Ancient of Days" (7:12–14). If the "son of man" is worshiped (vv. 13, 14; Rev. 5:8–14) and His "hair" is identical to that of the "Ancient of Days" (Dan. 7:9; Rev. 1:14), then He is like or is Himself the "Ancient of Days." This should not surprise us because we

---

[220] Mueller does a word study on the concept of Jesus as coming from God. He particularly attempts to show that the concept of Jesus as coming from the Father does not refer to Him having a beginning in the past, but His "incarnation" ("Did Jesus Emanate from the Father?" *Biblical Research Institute*, p. 3).

have established that Jesus is also the "Alpha and Omega," the "First and the Last," the "Beginning and the End," "eternal life," and even the "true God" (Rev. 22:12, 13; 1 John 1:2; 5:21). Paul observed the same when he described Christ this way: "For in him [Jesus Christ] all things were created: things in heaven and on earth ... all things have been created through him and for him. He is before all things, and in him all things hold together" (Col. 1:16, 17).

<u>Possible Reasons Why Jesus Was Denied, Rejected, and Crucified</u>. If John's visions and discourses revolved around Jesus' origin, identity, authority, and divinity, then it is possible that the false prophets had something to do with these. Perhaps they may have denied Jesus' Christology and claim to be of Davidic linage or the one Moses and the prophets "wrote about." To those who knew the Scriptures, Jesus' claim to be from "the beginning," "above," or even the "sent of God" may have seemed utterly preposterous (see John 7:48, 49). This is because unlike Moses and David, Jesus neither fights nor liberates any nation. When pressured to confess that He is a deceiver, He remained silent. Then when hanging on the tree, the oppressors taunted, "if you are the Christ, come down." He never came down. Instead, He died. He was buried. His opponents and crucifiers may have perhaps felt vindicated because if He was the one about whom Moses and the prophets wrote, He would not have died. "The crowd spoke up," wrote John, "'We have heard from the Law that the Christ will remain forever, so how can you say, 'The Son of Man must be lifted up'?" (John 12:34).

Therefore, to His opponents, His death was the ultimate evidence that Jesus was not who He claimed to be. The hopes of those who believed in Him were dashed. Cleopas' response to that "visitor to Jerusalem" sums up their feelings: "Jesus of Nazareth, who was a prophet mighty in deed and word ... the chief priests and our rulers delivered Him up to the sentence of death, and crucified Him. But we *were hoping* that it was He who was going to redeem Israel" (Luke 24:19–21, NAS, emphasis supplied). Implied here is that their hopes were, at least initially, shattered.

<u>Jesus and the Holy Spirit</u>. Did He come back to life after three days? Did He ascend to Heaven afterwards? To those who crucified Him, there

was no evidence that these events actually occurred.[221] Assuming that to be true, the Jews refused to investigate the resurrection claims because they feared uncovering the truth. However, they must dismiss one more hurdle to make their case as watertight and compelling as possible. If Jesus was the Christ, He would have "come baptizing," but He baptized no one. Instead, it was John the Baptist who came baptizing—who even baptized Jesus! That would make a good case for the baptizer being greater than the one being baptized.

Therefore, the Pentecost phenomenon must have had something to do with the ministry of John the Baptist rather than Jesus. The opponents of Jesus may have further claimed to have access to and know God apart from Jesus (see John 8:41; 1 John 2:4, 23). The Jews who saw themselves as "disciples of Moses" held that John was of God, but "this fellow [Jesus], we don't even know where He comes from" (John 9:28, 29). If the false prophets of Revelation, the antichrists of 1 and 2 John, or the Jews of the Gospel of John had such a conception, it appears quite convincing.[222]

Jesus the Lamb of God. However, just when they thought they had figured it out, they forgot one critical aspect about the Coming One: Jesus' identity as the "Lamb of God" who must die in order to take away the sins of the world. His opponents did not know that the Messiah voluntarily laid down His life for His friends. He was the Lamb who liberates, not just Israel, but the whole world from slavery to sin (see John 1:29; 8:31–36; Heb. 9:15; 1 John 2:2).

Therefore, the beloved John heard a "mighty angel" introduce the Lamb as the "Lion [and the] Root of David." This Lamb later transforms into a "Lion," "King," "Michael," the "male child," "Word of God," Son of Man,

---

[221] While the believers rejoiced in the resurrection account, the Jews spread the rumor that Jesus' body was stolen by the twelve disciples. By the time Matthew wrote his Gospel, these two views were popularly held (see 28:15).

[222] E. G. White stated that there were issues between the followers of John the Baptist and the followers of Christ: "These disciples [of John] had been envious of Christ when He seemed to be drawing the people away from John. They had sided with the Pharisees in accusing Him when He sat with the publicans at Matthew's feast. They had doubted His divine mission because He did not set the Baptist at liberty" (*The Desire of Ages*, p. 361).

"Son of God," Son of David, a High Priest, and a host of other divine characters. In the Gospel of John, however, it was John the Baptist who introduced Jesus as the "Lamb of God" to his disciples. Then similar to Revelation, that Lamb also transforms Himself into the "King of Israel," "son of God," "the Christ," and "the one Moses and the prophets wrote about."

CONTEXTUAL IMPLICATIONS

<u>Contextual Issues</u>. It is against such a background that literally every page in Revelation is stained with blood, every garment a saint wears is bathed in blood, and even the Lamb and the Rider on the white horse are "dipped in blood." We watch as the blood from that slain Lamb in the pages of Revelation now begins to spill over into the Gospel, epistles, and Hebrews. In the Gospel, the Lamb sets His mind on Calvary and voluntarily lays down his life for his friends (see John 10:18; 1 John 3:16). First John sees Christ as coming through "water and blood" (5:6, 8). Similarly, Hebrews boasts of a better blood that must be shed for the remission of sins (Heb. 9:14, 22).

However, the Jews did not expect a spineless Lamb to come. Their expectation of the Messiah was entirely different, as captured well in these words:

> They [the Jews] had not studied the Scriptures with a desire to conform to the will of God. They had searched for prophecies which could be interpreted to exalt themselves, and to show how God despised all other nations. It was their proud boast that the Messiah was to come as a king, conquering His enemies, and treading down the heathen in His wrath. Thus they had excited the hatred of their rulers.[223]

Then in Revelation, the mutating Lamb even meets those expectations when the great harlot and her daughters, the beasts and their horns, and

---

[223] *The Desire of Ages*, pp. 65, 66.

the dragon and his angels make war against Him. The Lamb overcomes "them because he is the Lord of lords and the King of kings" (17:14). "Even those who pierced him ... will mourn," saying, "Fall on us and hide us from the face of him who sits on the throne and from the wrath of the Lamb!" (1:7; 6:16). Further, "out of the mouth" of the Rider on the white horse "comes a sharp sword with which to strike down the nations ... He treads the winepress of the fury of the wrath of God Almighty" (19:15).

The issues that confronted the early church revolved around the origin, identity, and authority of Jesus. The life of Jesus of Nazareth was scrutinized in the light of OT prophecies, types, rituals, and characters. For these reasons, the NT writers not only argued for Jesus' Messiahship; they also advanced the argument to an entirely new level, claiming that Jesus of Nazareth is not only the anticipated Messiah, but also preexisted and is divine. In this sense, Revelation shares the same theological and contextual background with the other NT books.

CONCLUSION

The "Revelation of Jesus" is infused with Christological names, titles, designations, roles, and imageries. We have noted at least two passages in Revelation that contain a high concentration of these (1:5–7; 19:11–16). Just as the Rider of the white horse is soaked in blood, so is the passage bathed in Jesus' names and titles. However, the *actual* visions in 1:12–16, 5:1–8, and 12:1–9 are intended to capture numerous portraits of Christ as alluded to in the Old and New Testaments. While discussing the life of Jesus, a Christian author wrote, "The true interpreter must come. The One whom all these types prefigured must explain their significance."[224] Jesus not only came to explain their significance, but actually He was the Significance.

---

[224] Ibid., pp. 33, 34.

15.
EPHESUS: HIM WHO HOLDS THE SEVEN STARS

To the angel of the church in Ephesus write: These are the words of him who holds the seven stars in his right hand and walks among the seven golden lampstands. I know your deeds, your hard work and your perseverance. I know that you cannot tolerate wicked people, that you have tested those who claim to be apostles but are not, and have found them false. You have persevered and have endured hardships for my name, and have not grown weary. Yet I hold this against you: You have forsaken the love you had at first. Consider how far you have fallen! Repent and do the things you did at first. If you do not repent, I will come to you and remove your lampstand from its place. But you have this in your favor: You hate the practices of the Nicolaitans, which I also hate. Whoever has ears, let them hear what the Spirit says to the churches. To the one who is victorious, I will give the right to eat from the tree of life, which is in the paradise of God. (Revelation 2:1–7)

JESUS IN EPHESUS

The Seven Stars, Seven Lampstands, and Jesus

Jesus' Right Hand. To the Ephesians, Jesus was introduced as the One "who holds the seven stars in his right hand and walks among the seven golden lampstands." The "seven stars" are the "seven angels of the seven churches," while the seven lampstands are "the seven churches" (Rev. 1:20).

Note that Jesus holds the seven stars in His right hand. Among other things, the right hand signifies power and unlimited authority. "Your right hand, O Lord was majestic in power. Your right hand, O Lord shattered the enemy" (Exod. 15:6). After seeing the vision of the "Son of Man," John "fell as though dead." However, Jesus came and placed His right hand on John and revived him (see Rev. 1:17). The Lord's right hand is able to both shatter the enemies and revive fallen saints.

The use of the right hand or the act of holding someone or something in the right hand suggests ownership and security, for Jesus said, "no one can snatch them out of my hand. My Father who has given them to me is greater than all; no one can snatch them out of my Father's hand" (John 10:28, 29). If no one (including Satan) can snatch them out from His grip, and especially if God does not forsake His subjects, then the power to either remain or walk out from His hand rests solely on those being held.

Jesus said, "no one can snatch them out of my hand. My Father who has given them to me is greater than all; no one can snatch them out of my Father's hand" (John 10:28, 29). If no one (including Satan) can snatch them out from His grip, and especially if God does not forsake His subjects, then the power to either remain or walk out from His hand rests solely on those being held.

<u>Stars Shine in Jesus' Hand.</u> Because Jesus also appeared to the believers in Sardis as holding seven stars, an elaborate discussion on the definition and significance of this imagery will be provided in chapters 19 and 20. Also, the idea of wearing a long robe and walking among the seven golden lampstands signifies Jesus' priestly roles. For discussion on this, refer to chapter 13.

<u>Jesus at the Center of the Church and Heaven.</u> Jesus "walks among the seven golden lampstands [churches]." The Greek word translated "among" is *miseō*, which literally means "in the midst," "middle," or

"at the center" of something or some persons. Jesus is here seen walking around in the middle or center of the seven churches. The same word is used in Revelation 5:6, where "the Lamb" is seen "standing in the center [*miseō*] of the throne" in heaven. What does this tell us about Jesus? In chapters 4, 5, and 7, the throne, with "him who sat on it," is presented as the nerve center of all that goes on in heaven, earth, and under the earth and sea. That throne is surrounded by "four living creatures," "seven spirits of God," "twenty-four elders," "those who were sealed: 144,000 from all the tribes of Israel," a great multitude from every nation "that no one could count," and myriads of angels that number "ten thousand times ten thousand." In the center of this spectacular worship scene in heaven stands Jesus.

He who is at the center of what goes on in the church, world, and heaven was the One who was rejected, tortured, and killed by evil men at Calvary. In the book of Revelation, the same Person who occupies the center of both worlds actually longs to be at the center of our individual lives and homes. "Here I am!" He declares, "I stand at the door and knock. If anyone hears my voice and opens the door, I will come in and eat with him, and he with me" (Rev. 3:20).

The Ephesians and Jesus

The One who holds the "seven stars" and "walks among the seven lampstands" says to the Ephesians, "I know your deeds" (Rev. 2:2). He then proceeds to itemize the nature of those deeds as follows:

Good deeds	Bad deeds	Challenge
"hard work," "perseverance," "endurance"	"you have forsaken your first love"	"Repent and do the things you did at first"
"cannot tolerate wicked men"	"remember the height from which you have fallen"	"remember the height"
Arguing and contending with "false prophets," "the Nicolaitans," and "have not grown weary."		

Although Jesus commends them for their noble deeds, He also points out their weaknesses and how to amend them. Three aspects of these divine assessments are discussed as follows: 1) the nature of their "first love," the "height from which they have fallen," and "the things [they] did first," 2) the relationship between these noble deeds and their "first love" experience, and 3) the divine call to "remember," "repent," and "do" the things they did at first.

The "first love," "first works," and "height"

Introduction. A relationship exists between the saints' "first love" experience, the things they "did at first," and "the height" from which they have fallen. The text says that the Ephesians had reached a spiritual height because they did certain deeds of righteousness at the initial stages of their Christian life. However, because they no longer "do the things [they] did at first," they have fallen from that height. This scenario begs these questions: What was their "first love"? What did that love compel them to do? What was the nature of the height from which they had fallen?

Things They Did at First. Acts 19 documents the experiences of the Ephesians' first encounter with Christianity. Paul reasoned with the Jews in Ephesus for three months in the synagogue, but "when they refused to believe … Paul left them." He then taught the believing "Jews and Greeks" in the "lecture hall of Tyrannus" for two years (vv. 8–10). Paul's teaching was accompanied with "extraordinary miracles" to the extent that 1) "fear fell on them [the believers]," and the "name of the Lord Jesus was magnified," 2) "many who had believed came confessing and telling their deeds," 3) those who had practiced magic brought their books worth 50,000 silver coins and burned them in public,[225] and 4) "the word

---

[225] If one silver coin is a denarius, a day's wage in today's equivalent would be $80 (that is, at $10/hour). That means that 50,000 silver coins would be about $400,000 and $600,000.

of the Lord grew mightily and prevailed." The following table documents these deeds of righteousness:

First Love	First works	Results
Fear	Daily heard the word of God for "two years"	"name of the Lord was magnified"
Reverence	"many who believed ... confessed" their sins.	"word of the Lord grew mightily and prevailed"
Awe	Magicians stopped their art and burned their books in public.	Silversmiths lost business, "temple of the great goddess Artemis will be discredited"

The First-love Experience. Unlike most churches, the church at Ephesus was built on rare precious gems. Some of those gems include "fear," "reverence," and "awe." Concerning these, the author of Hebrews wrote, "worship God acceptably with reverence and awe, for our 'God is a consuming fire'" (Heb. 12:28, 29). Notice that it was fear and reverence for God that moved the Ephesians to believe in the Lord Jesus Christ, confess their evil deeds, cease their magic arts, and burn their books. As they, in fear and trembling, emptied themselves of these things, the "word of the Lord grew mightily" and the "name of the Lord Jesus was magnified." Since the "fear of the Lord is the beginning of wisdom" (Prov. 1:7; 9:10), the Ephesian church was founded on that commodity. If these aspects constituted their "first love" and "first works" experiences, then what is the significance of the height from which they had fallen?

The Spiritual Height. Note the entries in the "Results" column. The text says that "the name of the Lord was *magnified*" and the "word of the Lord *grew mightily*" (emphasis supplied). The terms "magnified" and "grew mightily" denote some type of an upward and outward increase. The two things that grew and increased among the Ephesians were the "name of the Lord" and the "word of the Lord." If the name and word denote the character, life, and power of Christ, then these were perfectly reproduced in the lives of the Ephesian saints. The "name" and the "word of the Lord" were established and grounded in the "fear of the Lord" and grew and increased mightily within the lives of the believers. Therein lies the height that they had reached when they first believed.[226]

Ephesians' Current "works" and the "first love"

The church that began with fear, awe, and reverence now demonstrates a militant spirit as they battle with wicked men, dispute with false apostles, and hate the practices of the Nicolaitans. Also note that the Ephesians are commended for their hard work and the ability to endure hardship and not become weary. Could it be that an independent and militant spirit replaced the spirit of fear, love, awe, reverence, and dependence on God?

Challenge, Warning, and Promises

A Call to Remember. The Orator issues a challenge, followed by a series of promises. He urges the church to "remember," "repent," and "do" the things she did before. The Orator does not specify what these things were.[227] However, in using the word "remember," He appeals to their past experiences and memories. John often applies the same method in 1 John. He wrote, "I do not write to you because you do not know the truth, but because you know it." "See that what you have heard from the beginning remains in you" (1 John 2:21, 24). These and other passages do not indicate the actual contents of what they may have heard or known, but are intended to evoke their memories.

---

[226] For further discussion on the concepts of "name," "word," and "commandment" as the key issues among the seven churches, refer to chapter 21 of this study.

[227] Revelation 21:7−8 identifies two classes of people: The overcomers who inherit the kingdom and those who are cast into the lake of fire. Here the "overcomers" are contrasted with the "cowardly, the unbelieving, the vile, the murderers, the sexually immoral, those who practice magic arts, the idolaters and all liars." In Acts 19:19, many who practiced magic arts brought their books and burnt them. There is a possibility that some who "fell from the height" must be involved in these. Perhaps those who forsook witchcraft and burned their books also returned to their old ways. Since we do not have clear contextual evidence, we can only speculate.

<u>All True Repentance Begins with Remembering</u>. A call to remember is important because all true repentance begins with recalling the past. Such was the case with the prodigal son. Luke wrote, "When he came to his senses, he said, 'How many of my father's hired men have food to spare, and here I am starving to death! I will set out and go back to my father and say to him: Father I have sinned against heaven and against you. I am no longer worthy to be called your son; make me like one of your hired men.' So he got up and went to his father." (Luke 15:17).

<u>Remembrance, A Means to an End</u>. The call to remember is not an end in itself. Its main purpose is to evoke the best experiences of the past in order to facilitate a genuine repentance. As repentant souls remember the past, especially their "first love" experience and the lofty spiritual height from which they may have fallen, they have to come to their senses. Then they must say with the prodigal son, "I will set out and go back to my father" and then do the works they did at first, thus reclaiming both the lofty height and "first love" experience. The following diagram attempts to capture these discussions:

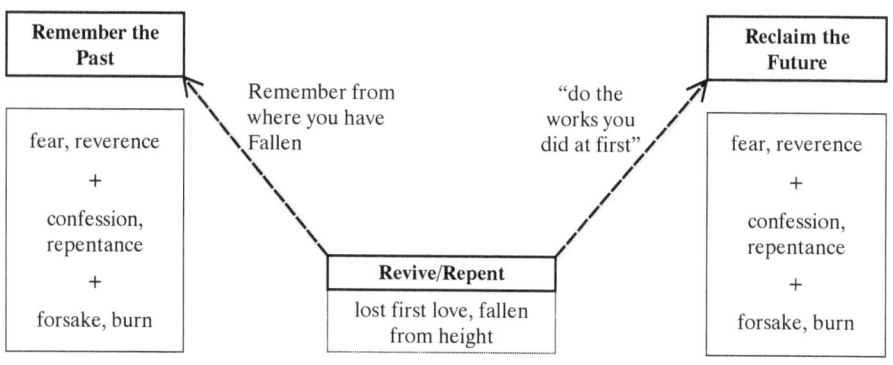

The Ephesians' first-love experience went from fear and reverence to public verbal confession, which then led to noble deeds and works of love. They then proceeded to burn the books that had sustained their livelihood—a fitting testament to the fact that they had forsaken their evil practices and witchcraft. This shows that a complete repentance may begin with the fear of the Lord and verbal confession, but it must translate into real works. The forsaking of cherished sins and burning of "books" must take place. Only when the soul is fully emptied of self and sin can the name and the word of the Lord grow mightily in one's life.

Rewards and Promises. If the Ephesians repent, Jesus promises them the "right to eat from the tree of life, which is in the paradise of God." However, should they refuse to repent, the Orator threatens to remove their lampstand from its place.

> *The Ephesians' first-love experience went from fear and reverence to public verbal confession, which then led to noble deeds and works of love. They then proceeded to burn the books that had sustained their livelihood—a fitting testament to the fact that they had forsaken their evil practices and witchcraft.*

OPPONENTS IN EPHESUS

Various Perspectives

Several opponents are mentioned in each of the seven letters, as well as Acts and other Pauline epistles. A comprehensive study on these characters and their related works are important for a number of reasons. First, being that such approaches serve to reveal the dynamics and relationship that exist between the villainous characters in both sections of the book (Rev. 1–3 and 4–22). Second, understanding the characters and their activities in both sections of the book serves to reinforce the fact that the text was comprehensible and applicable to John and his initial audience. Finally, such an approach serves to enhance our understanding and appreciation of the entire text. Therefore, in this study, we shall discuss the opponents in the church of Ephesus as revealed in Revelation, Acts, and Ephesians.

<u>Opponents According to Revelation</u>. The Ephesian oracle features two groups of opponents. The first group is identified as the "wicked people." Who are they, and why are they described as such? The wicked people are further defined as those who had "claim[ed] to be apostles but are not." If these people had claimed to be sent of God, then they were God-believing and good moral people (see Rom. 2:17; 10:2).

The "wicked people" and the "wicked works." The activities of the opponents ("false prophets," "liars," and "antichrists") in the epistles of John are described as "wicked works" (2 John 11). Whether or not a relationship exists between these characters and the activities in these two documents is unclear. However, several things are clear: 1) The opponents in both books have antichristological tenets, 2) Among others, the opponents in both books are called "false prophets," 3) Opponents in both books are God-believing, good moral people who "are zealous for God" (Rom. 10:2; 2:17),[228] and 4) They are called "wicked people" and involved in "wicked works," probably because of their rejection of Jesus as the Christ.

The Teaching and Practices of the Nicolaitans. The second group of opponents consists of the Nicolaitans, who are described as being involved in evil practices. While the Ephesians are accused of being involved in these practices, those in Pergamum are charged with holding to the *"teaching* of the Nicolaitans" (Rev. 2:15, emphasis supplied). Who are the Nicolaitans, and what were their teachings and practices?[229] Did the "wicked men," "false apostles" and "Nicolaitans" have any role in the believers' fall from their lofty

---

[228] A classic example of these opponents are "Pharisees." A good Pharisee defined himself this way: "God, I thank you that I am not like other people—robbers, evildoers, adulterers—or even like this tax collector. I fast twice a week and give a tenth of all I get" (Luke 18:11, 12). And he was correct; he certainly did all the right religious things ..., but for the wrong reasons. It is possible that John dealt with the same people.

[229] Scholars propose various theories to determine the identify of the Nicolaitans. Maxwell, cites Irenaeus (a second century church father) and says that the Nicolaitans were Christians who were indifferent about sexual purity. See C. Mervyn Maxwell, *God Cares, Vol. 2*, pp. 99–100. Ferrerro, Alberto discusses various views which associate these opponents with Gnostics and others, and wonders if Nicolaitans were associated with Priscillians. See his article, "Prscillian and Nicolaitism." *Vigilae Christianae* 52, no. 4 (November 1998): 382–392. Stefanovic, however, makes an interesting observation when he sees a parrallel between the Nicolaitans and Balaamites. See *The Revelation of Jesus Christ*, pp. 115–116. For various reasons, we shall go with Stefanovic. The main reason being that

heights? The text does not provide any direct answers to these questions. However, we shall investigate what Luke and Paul said about their opponents.

Opponents According to Acts. As indicated earlier, Acts 19–20 contains the history of the Ephesians' first encounter with Christianity. Luke described certain opponents as "savage wolves" (20:29). These wolves were all Jews and fell under one of two categories. One group consisted of the "obstinate" Jews who "refused to believe [in Jesus] and publicly maligned the Way" (19:9). Paul reasoned with this group for more than three months in the synagogue, but they rejected him, his message, and his Jesus (19:8, 9).

The second group consisted of certain Jews who believed at first, but later abandoned their faith. Having this group in mind, Paul stated in his final address, "I know that after I leave, savage wolves will *come in among you* and will not spare the flock. Even *from your own number* men will arise and distort the truth in order to draw away disciples after them. So be on your guard!" (Acts 20:29–31, emphasis supplied). Paul further divided these "believing wolves" into two groups: those who "will come in among you" and those already "from your own number," referring to some Jews who would be baptized after Paul's departure and some who were already members of the faith at the time. The following diagram shows these "wolves."

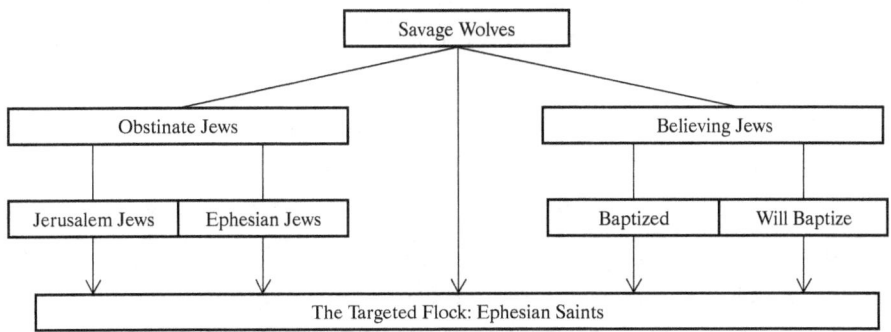

At this stage, it is also important to insert one more group: the twelve men—the former disciples of John the Baptist who were re-baptized into

---

John frequently uses multiple names and designations to identify a group or a single character. And we think that this falls into this category. See the discussions on the opponents in chapter 20 and 22.

Christ by Paul (see Acts 9:7). These men had previously been baptized into John's baptism, but upon hearing about Jesus, they were re-baptized. When Paul laid his hands on them, they received the Holy Spirit and spoke in tongues (see 19:4–6). Then when Paul "entered the synagogue and spoke boldly for three months," these "twelve disciples" were with him. Afterwards, when Paul left the synagogue, "he took the [twelve] disciples with him" (v. 9).

Three years later, when Paul gave his final address to the Ephesian elders at Miletus, some or most of these men may have been present. This group is emphasized because some among them may have become "savage wolves" after Paul's departure. He said with confidence, "I know that after I leave, savage wolves will come in among you and will not spare the flock. Even from *your own number* men will arise and distort the truth in order to draw away disciples after them." (Acts 20:29–31, emphasis supplied).

<u>Opponents According to Ephesians</u>. In the letter to the Ephesians, Paul did not directly mention any opponents. There are, however, two muted references to opponents of Jewish descent. The first reference is in 2:11, where they are called "the circumcision" party. This party consisted mostly of Jewish Christians who pushed for Gentile converts to be circumcised. In Ephesus, this was not a peripheral issue. Paul wrote extensively about and against this group and refuted their claims in three of the six chapters (3–5).

The second group of opponents, according to Paul, consisted of "those who are disobedient." At the time the apostle wrote this letter, the disobedient group was at work, for the text says, "the spirit who is now at work in those who are disobedient" (Eph. 2:2). These are not merely unconverted or unevangelized Gentiles per se, but this group consisted of Jews who were disobedient to the truth. In other words, they may have known or had access to certain truths, but forsook or simply refused to obey them. Instead, they allowed a different spirit, a spirit of disobedience to dictate their lives.

<u>Analysis of Opponents</u>. Are the opponents according to John, Luke, and Paul the same? There is insufficient information to draw this conclusion. Nevertheless, we have far less reason to think otherwise.

Certain characteristics are common to all opponents, as summarized below.[230]

Sources	Opponents' Designations	Nationality	Activities
Revelation (John)	"wicked men," "false apostles"	Jews	"endured hardships for my name's sake" (Rev. 2:3)
	"Nicolaitans"	Jews	"practice of Nicolaitans"
Acts (Luke)	"Savage wolves," "obstinate Jews," former Jewish Christians	Jews	"anti-Way," "name of the Lord" + "word of the Lord"
	Ephesian locksmiths	Gentiles	Opposed the Pauline team and Jews
Ephesians (Paul)	"the Circumcision" party, "the disobedient"	Jews	Circumcision + Jesus, "disobedient" + "spirit"
1 and 2 John	"antichrists," "false prophets," "lairs," "deceivers"	Jews	"wicked works," "deny Christ," claim another anointing and Spirit, "deny the Lord's name"

Here we make several important observations:

1. *Gentile and Jewish Opponents*. First, the "locksmith" related issue is partly for financial and partly for religious reasons. Although it was an issue that threatened the church and its leadership at Ephesus, it is not mentioned in other writings. Apart from the locksmiths, the remaining opponents are all Jews—both Jerusalem and diaspora Jews, as well as obstinate and disobedient Jews and current and future believers.
2. *The "name" of Jesus as the Core Issue*. The core issue that runs through all of the previously mentioned sources has to do with the "name," which is mentioned variously by different authors. Luke called it "the Way," "name of the Lord," "word of God," or "Jesus." In Revelation, the Orator commends the Ephesians for enduring "hardships for my

---

[230] We have not discussed the opponents in the epistles of John because we do not know if they were written to the Ephesians. However, they are included in the following table because they share many similarities with Revelation, considering that both were written by the same author.

name" (Rev. 2:3). In Ephesians, Paul presented Jesus as the destroyer of the "wall of separation," thus uniting the circumcised and uncircumcised parties. Then in the epistles of John, the opponents are associated with either denying that "Jesus is the Christ," failing to "acknowledge Jesus Christ," or the "Name" of Jesus (2 John 7; 3 John 7).

3. *Strong Anti-Jesus Sentiment Among the Opponents.* A sentiment *against* Jesus comes through quite strongly. The opponents of the church at Ephesus were obstinate and disobedient, especially they "refused to believe and publicly maligned the Way" (Acts 19:9). In Revelation, the opponents are actively engaged in fighting against Jesus, and He is either threatening to fight back (see Rev. 2:16, 23) or actually fighting back (see Rev. 6:2). Revelation also states that the entire diabolical confederacy "will make war against the Lamb, but the Lamb will overcome them" (Rev. 17:14; 19:11–21). Note that the war is "against the Lamb," which is against Jesus as the Christ. This would, therefore, make the opponents the antichrists. Although the concept of engaging in warfare against Christ is used in Revelation, the exact term ("antichrist") is not used there. John, however, designated his opponents in 1 and 2 John as "antichrists" (1 John 2:18; 4:3; 2 John 7).

4. *"Wicked works" from "false prophets" and "wicked men."* In Revelation, John described the false prophets as "wicked men," whereas in 2 John, the activities of the false prophets are called "wicked works" (v. 11). One wonders if the wicked men of Revelation produce those wicked works in 2 John.

5. *Opponents Are Mostly Former Believers.* A final observation concerns prima facie evidence that the opponents of Revelation, Acts, Ephesians, and 1 and 2 John are former members of the faith community. In Acts, Luke identified a segment of the opponents as former members. These opponents have not only forsaken their faith, but are also trying to persuade other members to join them (see Acts 20:29–31). The opponents in 1 and 2 John are similar to those whom Luke describes. "They [the antichrists/false prophets] went out from us, but they did not really belong to us. For if they had belonged to

us, they would have remained with us; but their going showed that none of them belonged to us" (1 John 2:19). In 2 Thessalonians, Paul wrote about a great "apostasy" or "falling away" that must precede the second coming. Whether the opponents in Revelation, especially those described in Ephesus, were former members is unclear.[231] However, note the second beast of Rev. 13:11. When that beast came up out of the earth, it resembled a lamb but later changed and spoke like a dragon; a clear indication that certain members of the faith community had, in due time, turned away from and against Christ. The same concept is also apparent in 2 Peter and Hebrews, where former members fall away from the faith and set themselves against God.[232]

Acts	1 and 2 John	2 Thessalonians	Revelation
"from your own number" (20:30)	"they went out from us" (2:19)	"falling away first" (2:3)	Two lamb-like horns of the land-beast (13: 11–18)
"obstinate Jews" (19:9)	"wicked work" (2 John 11)		"wicked people" (2:2)
"ravenous wolves," "many will arise" (20:29–30)	"false prophet and deceivers" (4:1–3; 2 John 7)	"man of lawlessness shall come" (2:9)	"false apostles" (2:2)
"maligned the Way" (19:9)	"antichrist" (4:1–3; 2 John 7)	those disobedient to Jesus will be punished (1:7–8)	dishonor the name (2:3)

Summary

The similarities between the opponents, their nationality, the core issues, and their attitude toward Jesus Christ in each of these books is revealing on a number of levels. First, these similarities suggest that John,

---

[231] A detailed discussion on this will be provided in a later work when we study Revelation 13. Also, note the language in Revelation 14:4: "They follow the Lamb wherever he goes." Implied here is the concept of faithfulness and perseverance, while those described in 13:11 may have disassociated themselves from the Lamb.

[232] Similar references are prominent in 2 Peter 2:20–22; Matt. 24:15–25 and Hebrews 6:4–8.

Paul, Luke, and other early writers dealt with similar (if not the same) opponents and issues. Second, Revelation's socio-cultural background is nearly identical to that of the other NT books.

RELATIONSHIP BETWEEN REVELATION 1-3 AND 4-22

In this section, a set of common materials between Revelation 1-3 and 4-22 will be analyzed. The purpose is to show that the early readers who read and understood the messages of Revelation 1-3 could also understand those of 4-22, and that these two messages are almost identical. However, if there are any differences, those differences are minimal.

The Tree of Life. As previously discussed, the repentant soul is promised the right to "eat from the tree of life, which is in the paradise of God" (2:7). This promise is fulfilled twenty chapters later. "On each side of the river stood the tree of life, bearing twelve crops of fruit, yielding its fruits every month. And the leaves of the tree are for the healing of the nations" (22:2).

In the messages of Revelation 1-3, the promise consisting of the tree of life is made only to the believers at Ephesus. This does not mean that the overcomers from the other churches would not have access to this tree, but that the saints in Ephesus could relate to this promise on a more personal level. It is a promise made *to* them, and seeing the same promise reiterated in chapter 22 could have awakened a keen interest in them. Perhaps if I was a member of the Ephesus church when this letter was first read, I would have wanted to know if John actually saw anyone wandering around that tree. If he did, I would be even more curious to know if he could recognize *anyone* in my church. As we proceed to discuss the other six churches, the relationship between the two sections of Revelation will become more pronounced.

16.

SMYRNA: HIM WHO IS THE FIRST AND LAST

> To the angel of the church in Smyrna write: These are the words of him who is the First and the Last, who died and came to life again. I know your afflictions and your poverty—yet you are rich! I know the slander of those who say they are Jews and are not, but are a synagogue of Satan. Do not be afraid of what you are about to suffer. I tell you, the devil will put some of you in prison to test you, and you will suffer persecution for ten days. Be faithful, even to the point of death, and I will give you life as your victor's crown. Whoever has ears, let them hear what the Spirit says to the churches. The one who is victorious will not be hurt at all by the second death. (Revelation 2:8–11)

JESUS IN SMYRNA AND THE IMPLICATION

Jesus appeared to the believers at Smyrna as "the First and the Last, who died and came to life again." Just as in the Ephesian address, the dual title here mirrors the condition of the church in a number of ways, but for our purposes, we will discuss only two of them. First, these and other designations were carefully employed to address some pressing issues that the churches had. To the believers at Smyrna, Jesus' designations of "First and the Last" and "who died and came to life again" were intended to address issues surrounding death and resurrection. Second, the same titles were also intended to address the issues of doubts, fears, and uncertainty in the midst of affliction.

Jesus as the "First and the Last" to the Dead

<u>Jesus as the "First and the Last."</u> To the church at Smyrna, Christ is identified as the one "who is the First and the Last" and "who died and came to life again." Earlier in our discussion on Revelation 1:4–8, we observed two aspects of the title "First and the Last" (Rev. 2:8; 1:17). The first one was that this title for Jesus is thematically related to two other titles: "Alpha and Omega" and the "Beginning and the End," which are used for God. The second was that all of these divine titles are actually applied to both Jesus and God. However, we did not adequately discuss any contextual, theological, or ecclesiastical significance that any of these titles may have had for the believers' lives. We will do this now.

What, then, do these titles, "the First and the Last" in particular, teach us about the condition of the believers in Smyrna? As stated earlier, this title encompasses 1) the issues surrounding the believers' death and resurrection and 2) uncertainties among the believers in the face of persecution.

<u>Believers' Death and Resurrection (Revelation 1–3)</u>. In both instances where the title "First and Last" is attributed to Jesus, it is used in association with His death and resurrection, but therein contains a subtle message addressed to the saints. In fact, these veiled or somewhat indirect messages are intended to address issues surrounding death and resurrection among believers. Consider Rev. 1:17–18 and 2:8–11:

Revelation 1:17–18	Revelation 2:8–11
"I am the *First and the Last*. I am the living One. I was dead and behold I am alive for ever and ever! And I have the *keys of death and Hades*" (emphasis supplied).	"the *First and the Last*, who died and came to life again ... Be faithful, to the point of death, and I will give you the *crown of life* ... He who overcomes will not be hurt at all by the second death" (emphasis supplied).

<u>Analysis of the Passages</u>. A few observations can be made. First, in both texts, Jesus' designation as "First and the Last" is used in conjunction with His own death and resurrection. For instance, in Rev. 1:17–18,

the designation is used with "I was dead and behold I am alive for ever." The same is also true for Rev. 2:10–11. Second, the implication of Jesus' titles and deeds for the believers' lives are stressed. The fact that He is seen having the "keys of death and Hades" (Rev. 1:18) and rewards overcomers with the "crown of life" speaks to the believers at Smyrna. The indirect message communicated here is that the One who died and is now "alive forever and ever" has the power to bring to life the saints who had died, are dying, or would die in the future. This perhaps is why the churches are urged to "be faithful even to the point of death" (Rev. 2:10) and not "shrink from death" (Rev. 12:11). Furthermore, among other things, a crown of life is promised to those who overcome Satan "by the blood of the Lamb" and by their own blood.

The use of Jesus' titles and deeds in the text is not merely to display His accomplishments. These designations have a direct bearing on the condition of the churches being addressed.

Believers' Death and Resurrection. All of Revelation is saturated with the concepts of death, resurrection, and final rewards. The following table shows the pervasiveness of these teachings: (See Table that follows).

The Implication of Jesus' name for the Believers. The use of Jesus' titles and deeds in the text is not merely to display His accomplishments. These designations have a direct bearing on the condition of the churches being addressed. Revelation explicitly states that there were known deaths from John's past [e.g., "Antipas" of Pergamum (Rev. 2:13), "the souls of those who had been slain" (Rev. 6:9), "prophets," "saints," and "servants" (Rev. 18:24, 19:2)].[233]

The Impending Persecution and Death. Revelation also speaks of an impending worldwide persecution that would last for "a while" or "ten

---

[233] By the time the Gospel of John was written, the apostle Peter had already died (see John 21:19).

Titles	"I am the First and the Last. I am the living One. I was dead and behold I am alive for ever and ever! And I have the keys of death and Hades" (1:17, 18)	"the First and the Last, who died and came to life again … Be faithful, even to the point of death, and I will give you the crown of life. … He who overcomes will not be hurt at all by the second death" (2:10, 11)	"I am the Alpha and the Omega, the Beginning and the End … He who overcomes will inherit all this. But the cowardly … will be in the fiery lake" (21:6–8)		"Behold, I am coming soon! My reward is with me, and I will give to everyone according to what he has done. I am the Alpha and the Omega, the First and the Last, and Beginning and the End" (22:12, 13)
Keys	"I was dead and behold I am alive for ever and ever! And I have the keys of death and Hades" (1:17, 18)	"these are the words of Him who is holy and true, who holds the keys of David" (3:7)	The rider on the pale horse was named "Death, and Hades was following close behind him" (6:8)	"the [fallen] star was given the key to the shaft of the Abyss" (9:1)	"an angel coming down out of heaven, having the key to the Abyss and holding in his hand a great chain. He seized the dragon … and bound him for a thousand years" (20:1, 2)	"The sea gave up the dead that were in it, and death and Hades gave up the dead that were in them …" (20:12)	"Another book was opened which is the book of life … Then death and Hades were thrown into the lake of fire. The lake of fire is the second death. If anyone's name is not found written in the book of life, he was thrown into the lake of fire" (20:12–15)
OK To Die	"the First and the Last, who died and came to life again … Be faithful, even to the point of death, and I will give you the crown of life. … He who overcomes will not be hurt at all by the second death" (2:8–11)	"They [the slain souls] called out in a loud voice, 'how long Sovereign Lord … and avenge our blood?' … wait a little longer, until" those who "were to be killed … was completed" (6:9–11)	"They overcame him by the blood of the Lamb and by the word of their testimony; they did not love their lives so much as to shrink from death" (12:11)		"This calls for patient endurance on the part of the saints who obey God's commandment and remain faithful to Jesus. Then I heard a voice from heaven say; 'Write: Blessed are the dead who die in the Lord from now on.' 'Yes,' 'says the Spirit, 'they will rest from their labor, for their deeds will follow them'" (14:12, 13)

16. Smyrna: Him Who Is the First and Last

Resurrection									
"the First and the Last, who died and came to life again ... Be faithful to the point of death and I will give you the crown of life.... He who overcomes will not be hurt at all by the second death" (2:10, 11)		"They [the slain souls] called out in a loud voice, 'how long Sovereign Lord ... and avenge our blood?' ... wait a little longer, until" those who "were to be killed ... was completed" (6:9–11)		"after the three and the half days, a breath of life from God entered them and they stood on their feet" (11:11)		"And I saw the souls of those who had been beheaded because of their testimony about Jesus and because of the word of God. They had not worshiped the beast or its image and had not received its mark on their foreheads or their hands. They came to life and reigned with Christ a thousand years" (20:4)		"The sea gave up the dead that were in it, and death and Hades gave up the dead that were in them ... Then death and Hades were thrown into the lake of fire. The lake of fire is the second death. If anyone's name was not found written in the book of life, he was thrown into the lake of fire" (20:13–15)	

Rewards									
"and behold I am alive for ever and ever" (1:18)	"eat from the tree of life" (2:7; 22:2, 14, 19)	"I will give you the crown of life" (2:10; 3:11)	"book of life" (3:5; 13:8; 17:8; 20:12, 15; 21:27)	"living creatures" (4:6)	"seal of the living God" (7:2); "living Father" (John 6:57)	"springs of living water" (7:17; 21:6; 22:1, 17)	"swore by Him who lives for ever and ever" (10:6)	"breath of life from God" (11:11)	"and they will live for ever and ever" (22:5)

days." That persecution would target those who "keep the commandments of God" and "have the testimony of Jesus." The text reveals that many would be killed.

Believers Encouraged to Face Death. In the face of this, the saints are encouraged not to fear death. In fact, Revelation pronounces blessings upon those who would be killed. "Blessed are the dead who die in the Lord from now on" (Rev. 14:13; see also Matt. 10:28). This is contrasted with the unbelievers' quest for death in the end of time. The period covering the seven last plagues and the Second Coming is presented as a day of terror for the wicked. During this time, the opponents of Christ will not only cry to the rocks to "fall on us and hide us from the ... wrath of the Lamb," but also "seek death." "But [they] will not find it; they will long to die, but death will elude them" (Rev. 6:16; 9:6). In the light of this, it would seem preferable to "die in the Lord from now on" than to "seek death" with the wicked later.

Death, Dead, Dying, and Jesus. To the dead, dying, and soon-to-die, Jesus comes through as the "First and the Last" and the "Living One" who "holds the keys of death and Hades." He is not only able to bring the dead back to life, but He also promises them great rewards such as the "crown of life," "tree of life," "water of life," and eternal life (Rev. 20:4).

Death, Resurrection, and Eternal Life in New Testament Literature

<u>Johannine Books</u>. The issues of death, resurrection, and eternal life are not unique to Revelation. The other Johannine writings and all the NT literature discuss these themes extensively, perhaps an indication that these were serious issues during that era. The following table provides a general survey of these occurrences (especially in the Johannine books).

What John's four other books teach concerning life, death, and resurrection are similar to that of Revelation. However, the tone, mode, and tempo are increased in John's latter works, as seen in the following examples:

16. Smyrna: Him Who Is the First and Last

Titles	"eternal life" (1 John 5:20)	"Word of life" (1 John 1:1)	"I am the resurrection and the life" (John 11:25)	"bread of life" (John 6:35)	"leaving water" (John 4:10; 7:38)	"I am the way and the truth and the life" (John 14:6)	
Possessions	"in him was life" (John 1:4)	"for as the Father has life in himself, so he has granted the Son to have life in himself" (John 5:26)	"The words I have spoken to you are spirit and they are life" (John 6:63)	"You have the words of eternal life" (John 6:68)	"my flesh is the real food" (John 6:55)	"my blood is real drink" (John 6:55)	"spring of water welling up to eternal life" (4:14; 7:38)
Prerequisite	"eternal life" (John 3:15, 16; 4:14)	"springs of water" (John 4:14, 38, 39)	"my blood is real drink" (John 6:55)	"If anyone eats of this bread, he will live forever" (John 6:51, 58)			
Urged to die	"The man who loves his life will lose it, while the man who hates his life in this world will keep it for eternal life. Whoever serves me must follow me; and where I am, my servant also will be" (John 12:25, 26)			"And we ought to lay down our lives for our brothers" (1 John 3:16).			
Resurrection	"for just as the Father raises the dead and gives them life, even so the Son gives life to whom He is pleased to give it" (John 5:21)	"a time is coming and has now come when the dead will hear the voice of the Son of God and those who hear will live" (John 5:25)	"Do not be amazed at this, for a time is coming when all who are in their graves will hear his voice and come out—those who have done good will rise to live, and those who have done evil will rise to be condemned" (John 5:28, 29)	This is God's will, "that I shall loose none of all that He has given me, but raise them up at the last day" (John 6:40, 44, 54)	"your brother will rise again" (John 11:23, 24)	"He who believes in me will live, even though he dies; and whoever lives and believes will never die" (John 11:25)	
Rewards	"eternal life" (John 6:40, 54).	"he will live forever" (John 6:51, 58).	"mansions" (John 14:2)				

1. *Subtle and Explicit Statements.* Unlike the Apocalypse, in the Gospel of John, the veil of subtlety is removed and the concepts of death, resurrection, and eternal life are explicitly developed. Let us take Jesus' designations as an example. In Revelation, He was merely identified as "the Beginning and the End." However, in the Gospel of John, Jesus assumes, among others, the dual identity of being both "the Resurrection and the Life."
2. *Jesus Possesses and Performs.* Jesus' designations, "eternal life," "Word of life," "bread of life," "water of life," and "life," are derived from the fact that He either possesses or has the capacity to perform what those designations suggest. For instance, He is called the "Word of life" in 1 John 1:1 because He has "the words of eternal life" (John 6:68). Similarly, He is described as "eternal life" (1 John 5:20) because He both possesses (see John 1:3; 5:26) and gives eternal life to those who come to Him (see John 4:14; 7:38). He is called the "bread of life" because He is both "the living bread that came down from heaven" and gives the true bread to those who come to Him (John 6:48, 51).
3. *Blessed to Die.* Similar to Revelation, the Gospel also urges believers not to shrink from death (see John 12:25, 26; 1 John 3:16).
4. *Resurrection.* As in Revelation, John's other books explicitly teach about the reality of a "last day" resurrection. However, in the Gospel, the resurrection of Lazarus serves as a guarantee or precursor to the last-day resurrection doctrine.
5. *Eternal Rewards and Punishments.* Both books teach that believers will rise to eternal life, while evildoers rise to eternal condemnation.
6. *Rewards and Incentives.* Finally, in Revelation, Jesus promises to give the overcomers "eternal life," "crown of life," "tree of life," and "water of life." These are rewards that Christ will give to believers in the future. Therefore, they are nuanced eschatologically. However, in the epistles and Gospel, the same commodities serve a dual purpose. They function as both end-time rewards and incentives that a believer can have here and now.

Acts and the Synoptic Traditions. The resurrection was indeed a contentious issue among the religious leaders in the first century. The Sadducees, who held that the Pentateuch had more inspired authority than other OT books did, denied the resurrection. However, the Pharisees believed in a literal, bodily resurrection. The Scripture records several instances where Jesus, Paul, or other apostles encountered this issue (see Matt. 22:23, 24; Mark 12:18–27; Acts 23:6–8).

Pauline Epistles. The Pauline epistles also indicate the resurrection as a debated issue. In 1 Thessalonians, he wrote, "Brothers, we do not want you to be ignorant about those who fall asleep, or to grieve like the rest of men, who have no hope ... For the Lord himself will come down from heaven, with a loud command ... and the dead in Christ will rise first" (4:13–16). The Thessalonian believers were "ignorant about those who fall asleep." This theological misunderstanding undoubtedly had implications for their attitude and practice. Paul therefore wrote to correct those erroneous understandings.

Further, the topic of the resurrection also proved to be a debated subject among the Gentiles. Consider, for instance, the Pauline address to the Epicurean and Stoic philosophers in Athens. Those gathered in the Areopagus Hall listened to Paul with great interest, but "when they heard about the resurrection of the dead, some of them sneered," and the discussion was terminated (Acts 17:32).

Petrine Epistles. The apostle Peter's two letters were circulated through a wider geographical location ["throughout Pontus, Galatia, Cappadocia, Asia, and Bithynia" (1 Peter 1:1)], which included the seven churches of Revelation. In his second letter, he wrote:

> Above all, you must understand that in the last days scoffers will come, scoffing and following their own evil desires. They will say, "Where is this 'coming' he promised? Ever since our ancestors *died*, everything goes on as it has since the beginning of creation."... But do not forget this one thing, dear friends:

> With the Lord a day is like a thousand years, and a thousand years are like a day. The Lord is not slow in keeping his promise, as some understand slowness. Instead he is patient with you, not wanting anyone to perish, but everyone to come to repentance. But the day of the Lord will come like a thief. (2 Peter 3:3, 4, 8–10, emphasis supplied)

Peter made important contributions to the issues of death and resurrection in the early church. First, he seemed distressed with some opponents whom he describes as "false prophets." These opponents were once believers but have left the fellowship and now actively deny "the Sovereign Lord who bought them" (2 Peter 2:1). They have "cleverly invented" and "introduce[d] destructive heresies" aimed at bringing the "way of truth into disrepute" (1:16; see also 2:1, 2). These opponents were not ignorant of the body of Scriptures. According to Peter, the concoction of their destructive heresies resulted from distorting Pauline and "other [possibly the Old Testament] Scriptures" (3:16).

Second, Peter mentioned that "Paul also wrote ... speaking in them of these matters" (3:15–16). By "these matters," Peter could have been referring to anything "hard" contained "in all his [Paul's] letters." However, the immediate context shows "these matters" to mean the contents of 1 and 2 Thessalonians, particularly the tension between the believers' death and Christ's apparent delay (1 Thess. 4:13–5:11; 2 Thess. 2:1–13).

Finally, note how Peter summed up the scoffers' arguments. He particularly combined Christ's delay and the issue of death and resurrection. The rhetorical question ("Where is this coming he promised?") may have been used by the false prophets to point out the reality that Christ has not yet returned as expected. However, the very next line, "Ever since our fathers died, everything goes on as it has since the beginning of creation," is intended to refute the claims against the resurrection. The false prophets seemed to have scoffed at the believers for holding onto the hope of Christ's return as older members began to die out. This is exactly the same argument Paul made in his two letters to the Thessalonians.

In this regard, John's teaching on Christ's delay, the believers' death, and the resurrection in Revelation and other books are similar to that of Petrine, Pauline, and other NT traditions.

CONTEXTUAL AND THEOLOGICAL ISSUES

Jesus as the "First and the Last" to the Dead, Dying, and Those About to Die

A broad survey of the topic of death and resurrection suggests the following:

Death and Resurrection Among Gentiles. The non-believing Gentiles, Sadducees, and certain Jewish and Gentile believers had issues concerning the doctrine of the resurrection. Following Paul's address at Athens, only one "member of Areopagus," Dionysius, and a "few [other] men became followers of Paul and believed" (Acts 17:34). This means that most of the Gentile thought leaders dismissed the teaching and described Paul as a "babbler" (v. 18). If all Gentile converts addressed in Revelation once held or still hold a similar concept about death, then them being unsettled on the topic of death and resurrection is likely.

> *Paul acknowledged a widespread ignorance among the believers. Perhaps the issue arose among younger believers or those living when the older ones began to die out, especially if they were taught that Jesus would return soon, possibly in their lifetime. However, His seeming delay, coupled with the death of older believers (including the apostles), challenged their own convictions and expectations.*

Death and Resurrection Issue Among Believers. In 1 Thessalonians, Paul acknowledged a widespread ignorance among the believers. Perhaps the issue arose among younger believers or those living when the older ones began to die out, especially if they were taught that Jesus would return soon, possibly in their lifetime. However, His seeming delay, coupled with the death of older believers (including the apostles), challenged their own convictions and expectations.

<u>Death, Resurrection and the Delay</u>. The early church expected Christ to return in their lifetime. Against such a backdrop, when the Lord's apostles began to die out, it affected the mood of the saints.

The Apostles Indicate the Delay and Their Own Death. These sentiments are fully reflected in the NT writings, particularly in how the apostles themselves shifted their own positions when they realized that they would not live to see the Lord return. When they began their ministry, they identified themselves with titles such as "apostle," "shepherd," and "elder." Further, they talked and wrote as if they were living in the last days and Christ would return in their *own* lifetime. However, when it became apparent that they would die, these same titles were increasingly transferred to Jesus Christ, for they knew that He alone would outlive them. The following table uses the lives and writings of Peter, John, and Paul to illustrate this point:

	Second Coming, Disciples, and Titles		Delay, Disciples, and Titles	
Apostles	*Christ coming in their lifetime*	*Disciples as apostles, shepherds*	*Delay & indicate their death*	*Christ as apostle, Shepherd*
Peter	"last days" (Acts 2:17)	"your apostles" (2 Peter 3:2); "feed my sheep [shepherd]" (John 21:15–18)	"after my departure" (2 Peter 1:14, 15); "the kind of death" Peter would die (John 21:19); "a day is like a thousand years" (2 Pet. 3:8)	Jesus "the Shepherd and Overseer of your souls" (1 Peter 2:25)

	Second Coming, Disciples, and Titles		Delay, Disciples, and Titles	
Apostles	*Christ coming in their lifetime*	*Disciples as apostles, shepherds*	*Delay & indicate their death*	*Christ as apostle, Shepherd*
John	Some "will not taste death" (Matt. 16:28; see also John 21:20–23)	"his servant John," "I, John" (Rev. 1:1, 9)	"Jesus did not say that he would not die" (John 21:23; Rev. 6:10, 11)	"Jesus, the apostle and high priest" (Heb. 3:1), and Jesus the "great Shepherd" (13:20)[234]
Paul	"we who are still alive and are left" (1 Thess. 4:17)	"Paul ... an apostle of Jesus Christ" (1 Cor. 1:1)	"time has come for my departure" (2 Tim. 4:6)	

This table is self-explanatory. We will use Paul and Peter's cases as examples. In reference to those who would live to see Christ come, Paul wrote, "we who are still alive." Observe that at the time he wrote this, he saw himself among those who would be living at that time. However, by the time he wrote 2 Timothy, his tone changed. He wrote about his "departure." Peter and John did the same thing. They wrote about some "not tast[ing]" death. However, a little later, they wrote about their departure also. Then they increasingly transferred their own titles of "shepherd," "overseer," and "apostle" to Jesus.

Contextual Significance. As demonstrated, the issues surrounding life, death, and the resurrection are not only mentioned in Revelation 1–3, but are prevalent in the major prophetic sections of 4–22 and other NT writings. This indicates two things. First, the pervasiveness of this teaching in the entire Apocalypse shows that the early readers understood all the prophecies to be applicable to them. Therefore, the argument that the life, death, and resurrection messages of Revelation 1–3 were for the early church but the same themes found in 4–22 were reserved for those living 300 years later appears questionable. Second, it reveals that the theological

---

[234] It is widely held that Hebrews was written by Luke or apostle Paul, but there is sufficient indication that John may also have written it. (Refer to our discussion elsewhere in this book) For this reason, Jesus' titles such as "apostle," "high priest," and "Shepherd" are presented as being from either of them.

and cultural context in which Revelation was conceived is, in many ways, similar to the setting in which the rest of the NT writings were conceived.

Jesus as the "First and the Last" to the Fearful

Courage and Hope to the Fearful. Kenneth A. Strand writes that Revelation was written to "give comfort and hope to oppressed and downtrodden servants of God in their time of critical need."[235] In this regard, the very use of Jesus' titles such as "First and the Last," "Alpha and the Omega," and "Beginning and the End" were intended to do just that—inspire hope and courage among the afflicted and fearful saints. The Smyrnaeans are portrayed as a severely persecuted group, battling slander from the "synagogue of Satan." However, they were also "about to suffer" a "ten day" affliction consisting of imprisonment and death. To this, Jesus disclosed Himself as the "First and the Last."

> *To the fear-stricken, persecuted, and hopeless, Jesus appears as the "First and the Last." The use of this divine title is intended to instill courage and hope. He who says "I am the First and the Last" is able to both bring His saints back to life and "wipe every tear from their eyes."*

Courage and Hope to the Author and Smyrnaeans. To help us appreciate these titles, let us consider what the "First and the Last" meant to the author. A few verses before Jesus introduced Himself as the "First and the Last" (Rev. 1:17–18), John "fell down as though dead" after seeing the glorified Christ, but Jesus said to him, "Do not fear; I am the First and the Last." To a fear-stricken John, this title not only spoke words of hope and courage to him, but also resuscitated him. Like John, the believers at Smyrna also had reasons to be

---

[235] Kenneth A. Strand, "Foundational Principles of Interpretation," in Symposium on Revelation—Book I, ed. Frank B. Holbrook, (Hagerstown, Maryland: Review and Herald Publishing Association, 1992), p. 16.

fearful. Their fear stemmed from the current afflictions they were undergoing and what they were soon to suffer. Therefore, to both John and the believers at Smyrna, Jesus appeared to them as the "First and the Last."

Jesus	John	Smyrnaeans	Notes/Reasons
"I am the First and the Last" (Rev. 1:17; 2:8)	"fell at his feet as though dead" (Rev. 1:17).	"Be faithful, even to the point of death" (Rev. 2:10b)	"resurrection"
"I am the First and the Last" (Rev. 1:17; 2:8)	"do not fear" (Rev. 1:17)	"Do not be afraid of what you are about to suffer" (Rev. 2:10a)."	"courage" and "endurance"

To the fear-stricken, persecuted, and hopeless, Jesus appears as the "First and the Last." The use of this divine title is intended to instill courage and hope. He who says "I am the First and the Last" is able to both bring His saints back to life and "wipe every tear from their eyes." So implicit in the use of the title "First and the Last" is a divine appeal to trust in Him with all our past, current, and future uncertainties, afflictions, fears, and even death.

"I know your afflictions and your poverty—yet you are rich"

Poverty-Rich. Unlike the Ephesians, the Orator did not say anything about Smyrna's past. He merely acknowledged their present predicament and impending afflictions, saying, "I know your afflictions and your poverty—yet you are rich" (Rev. 2:9). We have previously discussed the afflictions, uncertainty, and fear components. Now we shall turn to the "poverty–rich" contradictions. However, this term cannot be discussed in isolation, but must be studied comparatively with similar passages elsewhere.

Rich-poor. The Orator said to the Laodicean church, "You say, 'I am rich; I have acquired wealth and do not need a thing.' But you do not realize that you are … poor … I counsel you to buy from me gold refined in the fire, so you can become rich" (Rev. 3:17, 18). To those in "poverty," Christ describes them as "rich," while those who claim to be "rich" He calls "poor." To the poor, He counsels them to "buy gold refined in the fire" so that they can "become rich." If the Smyrnaeans are considered "rich," then it can be assumed that they have "bought [the] gold refined by fire." What then is this "gold"? A study on what constitutes refined gold is important because it is this that makes one either "rich" or "poor."

A Comparative Analysis of Smyrna and Laodicea. A general comparative analysis of the churches of Smyrna and Laodicea is as follows:

Smyrnaean Condition	Assumed to Have	Laodicean Condition	Does Not Have
In "poverty ... but she is rich" (2:9)	"gold refined by fire" (implied)	"rich, acquired wealth" (3:17)	"does not know that she is poor" (3:18)
"afflictions" (2:9)	symbols of fire (implied)	"do not need a thing" (3:17)	
"persecutions" (2:10)	symbols of fire	"wretched" (3:17)	
"prison" (2:10)	symbols of fire (implied)	"pitiful" (3:17)	"I counsel you" (3:18)
"death" (2:10)	symbols of fire (implied)	"poor" (3:17)	"gold refined by fire" (3:18)
"white clothes"		"blind" (3:17)	"eye salve" (3:18)
an impending "ten-day persecution" (2:10)	"white clothes" (implied)	"naked" (3:17)	"white clothes" (3:18)
	"hot" (implied)	"lukewarm—neither hot nor cold" (3:16)	"either one or the other" (3:15)
"rebuke and discipline" = "gold refined by fire"		"those whom I love, I rebuke and discipline" (3:19a)	"be earnest and repent" (3:19b)
Jesus inside		"behold I stand at the door and knock" (3:20)	
Promised "crown of life" + "escape second death" (2:10, 11)		Promised the "right to sit on the throne" (3:21)	

The following can be deduced from this table:

1. *The Rich.* The Smyrnaeans who are currently being slandered by the "synagogue of Satan" are pronounced as being "rich," while the

Laodiceans are associated with a life of ease, comfort, and material wealth are labeled as "poor."

2. *Trials—the Refiners Fire*. Christ says of Laodicea, "those whom I love I rebuke ... Be earnest and repent," but the saints in Smyrna who are characterized as enduring affliction, persecution, prison, and death are encouraged to "be faithful, even to the point of death." The inference here is that the "gold tried by fire" is a byproduct of trials, afflictions, and struggles. "Temptation, poverty, adversity, is the very discipline needed to develop purity and firmness."[236] Therefore, the faithful saints attract the wrath from the "synagogue of Satan," while to the "lukewarm," Christ comes across as the *Rebuker*.

3. *White Robes*. The Orator assesses the Laodiceans as being naked and offers them white clothes. The Smyrnaeans, however, are assumed to have received and are clothed with the same. Revelation 19:8 defines "white clothes" as the "righteous acts of the saints." Revelation 7:13–14 adds another dimension to this definition. One of the elders had rhetorically asked John, "Who are these arrayed in white robes and where did they come from?" He then answered, "These are they who have come out of the great tribulation; they have washed their robes and make them white in the blood of the Lamb."

How do we reconcile these two strands of thought? In the midst of great tribulation, those who persist in righteous acts are considered as having washed their robes, making them white in the blood of the Lamb. The Smyrnaeans, who were handling afflictions gracefully, are further admonished, "I tell you, the devil will put some of you in prison to test you, and you will suffer persecution for ten days. Be faithful, even to the point of death, and I will give you the crown of life" (2:10). They are basically told to persevere. However, the Laodiceans do not experience any afflictions, or if they do, their responses do not constitute "righteous acts" or "endurance." They probably used their power, wealth, and affluence to either fend off or absorb afflictions.

---

[236] White, *The Desire of Ages*, p. 29.

4. *Significance of Christ Standing at the Door.* To the Laodiceans, Christ is pictured as standing at the door and knocking. If He is knocking, then He has not been granted the permission to enter the house (see 3:20). Consequently, His influence is absent in the lives of the Laodiceans.
5. *The Correct View of Reality.* To the church at Smyrna, Christ said, "I know your afflictions and your poverty—yet you are rich!" (2:9). However, to the church at Laodicea, it's the other way around. There, He said, "Because you say, 'I am rich, have become wealthy, and have need of nothing'—and do not know that you are wretched, miserable, poor, blind, and naked" (3:17). The Laodiceans have allowed their wealth and social status to enter into and fill their minds and hearts. This explains why Christ is seen standing outside and knocking. Furthermore, they are described as those who do not know their actual condition. Because they see themselves through the lenses of their own wealth and status, all they could see is a life of abundance, ease, and comfort, while the Smyrnaeans, who saw themselves through Christ, saw something entirely different!
6. Finally, a similarity exists between the Laodiceans and the opponents in Smyrna. Note the following passages:

Revelation 2:9	Revelation 3:17
"I know the slander *of those who say they are Jews and are not*, but are a synagogue of Satan."	"*You say, 'I am rich*; I have acquired wealth and do not need a thing.' *But you do not realize that you are* wretched, pitiful, poor, blind and naked."

These two groups have a mental awareness of their own identity. The identity of one group stems from their heritage and nationality, whereas the other comes from their wealth and possessions. Their view of reality was heavily colored by their race and wealth.[237] Note the effects of these perspectives. For the Laodiceans, Christ was no longer part of their fellowship. He was not even inside. He had been pushed out. Conversely,

---

[237] The opponents in Philadelphia were exactly the same as those in Smyrna. For further discussion on the issue of being a *false* Jew, refer to chapter 21.

those who prided themselves in their Jewish heritage did not even realize that they had become the synagogue of Satan.[238] Thus, the latter group positioned itself in diametrical opposition to Jesus Christ. Like the Laodiceans and the synagogue of Satan, if one's life is not built and established on a proper foundation (i.e., Christ), he or she can be an enemy of Christ and may not even be aware of it. The following table summarizes the discussion on the three institutions: Smyrna, Laodicea, and the synagogue of Satan.

Attitude	Smyrna	Laodicea	Synagogue of Satan
Awareness	They know their condition (2:9)	"you do not realize that you are ..." (3:17)	They do not know on whose side they are (2:9)
Results	Rich, robed in white, crown of life (2:10)	Poor, blind, naked, will be spewed out (3:17)	Not real Jews, synagogue of Satan, enemies of Christ (2:9)
Persevere	"Faithful" to Christ (2:10)	"do not need a thing" (3:17)	"Slander Christ" (2:9)
Pursuits	"They follow the Lamb wheresoever He goes" (14:4)	They pursue wealth, riches, and treasure (3:17)	Crusade against Christ (2:9)
Foundations	Jesus Christ (2:8)	Wealth: "I am rich" (3:17)	Nationality: They "say they are Jews and are not" (2:9)

A Comparative Study of the Churches at Smyrna and Ephesus

A comparative study of the Ephesians and Smyrnaeans also reveals another dimension to our discussion. One church consisted of saints who were militant and combative, while the other consisted of those who were meek, gentle, and submissive.

---

[238] Note the similarity we find in John the Baptist's castigation of the Pharisees during his ministry. Those who came prided themselves in their Abrahamic heritage, but they did not know that they had become like a "brood of vipers" (Luke 3:7–9).

Ephesus	Smyrna
"cannot tolerate wicked men," "tested those who claim to be apostles … and have found them false" (2:2)	"I know your afflictions and poverty," false Jews (synagogue of Satan) slander you (2:9)
"persevered and endured hardship," "did not grow weary" (2:3)	"Do not be afraid of what you are about to suffer"; Some into prisons, others persecuted; "Be faithful, even to the point of death" (2:10)
She is combative, lost first love, fell from height; dry; no longer does what she used to do (2:4–5)	Fearful, uncertain about the duration of suffering, intensity of afflictions, doubted divine leading
A fighter church that fights by herself (2:2, 3)	A submissive (perhaps meek) church; has inner resolve; trusted God to avenge their enemies (Note that in Pergamum, Christ is the fighter who fights for the church and against sinners) (2:10, 16)
Christ issues warnings and threats (2:4, 5)	Christ offers encouragement and promises (2:10, 11)
Threatened with removal of lampstand (2:5)	Promised the crown of life (2:10)

Regarding their works, both churches were commended for doing the right thing and urged to persevere. Although these churches had the same or similar opponents, they reacted to them differently. The Ephesians are described as those who "cannot tolerate wicked men" and had also gone to great lengths to falsify their opponents' claims to apostleship. They had "persevered … and did not grow weary" in their mission. Ephesus was a combative, offensive, and militant church. Although a disputing, disproving, arguing, and justifying spirit has some values, it typically functions at the expense of genuine graciousness. A militant spirit is usually counterproductive and always rubs against such divine commodities as holy fear, reverence, awe, and a tender devotion to Christ. It also dries up the well of compassion towards humanity, and the soul eventually becomes as dry as the hills of Gilboa. This appears to be the life and experience of those in Ephesus. No wonder why Christ urged them to reclaim their "first love" experience.

However, the Smyrnaeans handled their afflictions and opponents in an entirely different manner. They demonstrated a meek and submissive spirit. In their afflictions and poverty, they were encouraged to be "be faithful, even to the point of death." They were advised against exhibiting a combative or retaliatory spirit. As their Lord was led to the slaughter and yet opened not His mouth, the Smyrnaeans quietly passed through their own crucibles. Perhaps they had allowed Christ, who fights with "the sword of [His] mouth," to fight for them and avenge their blood (Rev. 2:16). Thus, their only cry may have been to the Lord, saying, "How long, Sovereign Lord, holy and true, until you judged the inhabitants of the earth and avenge our blood?" (Rev. 6:10).

> *Although a disputing, disproving, arguing, and justifying spirit has some values, it typically functions at the expense of genuine graciousness. A militant spirit is usually counterproductive and always rubs against such divine commodities as holy fear, reverence, awe, and a tender devotion to Christ.*

OPPONENTS IN SMYRNA

Opponents and Their Activities in the Current War

<u>False Jews</u>. The opponents in Smyrna were diversely described. One group consisted of those who claimed to be "Jews and are not, but are a synagogue of Satan." This is not a case of mistaken identity. As far as ethnicity is concerned, these people were genuine and authentic Jews. During His ministry, Jesus did meet them. To their claim "We are descendants of Abraham," Jesus responded:

> I know you are Abraham's descendants. Yet you are ready to kill me. ... If you were Abraham's children ... then you would do the things Abraham did. As it is you are determined to kill me ...

> Abraham did not do such things. You are doing the things your own father does. ... You belong to your father, the devil; and you want to carry out your father's desire. He was a murderer from the beginning, not holding to the truth, for there is no truth in him. When he lies, he speaks his native language, for he is a liar and a father of lies. (John 8:37, 39–41, 44)

As shown here, Jesus did not dispute their physical, Abrahamic descent and linage, but He pointed out that their words, deeds, and characters were un-Abrahamic and more like that of the devil. Christ, therefore, called them liars, murderers, and children of Satan. Like the opponents at Ephesus, they were aggressively involved in an antichristological crusade.[239]

Blasphemy. One of the activities in which the opponents were involved is "slander[ing]" the name of Jesus Christ (Rev. 2:9). The Greek word translated "slander" is *blasphēmian*, from which we get the word "blasphemy." The same word is used more than three times to describe the name, title, and activities of the sea beast of Revelation 13 (vv. 1, 5, 6).

Satan Behind Blasphemies. These opponents are described as emanating from the "synagogue of Satan." The term "Satan" denotes the adversarial title for the chief enemy of Jesus Christ. Therefore, when the activities of the Jews are described as blasphemous, antichristological, and emanating from Satan, these descriptions resemble the sea beast of Revelation 13.

Opponents and Their Activities in the Impending War

The Current and Impending Wars. At the time John wrote Revelation, the Smyrnaeans were grappling with blasphemies from the synagogue of Satan, but the Orator also warned of an impending ten-day tribulation. Therefore, there are two wars in focus here. The same two wars—one current and the other impending—are also featured in other parts of

---

[239] For more discussion on the (Jewish) nature of the opponents, see chapter 16 and 17, especially the discussion on the opponents of Philadelphia.

Revelation. Christ said to the saints in Philadelphia, "Since you have kept my command to endure patiently [in the current conflict], I will also keep you from the hour of trial that is going to come upon the whole world to test those who live on the earth" (Rev. 3:10). Then God tells those slain in the current persecution to "wait a little longer, until the number of their fellow servants and brothers who were going to be killed as they had been was completed [in the impending war]" (Rev. 6:11; see also chs. 12–14). Thus, the text consistently presents two wars, and the duration of the second is variously described as "ten days," "the hour of trial,"[240] and "a little longer." (For two wars in Matthew 24, see chapter 5).

The Accuser—the Enemy in Revelation 1–3 and 4–22. The opponent in the impending tribulation is identified as *diabolos*, typically translated as "devil," meaning "a slanderer or accuser." Although the titles "Satan" and "Devil" refer to the same character, they nevertheless signify different roles that the enemy plays.

Satan is also referred to as the "accuser" in Revelation 12:10. "For the accuser [Gr. *katēgōr*] of our brothers who accuses them before our God day and night has been hurled down." Two verses later, the "accuser [*katēgōr*]" is identified as the "devil" (v. 12). These similarities indicate a relationship between the opponents in Smyrna and the adversarial characters in Revelation 12 and 13, which are further explored in the next section.

RELATIONSHIP BETWEEN REVELATION 1–3 AND 4–22

Relationship Between the Smyrnaean Conflict and Revelation 12–13

A striking similarity exists between the opponents and their activities at Smyrna and in Revelation 12 and 13. The following table shows the relationship between these two passages:

---

[240] For the reference to the "hour of trial," see Revelation 17:12.

Opponents	Current Conflict	Impending Conflict
The "synagogue of Satan" in Smyrna (Rev. 2)	1) Opponents: Jews, synagogue of Satan 2) Their activities involve blasphemy (Gr. *blasphemē*) 3) Saints: have "the word of God and the testimony of Jesus" (1:9)	1) Conflict: "ten day tribulations" 2) Opponent: Devil, the Accuser 3) Activities: imprisonment, persecution, and death 4) Saints: commandment keepers with testimony of Jesus (6:9–11; 12:17; 14:12)
Dragon (Rev. 12)	1) Dragon pursued the birth mother for 1,260 days (vv. 13–16) 2) Earth opens its mouth, helps woman flee	"The Dragon was enraged at the woman and went off to make war against the rest of her offspring—those who obey God's commandments and hold to the testimony of Jesus" (v. 17)
Sea/Land Beasts (Rev. 13)	1) Dragon gives throne to the sea beast; the sea beast's name, words, and activities are saturated with blasphemy (Gr. *blasphemē*) 2) Persecutes for 1,260 days/forty-two months (vv. 1–10)	1) Dragon and sea beast behind the land beast, which exercises the sea beast's authority 2) Makes all worship the sea beast and its image. Those who refuse will be killed (vv. 11–18)

It is possible that the Smyrnaeans (and the early church) must have seen their two conflicts, the current and impending, in the light of what is written in 12 and 13 and also alluded to elsewhere (see 6:9–11; 14:12–14; 17:12). This is because of the following reasons:

1. *Presence of Two Wars in Revelation.* In Revelation 1–3 and 4–22, two separate conflicts are stressed: the current conflict and the impending one. The two wars are heavily featured in the Smyrnaean and Philadelphian addresses (see Rev. 2, 3), the fifth seal (Rev. 6), and Revelation chapters 12, 13, and 17.
2. *The Duration of the Impending War.* Apart from the current conflict, the duration of the impending one is variously described as a "ten day" conflict, an "hour of trial," "a little longer," or just "one hour" (Rev. 17:12).
3. *The Opponents of the Impending War.* The opponents of the impending war in both sections of Revelation (1–3 and 4–22) are similar. For instance, the opponent in Smyrna and Philadelphia is Satan and those

coming from his "synagogue." In the same churches, the enemy is also described as the "devil" or "accuser" (2:9, 10; 3:9). These are the same titles featured in chapters 12 and 13. For instance, the enemy is called the "dragon," "Satan," the "devil," and the "accuser" (12:7–10, 15–17).

4. *Blasphemies Against Christ*. As the names of the opponents suggest, the enemy uses multiple schemes in the conflicts, but all of them are united against the person of Jesus Christ. For instance, the opponents in Smyrna "slander" or "blaspheme" His name, whereas the sea beast of Rev. 13 is literally covered in "blasphemous names."

5. *Saints Keep Testimonies and Commandments*. Further, those who Satan targets in the early church (including the Smyrnaeans) and Revelation 12 and 13 are described as having the "commandments of God" and "the testimony of Jesus" (1:9, 10; 12:17; see also 6:9–11; 14:12–14).

6. Further, the same Greek term is used to describe the saints in both sections of the book. The faithful saints in Sardis are described as "a few people [*loitois*]" (3:4), whereas the saints who attracted the enemy's wrath in 12:17 are described as "the rest of her offspring [*loipōn*]." In both cases, the same Greek is used. One wonders if these similarities meant anything to the early church.

With such similarities as these, it is hard for one to deny that the early church did understand the prophecies of Revelation. If the early church, especially the Smyrnaeans, understood the contents of Revelation 12 and 13 within their own context, then one must first seek to understand what 4–22 meant to them before determining what they mean to us. That includes identifying the two beasts of chapter 13, their activities, and the saints of God (see 12:17), which we have partially discussed in 1:9. The remaining portion will be discussed more fully in Revelation 12 and 13.[241]

---

[241] Revelation 12 and 13 are not discussed in this work.

17.

PERGAMUM: HIM WHO HAS A SHARP, DOUBLE-EDGED SWORD

To the angel of the church in Pergamum write: These are the words of him who has the sharp, double-edged sword. I know where you live—where Satan has his throne. Yet you remain true to my name. You did not renounce your faith in me, even in the days of Antipas, my faithful witness, who was put to death in your city—where Satan lives. Nevertheless, I have a few things against you: You have people there who hold to the teaching of Balaam, who taught Balak to entice the Israelites to sin by eating food sacrificed to idols and by committing sexual immorality. Likewise you also have those who hold to the teaching of the Nicolaitans. Repent therefore! Otherwise, I will soon come to you and will fight against them with the sword of my mouth. He who has an ear, let him hear what the Spirit says to the churches. To him who overcomes, I will give some of the hidden manna. I will also give him a white stone with a new name written on it, known only to him who receives it. (Revelation 2:12–17)

JESUS IN PERGAMUM

To the church in Pergamum, the city "where Satan lives," Jesus comes across as the one who "has a sharp, double-edged sword" coming from His mouth. This description appears three times in Revelation. It first appears in the vision of Rev. 1:12–16. The same is also used to describe the Rider on the white horse in Rev. 19:11–16. In both of these occurrences, the "double-edged sword" is one of many descriptions used to describe Jesus, but to the Pergamumites, the "double-edged sword" is featured prominently. What, then, is the definition and significance of this title?

The Double-edged Sword of Christ

Revelation 1 states that the sword came "out of his mouth" (v. 16).[242] What John literally saw was Christ's "tongue." If the tongue is a symbol for words or uttered thoughts, then that which comes from Jesus' mouth is "words," "true words," "truth," or the "word of God." Therefore, the Rider with the sharp-sword of 19:11–16 is even called the "Word of God" (vv. 13–15). Concerning this, the author of Hebrews wrote, "For the word of God is living and active. Sharper than any double-edged sword, it penetrates even to dividing soul and spirit, joints and marrow; it judges the thoughts and attitudes of the heart" (Heb. 4:12).

In Ephesians, Paul coined the term "sword of the spirit" to mean the "word of God (6:17). Therefore, that sharp sword represents the life of Jesus Christ, the word of God that came from and through Jesus Christ, and the Spirit of God promised by Jesus Christ. The following table summarizes these thoughts:

"Word of God" (Heb. 4:12, 13)	"The Rider" (Rev. 19:11–16)	"Son of Man" (Rev. 1:16; 2:12)
"sharper ... doubled-edged sword" (v. 12)	"double-edge sword" (v. 15)	"sharp double-edge sword" (1:16; 2:12)
"word of God" (12)	"word of God" (13)	"son of Man" (1:13)
"living and active. It penetrates even to dividing soul and spirit, joints and marrow" (13)	"beast, kings of the earth and their armies were "killed with the sword that came out of the mouth of the rider" (19, 20)	"come to you and fight against them with the sword of my mouth" (2:16)

---

[242] The term "sword" is also used twice in Revelation 13:10: "If anyone is to be killed with the sword, with the sword they will be killed."

Sword of the Sea Beast

<u>Blasphemies from the Beast</u>. The "word of God" in the form of a double-edged sword comes from the mouth of Jesus Christ. However, in Revelation, other "swords," "tongues," or "words" also proceed from other mouths. One of those being the sea beast of chapter 13. "The beast was given a mouth to utter proud words and blasphemies ... He opened his mouth to blaspheme God, and to slander his name and his dwelling place and those who live in heaven" (vv. 5, 6). Similar to Christ's "sharp double-edged sword" that fights and kills, this beast's proud and blasphemous words also have the power and authority to kill (see v. 7). The upcoming table provides a comparative analysis of these two characters.

The Sea Beast and the Rider on the White Horse. The comparison between this beast and the Rider is quite revealing. They have about a half dozen characteristics in common.

Sea Beast (Rev. 13:1–10)	Rider on the White Horse (Rev. 19:11–21)
"on each head a blasphemous name," a total of seven or more names (v. 1)	"His name is the Word of God" (v. 13). But the Rider has more names—at least fifteen
"mouth to utter proud and blasphemous words" (v. 5)	"out of his mouth comes a sharp sword" (v. 15)
"one of the heads ... seemed to have a fatal wound, but the fatal wound had been healed" (v. 3a)	"He is dressed in a robe dipped in blood" (v. 13), thus signifying that He has also been fatally wounded.
"The whole world was astonished and followed the beast" (v. 3b)	"The armies of heaven were following him" (v. 14). Also, "they [144,000] follow the Lamb wherever he goes" (14:4)
"he was given authority over every tribe, people, language and nations" (v. 7b)	He will "strike down the nations, 'He will rule them with an iron scepter'" forever (v. 15)
"was given power to make war against the saints and conquer them" for "forty-two months" (vv. 5, 7a); "who is like the beast? And who can make war against him?" (v. 4)	"with justice he judges and makes war" (v. 11); "But the beast was captured" and "thrown alive into the fiery lake of burning sulfur" (v. 20); "The lake of fire is the second death" (20:14)

We will briefly discuss the common characteristics:

1. *Total Number of Names*. The Rider and beast are featured as having multiple names—the Rider with fifteen and the beast with at least seven.
2. *The Characters have a Mouth*. From the mouth of the Rider comes the "Word of God," while "proud and blasphemous words" proceed from the mouth of the beast.[243]
3. *Authorities of the Characters*. Although both of these mouths have the power and authority to inflict harm, the beast obviously has limitations. It "makes war against the saints" for a limited forty-two months, while the Rider can and will capture, strike, and burn the beast forever!
4. *Deadly Wounds*. Both the beast and Rider have suffered a fatal wound, but survived. The beast suffered a "fatal wound," whereas the Rider comes in a robe "dipped in [His own] blood" (Rev. 13:3; 19:13).
5. *Huge Following*. Both characters have a huge following. The "whole world … followed the beast," while "the armies of heaven" followed the Rider on the white horse. Concerning Christ's following, the Jews wondered, "Look how the whole world has gone after him [Jesus]" (John 12:19).

> *Although both of these mouths have the power and authority to inflict harm, the beast obviously has limitations. It "makes war against the saints" for a limited forty-two months, while the Rider can and will capture, strike, and burn the beast forever!*

<u>The Beast of Revelation 13 and the Little Horn of Daniel 7</u>. Incidentally, the little horn of Daniel 7 is similar to the first beast of Revelation 13. Apart from the blasphemous mouth, these two powers also have other things in common, as shown in the following table:

---

[243] Compare this beast with the "little horn" of Daniel 7. Both are featured as having a "mouth" that speaks blasphemous words.

Daniel 7	Revelation 13
"little horn" (v. 8)	Sea beast with "blasphemous names" (v. 1)
"a mouth that spoke boastfully" (v. 8), "boastful words" (v. 11), "mouth that spoke" (v. 20)	"was given a mouth to utter proud words and blasphemies" (v. 5)
"He will speak against the Most High and oppress His saints" (v. 25)	"he opened his mouth to blaspheme God, and to slander his name and his dwelling place and those who live in heaven" (v. 6)
"for a time, times and half-a-time" (v. 25)	"exercise his authority for 42 months" (v. 5)

The relationship between these two powers will be thoroughly discussed in Revelation 13, but a quick glance at the table reveals that 1) the two powers have a mouth that speaks boastfully, 2) both mouths speak against the "Most High," His name, dwelling place, and those who live in heaven, and 3) both powers make war against the saints of God for forty-two months. These similarities suggest that these two powers are identical.

The Swords of the Land Beast, Image, and Dragon

The land beast of Revelation 13:11–18 is also portrayed as having a mouth that speaks "like a dragon" (v. 11). With the help of the false prophets, this beast gives "breath to the image of the first beast, so that it could speak and cause all who refused to worship the image to be killed" (v. 15). Here we have the "dragon," "land beast," and "image" all having mouths and speaking great and blasphemous words. Further, similar to the sharp, double-edged sword coming out of Christ's mouth, three frog-like evil spirits are seen coming out of the "mouth of the dragon," "mouth of the beast," and "mouth of the false prophets" (Rev. 16:13, 14). Note that these three frog-like spirits are responsible for all the deceptive work prior to the final tribulation.

The Sword of the Saints of God

The saints of God also have mouths that speak. "They overcame him [Satan] … by the word of their testimony" (Rev. 12:11). Speaking of the same group, John wrote, "They follow the Lamb wherever he goes … No lie was found in their mouths; they are blameless" (Rev. 14:4, 5).[244] The following table summarizes the characters, their mouths, and activities:

Character	Mouth/Words
"son of man" (1:13)	"a sharp double-edged sword" (1:16)
rider on the white horse (19:11)	"a sharp sword with which to strike down nations" (19:15)
"beast coming out of the sea" (13:1)	"a mouth to utter proud words and blasphemies and to exercise his authority for forty-two months" (13:5)
"beast coming out of the earth" (13:11)	"spoke like a dragon" (13:11)
"the image of the first beast" (13:15)	The land beast breathes life into the image. The image speaks and causes the saints to be killed (13:15)
"The dragon" (chs. 12, 13; see also John 8:44)	"When he lies, he speaks his native language, for he is a liar and the father of lies" (John 8:44)
The saints (Rev. 12:11; 14:12)	1) "no guile was found in their mouth" (12:11) 2) overcome Satan with "words of their testimony" (12:11)

Summary on Swords, Tongues, and Words

The following can be deduced from the previous discussion:

1. The sharp sword coming from the Rider's mouth represents the true words of God as uttered by Christ. Swords or words are also described as coming from the mouths of other characters. From the mouths of Satan, the beast, and false prophets proceed guile, falsehood, lies,

---

[244] Paul's language also evokes a similar imagery. "Pray also for me," he said to the Ephesians, "that whenever I open my mouth, words maybe given me" (Eph. 6:19). Although Scripture is filled with tongue/mouth-related passages, we will consider only three passages. The first concerns Paul's reference to the sword as the "sword of the spirit." He proceeded to explain that the sword of the Spirit is the "word of God" (v. 17).

The third passage about the mouth and tongue is in James 3: "The tongue is a small part of the body, but it makes great boasts. ... The tongue is also a fire, a world of evil among the parts of the body. It corrupts the whole body, sets the whole course of one's life on fire, and is itself set on fire by hell. ... no human being can tame the tongue. It is a restless evil, full of deadly poison" (vv. 5, 6, 8).

deception, blasphemy, and "wine of her adulteries." From the saints, however, "no guile was found in their mouth." This means that truth proceeds from the mouths of the saints.

2. The swords that proceed from the dragon and his team have certain power to inflict fatal wounds. However, the hurt they inflict has limitations. This is because the passive language in Revelation 13:5–7 shows that their mouths, words, and activities are controlled by God. Also, the death they administer is the first death, whereas Christ administers the second death.

3. The saints, on the other hand, have swords ("word of their testimony") that can overcome Satan and his agents, even if it means *through* their own blood (see 12:11; 6:9–11).

4. The sword that proceeds from the mouth of Christ is emphatically described as "sharp" and "double-edged," signifying precision, incisiveness, and finality. The term "double-edged" could suggest the dual role of Christ's sword. For instance, the same sword that protects, defends, and saves the saints is also the same that administers justice to the dragon and his allies.[245]

5. Therefore, the great controversy primarily involves words and thoughts. It is essentially a battle of the mind, the casualties of which may be diversely manifested. In this case, Paul was correct when he said, "For our struggle is not against flesh and blood, but against the rulers, against the authorities, against the powers of this dark world and against the spiritual forces of evil in the heavenly realms" (Eph. 6:12).

What then is the implication of the use of the "sharp double-edged sword" in the Pergamum address?

---

[245] Note that the saints are saved because they keep the "word of God," while the same "word of God [sword]" captures and throws Satan and his agents "alive into the fiery lake of burning sulfur" (Rev. 19:19–21). Hence, the phrase "With justice he judges and makes war" (v. 11).

Implication of the Two-edged Sword on the Balaamites and Nicolaitans

The city of Pergamum was Satan's turf. The archenemy of God had his throne in Pergamum and operated from there (see Rev. 2:13). Despite this, the church at Pergamum had remained faithful. Accordingly, the Orator mostly commended them, but He also had "a few things against" them. Christ proceeded to identify two groups of people—those who hold the teachings of either Balaam or the Nicolaitans—and summoned them to repent (see vv. 14, 15). However, should they refuse, He warned that he would come and "fight against them with the sword of [His] mouth" (v. 16).

The sword which Jesus spoke of is used elsewhere as the ultimate weapon against His sworn enemies (see 19:15, 21; also Ps. 149:6–9). If Christ was threatening to use that weapon against the Balaamites and Nicolaitans, then it is possible that these groups were guilty of something heinous. Whatever the nature of their sins may have been, a few things are clear.

"<u>Hold the teachings.</u>" First, these two groups are identified as those "hold[ing] the teachings of Balaam" and "hold[ing] the teachings of Nicolaitans." The Greek term used for "teachings" is *didachēn*, from the root word *didachē*, meaning a body of teachings, instructions, or doctrines. Revelation is replete with the concept of individuals or groups holding or being in possession of a body of teachings, doctrines, commandments, words, or testimonies. The following table identifies the people and the body of teachings that they possessed:

Groups of People	Body of teachings held
Pergamum	• "teachings of Balaam and the Nicolaitans"
Thyatira	• "You tolerate that woman Jezebel ... By her teaching [Gr. *didaskei*] she misleads my servants" (2:20) • "Now I say to the rest of you in Thyatira, to you who do not hold to her teaching and have not learned Satan's so-called deep secrets ... hold on to what you have until I come" (2:24, 25)
Philadelphia	• "you have kept my word and have not denied my name" (3:8) • "hold onto what you have so that no one will take your crown" (3:11)

Groups of People	Body of teachings held
Those whose "names are not in the Lamb's book of life"	• those who accepted the "blasphemies" of the beast "wondered after the beast" (13:3–8) • "all the nations drank the maddening wine of her [Babylon] adulteries" (14:8; 17:4; 8:3)
"saints"	• "Blessed is he who reads, hears, and takes to heart what is written [word of God and the testimony of Jesus] in it" (1:2, 3); "keep the word of God and have the testimony of Jesus" (6:9–11; 12:17; 14:12; 22:7)

However, the saints of God are identified as having, holding onto, keeping, or being in possession of either the "commandment [Gr. *entolē*]" or "word [Gr. *logon*] of God," as well as the "testimony [Gr. *marturia*]" or "faith [Gr. *pistis*] of Jesus."

Whatever constituted the exact nature of these bodies of teachings, two points are noteworthy. Eternal life or eternal damnation depends on what one does with these bodies of teachings. Those who "read," "hear," keep," "do," and share the commandments of God and the testimony of Jesus will be raised from the dead and rewarded with a crown of life. However, those who hold onto the teachings of Balaam, the Nicolaitans, or Jezebel, or Satan's deep secrets or the blasphemies of the beast, or drink the "wine of [Babylon's] adulteries" will be cast into the "lake of fire" (Rev. 14:8). This also underscores the fact that "teachings," "doctrines," and "commandments" do matter in Christianity. Therefore, the reading, hearing, and holding onto a correct set of teachings is the bedrock for a genuine relationship between believers and their God.

> *This also underscores the fact that "teachings," "doctrines," and "commandments" do matter in Christianity. Therefore, the reading, hearing, and holding onto a correct set of teachings is the bedrock for a genuine relationship between believers and their God.*

Teach the Teachings. Second, they not only hold these bodies of teachings, but are also actively involved in teaching others to do so. The text reads, "teachings of Balaam, who taught Balak to entice the Israelites to sin" (Rev. 2:14). In the ancient account, Balaam had taught Balak to entice the Israelites, leading them to immorality and idolatry. This in turn kindled the Lord's anger, and 24,000 Israelite men perished in the plains of Moab (see Num. 25–31).

The Greek term translated "entice" is *skandalon*, from which we get the English word "scandal," which means "cause for stumbling" or "trap." When Balaam realized that he could not invoke a curse upon God's people, he resorted to lay an enticing trap. His instructions to Balak were intended to cause the Israelites to turn from their God. They were first lured into immorality, which then led to idolatry. Thus, the "worshiping of the Baal of Peor" replaced the worship of the true, living God (Num. 25:3).

Eating, Drinking, Accepting the Teaching, and Sexual Immorality. In Numbers, the worship of Baal involved eating, drinking, and sexual immorality. In the Pergamum narrative and elsewhere in Revelation, false worship also involves eating of food sacrificed to idols, drinking of the "wine of her adulteries," and being involved in inappropriate sexual relations.

The situation in Peor, however, involved literal food and sexual immorality, where the Israelite "men began to indulge in sexual immorality with Moabite women" (Num. 25:1). The Moabite women then proceeded to invite them to the "sacrifices of their gods." This eventually led them to eating, drinking, and bowing down to foreign gods (vv. 2, 3). Thus, immorality and idolatry are inseparable in that one paves the way for the other.

Symbolic or Literal Harlotry. The language in Revelation invokes a similar imagery. However, one must determine if the Orator is addressing a situation that involved a literal or symbolic harlotry issue. If real sexual immorality is in focus in Revelation, one would expect a literal woman, real sacrifices, and real idols, but the setting does not favor such a literal interpretation. The text, however, shows the apocalyptic woman to be either a church or institution—that is, either a local synagogue or an organized religious entity. In the messages to the seven churches, each church is warned against either the "synagogue of Satan," the "woman Jezebel," "false Jews," "false apostles," or "the throne of Satan." In the rest of Revelation (4–22), we find the bride of the Lamb, Babylon the harlot, her adulterous daughters (chs. 12, 14, 17, 18), the throne of Satan, and the two beasts that sat on it (ch. 13).

Significance of Holding a Body of Teachings. The fact that Christ directly addresses the Balaamites and Nicolaitans shows that they have not yet left the fellowship. They are still members of the faith community. In fact, the Balaamites and Nicolaitans themselves may not even be aware of their real condition. However, at the time Christ addressed them, they were seen actively working *for* Satan. Note that Satan gains entrance into the life of believers through what they hold. These individuals cling to a body of teachings that originated from either the "synagogue of Satan" or "the throne of Satan," which has opened the door for the enemy to infiltrate their lives. "Every sinful desire we cherish affords him [Satan] a foothold. Every point in which we fail of meeting the divine standard is an open door by which he can enter to tempt and destroy us. And every failure or defeat on our part gives occasion for him to reproach Christ."[246]

Christ with the Mouth of a Sharp Sword. Satan works better when he works from within. In Pergamum, Satan may have manifested his physical presence by establishing a "throne," but to him, having a throne nearby was of no use if he could not access the rank and file of his targets. While the saints in this city were focused on their opponent's visible "throne," they were not even aware that he had actually infiltrated their camp. It is only the One whose eyes are like "blazing fire" and "search hearts and minds" that has seen it and warns His people.

Satan's agents (in this case, the Balaamites and Nicolaitans) adhering to a set of adulterated doctrines is one thing, but the fact that they are actively involved in teaching and influencing other believers makes their activities repugnant before Christ. Perhaps this has called for the use of His ultimate weapon. Years earlier, Jesus taught, "Things that cause people to stumble

---

[246] White, *The Desire of Ages*, p. 125.

are bound to come, but woe to anyone through whom they come. It would be better for them to be thrown into the sea with a millstone tied around their neck than to cause one of these little ones to stumble" (Luke 17:1, 2).

When Christ threatens the Balaamites and Nicolaitans with the "sharp double-edged sword," He is seeking to unclench the fists of those who hold to these deadly doctrines and ultimately uproot the enemy's foothold from their lives.

Pergamum—Throne of Satan

Of all the cities, Pergamum is enlisted as the "city where Satan lives" because his throne is there. This makes Pergamum the enemy's headquarters. Revelation provides a glimpse of what the enemy does with his throne. "The dragon gave the [sea] beast his power and his throne and great authority" (Rev. 13:2). Note what happens next. The sea beast then shares this authority with the land beast (see vv. 11, 12). In other words, Satan basically shares his throne with his followers.

This is similar to what Christ does with His throne. That "great white throne" belongs to God (see chs. 4, 5; 20:11), but by virtue of His victory, Christ has earned the right to sit "down with the Father on His throne" (3:21). Similar to the dragon and the beast, Christ also has the right to invite those deserving to sit with Him. "To him who overcomes, I will give the right to sit down with me on my throne." The diagram below shows these relationships:

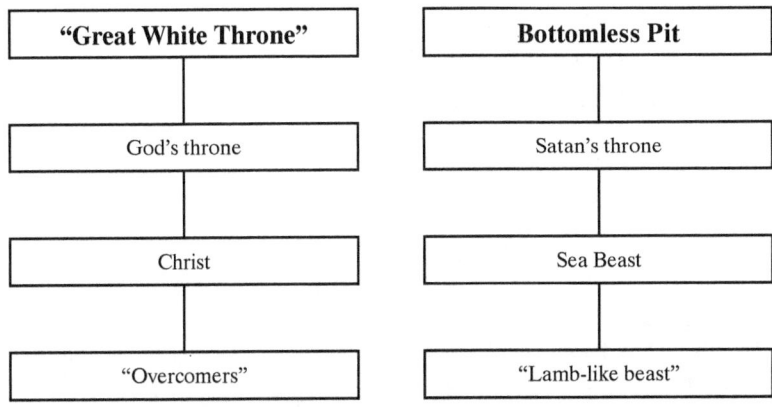

Satan's Structure, Organization, Servants, and Commodities

Although Satan shares his throne with the sea and land beasts, he actually oversees an extremely sophisticated operation. The following table provides a brief overview of that machinery:[247]

Features	Details
Satanic throne	• Administers or executes his "wicked works" from his throne in "Pergamum" (and the bottomless pit)
Satanic Institutions	• Although Satan has his throne in Pergamum, he operates from synagogues in other cities • Smyrna and Philadelphia are each stated as having a "synagogue of Satan," but this does not mean that there were no synagogues in other cities. Wherever there was a Jewish population, there was a synagogue.
Agents of Satan	• Satan deploys an army of agents in all churches. Some of them include "wicked men," "false apostles," "false Jews," "Jezebel, who calls herself a prophetess," "liars," "Balaamites," and "Nicolaitans."
Teachings	• The main commodity Satan designs, manufactures, markets, and sells (in his organization) includes falsehood, lying, and deceptions (e.g., "teachings of the Nicolaitans," "teachings of Balaam," and the "depths of Satan"). These false teachings, when conceived, give birth to wicked works (sexual immorality, food for idols, compromise, poverty, affliction, slander). The diabolical teachings and doctrines always pave the way for various works of iniquity.
Strategy	• "teach"—indoctrinate, convince, persuade • "accuse"—the saints and the true teachers/apostles • "warn," "threaten," "afflict," and "kill" • "seduce," "sexual immorality," "food," "idolatry"—Balaam, Balak, Jezebel • "weak"—spiritual lethargy, self-inflicted death, lazy, slow • "wealth," "materials"—Laodicea • "deception"

---

[247] The table is based mainly on Revelation 1–3. In the rest of Revelation, especially chapters 12–20, the enemy's activities are heavily featured.

Features	Details
Satanic Aim	• Denounce and dishonor the "name of Jesus," "faith in Jesus," "testimony of Jesus," "commandments of God," "spirits of God," "temple of God," "blood of the Lamb" • Prevent saints from following the Lamb, drinking from the springs of living water, receiving eternal life. • Instead of "water of life" and an infusion of the Lamb's blood into the saints' life, Satan desires to inject his poisons and the "wine of her adulteries" into our lives (see Sardis). • Instead of magnifying Jesus (e.g., Ephesian's first love), one magnifies self (Laodicea). • His ultimate aim is "death," even the "second death."
Satanic Method	• Satan values structure, organization, unity, diversification, and multiplication of methodologies, personality, strategy, specificity, locality, and issues. • Satan has advanced and well-developed plans. Strategies are tailored toward locality, personality, concerns, issues, needs, strengths, and weaknesses. • Where "holy fire" is blazing, Satan establishes his throne and synagogue and sends his able agents. However, in Sardis and Laodicea, where people are either "about to die" or "lukewarm," Satan's agents are manifestly absent. This also informs us of the enemy's intelligence and resourcefulness.

OPPONENTS

Opponents in Revelation 1–3

Regarding opponents, it is important to do a comparative analysis of them in the seven churches:

Churches	Opponents	Nature of the Opponents
Ephesus	"wicked men," "false apostles"	"apostles" who claim to be sent of God, Jews
Smyrna	"false Jews," "synagogue of Satan"	"Jews" as coming from the "synagogues"; thus, they are Jews
Pergamum	"throne of Satan," "Balaamites," "Nicolaitans"	possibly Jews
Thyatira	"Jezebel," "depths of Satan"	"Jezebel," probably an institution or a church

Churches	Opponents	Nature of the Opponents
Sardis	"you are dead," "about to die," "what you have heard, received, obey it"	internal weakness; their faith is likely weakened by the Jews
Philadelphia	"liars," "false Jews," "synagogue of Satan"	"Jews" from the "synagogues"; Jews
Laodicea	"wretched, "pitiful," "blind," "naked," "lukewarm"	Laodiceans read Colossians, addressed Jew-related issues, thus Jews caused problems (Col. 4:16)

Jewish Nature of the Opponents

All the opponents in the seven churches are of Jewish origin. Those in Smyrna and Philadelphia are described as "false Jews" who have come out from the "synagogue of Satan." Those wicked men in Ephesus are described as "false apostles," signifying their claims as being sent of God. Those in Pergamum and Thyatira are described as either "Balaamites," "Nicolaitans," or those who entertain the woman Jezebel and hold to her teachings. The opponents in Pergamum hold the *didachē*, while those in Thyatira possess the "depths of Satan."

Both of these teachings have a deadly influence on the believers. No external or internal opponents are mentioned in the two remaining churches (Sardis, Laodicea). Perhaps Satan does not want to waste his time and resources on them, seeing that one of them is almost "dead" and the other "lukewarm." However, that does not mean that there are no Jewish opponents in these two churches. In fact, the apostle Paul urged the Laodiceans to read the letter he wrote to the Colossians. In it, he mainly refuted the claims of the Jewish opponents (see Col. 4:16). Therefore, in the seven churches, the opponents are mostly of Jewish origin.[248]

---

[248] For further discussions on this, see the chapters on Smyrna and Philadelphia.

REWARDS FOR FAITHFULNESS

Satan operated out of Pergamum. "Yet you remain faithful to my name" and you "did not renounce my name" (Rev. 2:13a). The church at Pergamum is commended for not merely surviving, but thriving right under the nose of the enemy. Note that being faithful to Jesus' "name" and refusing to renounce their "faith in Him" was not something they developed overnight. The church seems to have a long history of remaining faithful to Jesus. "You did not renounce your faith in me, even in the days Antipas, my faithful witness, who was put to death in your city [Pergamum]" (v. 13b).

Because of Antipas' exemplary living, he is revered as "my faithful servant." If the saints in Pergamum remain faithful, as did Antipas, then Christ promises to reward their faithfulness with the "hidden manna" and "a white stone with a new name written on it, known to none but only him who receives it." The object in view is a white stone that has a secret name. What does Revelation teach about the elements "white," "stone," and a "secret name"?

The Color White. The color white is heavily mentioned in the book. First, God is enthroned on a white throne. Second, Jesus' hair is described as "white as wool" and "white as snow." He is also seen riding on a white horse twice in the text. In Revelation 6:2, a warrior with a bow in His hand rides out on a white horse. Then in chapter 19, Christ is pictured as riding on a white horse to strike the nations with a sharp, double-edged sword. Third, the angels are seen robed in white. Finally, the saints who have washed their robes in the Lamb's blood are arrayed in white. White, therefore, is a color that is closely associated with and represents the purity, holiness, and righteousness of God, the Lamb, angels, and His saints.

The Stones. Stones are featured in Revelation 4 and 21. Chapter 4 describes the appearance of the enthroned One this way: "And the one who sat there had the appearance of jasper and a carnelian. A rainbow, resembling an emerald, encircled the throne" (v. 3). Revelation 21:11

describes the dwelling place of God: "It shone like the glory of God, and its brilliance was like that of a very precious jewel, like a jasper, clear as crystal." Similar precious stones are used to describe the twelve gates and twelve foundations of New Jerusalem. For instance, the "twelve gates were twelve pearls, each gate made of a single pearl" (v. 21). Each one of these gates featured the names of the twelve tribes of Israel.

Similarly, the twelve foundations, each bearing one of the disciple's name, were made of "every kind of precious stone" (v. 19).[249] The walls of the city are made of jasper, and the city itself is made of "pure gold" (v. 18). Hence, the precious stones are used in association with God, His dwelling place, the gates and foundations of His city, and those who live (or will live) there. The white stones, therefore, speaks of the quality, rarity, purity, durability, permanence, and eternal value of God, godly things, godly principles, and godly people.[250]

<u>The Name that No One Knows</u>. Concerning "a new name written on it, known only to him who receives it," there are several clues. The fact that no one knows does not imply secrecy, but that it is unique, exquisite, and tailor-made. If the value of any precious stone depends on its rarity, then here we are allowed to see a "one of a kind" stone. With that said, why does only the concerned overcomer know the name? The stone that overcomers receive is contrasted with the stones that bear the names of the patriarchs and apostles. The names inscribed on the stones belonging to the patriarchs and apostles are no longer secret. The reader is already told of what those stones are made.

This, perhaps, is because they (except John) are dead, and their eternal rewards are, to a large degree, guaranteed. They have fought a good fight and secured those rewards (cf. 6:9–12). However, to those living,

---

[249] The twelve precious stones are stated as follows: "The first foundation was jasper, the second sapphire, the third chalcedony, the fourth emerald, the fifth sardonyx, the sixth sardius, the seventh chrysolite, the eighth beryl, the ninth topaz, the tenth chrysoprase, the eleventh jacinth and the twelfth amethyst" (Rev. 21:19, 20).

[250] "Gold there is, and rubies in abundance, but lips that speak knowledge are a rare jewel" (Prov. 20:15).

the fact that the name is "known only to him who receives it" means that they have yet to secure those rewards. They are still making decisions, and the messages addressed to them in the book of Revelation are intended to facilitate those decisions.[251] Since the addresses still have battles to fight and opponents to overcome, the names on those stones must remain undisclosed. In fact, this makes them become more like Christ, who also has a "name written on him that no one knows but he himself" (Rev. 19:12).[252]

RELATIONSHIP BETWEEN REVELATION 1–3 AND 4–22

Regarding the relationship between Revelation 1–3 and 4–22, the following can be noted:

1. *Satan, His agents, and Activities*. Satan, his throne, agents, and activities that saturate the seven messages are also featured in Revelation 12–19. If Satan has his "throne" set in Pergamum, then when the first readers (those in Smyrna, Philadelphia, and Pergamum, in particular) read chapters 12 and 13, they must have undoubtedly understood the prophetic messages as being applicable to them also.
2. *Swords out of Mouths*. Christ's designation as having a "sharp double-edged sword" out of His mouth stands in contrast to other "mouths," such as the mouths of the dragon, the beast and its image, the false prophets, and the saints of God. To those in Pergamum who not only held the teachings of the Nicolaitans but also taught others the same, Christ warned of striking them with a "sharp sword." Because the

---

[251] This is similar to the fifth seal (see Rev. 6:9–12). In the fifth seal, those slain were given and have already secured "white robes." However, the living who are crying "how long" have yet to secure them. They still have battles to fight, decisions to make, and dangers to face.

[252] Moreover, Christ also has a name that is known only to Himself (see Rev. 19:12). This account conveys the concept of being mysterious. In this case, the harlot of Revelation 17 bears several designations. The first one identifies her as the "Mystery." Her other titles are "Babylon the Great, the Mother of Prostitutes, and of the abominations of the earth" (v. 5). Perhaps these mysteries signify the mystery of God and sin.

opponents use words and teachings to cause the downfall of the saints, Christ also uses the "sword [mouth, tongue, or words]" to threaten them. The occurrence of the terms "sword," "mouth," or "tongue" in different parts of Revelation serve to connect the two parts of Revelation. This and other themes previously studied serve to narrow any differences that may exist between Revelation 1–3 and 4–22.

3. *Secret Names*. A white stone having a strange name that no one knows shares considerable similarity with Christ, who also has a similar name, and the patriarchs and apostles whose names are already in the public domain. Further, "Babylon the Great" of Revelation 17 also boasts of not merely having a mysterious name, but of *being* the "Mystery." Even the mention of the "hidden manna" only serves to heighten the mysteriousness that envelops the book and greatly increases the volume of common themes between these two sections (1–3 and 4–22).

> *Concepts and characters such as "false Jews," "false apostles," "liars," and "synagogue of Satan" seem to suggest that the theological milieu in which Revelation emerged is not totally removed from the issues that Paul, Peter, and Luke discussed in their works.*

4. *The Theological Context of Revelation*. Finally, concepts and characters such as "false Jews," "false apostles," "liars," and "synagogue of Satan" seem to suggest that the theological milieu in which Revelation emerged is not totally removed from the issues that Paul, Peter, and Luke discussed in their works. This will become increasingly clear as we discuss the remaining churches.

18.

THYATIRA: SON OF GOD, WHOSE EYES ARE LIKE BLAZING FIRE

To the angel of the church in Thyatira write: These are the words of the Son of God, whose eyes are like blazing fire and whose feet are like burnished bronze. I know your deeds, your love and faith, your service and perseverance, and that you are now doing more than you did at first. Nevertheless, I have this against you: You tolerate that woman Jezebel, who calls herself a prophetess. By her teaching she misleads my servants into sexual immorality and the eating of food sacrificed to idols. I have given her time to repent of her immorality, but she is unwilling. So I will cast her on a bed of suffering, and I will make those who commit adultery with her suffer intensely, unless they repent of her ways. I will strike her children dead. Then all the churches will know that I am he who searches hearts and minds, and I will repay each of you according to your deeds. Now I say to the rest of you in Thyatira, to you who do not hold to her teaching and have not learned Satan's so-called deep secrets, (I will not impose any other burden on you): Only hold on to what you have until I come.' To him who overcomes and does my will to the end, I will give authority over the nations—'He will rule them with an iron scepter; he will dash them to pieces like pottery'—just as I have received authority from my Father I will also give that one the morning star He who has an ear, let him hear what the Spirit says to the churches. (Revelation 2:18–29)

JESUS IN THYATIRA

How Jesus Is Introduced in Each of the Seven Churches

To the believers in Thyatira, Jesus Christ appeared as the "Son of God, whose eyes are like blazing fire and whose feet are like burnished bronze." In this divine designation, three names or descriptions are stitched together: 1) the "Son of God," 2) the One whose "eyes are like blazing fire," and 3) the One whose "feet are like burnished bronze." Before we discuss each of these in detail, we will first consider how Jesus is introduced in each of the seven churches.

The Seven Churches	Designations	Comments
Ephesus	• the one "who *holds* the seven stars in His *right hand* and *walks* among the seven golden lampstand" (2:1)[253]	Jesus "holds the seven stars in his right hand" + "walks" among the "seven golden lampstands"
Smyrna	• "First and the Last, who *died and came to life again.*" (2:8)	Who He is and His deeds
Pergamum	• "sharp, double-edged sword" coming out of His *mouth* (2:12, 16)	Physical features
Thyatira	• "Son of God" • "whose eyes are like blazing fire" • "burnished bronze" feet (2:18)	Names and physical features
Sardis	• "who *holds* the seven spirits of God and the seven stars" (3:1)	"holds the seven spirits of God" + holds the "seven stars"
Philadelphia	• "who is holy and true, who *holds* the key of David. What he opens no one can shut, and what he shuts no one can open" (3:7)	"holds the keys of David"
Laodicea	• "Amen, the faithful and true witness, the ruler of God's creation" (3:14)	Names and characters

---

[253] The emphases in all passages are supplied.

The Orator stresses a particular aspect of Himself and then draws a corresponding message that applies to each of the seven churches. To the church at Thyatira, the glorified Christ is presented as the "Son of God." With this, two specific characteristics are pointed out: His "blazing eyes" and "feet of burnished bronze." In the discussions that follow, we shall seek to address two questions: What do these identifying characteristics mean? and what is their significance for the saints in Thyatira?

Meanings and Implications

Son of God. In the vision of Revelation 1:10–20, John saw someone like a "Son of Man," but to those in Thyatira, Jesus Christ introduced Himself as the "Son of God." The Orator almost always pointed to a particular aspect of the vision of the Son of Man, but in this instance, the author added *new* material. Jesus' designation used here does not appear in the vision. This, however, is not a unique case. There are also other such changes. For instance, in the address to the believers in Sardis, Jesus came across as the One who "holds the seven spirits of God and the seven stars" (3:1). In the vision, however, Jesus only "holds the seven stars." The "seven spirits" were not part of that vision (see 1:16).

> *If Jesus' claim to be the "Son of God" had attracted the wrath of the opponents and landed Him at Golgotha, then Revelation is cautiously reinforcing the same argument.*

Core of the Christological Issue. Do these reflect an authorial error, or is it intentionally crafted? As we have seen earlier, this is part of the literary craftsmanship, where One like the "Son of Man" is intentionally elevated to assume the title "the Son of God." According to the Gospel of John, this designation is at the core of the Christological debate. "For this reason they tried all the more to kill him; not only was he breaking the Sabbath, but he was even calling God his own Father, making himself equal with God" (John 5:18). Therefore, if Jesus' claim to be the "Son of God" had attracted the wrath of the opponents and landed Him at Golgotha, then Revelation is cautiously reinforcing the same argument.

<u>Jesus Against the Prevailing Expectation</u>. The Jewish aristocrats condemned Jesus as "this fellow," signifying Him as an imposter (see John 9:28, 29), and His death was heralded as the climactic evidence of their claims (see Mark 15:31, 32). It seemed to confirm in the opponents' minds that He was not the coming Messiah, not the Prophet about whom Moses wrote, and certainly not the Son of David, because Jesus died without liberating Israel or reigning on David's throne as was eagerly expected.

In the face of this, the hopes of those who thought Jesus was the Messiah were devastated. They were genuinely baffled—at least initially. Later, the Holy Spirit opened their eyes to see two things. The first concerns the imagery of the "Messianic Lamb." Although Jesus was the Prophet, the One about whom Moses wrote, the anticipated Messiah, and the Son of David, He must first *be* the Lamb of God. "How foolish you are," the Visitor to Jerusalem rebuked Cleopas and his friend at Emmaus, "and how slow to believe all that the prophets have spoken! Did not the Messiah have to suffer these things *and then* enter his glory?" (Luke 24:25, 26, emphasis supplied; see also Luke 17:25). The Jewish nation was so focused on the Messiah coming like Elijah, Moses, the Prophet, and David, that they forgot that He was first going to come as a "lamb" and the Suffering Servant (see Acts 3:18).

The second source of hope was supplied by Daniel's prophecies, especially the vision concerning the one like the "Son of Man" and the "Ancient of Days" (see Dan. 7 and 10).[254] As we have seen earlier, this divine character in Daniel is evoked in Revelation 1:12–16. However, with the emphatic and intentional use of the title "Son of God," heaven seems to be saying that Jesus of Nazareth is not merely a human prophet who was "snatched up to God" in the same way Moses and Elijah were. He is not just another human— "Prophet," "Son of David," or the One about whom Moses wrote—who

---

[254] For more detailed information, see the discussion on the vision of Revelation 1:12–16.

happens to have a divine anointing or the Father's "seal of approval" (John 6:27), but He is greater than all who prefigured Him.[255] He not only existed before the patriarchs, prophets, and kings, but also He was their very God. "I tell you the truth," Jesus answered His critics, "before Abraham was, I am" (John 8:58). While the Jews expected the "Lord to raise up [for them] a prophet like me [Moses] from among your own brothers" (Deut. 18:15), God sent His "only begotten Son." While Israel waited for an earthly emissary, God sent a heavenly One. It is this Man that now identifies Himself as the Son of God. Therefore, throughout Revelation and the rest of NT literature, Christ's preexistence and divine attributes are given prominence.

The "Son of God" Described as Having "eyes" of "blazing fire"

The Greek phrase translated "blazing fire" is *phloga puros*,[256] which literally means "flames of fire." The description of Jesus' eyes as "flames of fire" is one of two features—the second being His feet of "burnished bronze." As noted earlier, John's description of Christ in Revelation 1:12–16 is similar to the divine characters of Revelation 10, Daniel 7, and Daniel 10. However, the phrase "flames of fire" appears three times in Revelation (1:14; 2:18; 19:12). Although the exact phrase is not used, the same concept also occurs in Hebrews 4:12–13, Revelation 4 and 5, and the Gospel of John. Since we have already discussed Revelation 1:14, we will now consider the other passages.

Christ's Blazing Eyes in Revelation 2. In the immediate context, Christ's fiery eyes are used in conjunction with the fact that He searches hearts and minds—that is, His ability to see what human eyes cannot see. Thyatira's inability to see as God sees has resulted in their toleration of the woman Jezebel. They were misled and played into her harlotry. However, the glorified Christ reveals to the saints what He intends to do with

---

[255] See Edmund Little, *Echoes of the Old Testament*, ed. J. Gabalda et al (Paris: Rue Pierre et Marie Curie, 1998), pp. 40, 41.

[256] The root word for *phloga* is *phlox*.

Jezebel and her children. "I will strike her children dead. Then all the churches will know that I am he who searches hearts and minds, and I will repay each of you according to your deeds" (v. 23).

Christ's Blazing Eyes in Revelation 19. The reference in Revelation 19:12 infers a similar intention. The Rider is called "Faithful and true," and "with justice he makes war." Then in verses 20 and 21, the One whose "eyes are like blazing fire" (vv. 11, 12) captures the beast and his image, throws them "alive into the fiery lake of burning sulfur," and kills their followers with the "sword that came out of the mouth of the rider on the horse."

In both of these passages, Christ's ability to see hearts and minds is prominently featured. Therefore, when He executes judgment, His judgments are thorough, fair, and final. Years ago, God said to the prophet Samuel, "Do not consider the appearance or the height ... Man looks at the outward appearance, but the Lord looks at the heart" (1 Sam. 16:17). This resulted in God appointing David, the youngest and least likely candidate, to be the king of Israel. David stood in contrast to Saul, who embodied man's choice and was appointed king based on his appearance and height (see 1 Sam. 10:23, 24).

The "Word of God" and "God" as the Blazing Eyes in Hebrews 4:12–13. In Hebrews, it is God's eyes that see everything. "For the word of God is living and active. Sharper than any double-edged sword, it penetrates even to dividing soul and spirit, joints and marrow; it [word of God] judges the thoughts and attitudes of the heart. Nothing in all creation is hidden from God's sight. Everything is uncovered and laid bare before the eyes of him to whom we must give account."

Unlike Revelation, here it is the "word of God" that "judges the thoughts and attitudes of the heart," and it is God's eyes that see everything, but the context still remains the same. In the two previous passages, the discussions on the blazing eyes are hatched within the context of the divine judgment. The same is also true in Hebrews 4.

Holy Spirit as the "blazing eyes" of Jesus Christ. When we leave the pages of Revelation, we see both the Word of God and God Himself assuming a similar role as the blazing eyes of Jesus Christ. Although the phrases "blazing" and "fiery eyes" are mentioned in Hebrews, the author made it abundantly clear that the eyes to which he refers are similar to, if not the same as, those in Revelation. However, a closer investigation reveals yet another aspect. The "blazing eyes" of Christ are equated with the "spirits of God." Compare the following passages:

Revelation 4:5	Revelation 5:6
"Before the throne seven lamps were *blazing*. These are the seven spirits of God."	"He [the Lamb] had seven horns and seven *eyes*, which are the seven spirits of God"

Several things are noteworthy. First, the term used for Jesus' eyes, in the Greek, is *phlox pur*, which means "flames of fire." However, that which burns before the throne is not *phlox pur*. It is *lamptades puros*, which means a "lamp of fire."[257] This means that they are conceptually and functionally identical, but lexically different. Second, according to Rev. 5:6, the seven "lamps of fire" are the "seven eyes" of the Lamb. This means that the "seven lamps of fire" are actually the "seven spirits of God." That is, "seven lamps of fire" = "seven eyes of the Lamb" = "seven spirits of God." Therefore, Christ's ability to search the hearts and minds is contingent on or manifested through the "spirits of God."

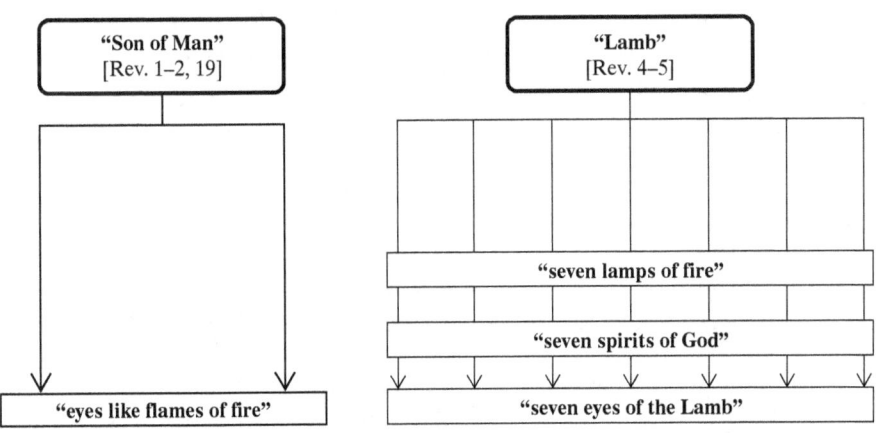

---

[257] Revelation also describes "Wormwood," that "fallen star" of Revelation 8:10–11 as a καιμενος ως λαμπας "blazing like a torch." The term for "torch" is *lampas*, which is translated as "lamp" elsewhere. This means that the usage in Revelation 4:5 is almost identical to the "fallen star" of 8:10–11. Further, similar to Christ's eyes as "flames of fire" in chapters 1, 2, and 19, in Hebrews 1:7, the "angels" of God are described as "flames of fire [*puros phloga*]." Note that the same Greek terms that were used to describe the eyes of Christ in 1, 2, and 19 are used to describe "angels" here.

As noted earlier, Jesus' eyes were described as "flames of fire," but here the "spirits of God" are described as "lamps of fire." Though the terms "flames" and "lamps" are not exactly the same, both are thematically and functionally the same. This etymological difference may merely indicate variation, a common literary feature in Revelation. We have earlier seen how Jesus Christ was variously described as the "First and the Last," the "Alpha and the Omega," or the "Beginning and the End." Therefore, the terms "flames" and "lamps" are used similarly, where the differences in branding are intended to merely enrich the meaning.

"Flames of Fire," "lamps of fire," and "tongues of fire." Jesus' eyes are likened to "flames of fire" (Rev. 1:14, 2:18, 19:12). Then in Revelation 4 and 5, the Holy Spirit is described as the "lamps of fire" and equated with the eyes of Jesus. However, in the Pentecost narrative, the pouring out of the Holy Spirit is described as *glōssai ōsei puros*, which is translated to mean "tongues of fire." Whether it be "flames of fire" on the Lamb's head, "the lamps of fire before the throne," or "the tongues of fire" at Pentecost, they all describe the Holy Spirit's role at various places and different times. Nevertheless, one thing is clear: the Holy Spirit is intricately related to and an inseparable part of Christ because He functions as the "eyes" of Jesus.[258]

All-seeing Eyes of Jesus in the Gospel of John. In the other Johannine writings, particularly in the Gospel, the phrase "blazing eyes" is not mentioned. However, the writer did provide sufficient evidence to show that Jesus is indeed divine and "searches the hearts and minds" of people. The following table provides a general survey of this concept:

Text		Comments on the Context
2:24	"He knew all men ... for he knew what was in a man"—***Believers***	"many people ... believed in his name" but He did not trust their sincerity because He knew the hearts and minds of men.
4:39	"He told me everything I ever did"—***Samaritan Woman***	Many in Samaria believed in Jesus because of the woman's testimony.

---

[258] John the Baptist had also prophesied that Jesus would baptize with the "Holy Spirit and with fire" (Matt 3:11, Luke 3:16).

Text		Comments on the Context
6:64	"Yet there are some of you who do not believe"—***Judas***	"For Jesus had known from the beginning which of them did not believe and who would betray Him."
7:24	"stop judging by mere appearances, and make a right judgment"—***The Jews***	Judgment based on "mere appearances" versus "right judgment," based on the truth and motives of the heart and mind.
21:15–17	"Lord, you know all things; you know that I love you"—***Peter***	This was in response to the last of the resurrected Jesus' three questions—"Do you love me?" Peter's response acknowledged that Jesus knew even his thoughts.

As the above passages reveal, Jesus can see both the outward appearances and the intents of the heart. He also knows things that are not yet spoken or uttered in secret, as well as the present and future.[259] However, the main focus of Jesus' blazing eyes is to show that He sees and knows all people. Because nothing is hidden before His all-seeing eyes, He executes judgments accordingly.

<u>Context of the Usage of Jesus' Blazing Eyes.</u> Before we explore the concept in more detail, the following is a brief survey of the context of each usage of Jesus Christ's fiery eyes:

> *Jesus can see both the outward appearances and the intents of the heart. He also knows things that are not yet spoken or uttered in secret, as well as the present and future. However, the main focus of Jesus' blazing eyes is to show that He sees and knows all people. Because nothing is hidden before His all-seeing eyes, He executes judgments accordingly.*

---

[259] Jesus' ability to know all things about all people could be attributed to his "blazing eyes." These statements in the Gospels could also stem from Jesus' own confession to each of the seven churches with statements that begin with the phrase "I know you," "I know where you live," "I know your deeds," etc.

Text	Eyes	Function
Rev. 2:18 (1:14)	"blazing eyes" of Jesus	Judgment: will punish Jezebel
Rev. 19:11, 12	"blazing eyes" of Jesus	Judgment: will punish the beast, image, and their followers
Rev. 4:5, 5:6	"seven blazing lamps" are the spirits	"wrath of the Lamb" (Rev. 6:16)
Heb. 4:12, 13	All-seeing "eyes" of God	Judgment: all creation will give an account

The context of each usage of Christ's blazing eyes has divine judgment in focus. John the Baptist had said likewise: "I baptize you with water. But one more powerful than I will come ... He will baptize you with Holy Spirit and with fire. His winnowing fork is in his hand to clear his threshing floor and to gather the wheat into his barn, but he will burn up the chaff with unquenchable fire" (Luke 3:15–17; Matt. 3:11, 12). We now turn to the opponents in Thyatira and the significance of Christ's blazing eyes for them.

OPPONENTS AND THEIR SIGNIFICANCE

Jezebel the Prophetess

What then is the implication of Jesus' blazing eyes for those in Thyatira? This question cannot be considered without discussing the opponents.

Jezebel the Prophetess. The opponent in Thyatira is described as "Jezebel." Jezebel "calls herself a prophetess" and has many children, but she is portrayed as being involved in "sexual immorality." This cannot be taken literally, as the imagery of having sexual relations or using the same bed involves erroneous doctrines, where the "prophetess'" is involved in teaching or deceiving Christ's servants. Jezebel's teachings are described as "Satan's ... deep secrets," which she has used to mislead even the very elect in Thyatira.[260]

---

[260] Ekkehardt Mueller, "Fornication." *Biblical Research Institute*, p. 3. Mueller also shows that references to fornication and adultery in Pergamum, Thyatira, and Babylon are all symbolic. https://1ref.us/10i (accessed February 13, 2020).

Christ says He has given Jezebel sufficient "time to repent," but at the time the letter was read, she had not yet responded favorably. Also, "she is unwilling" to do so in the future. Christ therefore makes two pronouncements. First, He will throw Jezebel into a "bed of suffering." Second, her children will be stricken dead. He then makes an urgent appeal to His children who have been misled into "sexual immorality" to repent. However, should they refuse to repent, He will also cause them to "suffer intensely" in the same "bed."

The Opponents in Ephesus, Pergamum, and Thyatira. "Wicked men," "Balaam," and "Jezebel" are the names of the opponents in Ephesus, Pergamum, and Thyatira, respectively. Although different labels are used to describe each of these opponents, they are similar in several ways. The following table shows these similarities:

Features	Ephesus	Pergamum	Thyatira
Satan	Satan's agents	"Satan's throne"	"Satan's deep secrets"
Opponents	"wicked men," "false apostles"	"Balaam," "Nicolaitans"	Jezebel, a prophetess
Nationality of opponents	Jews	Jews	Jews
Teachings	The "false apostles" had a set of teachings or doctrines	"teachings of Balaam" and teachings of Nicolaitans	"You tolerate that woman Jezebel" and "Satan's deep secrets"
Activities	"you cannot tolerate wicked men," "tested" and found them false	"you have people there who hold to the teachings of Balaam"	"misleads my servants"
Level of compromise	No compromise: No "idol food," no "sexual immorality"	Compromised: "eating foods sacrificed to idols," and "committing sexual immorality"	Compromised: "eating food sacrificed to idols" and involved in "sexual immorality"

Single Entity or Character with Many Names. A few aspects of this table need to be stressed. First, as mentioned earlier, Revelation gives multiple names, titles, or designations to label a single concept or character. For instance, Jesus is called the "word of God," the "Lamb," "Michael," the "male child," "Son of Man," "Son of God," the Rider on the white horse, the "King of kings," and the "Lord of lords." Similarly, the enemy is described as "Satan," the "dragon," "devil," "the star that had fallen from the sky," "the accuser," and "Wormwood." The same is also true with the beast, its image, and the saints of God.

The list here is not comprehensive, but the reason why this is highlighted is because most of the opponents in the seven churches represent the same entity. They derive from the same place—the "throne of Satan" or the "synagogues of Satan." They possess similar or the same teachings and doctrines, and their activities in most of the churches are identical. However, they differ in two ways. In each of the churches, these opponents assume a different label befitting their works. (This is exactly the same way Christ presents Himself to each of the seven churches). Also, the manner in which each of the seven churches responds to these opponents is markedly different.

Saints' Responses to Opponents Differ. Second, some members of Pergamum "hold the teachings of Balaam," demonstrating the success the Balaamites had in and among the Pergamumites. Jezebel in Thyatira has a similar result. The believers in Thyatira not only tolerated Jezebel, but even worse, some of their prominent leaders were misled. This shows the level of success Jezebel had in Thyatira.

Where these two churches failed, the Ephesians had tremendous success over the same opponents. They did not tolerate their wicked opponents. They tested and falsified these men's claims to apostleship. Perhaps this is the reason why there is no mention of eating "food sacrificed to idols" or "sexual immorality" among the Ephesians. The saints in Pergamum and Thyatira, however, had compromised and are represented as eating of ritualistic foods and committing "sexual immorality."[261]

---

[261] Committing spiritual adultery is a common issue in both Revelation 1–3 and 4–22. Our current discussion is limited to only three churches (Ephesus, Pergamum, and Thyatira). As we shall see later, the saints in Sardis are commended for their victory over the adulterous woman.

Jezebel the Prophetess and Babylon the Harlot of Revelation 17 and 18

Whereas the relationship between the opponents in Ephesus, Pergamum, and Thyatira are obvious, the similarities between the "Jezebel" of Thyatira and "Babylon" of Revelation 17 and 18 is even more striking. Carefully note the following table of similarities:

Jezebel of Thyatira (Rev. 2:18–29)	Babylon, the Harlot (Rev. 17–18)
"woman Jezebel" (v. 20)	"Babylon ... the Mother of Prostitutes" (vv. 3, 5)
"calls herself a prophetess" (v. 20)	"great prostitute," calls herself "a queen," a fallen church (17:1; 18:2, 7)
"By her teaching she misleads my servants" (v. 20)	"made the whole world drink the poison," "teaching" (17:2; 18:3)
"sexual immorality" (v. 20)	"committed adultery" (17:2, 5; 18:3, 9)
"eating of food sacrificed to idols" (v. 20)	"intoxicated with the wine of her adulteries" (17:2, 4; 14:18; 18:3)
"given her time to repent" (v. 21)	Given over "1260 days." Now "her sins are piled up to heaven" (18:5)
partners sleep with her on her bed (v. 22)	"kings, rulers, and princes" commit adultery with her (17:2; 18:3, 9)
"I will strike her children dead" implies, Jezebel is a mother, has children, and children as evil as mother (v. 23)	"BABYLON ... THE MOTHER OF PROSTITUTES" implies she has children who are prostitutes too (17:5)
"I will cast her on a bed of suffering ... and make those who commit adultery with her suffer intensely" (v. 22)	"The beast and the ten horns ... will hate the prostitute. They will bring her to ruin and leave her naked" (17:16), "she will be consumed by fire" (18:8).
"all the churches will know" that I judge and punish fairly (v. 23)	"the beast and the ten horns will hate the prostitute" (17:16), "pay her back double for what she has done" (18:6)
God punishes and repays (v. 23)	Just and fair God, rewards and punishes (18:6, 7)
"*to loitois*" faithful ones are asked to "hold on to what you have" (v. 24)	"*loitois*," "*loipōn*" they hold or "obey God's commandments and hold to the testimony of Jesus." They are urged to hold them till the end (ch. 14; 12:17)

Jezebel of Thyatira (Rev. 2:18–29)	Babylon, the Harlot (Rev. 17–18)
"Satan's so-called deep secrets" (24)	"Mystery, Babylon the Great" (17:5)
Partners are urged to repent of her sins (22)	God's people are urged to "come out of her" (18:4, 5)
Christ comes through as one having fiery eyes (18)	The Rider on the white horse also comes as one having "fiery eyes" to execute judgment on the beast and its image (19:12)

<u>Volume of Similarities</u>. Jezebel of Thyatira and Babylon share more than fifteen characteristics, some of which include the following: 1) Both are presented as female, seductive prostitutes who have multiple sexual partners; 2) Both characters have children who are as evil as they are; 3) Their characters and conducts are wrapped in mystery and secrecy; 4) Both women have a body of teaching with which they pursue followers and intoxicate God's servants; 5) God has given both of them sufficient time and opportunities to repent, but they have beat back every wave of divine mercy and continued in their disobedient path; 6) In the end, God will execute punishment on both; and 7) even the nature of the punishment is similar. For Thyatira, Jezebel and her lovers are cast into a "bed of suffering" and suffer intensely, while in Revelation 17, the same multi-horned beast on which she rides turns around and brings her to total ruin. Such volume and quality of similarities suggest that the two characters are almost identical.

Further, it is possible that John and his audience may have seen the relationship between Jezebel and Babylon. If the whole prophetic message was comprehensible and applicable to John and his initial audience, then for one to maintain that Revelation 4–22 was not for them is against the spirit of the text. This does not mean that the same prophecies do not apply to our time, but that those who read them for the first time at least thought the entire message was for them.

<u>An Appeal to Those with Jezebel and Babylon</u>. The letter to the saints in Thyatira states that Jezebel has been given sufficient time to repent, but she has not and does not intend to change, so the appeal

is made to her partners to "repent of her ways [sins]" (2:22). This appeal is exactly the same appeal made to those seduced by Babylon the Great. "Come out of her, my people, so that you will not share in her sins" (18:4).

<u>The Remnant</u>. When Jezebel deceived most of the saints and the Lord's servants, the remaining faithful ones were described as the "rest of you [Gr. *to loitois*]." The Greek word used to describe the faithful few is exactly the same word that is used to describe the remnant of Revelation 12:17—those who keep the commandments of God and have the testimony of Jesus.

<u>The Word of God and the Testimony of Jesus</u>. The remnant in Thyatira was urged to "only hold on to what you already have until I come" (2:25). However, one is not told of what those things consisted. Earlier in 1:9, we were informed of certain things the seven churches had in common. The prominent one in this list includes "the word of God and the testimony of Jesus." If the *loitois* in Thyatira held on to the same commandments and testimony, then these are exactly the same commodities of which the *loitois* of Revelation 12:17 are in possession.[262]

<u>Jesus as Having Fiery Eyes</u>. Finally, in both cases, Jesus Christ is presented as having "eyes like flaming fire." To Jezebel, the One with fiery eyes who searches hearts and minds says He will repay her for her works. Then to the harlot of Babylon, the One with the fiery eyes captures the beast, his image, and the false prophets, slays them with the sword from His mouth, and throws them into the fiery lake.

These and other similarities lead us to certain inescapable conclusions: 1) the text in its entirety may have been read, interpreted, and understood by the early church, 2) the prophecies therein are comprehensible and applicable to the early church, 3) the early church could have also identified some of these adversarial characters and institutions

---

[262] Those in Revelation 12:17 are briefly described in 17:14 as "his called, chosen and faithful followers." Therefore, we have the same "remnant" in view in all three places.

in their own time and context, and 4) the prophecies of Revelation have a dual application and did speak to the early church as much as they speak to us today.

Early Readers' Comprehensibility

<u>High Comprehensibility Narrows the Amount of Differences</u>. The volume of similarities between the opponents in the seven churches (Rev. 1–3) and the Babylon in Revelation 14–18 or the beast in 13 not only serves to aid our understanding of the early church's comprehensibility and applicability of the text, but also further narrow the level of differences that may exist between these two sections of the text.

<u>The Effects of Dissecting the Text and Its Remedy</u>. One of the problems a modern reader encounters is the plurality of opponents within the seven churches (1–3) and in rest of Revelation (4–22). Because each of these opponents assumes a wildly different label, name, designation, or description, one is led to believe that they are totally different characters. Any possibility of them being the same is immediately dismissed. Then when one proceeds to divide the text (1–3 and 4–22) and place the sections hundreds or thousands of years apart, it only serves to compound our comprehensibility issues. Therefore, the fundamental questions we need to ask are, What did the text mean to the early church? How did the early church view the opponents? How did they read the two sections of Revelation? If there is a high degree of similarities between Jezebel and Babylon, then could it be that the early church may have seen these two characters as being one and the same? Could it be that the early church may have seen the opponents in Ephesus, Pergamum, and Thyatira as consisting mostly of the same characters?

The literary feature in Revelation whereby a single character assumes multiple names and titles helps us make sense of some of these issues. Furthermore, to the early church, the opponents, whether they were the Balaamites, Nicolaitans, Jezebels, "wicked men" from the "synagogues of Satan," "false Jews, "false apostles," "false prophets," or the "sea beast," "land beast," or even "Babylon the Great," represent some distinctly identifiable personalities, characters, or institutions in their time. Therefore, one of the aims of this study is to investigate those characters. This is because if we can form some opinion on what these messages meant to the early church, then it will elucidate our understanding of the same prophecies in our time.[263] Paulien puts it this way: "The book of Revelation was definitely written to people in its time and place. It definitely meant something to them, and the more we can understand what they understood, the better our understanding of the book will be."[264]

Dual-Intentionalism Reveals God's Sovereignty

The messages of Revelation speak so eloquently of God's sovereignty and wisdom, especially in using the same concepts and entities to speak to a people then and now. The opponents that existed then also exist today, for there is really "nothing new under the sun." This is 'dual intentionalism' at work. In a dualistic method, the prophecies that had a more literal fulfillment in a specific locality in the past, now have a wider and grander application in our time and context. Therefore, an attempt to determine what Revelation (both 1–3 and 4–22) meant to the initial readers will serve to enhance our understanding and appreciation of the prophecies.

Significance

Perhaps the core message God was attempting to communicate to His fledgling church is that His "blazing eyes" see everything. Just as He punished Balaam for his role in seducing the Israelites into immorality and

---

[263] This is especially crucial because the Adventist church admits that her prophetic messages of Revelation are drawn mainly from the last half of the book, chapters 12–22 (*Symposium on Revelation—Book II*, p. xiii).

[264] Paulien, "Simply Revelation, Part One," p. 2. See also Joh Paulien, "The Seven Heads of Revelation 17," p. 17. Taken from original manuscript.

idolatry, so will He punish spiritual Balaams, the "wicked men," and the "Jezebels" of Revelation. Even Babylon, whose "maddening wine of her adulteries" has made all nations drunk, will be served a "double portion from her own cup" (Rev. 18:6). Such divine assurances are very appropriate for a distressed church that screams "how long?" day and night (see Rev. 6:9–11).

Punishment and Rewards

To the Thyatirans, Christ said, "I know your deeds, your love and faith, your service and perseverance, and that you are now doing more than you did at first" (2:19). To these faithful followers, He promised, "I will repay each of you according to your deeds." Therefore, "hold onto what you have" (vv. 23, 25). He who threatens to punish the wicked also promises to reward His faithful followers. This theme of punishment and reward that is based on one's works is a thread that runs throughout Revelation. We will pick this up in a later discussion.

> *He who threatens to punish the wicked also promises to reward His faithful followers. This theme of punishment and reward that is based on one's works is a thread that runs throughout Revelation.*

RELATIONSHIP BETWEEN REVELATION 1–3 AND 4–22

The amount of similarities between the Thyatiran message and Revelation 4–22 serves to narrow any differences that may exist between these two sections. For specific similarities between the Thyatiran address and the Babylon of 14–19, refer to earlier discussions in this chapter. Additionally, we have thus far identified numerous literary, linguistic, and thematic relationships that exist between these two sections of Revelation. In the table below, we enlist these similarities for emphasis:

Revelation 1–3	Revelation 4–22
1/Ephesus Address (2:1–7)	*See also Rev. 22:2*
• Promised "tree of life" (2:7)	• "tree of life" (22:2)
2/Smyrna Address (2:8–11)	*See Rev. 12, 13*
• Two wars—current war and future "ten-day" war • War is waged against those who keep God's commandments and have Jesus' testimony • War originates from "Synagogue of Satan," and they are involved in "blasphemy" against God. • Devil is described as "accuser" (2:10)	• Two wars—current 1,260 days war and future war on "remnant" (12:17) • War waged against those with God's commandments and Jesus' testimony • War from dragon and beast, who are covered in blasphemous names • Satan or devil is described as "accuser" (12:10)
3/Pergamum Address (2:12–17)	*See Rev. 12, 13*
• "throne of Satan" • Christ comes with "sharp sword" to judge opponents • Rewards: white stones	• "Satanic throne" (13:2) • Dragon, beast, land-beast, and image have mouths/swords to kill too • Rewards: precious stones (chs. 21, 22)
4/Thyatira Address (2:18–29)	*See Rev. 14, 16–18*
• Jezebel the prophetess • Prostitute, seduces saints • Faithful saints as "remnant" (2:24) • Remnant have "the commandments of God and testimony of Jesus"	• Babylon the harlot (ch. 17) • Prostitute, seduces saints • Faithful saints as "remnant" (12:17) • Remnant have "the commandments of God and testimony of Jesus" (12:17)

CONCLUSION

The adversarial characters, groups, and institutions in the seven oracles (Rev. 1–3) have a strong relationship with the material in 4–22. The manner in which Christ is presented in these two sections of the book corresponds as well. As we proceed with the three remaining oracles, it will become abundantly clear that these two sections of Revelation are identical. Such an approach in turn minimizes most of the comprehensibility, applicability, and exegetical issues.

19.

SARDIS, PART I: HIM WHO HOLDS THE SEVEN SPIRITS AND STARS

> To the angel of the church in Sardis write: These are the words of him who holds the seven spirits of God and the seven stars. I know your deeds; you have a reputation of being alive, but you are dead. Wake up! Strengthen what remains and is about to die, for I have not found your deeds completed in the sight of my God. Remember, therefore, what you have received and heard; obey it, and repent. But if you do not wake up, I will come like a thief, and you will not know at what time I will come to you. Yet you have a few people in Sardis who have not soiled their clothes. They will walk with me, dressed in white, for they are worthy. He who overcomes will, like them, be dressed in white. I will never blot out his name from the book of life, but will acknowledge his name before my Father and his angels. He who has an ear, let him hear what the Spirit says to the churches. (Revelation 3:1–6)

CHRIST IN SARDIS

The "Son of Man" introduces Himself as the One "who holds the seven spirits of God and the seven stars" in His hand. Before we discuss the content of His actual words, we shall first seek to establish the definition, significance, and implication of this self-disclosure. What do the "seven spirits" and "seven stars" mean? What does it mean to have them in His hand? For information concerning the seven spirits, see our previous discussions in chapter 8 and 18 of this study. We shall, however, begin this discussion with some aspects of the seven spirits.[265]

A Review on the Seven Spirits

<u>Seven Spirits for All the earth</u>. Christ is pictured as having "seven spirits" and "seven stars" in His hand. The discussion on the stars will be done later. Here we continue the discussion on the seven spirits. There is much scholarly discussion as to whether or not the seven spirits were for the seven churches or the whole world. Scholars who subscribe to the latter viewport usually do so at the expense of its immediate context. Stefanovic, for example, offers two reasons for such an approach. First, because the OT treats the number seven as a sacred number that denotes perfection or completeness, the seven spirits are for the whole world and not just for the seven churches.

Second, because Revelation heavily features the number seven—in its structure, the total number of churches addressed, the lampstands, eyes, horns, angels, trumpets, bowls, and seals—the seven spirits here are assumed to have a similar universal significance.[266] Considering the broader narrative regarding this number, one can appropriately conclude that the seven spirits could refer to the totality of the Holy Spirit sent "out into all the world" (Rev. 5:6)."[267]

The Seven Spirits and Dual-Intentionalism

Whereas the methodology used and the subsequent conclusions at which we arrived are valid, this approach does not account for the immediate context. The core exegetical question—What exactly did the seven spirits mean to the addressees, especially the seven churches?—is not addressed at all.

---

[265] Due to its length, the discussion on Sardis has been divided into two chapters.
[266] Stefanovic, pp. 63, 64, 202. Maxwell is also of the same opinion. See, *God Cares*, Vol. 2, p. 68. See also, Aune, *Revelation* 1–5, pp. 115–116. Aune considers the "seven churches" as a "symbol of universal church," p. 130.
[267] Stefanovic, p. 204.

The "seven spirits" sent to both the Local and World Churches. The "seven letters" were addressed to the "seven angels of the seven [literal] churches" (Rev. 1:20; 22:16). If the "seven angels" that Christ holds "are the seven angels of the seven churches" (Rev. 1:20), then there is no reason to think that the "seven spirits" are not. In the passage under study, the glorified Christ holds the "seven stars [angels]" and "seven spirits" and walks among the seven churches. The emphatic use of the number seven here is perhaps intended to reinforce a single message. The first readers probably felt the seven spirits were intended for *them*. Christ sent the seven spirits to the seven literal churches. The Divine Orator undoubtedly used a series of sevens to personalize the message. Acknowledging this reality answers our primary exegetical question: What did the text mean to the original readers?

> *Although the text may have meaning for us today, we cannot ignore what it may have meant to its first readers. He who gave the prophecies sought to respond to the immediate issues confronting the seven literal churches, while simultaneously having His eyes fixed on future global scenes.*

Yet Christ left sufficient evidence to show that the seven spirits also embody the totality of the "spirits of God sent out into all the earth" (Rev. 5:6). Jesus, who sent the seven spirits to the seven literal churches, is also the One who sent or sends the seven spirits to all the earth. He who holds the "seven spirits in His hand" in Revelation also holds "everything," including "the Spirit without limit," in His hand in the Gospel of John (3:34, 35). Therefore, the seven spirits having some sort of a dual significance is more in harmony with the intent and spirit of the text.[268]

Dual Application. What then does this passage about the seven spirits mean? This encompasses the core of a methodological issue. A dual

---

[268] For a thorough discussion on the spirits or Holy Spirit, refer to chapter 8.

application for the prophecies of Revelation seeks to address the questions, What did the text mean to the seven churches in Asia Minor? and what does it mean to us today? Although the text may have meaning for us today, we cannot ignore what it may have meant to its first readers. He who gave the prophecies sought to respond to the immediate issues confronting the seven literal churches, while simultaneously having His eyes fixed on future global scenes. Therefore, the same prophecies that spoke to the seven literal churches in Asia Minor also speak to a wider community today.

The Seven Stars

What then are the "seven stars"? The phrase "seven stars" appears four times in Revelation 1–3, first appearing in 1:16. The second occurrence explains what the stars are: "The seven stars are the [seven] angels of the seven churches" (v. 20). The other two passages (2:1 and 3:1) quote 1:16, where the glorified Christ is seen holding the "seven stars in his right hand." In that case, we will explore both stars and angels together.

<u>Angels as Heavenly Messengers</u>. The Greek word for "angels" is *angelos*, which primarily refers to supernatural beings, especially angels, both fallen and unfallen. Aune, therefore, argues that the letters were indeed addressed to supernatural beings. He writes, "each church is represented in the heavenly world by an angelic figure who somehow personifies that church ... seems to be John's meaning."[269] Although Aune uses Revelation 1:20 ("The seven stars are the seven angels of the seven churches") to support this, his argument has two problems. First, he does not fully develop his view to show how he arrived at his conclusions. Second, this view presents a logistical issue. If indeed the messages were written to the angels, consider what would happen: the messages went from Jesus to John through an angel, then John addressed the seven heavenly angels. The angels then gave it back to John, who then gives it to the seven churches. Therefore, this theory has inherent issues.

---

[269] Aune, *Word Bible Commentary: Revelation* 1–5, pp. 131, 132.

Angels as Human Messengers. Because this proposition poses a logistical and logical concern, others prefer to have the word *angelos* translated as "human messenger," similar to an elder or bishop in each of the churches.[270] This proposition fits in very well with this interpretation, given that John was tasked to write and send it to the seven churches, so in this case, the seven stars might be translated as "seven [human] messengers."[271] However, a problem arises when there are other Greek words for "messengers," "apostles," "elders," or "envoys," but the Divine Orator does not use any of these. He consistently and intentionally uses the term *angelos* when addressing each of the churches (see Rev. 2:1–3:22). This emphatic use of the term *angelos* should make one wonder whether Christ actually meant heavenly angels. Therefore, this study is of the opinion that the "seven angels" could stand for both supernatural and human agents. This suggestion should not surprise us, as such rendering is tenable in Revelation. What follows next is a discussion on 'angels as both heavenly and earthly beings.' Additionally, discussion on 'angels as human church leaders,' is briefly stated in chapter 20 of this book.

The seven angels as both supernatural and human servants. This dilemma pushes us to explore another literary style in Revelation—one that is actually the opposite of two devices discussed earlier. First, in chapter 12 and 13 of this book, we extensively discussed the composite representation of Christ in Revelation. For instance, in Revelation 1, Christ is portrayed as the embodiment of all OT iconic priests, kings, priestly-kings, prophets and patriarchs. In this graphic representation, all these characters are subsumed into a single character—the "one like the son of man" (Rev. 1:13). Second, we have also seen how a single character assuming several identifications, names and brandings. For example, the "one like the son of man" in Revelation 1 is also the "Lamb" (Rev. 5), "male child" (Rev. 12), and the "Rider on the white horse" (Rev. 19). The same is also likened to

---

[270] For a brief overview on each of these views, see *Aune, Revelation* 1–5, pp. 108–112.

[271] This may be somewhat true. Consider the three angels of Revelation 14 flying midair with an "everlasting gospel to proclaim to every nation, tongue, and tribe," which raises the question, Who is actually proclaiming, the angels or the saints? Here, church leadership is personified as an "angel." The same could be true in Revelation 2–3. If so, that does not nullify the reality that angels do exist.

a "mighty angel" of Revelation 10. Then in Rev. 19, Christ is presented as having more than seven names and titles (vv. 11–16). In these two types, Christ is presented as a single character but bearing multiple imageries and titles. However, the literary style associated with the "seven angels" of Revelation 1–3 is the opposite of these two. In the "seven angels," we are seeing two distinct set of characters labelled and treated as *one* single entity. Stated differently, the "seven angels" represent both the seven literal angels and seven human church leaders. Therefore, the angels have a dual significance. This is not an uncommon literary construction in Revelation. The table below shows other examples of two separate characters blended together and addressed as a single entity.

Characters	Character 1	Character 2
"morning star"	Jesus Christ (Rev. 22:16)	Saint(s) of God (Rev. 2:28)
"144,000" (Rev. 7, 14)	sealed Jewish believers (Rev. 7: 4–5)	"first-fruit from the earth" (Rev. 14:1–3)
"First and Last," "alpha and Omega," etc.	God (refer to chapter 7)	Jesus Christ (refer to chapter 7)
"Three angels" (Rev. 14:6–9)	Three literal angels (Rev. 14:6–9)	"144,000" of Rev. 14:1–4 (17:14)
"armies of heaven" (Rev. 19:14)	Literal angels "of heaven" (v. 14)	End-time militant church for they are dressed in white robe (v. 14)
"seven angels" (Rev. 1–3)	Seven heavenly winged Angels	Human church leaders

A thorough discussion can be done in a future project, but for our purpose now, it is important to point out a few things.

- *The Morning Star.* Two distinct characters are described as the "morning star." In Rev. 2:28, Christ promises to give the "morning star" to the saints in Thyatira. Then in Rev. 22:16, Christ Himself is also described as the "bright morning star."
- *The 144,000.* As discussed in chapter 12, the "144, 000" is a single set of numbers that is used to identify two distinct groups of people with 144, 0000 each—that is, the 144, 000 sealed Jewish believers and the 144, 000 "first-fruit from the earth."

- *Names of Christ and God*. As was discussed in chapter 7, Jesus Christ and God share the exact same names, titles and designations. The same designations like "First and the Last" and "Alpha and Omega" that are used for God are also applied to Jesus Christ—thus establishing their oneness.
- *Three Angels*. The three angels who are seen flying in "mid-air" in Rev. 14:6–9 could refer to both three literal angels and/or the end-time militant saints of God assembled on Mount Zion (Rev. 14:1–4; 17:14; 19:14).
- *Armies of Heaven*. And finally, a similar case could be made for many other characters. For example, the "armies" that follow the Rider on the white horse of Revelation 19 are called "armies *of heaven*." The phrase "of heaven" suggests that these are literal heavenly angels. However, the fact that they are "dressed in fine linen, white and clean" implies that "the army" consists of those who "washed their robes and made them white in the blood of the Lamb" (Rev. 7:14). Therefore, just like the "three angels" of Rev. 14, these "armies" are both "of heaven" and earth.

The argument here is that the "seven angels" of Revelation 1–3 could mean *both* seven heavenly angels and seven human servants of God.

The Earthly and the Heavenly Churches. To further reinforce this argument, let us explore one more factor. John consistently presents the saints or the church of God as being both of earth and heaven. The table below captures these occurrences.

Characters	Earthly Church	Heavenly Church
"morning star"	A saint(s) of God (Rev. 2:28)	Jesus Christ (Rev 22:16)
"seven angels" (Rev. 1–3)	Human church leaders	Heavenly winged Angels
"Three angels" (14:6–9)	"144,000" of Rev 14:1–4. The saints "were given two wings of a great eagle" to fly to safety (Rev. 12: 14). In Rev. 14: 6–9, the same wings turn to "wings of mission"	The three angels of Rev. 14:6–9 can stand for three literal heavenly angels or it could also refer to the end-time militant church of God

Characters	Earthly Church	Heavenly Church
"armies of heaven" (Rev 19:14)	End-time militant church for they are dressed in white robe (v. 14)	Literal angels "of heaven"
The pure and faithful bride of Rev. 12	The earthly saints of God who believe in Christ are considered as entering or being in heaven	The bride is seen "in heaven" (v. 1). The "church of the firstborn" in "Heavenly Jerusalem" (Heb. 12:22–23)
"a great multitude … before the throne" (Rev. 7: 9)	Those who have "washed their robes and made them white in the blood of the Lamb" (7:14b), but have not yet "come out of the great tribulation"	"These are those who have come out of the great tribulation" (7:14a). They can "come out" by righteous death or at Second Coming
"twenty-four elders… were dressed in *white* and had *crowns of gold* on their heads" (Rev. 4:4)	Washing of robes in His blood is akin to coming to "Mount Zion, to the heavenly Jerusalem, the city of the living God. You have come to thousands upon thousands of angels in joyful assembly, to the church of the firstborn, whose names are written in heaven. You have come to God … to Jesus Christ" (Heb. 12:22–24)	If dressed in "white," they too came out of the great tribulation—either by death or 2nd Coming. Righteous dead and martyred saints have already secured their "white robes" (Rev. 6:11) and the "crowns of gold" (Rev. 4:4)

In the Apocalypse, the saints of God can be seen both in heaven and no earth. Consider the following examples. Thus far, we have stated the following: (a). that there are two "morning stars"—one in heaven (Christ) and another one promised to the saints in Thyatira; (b). that the "three angels" could refer to both the heavenly angels and the "144,000" militant church of God. Also notice that the 144, 000 are seen "standing on Mount Zion" (Rev. 14:1). If this Zion is the earthly one, then according to Hebrews, there is another Zion in Heaven (Heb. 12:22); (c). that the "armies of heaven," signifies both heavenly and earthly armies. To this list, we add the following:

(d). *The Pure Woman of Revelation 12.* This woman represents the church of God here on earth—from Eden to Bethlehem and then down to the present time. But notice that this church emerges from "heaven" and not from somewhere here on earth (Rev. 12:1).

(e). *The Great Multitude of Revelation 7:9*. Apostle John describes the "great multitude before the throne" in two ways. First, they are "those who have washed their robes and made them white in the blood of the Lamb." This description signifies the saints' initial faith in Christ and washing away of their sins. Second, the "great multitudes" are also described as those who "have come out of the great tribulations." If the first description of the saints signifies their initial faith in Christ here on earth, then the second description is intended to provide a preview of those who will eventually be saved (in heaven). Thus, the righteous are seen in two places—both here on earth and also in heaven.

(f). *The church of the firstborn*. As shown above, the saints who accept, believe, love, obey and follow Christ are considered as joining the heavenly assembly. "But you have come to Mount Zion, to the heavenly Jerusalem, the city of the living God. You have come to thousands upon thousands of angels in joyful assembly, to the church of the firstborn, whose names are written in heaven. You have come to God ... to Jesus Christ" (Heb. 12:22–24). Hebrews blurs the demarcation between the earthly and the heavenly churches and calls both churches the "church of the firstborn."

<u>Summary</u>. In summary, the wider context supports the "seven angels" as being both of heaven and earth. Other characters who are similar to this include: the morning stars, the three angels, the armies of heaven, the pure bride and the great multitude. Then when both churches—the heavenly/"thousands upon thousands of joyful assembly" (Heb. 12:22–24; Rev. 5:11–12; 7:11) and the earthly saints of God (Rev. 7:9–10; 12:1–2, 17;14: 1–5) are combined, the unified church becomes the "church of the firstborn" (Heb. 12:23).

Nevertheless, the questions that need to be asked are, If the letters were addressed to supernatural beings, then why? Was there a contextual issue that the Orator and author were trying to address? If so, then what was it? This study reexamines the textual evidences to determine these and other issues surrounding the "seven stars [angels]." In our discussion, three sets of evidences will be explored: 1) The concept of "stars" and "angels," 2) The significance of the seven stars and seven spirits being in the hands of Christ, and 3) The relationship between seven angels and seven churches.

The Use of Stars in Revelation

Occurrences of Stars in Revelation. In Revelation, as in other NT literature, stars signify angels and a host of other things. We shall briefly discuss each of them:

1. *Holy Angels of God.* From the start, Christ Himself says, "the seven stars are the [seven] angels of the seven churches" (1:16). Therefore, stars are holy angels of God.
2. *The Morning Star.* Jesus Christ promises to give the overcomers of Thyatira "the morning star" (Rev. 2:28). The exact meaning of this morning star is unclear. Peter described the "morning star" as something that can "arise in your hearts" (2 Peter 1:19). It probably refers to the "sure word of prophecies" and its fulfillment. It could also refer to a mighty angel. However, in Revelation 22:16, Jesus refers to Himself as the "bright morning star."
3. *Jesus Christ.* Revelation 10 describes a Christ-like character as "another mighty angel" (v. 1). The exact identity of this character is debated. Some think it is an angel, while others are of the opinion that it is Christ. Further discussions on this are provided towards the end of chapter 20 in this book.[272] There we have provided sufficient evidences to conclude that this character is Christ.
4. *Saints and Servants of God.* The pure woman of Revelation 12 is described as having "a crown of twelve stars on her head" (v. 1).

---

[272] Scholarly discussions on this are presented towards the end of chapter 20 in this book. The reason for doing this is because of the complex nature of this character. It is better to pick up the discussions after some critical, preliminary discussions in chapter 19 and the early part of chapter 20, so at this stage, one can either go there first or continue reading.

The same woman is also pictured as clothed with the sun and moon under her feet. This imagery is similar to Joseph's dream, where the twelve stars represented the twelve sons of Israel and the sun and moon represented Jacob and his wife (Gen. 37:9–11). At that time, Jacob and his household were the people of God. Daniel refers to God's end-time people as the "stars" and "brightness of the heavens;" "Those who are wise will shine like the brightness of the heavens, and those who lead many to righteousness, like the stars forever and ever" (Dan 12:3). The apostle Paul referred to the saints and servants of God as shining stars in a dark and crooked world (Phil. 2:15). Furthermore, Mephibosheth likened King David to "an angel of God" (2 Sam. 19:27). Whether in the Old or New Testaments, stars can also refer to the saints of God.

5. *Satan and His Fallen Angels.* The third and fifth trumpets describe "Wormwood" as the "great star, blazing like a torch [that] fell from the sky" (Rev. 8:10, 11; 9:1–11). Then chapter 12 describes an "enormous red dragon" sweeping "a third of the stars out of the sky" and onto the earth (vv. 3, 4). If Wormwood and the great red dragon represent the same entity, then both describe the fall of Satan and his angels,[273] who are described as *angelos* also. Further, the apostle Paul also described Satan as an "angel of light" (2 Cor. 11:14).

6. *False Apostles, Prophets, and Shepherds.* Finally, Jude referred to the false shepherds and counterfeit apostles as "wandering stars" in the universe (v. 13).

Summary. Therefore, in Revelation (and the NT), stars represent supernatural beings—Christ, angels of God, Satan, angels of Satan—and

---

[273] For a further discussion on this, see Ekkehardt Mueller's newsletter "The Beast of Revelation 17–A Suggestion," *Biblical Research Institute*, p. 2.

human servants of God or Satan.[274] The following table summarizes the occurrences of the term "stars" in Revelation and what they represent:

"Star" or "stars" in Revelation	Notes
"seven stars are angels" (1:16)	Angels, servants of God
Jesus Christ is the "bright Morning Star" (2:28; 22:16).	Christ (and His human servants)
"another mighty angel" (10:1)	Jesus Christ
"wandering stars" (Jude 13)	False shepherds/apostles
Pure woman with a crown of "twelve stars" (12:1); Saints "shine like stars in [this] universe" (Phil. 2:15)	The church, saints, and servants of God
"Wormwood," the "great star" that fell from the sky (8:10, 11; 9:1–11)	Satan
The dragon swept "a third of the stars out of the sky" and onto the earth (12:3, 4)	Satan and a third of the fallen angels

The Significance of the Seven Stars and Seven Angels in Christ's Hand

<u>Significance of Being in Someone's Hand</u>. Some important issues are noteworthy here. First, Christ has the "seven stars" and "seven spirits" in His hands. Revelation 1:16 states that the "seven stars" are in "his right hand." What, then, is the significance of being in the hands of someone? In Rev. 5:1, God is seen holding a scroll in "his right hand." If that signifies ownership and having authority over the scroll, a similar relationship can be assumed in Christ's case; that is, Christ has authority over *both* the seven spirits and seven angels.

<u>The Seven Spirits and Seven Angels in Christ's Hand</u>. This is quite consistent with the text. In our previous discussion on the "spirits of God," we noted how the seven spirits form the seven eyes of the lamb (Rev. 5:6), how Christ sent them out into the world, and how they work in submission to Him.[275] Because the seven angels are also in Christ's hand, it is possible to conclude that both of these entities have a similar role, and a similar

---

[274] In Matthew 2, the star has messianic significance.
[275] Refer to our discussion on the spirit and Christ in Revelation 1:4–7.

relationship to and with Jesus Christ. This means that He who gave the seven spirits also gave the seven angels to the seven churches, and they both work in total submission to Christ.

CHRIST, SPIRITS, ANGELS, AND THE SEVEN CHURCHES

Dual Positions and functions of Christ, Spirits, and Angels

<u>Dual Positions of Christ, Spirits, and Angels</u>. This rendering also makes three, not two, divine characters occupy a prominent position in both heaven and earth. For example, Jesus Christ, who is seen walking among the seven churches here on earth (see 1:10–20), also stands in the center of the throne in heaven (see 5:5–8). The seven spirits and seven angels who are seen addressing the seven churches (on earth) are also present "before the throne" in heaven.

Divine Beings	Earth	Heaven
Christ	"among the lampstands was someone like, 'a son of man'" (1:12)	"Then I saw a lamb ... standing in the center of the throne" (5:6)
Spirits	"the seven spirits of God sent out into all the earth," "He who has an ear, let him hear what the spirit says to the churches" (2:7; etc.)	"Before the throne, seven lamps were blazing. These are the seven spirits of God" (4:5; 5:6; 1:4)
Angels	"The seven stars are the seven angels of the seven churches" (1:20; 2:1, etc.)	"the seven angels who stand before God, and to them were given seven trumpets" (8:2)

<u>Dual Roles of Christ, Spirits, and Angels</u>. These three divine characters not only occupy prominent positions in both worlds, but they also play a dual role.

Jesus Christ's Dual Role. The Lamb who was slain and whose "blood ... purchased men for God" is the only Being who could stand in the center of the throne of God with His bloodied body. Because He has triumphed, He has not only earned the right to receive the scroll, but also "sit with the Father on his throne." The One before whom John falls "as though dead" is also the

One before whom the four living creatures, twenty-four elders, and myriads of angels fall down in worship! The Lamb who is heralded as the only worthy Being in the entire universe is the cord that binds earth to heaven.

The Spirits' Dual Role. Following His ascension, Christ sent the "seven spirits to all the earth," and they function as the "eyes of the lamb" here. Christ's ability to see the thoughts and minds of people is enabled by the Spirit of God who dwells in their hearts. Notice that these same seven "spirits of God" who play a crucial role in the life of the church here on earth also glow and burn before the throne in heaven. Thus, like the Lamb, the Spirit of God also plays an important role in both realms.

The Angels' Dual Role. Like the seven spirits, Christ also sent the seven angels to the earth. Unlike other angels, these seven angels are especially tasked to personally attend to the redeemed. Then they also have direct, unlimited access to the throne of God. Referring to these angels, Christ says, "their [little children's] angels in heaven always see the face of my Father in heaven" (Matt. 18:10). These special angels present the cries and anguishes of the saints to God. Then they bring back messages from God to humanity, and sometimes they are personally involved in executing divine judgments in response to prayers.[276]

For instance, in Revelation 8:2, we note "seven angels" involved in executing divine judgment on the disobedient. The same seven are also involved in pouring the seven plagues in chapters 15–17. These judgments are in direct response to the anguished cries of the saints in Rev. 6:9–12. The following table summarizes our discussion:

Divine Character	Believers' Concerns	Divine Response
Christ	Dead, with His own blood, purchased mankind for God	"He [Jesus] is able to open the scroll and its seven seals" (5:5), and to give the Spirit to the earth

---

[276] For instance, "How long" cries are assumed to have been carried up to God by the angels. The golden bowls with the incense is the anguish, cries, and tears of the saints (Rev. 5:8). Then in Revelation 8–11, the same angels are responsible for administering God's judgment—a direct response to the saints' prayers in chapters 5–6. We will develop this fully in a later project.

Divine Character	Believers' Concerns	Divine Response
Spirits	"hear what the spirit says," Christ's blazing eyes/spirits, sees the heart and executes judgments	"blazing fires before God," "blazing fires—spirits of God—are the eyes of the lamb" (5:6)
Angels	"the angels of the seven [earthly] churches" (1:20), "To the angel of the church in ... write" (2:1; etc.)	"The seven angels who stand before God ... were given seven trumpets" (8:2, 6); "their [little ones'] angels in heaven always see the face of my Father in heaven" (Matt. 18:10)

The Seven Messages: Christ, Spirits, and Angels

Just as these three entities occupy and perform special tasks in both heaven and earth, the same three are also involved in the communicating of the seven messages to the seven churches.

Christ and the Spirits. Each of the seven messages to the seven churches was orated by the glorified Christ, but each one ends as if it is coming from the "spirits." For instance, it begins with the formulaic "These are the words of him who ...," and a description of Christ follows. Then it ends with the appeal, "He who has ear, let him hear what the Spirit says to the churches." This is not an indication of contradiction, but of unity. Speaking of His own words, Christ says, "The words I have spoken to you are spirit" (John 6:63). Therefore, He and the Spirit are one, just as the Father and Son are one, so in this case, there is clear evidence that both Christ and the Spirit are involved in communicating the messages of Revelation to the seven churches.

Angels. Now to that list, we can add the angels because the messages dictated by Christ and the appeals made by the Spirit are addressed *to* the angel assigned to each church.[277] In this case, the same three divine beings

---

[277] Several observations are made here. First, at the outset, John identified God as the source of Revelation, which was given to him by Christ but through "his angel" (1:1). The angel in focus here is singular and obviously differs from the "seven angels" of chapters 2–3. In this case, the angel

that occupy the honored position in heaven (i.e., "before the throne"), have direct and unlimited access to God, and see the "face of [the] Father in heaven" are now actively involved in disseminating the seven messages to the seven churches on earth.

The involvement of Christ, the spirits, and the angels in the communication of the oracles demonstrates the value and solemnity of these messages. Because Christ stated, "The words I have spoken to you are spirit and life," eternal life and eternal damnation depend on these words (John 6:63). The author of Hebrews puts it this way; "For if the message spoken by angels was binding, and every violation and disobedience received its just punishment, how shall we escape if we ignore such a great salvation?" (Heb. 2: 2–3).

The Three Witnesses: Christ, Spirits, and Angels

<u>The Accuser and Three Witnesses Before the Throne</u>. The same three characters also have another important role. They who represent the believers "before the throne" are the ones who are united in bearing the testimonies to the believers here on earth.[278] In this sense, they function as "three witnesses" before the throne. Moses wrote that the testimonies of

---

here refers to the one that acts as John's personal guide throughout Revelation (especially chapters 4–22). However, this does not nullify the fact that even in the seven messages, as in the rest of Revelation, *one* angel is also involved in the communication process. That is, instead of "his angel," the "seven angels" are involved in the "seven messages." In other words, the seven messages come to John *through* the angel. Therefore, the route that the message takes is consistent with the spirit of the prologue of Revelation.

[278] The story even gets better. The angels who are each apportioned a church go from the church to the throne and back. They carry the prayers and burdens of the church—each member—specifically before the throne. Their job is not only to present a "report" but also our cases against the charges of the "accuser of our brethren." That angel is portrayed as being in the "presence of God," seeing His face, and pleading our case on our behalf. That includes the "How long" cry of the sixth seal. However, when the response finally comes, the Lord appoints the very same angels—"the seven who stand before the throne"—to receive the trumpets and blow them. How fittingly appropriate! That is justice at its best!

two or three witnesses are required to validate or settle a dispute in the Jewish legal system (see Deut. 17:6; 19:15; John 5:31–47; 8:14–18; 1 John 5:6–9), so in this context, we see "three witnesses" representing the saints before the throne in heaven. If Satan is the "accuser ... who accuses [us] before our God day and night," and Christ is the Chief Advocate, then the "spirits" and "angels" act as the second and third witnesses before the throne on our behalf (Rev. 12:10; see also 1 John 2:1).

> *If Satan is the "accuser ... who accuses [us] before our God day and night," and Christ is the Chief Advocate, then the "spirits" and "angels" act as the second and third witnesses before the throne on our behalf.*

The Courtroom Scene in Sardis. As if this was intended, a courtroom scenario is fittingly evoked in the Sardisian address. "I will never blot out the name of that person from the book of life, but will acknowledge that name before my Father and his angels" (Rev. 3:5). Here Christ is presented as the Attorney before His Father and the saints' angels. And, of course, the "seven spirits of God" are always before the throne.

Courtroom Scene in Hebrews. With all that goes on behind the scene, how solemn it is for us to hear "what the spirit says to churches."[279] Hebrews makes the same point: "Anyone who rejected the law of Moses died without mercy on the testimony of two or three witnesses. How much more severely do you think a man deserves to be punished who has trampled *the Son of God* underfoot ... and who has insulted the *Spirit of grace?*" (10:28, 29, emphasis supplied).[280]

---

[279] Jesus holding both the angels and spirits in His hand signifies His authority over both of them. Why is this important? The contextual issue the early church encountered concerning the Holy Spirit is fully discussed in Revelation 1:4. There we have suggested that the opponents not only denied Jesus of Nazareth's Christology, but also His divinity because He did not come baptizing. The Holy Spirit came after both John the Baptist and Jesus were dead. This could have provided fertile ground for opponents to claim that the manifestation of the Spirit was in direct response to John the Baptist's ministry.

[280] The same is reiterated in Hebrews 2:2–4: "For if the message spoken by angels was binding, and every violation and disobedience received its just punishment, how shall we escape if we ignore

CONTEXTUAL ISSUES: CHRIST AND ANGELS

Stars, Angels, and Spirits in New Testament Writings

Whether the imagery of Christ having authority over both the "spirits" and "angels" of God is intended to address any issues the early church encountered is unclear. For discussions on issues surrounding Jesus' relationship to the Holy Spirit, refer to chapter 8. However, if the early church encountered any issue that emphasized the worship of angels over Jesus, it remains to be investigated.

In all the NT literature, the clearest text concerning such a practice is Colossians 2:18: "Do not let anyone who delights in false humility and the worship of angels disqualify you for the prize." The phrase "worship of angels" in this context is a contentious one, and scholars are divided over the exact meaning of this passage. Some think it means "worshiping *with* the angels," whereas others suggest it denotes worship that is rendered *to* angels. However, even the methodologies used to arrive at these and other conclusions are contrived and convoluted.[281] The second passage that makes reference to angels submitting to Jesus Christ is 1 Peter 3:22. With such obscure passages, it is hard to reach a sound conclusion on this issue.

Angels Versus Jesus in Revelation

Revelation 1–3. Any discussion concerning the worship of angels in the early church must be within the parameters of known NT historical and textual contexts. In Revelation, we have four sets of passages that indicate angel–related issues. The first set concerns the passage under study, so we will proceed to discuss the other three passages.

Revelation 19. The second is John's attempt to worship the angel in Revelation 19. "At this I fell at his feet to worship him. But he said

---

such a great salvation [that is, the message "spoken to us by his Son"]? This salvation, which was first announced by the Lord, was confirmed to us by those who heard him. God also testified to it by signs ... and gifts of the Holy Spirit distributed according to his will."

[281] Refer to some of the major contemporary works of Aune, Ranko, and others.

to me, 'Do not do it! I am a fellow servant with you and with your brothers who hold to the testimony of Jesus. Worship God!" (v. 10). As if for emphasis, John repeated this encounter again in the epilogue (Rev. 22:8, 9). Whether or not this passage was intended to forbid the worship of angels in the early church is still unclear, but what is clear in these passages is that worship rendered *to* the angel in place of God is forbidden. Note that the angel that John attempted to worship is "his angel" through whom the prophecies came (Rev. 1:1).

Angels Command Mankind to Worship God. Further, although the angel acknowledged being the "servant" who "hold[s] to the testimony of Jesus," he actually instructed John to "worship God," but not Jesus. This same command first appears in the first angel's message of Revelation 14:6–7. "He [the first angel] said in a loud voice, 'Fear God and give him glory ... Worship him who made the heavens, the earth, the sea and the springs of water." Two things are clear: 1) angels restrain people from worshiping them, and 2) they command John and the whole world to worship the Creator God.

Worship Rendered to God and Jesus Christ (Rev. 4–5). However, the text does not say anything about rendering worship to Jesus. Despite this lack of explicit command to worship Jesus (in Revelation), the book is actually saturated with the *act* of worship being rendered to Him. In fact, the worship rendered to Christ is more than the worship rendered to God. For illustrative purposes, let us compare Revelation 4 and 5.

Worshipers	Worship of God	Worship of Jesus
"four living creatures"	Worship God who was, is, and is to come (4:8)	Worship Jesus (5:8–10, 14)
"twenty-four elders"	Worship God the Creator (4:9–11)	Worship Jesus (5:8–10)
"many [or all the] angels"	—	Worship Jesus (5:11, 12)
"every creature in heaven and on earth and under the earth and on the sea"	—	"To him who sits on the throne and to the Lamb" (5:13)

As the table shows, the volume of worship rendered to Jesus is more than that rendered to God.

1. *The Number of Texts.* There are only four verses that describe the worship rendered to God, whereas seven verses discuss worship offered to Jesus. Only in one place are both deities worshiped together. However, even that text occurs in the chapter that discusses Jesus Christ (Rev. 5) and not God (Rev. 4).
2. *The Number of Worshipers.* Only two groups of worshipers (twenty-four elders and four living creatures) worship God in Revelation 4, whereas seven groups of worshipers worship Jesus in chapter 5. For instance, the twenty-four elders and four living creatures worship Jesus twice, with all the angels and the creatures of heaven, earth, in the sea, and under the earth.
3. *Other Worshipers Worship God in Revelation 5, but Not in Revelation 4.* The twenty-four elders and four living creatures that worshiped God in Revelation 4 also worshiped Jesus in chapter 5. Four of the remaining five groups of worshipers (all heavenly creatures, earthly creatures, sea creatures, and those under the earth) render worship to both God and Jesus. However, the difference is that they do so only after Jesus had received the scroll from God in Revelation 5.
4. *Angels Worship Jesus Only.* In the final analysis, six out of seven groups of worshipers render worship to both God and the Lamb (in Rev. 4 and 5). The remaining group of worshipers directs their worship only to Jesus Christ. That group is the entire angelic host of heaven. Although the angels "encircle the throne and the four living creatures and the elders," they take a muted position when God is worshiped in chapter 4, but as soon as Jesus receives the scroll from God, a torrent of ecstatic worship arises from them. In a telling way, their worship is rendered *only* to Jesus Christ (see 5:12).

The angels' verbal confession to worship God (Rev. 14:6, 7; 19:10) and their prohibition from being worshiped (Rev. 19:10) speak one thing, but their actions speak another. They refuse to be worshiped and repeatedly command others to worship God, but their actual acts of worship are directed only to Jesus Christ. These passages in Revelation serve as important clues to unearthing issues concerning the worship of angels in the early church. Therefore, we will turn to Hebrews in the next chapter and continue this discussion.

20.
SARDIS, PART II

ANGELS, MOSES, AND JESUS IN HEBREWS

Superiority of Jesus over Angels and Moses

The book of Hebrews makes an elaborate contribution to the issues surrounding the worship of angels in the early church. Chapters 1–3 address new doctrines that were introduced by false teachers. These erroneous doctrines caused the believers to "drift away" from the truths that "[they] have heard" from the beginning (Heb. 2:1). The author then exalted the superiority of Christ over both the angels and Moses. The following section is a discussion on these issues.

Structure. Hebrews 1:1–2:4 discusses Christ's superiority over the angels. Then 2:5–18 provides reasons why Jesus became a man and suffered death. Finally, chapter 3 discusses Christ's superiority over Moses.

(1) Hebrews 1:1–2:4   Christ compared to Angels
(2) Hebrews 2:5–18   Reasons for Jesus' Incarnation and Death
(3) Hebrews 3   Christ compared to Moses

The Son Greater than the Angels (Heb. 1:1–2:4). The following table catalogues the differences between the angels and Christ in Hebrews 1:1–2:4:

Angels	Son
Inferior to the Son (1:4)	"Superior to the angels" (1:4)
Inferior names to that of the Son (1:4)	Has a superior name than that of angels (1:4)
Angels are like "winds" (1:7)	Relationship to Father: "Father-Son" (1:5)
"his servants flames of fire" (1:7)	"Firstborn" of creation (1:6)

Angels	Son
"God's angels worship him [Jesus]" (1:6)	"your kingdom" and "your throne will last forever and ever" (1:8)
"angels [are] ministering spirits" (1:14)	"sit at the right hand" of my throne (1:13)
"not to angels that he has subjected the world to come" (2:5)	But to the "son of man" that the "world to come" has been subjected (2:5)

As shown, the author likened the angels to "winds," "flames of fire," and "ministering spirits."[282] The Son, on the other hand, is proclaimed as "superior to angels," has a "superior name," is the "firstborn" of creation, and the very Son of God. The "throne," "kingdom," and entire "world to come [including angels]" have been subjected to Him. The angels, therefore, are subjected to the Son, and they even "worship him [Jesus Christ]."

<u>Why Jesus Was Made a Little Lower than the Angels</u>. Although Jesus is "superior," the "radiance of God's glory," and even the very "Son of God," He was "made a little lower than the angels." He took on "flesh and blood" and became like His brothers. The following table provides Christ's humanity and the rationale for it:

Jesus' Nature	Reasons Why Jesus Became "human" and "tasted death"
"Jesus," "son of man," "you made him [Jesus] a little lower than the angels" (2:6, 7a, 9a)	• In order to "taste death for everyone" (2:9) • So that he could sanctify men (2:11)
Jesus "shared in their humanity," putting on "flesh and blood" (2:14)	• "so that by his death he might destroy him who holds the power of death—that is, the devil" (2:14) • "free those ... held in slavery" by sin • Because He came to help "Abraham's descendants ... He had to be made like his brothers in every way" (2:17)

---

[282] Note that these two descriptions ("flames of fire" and "ministering spirits") bear several similarities with the descriptions of the "spirits of God" as discussed earlier. In fact, the phrase "flames of fire" is the phrase used to describe the "spirits of God" in Revelation 1:14, 2:18, and 19:12. Therefore, when the author of Hebrews described the angels as "ministering spirits," it is not surprising. The angels and Spirit do seem to share a lot in common. It is highly likely that both books were written by John, and he was attempting to make both the angels and spirits have a subordinate relationship to Christ. Both elements have somewhat of an equal status and role compared with that of Christ's.

Jesus' Nature	Reasons Why Jesus Became "human" and "tasted death"
"He [Jesus] had to be made like his brothers [Abraham's descendants] in every way" (2:17)	• so that He could "help ... Abraham's descendants" (2:16) • "so that he could become a merciful and a faithful high priest in service to God" (2:17) • so that he "might make atonement for the sins of the people" (2:17)
As a man, Jesus was "tempted" and suffered death (2:10, 18)	• to "make the author of their salvation perfect through suffering" (2:10) • "able to help those who are being tempted" (2:18)
"you crowned him [the Son of Man] with glory and honor and put everything under his feet" (2:7b, 8)	

Jesus' humanity is diversely described as "man," "son of man," "flesh and blood," "Abraham's descendant," and becoming "like his brothers in every way." The author did this in order to itemize the reasons why Jesus had to be made like "his brothers." He became a man in order to "help" people, help "his brothers," and help "Abraham's descendants." He did this by "tast[ing] death" to save "everyone," sanctify all people, destroy the "powers of death" and him who holds those powers (the devil), "free those ... [being] held in slavery," "make atonement for the sins of the people," "help those being tempted," and "become a merciful and a faithful high priest" for us.

Jesus Compared to Moses. Just as Jesus is superior to the angels, He is also superior to Moses. Among the Jewish patriarchs, none stands taller than Moses. It is said of Moses, "no prophet has ever risen in Israel like Moses, whom the Lord knew face to face" (Deut. 34:10). The greatest among man is now contrasted with the Son. Although both were faithful in God's house, the fact that one is a "servant" and the other a "Son" forever changes the dynamics, nature, and status of the two characters in that house.

Moses	Jesus
"Moses faithful" (3:2b)	"he [Jesus] was faithful" (3:2a)
"Moses was faithful as a servant in all God's house" (3:5). This makes Moses the "servant" of God.	"But Christ is faithful as a Son over God's house" (3:6). Unlike Moses, Jesus is the Son of God.
Moses found worthy of lesser honor than Jesus (by implication)	"Jesus has been found worthy of greater honor than Moses" (3:6)

ANGELS, MOSES, AND JESUS IN OLD TESTAMENT CONTEXT

Moses and Jesus: Old Testament Context

Two crucial questions must be asked at this point. What was the nature of the contextual issue that necessitated the author of Hebrews to establish Christ's superiority over both the angels and Moses? What does Hebrews teach about the worship of angels over and against Jesus Christ? The discussion that follows attempts to answer these and other related questions.

Jesus: Moses-like Prophet. First, it is important to recognize that the argument concerning Jesus Christ's superiority is a continuation of what we have discussed in Revelation 1:12–16 about the "One like a son of man." In that section, we established that Jesus is not only like Moses, Elijah, and David, but He is greater than all of them combined. Edmund Little writes, "In Moses, Jesus fulfills and transcends the Law. In Elijah, he fulfills and transcends the prophets. Both fade before the Incarnate Word as, in the synoptic gospels, they yield place to him on the Mount of Transfiguration."[283]

We also demonstrated how Jesus is presented as a King, High Priest, and High Priestly–King in the order of Melchizedek. However, unlike all of these human characters, offices, rituals, and types, Jesus is uniquely different because He alone is from the "beginning," "from above," the "eternal" one, "the Son of God," and even "the [very] true God" (1 John 5:20).

---

[283] Edmund Little, *Echoes of the Old Testament*, p. 41.

Here in Hebrews, the author continued the same discussion. However, Jesus' superiority over angels is a new material being introduced.[284] Therefore, in order to fully understand what is going on here and the exact nature of the issues with which the early church may have grappled, we must explore what Moses wrote about the "Coming One" in the Law. The Mosaic prophecy concerning the Coming One reads:

> The Lord your God will raise up for you *a prophet like me from among your own brothers*. You must listen to him. For this is what you asked from the Lord your God at Horeb on the day of the assembly when you said, "Let us not hear the word of the Lord our God nor see this great fire anymore, or we will die." The Lord said to me: "I will raise up for them a prophet like you from among their brothers; I will put my words in his mouth, and he will tell them everything I command him. If anyone does not listen to my words that the prophet speaks in my name, I myself will call him to account." (Deuteronomy 18:15–19, emphasis supplied).

According to this prophecy, the Jews anticipated the Coming One to be "like Moses," who is to be chosen from "among [their] own brothers." In short, they were anticipating a "man," "human," and "brother" from among themselves, not Someone from "above" or the "beginning," let alone the Son of God. If these false teachers had preached against Jesus' claims to divinity, then the author of Hebrews was seen refuting those claims. He stated that Jesus is the "Son of God" that bears the imprint of God Himself. However, He "shared in [our] humanity" by taking on "flesh and blood." More importantly, "for this reason," writes the author, "he [Jesus] had to be made like his brothers, in every way, in order that he

---

[284] Although Jesus' superiority over the angels is well articulated in Hebrews, it is not entirely "new" material in Revelation. As we have discussed, Revelation presents Jesus as superior to both mankind and angels.

might become a merciful and faithful high priest in services to God, and that he might make atonement for the sins of the people" (Heb. 2:17).

<u>Jesus: A Prophet Chosen from Among his "own brothers."</u> Second, note the manner in which the term "brother" is used. According to Moses, the coming prophet would be chosen from among their "own brothers." Revelation, the Gospel of John, and Hebrews all attempt to highlight Jesus as "our brother," perhaps an intentional attempt to make Him meet the existing expectations.

Deuteronomy 18:15	Hebrews 2:17	Revelation 19:10	John 20:17
"The Lord your God will raise up for you a *prophet like me from among your own brothers*. You must listen to him."	"For this reason he had to be *made like his brothers in every way*, in order that he might become a merciful and faithful high priest in service to God."	"I am your *fellow servant with you and with your brothers* who hold to the testimony of Jesus. Worship God!"	"Jesus said, 'Do not hold on to me, for I have not yet returned to the Father. Go instead to *my brothers and tell them, "I am returning to my Father and your Father, to my God and your God."'"*

The usage of the term "brothers" in the above passages is intended to confirm Jesus' brotherhood to the human family, as predicted by Moses in Deuteronomy. In Hebrews 2:17, Jesus was "made like his brothers" because He is a descendant of Abraham and came in "flesh and blood."

Then in Revelation 19:10, the angel told John that he was a fellow servant with John and his brothers. Note that the angel is a fellow servant with John, but he is not a brother of or to John.[285] Therefore, the argument here is that because the angels are "ministering spirits" and "flames of fire," they can never be "brothers" to the human family. Only Jesus Christ, who became "flesh and blood," is and can be called a "brother."

---

[285] However, the brotherhood to which the angel alluded is shared between John and his brothers. They are described as those who "have the testimony of Jesus." This phrase limits John's brothers to those living [prophets and apostles] during and after Jesus' first advent. However, as if to broaden John's circle of brothers or prophets, the angel further defined the "testimony of Jesus" as "the spirit of prophecy." This definition is broad enough to include the Old Testament and post-apostolic prophets.

Third, in John 20, Jesus' brotherhood to His disciples is reiterated three times: 1) Jesus calls the twelve "my brothers," 2) they are brothers because they have a common "Father," and 3) they are brothers because they have a common God.

The Angel and Jesus: Old Testament Context

<u>My Angel Will Go Before You</u>. Finally, when people made the golden calf at Horeb, God intended to punish them, but Moses intervened and pleaded, "But now, please forgive their sin—but if not, then blot me out of the book you have written" (Exod. 32:32). To this, the Lord replied:

> Whoever has sinned against me I will blot out of my book. Now go, lead the people to the place I spoke of, and *my angel* will go before you. ... Leave this place, you and the people you brought up out of Egypt, and go up to the land I promised on oath to Abraham, Isaac and Jacob, saying, "I will give it to your descendants." I will send *an angel* before you and drive out the Canaanites ... Go up to the land flowing with milk and honey. But I will not go with you. (Exod. 32:33, 34, 33:1–3, *emphasis supplied*)

When Moses heard "these distressing words" (v. 4), he implored, "If your presence does not go with us, do not send us up from here. How will anyone know that you are pleased with me and with your people unless you go with us? What else will distinguish me and your people from all the other people on the face of the earth?" Then the Lord God finally consented, saying, "I will do the very thing you have asked" (vv. 15–17).

Analysis. These conversations indicate an angel is described as "my angel." This angel is obviously highly ranked but not quite on equal footing with Christ. Nevertheless, one thing is clear: God tried to send "his angel" in place of Himself, but Moses protested against it. Now what does this have in common with the worship of the angel in the New Testament, especially in the writings of John and Hebrews? A few things are instructive.

Revelation's "his angel" and "My angel" in Exodus. Revelation is literally saturated with angels. There are angels standing "before God" (8:2), "around the throne" (7:11), "at the altar" (8:3), and some are holding the "four corners of the earth" (7:1). Other angels administer the seven trumpets and seven last plagues. However, one stands out among all these. In the prologue, John described this angel as "his [Jesus'] angel" (1:1), as if set apart from the rest. The same line is repeated in Rev. 22:16: "I, Jesus, have sent my angel to give you this testimony for the churches." It is a fact that *all* angels are His, but the manner and tone in which this particular angel is stressed as "my angel" implies a specific angel, perhaps one of which the author assumed his audience was aware. It is possible that Revelation's "his" or "my angel" could be the one God had announced as "my angel" in Exodus 32 and 33.

The Ranking and Position of "His angel" in Revelation. The channel God used to communicate Revelation also suggests the position and rank of that angel. For example, the prophecies go from God to the seven churches in this order: God →Jesus →His angel →John →seven angels →the churches. It is as if John went to some length to put this nameless angel in its proper place to occupy a position below Jesus Christ but above himself (human).[286] The same is implied in John 1:51: "'I tell you the truth,' Jesus says to Nathanael, 'you shall see heaven open, and the angels of God ascending and descending on the Son of Man.'" Here, Jesus is the ladder that actually connects heaven and earth.[287]

John's Attempt to Worship the Angel and the Colossians' Worship Thereof. Even John's aborted attempt to worship this angel, and the angel's response, indirectly address this issue. The angel's prohibition, "Do not do it" (Rev. 19:10), is not only intended to stop John from worshiping him at that moment, but also to stop the wider community from doing so. Besides, the angel-worshiping opponents that Paul castigated in Colossians are located approximately

---

[286] This is the very same point that Hebrews makes when it says that Christ is "superior to the angels" but mankind was "made a little lower than the angels" (Heb. 1:4; 2:7, 9).

[287] Further, concerning the "seven angels" John writes to, we have suggested that they represent both heavenly and earthly messengers. In chapter 19, we demonstrated how and why these characters can be both literal angels and human leaders. Here, however, they cannot be supernatural beings. They must represent seven elders in each of these churches. (See the discussion in chapter 19).

seventy miles from Sardis, but less than twenty miles from Laodicea. Peter, writing to almost the entire Gentile world, said, "Jesus Christ ... has gone into heaven and is at God's right hand—with angels, authorities and powers in submission to him" (1 Peter 3:22). Thus, the issue surrounding the worship of angels appears to have been a common one in this region.

The Angel's Testimony Against Worship of Angels. The angel's admission that "I am a fellow servant with you and your brothers who hold to the testimony of Jesus" does seem to put the issue to rest (Rev. 19:10). The very angel who is possibly being worshiped by the false teachers, testifies against such practices. He said that he was a "fellow servant" with John and others who hold to the "testimony of Jesus." Although he verbally directed John to worship God, he himself (with the rest of God's angels) are seen worshiping Jesus in Revelation 5:11–12. For these reasons, the author of Hebrews wrote, "Let all God's angels worship him [Jesus]" (1:6).

Contextual Issue

Our analysis of the evidence shows that the early church did have issues with angels. It is possible that the false prophets must have "cleverly invented stories" against Jesus' Christology, origin, and authority because they felt He was not like David, Moses, Elijah, or any of the OT characters. Since Moses wrote about the Coming One as being from "among our brothers," and like David, He must come from Bethlehem, the Jews were expecting an earthly emissary (see John 7:41, 42). Against this backdrop, the early church's claims that Jesus was from "above," "from the beginning," "from the Father," and the "Son of God" were unacceptable. However, should any heavenly or divine being that is worthy of our attention, it must be the "my angel" of Exodus 32:33.

The false prophets may have argued that the Christ—the Coming One, the One like Moses—must be One from among "our brothers." However, the only heavenly emissary mentioned as one whom God had attempted to send was "His angel." Further, God said, "I will send an angel before you and drive out the Canaanites ...." (Exod. 33:2). It is apparent that that angel is in focus in Revelation. Therefore, we find angels in almost every page in the apocalyptic book, but the angel that stands out is "his angel" of Revelation 1. According to the text, that angel occupies a position lower than Christ (vv. 1–3) and is a "ministering spirit" or "flame of fire," and such angels should not be worshiped (see ch. 19). On the contrary, we find this ranking angel and all God's angels worshiping Jesus Christ.[288] The following table summarizes the issues surrounding Christ and angels.

Book	Superiority and Worship of Christ over Angels
Revelation	Many angels sang in a loud voice "Worthy is the Lamb" (5:11, 12), "Do not do it [worship me]! I am a fellow servant with you and with your brothers, who hold to the testimony of Jesus. Worship God!" (19:10). See also Rev. 1–3, 5, 19, 22
Hebrews	"Jesus ... was made a little lower than angels now crowned with glory and honor" (2:9); "Let all God's angels worship him [the firstborn]" (1:6). See also 1:2–2:5
John	"angels of God ascending and descending on the Son of Man" (1:51)
Colossians	"Do not let anyone who delights in the ... worship of angels disqualify you for the prize" (2:18)
1 Peter	"Jesus Christ, who has gone into heaven and is at God's right hand—with angels, authorities and powers in submission to him" (3:21, 22)
Matthew	Angels are Jesus' servants (13:30, 39–41)

"ANOTHER MIGHTY ANGEL" OF REVELATION 10: ANGEL OR CHRIST?

The Divine Character of Revelation 10: Angel or Christ?

At this juncture, we turn to "another mighty angel" in Revelation 10. The identity of this angel has been debated for years. Stefanovic and others

---

[288] Up to this stage, we have not discussed the "mighty angel" of Revelation 10. The identity of this angel is debated among scholars. Some identity this angel as a literal angel, while others think he is Jesus Christ. As we shall see later, that angel is Jesus Christ. It is one of those Johannine arguments where the author presented Jesus Christ as both similar to *and* greater than Moses, David, or the high priest. To illustrate this further, John wrote that John the Baptist was not the Christ. He also denied that he was Elijah. Then he presented Jesus as both the Christ and Elijah (see John 1), while the other New Testament writers saw John the Baptist as the coming Elijah.

think that this divine character is a "special angel of exalted rank." They offer two main reasons for this view: 1) Christ is never called an angel in Revelation, and 2) "another mighty angel" suggests that this angel is like the earlier "mighty angel" of Revelation 5 who had introduced Christ.[289] Other scholars think that this character is Jesus Christ. William Shea, a representative of this view, clinically compares the angel of Revelation 10 with Christ in Revelation 1, Daniel 10, and other similar occurrences in Exodus, and concludes that these characters are identical. He especially offers four main evidences in support of this view: 1) the description of His feet, 2) His cloudy robes, 3) His radiating face, and 4) the rainbow over His head.[290] The text does appear to support both views. However, the problem with these views is that neither Shea nor Stefanovic make any attempt to address the broader contextual issue. If the divine character of Revelation 10 is "another angel," then why does he look almost like the "Son of Man" in Revelation 1? Or if the same is Christ, then why was He even labeled an "angel"? Is this indicative of a contextual issue that John and his initial audience encountered? If so, then what was the issue? To answer these and other related questions, we add three thematic and contextual reasons to the list Shea provides.

Jesus as the 'Mighty Angel': Further Evidences

<u>Label Versus Content Issue in Revelation 10</u>. First, the issues concerning the identity of the divine character of Revelation 10 just boils down to a labeling issue. The divine figure is labeled or identified as an angel, but the description of his anatomy, significance, nuances, content, and demeanor are more Christlike. Therefore, in such situation, the reader must choose to go by either the label or the actual content. One of the keys to addressing this issue was discussed earlier in chapter 12 of this book.

---

[289] See Stefanovic, *Revelation of Jesus Christ*, p. 326.
[290] See William H. Shea, "The Mighty Angel and His Message," in *Symposium on Revelation— Book I*, p. 290.

There, we extensively discussed the key words, concepts, imageries, and characters that have a dual definition, dual significance, or dual application. We noticed how a single word, concept, or character had two or more definitions or applications. Stated differently, in this literary construction, the word or label is the same, but the definitions, nuances, descriptions, significances, and contexts were wildly different. After a lengthy discussion, we concluded the study this way:

> In such a situation, one is left with the choice of either embracing the linguistic similarities (in this case, the "angel") and ignoring the differences in definitions, description, nuances and contexts; or accepting the differences as stated in the text, and then attempting to discover the reasons why the author may have used the same labeling. In other words, it is the articulated definition, the differences in nuances, and the immediate context of these terms that must provide the clue to addressing the labeling issue, and not the other way around.[291]

Considering the overall pattern of Revelation and other Johannine writings, it is appropriate to go by the above principle and see the angel of Revelation 10 as Christ Himself. Instead of the labeling or linguistic similarities, it is more reasonable to consider the definitions, nuances, content, and context of the character. Besides, Revelation does present Jesus Christ as an angel after all, for if stars are angels in Revelation, then Christ is both the "bright Morning Star" (22:16) and the "Star of Jacob" (Matt. 2:2, 9).

<u>Label Versus Content: a Literary Device</u>. Second, the labeling issue can be further explained this way. The character in Revelation 1 is called, labeled, or likened to a "son of *man.*" However, his description and demeanor show that He is the glorified Christ. He is like a "man," but He is much more than a man. Therefore, the "Christ" of Revelation 1 and 10 are

---

[291] For more details and discussion on this, refer to chapter 12 of this book.

part of another literary device. In chapter 1, Christ comes across like a "man" and dressed as one; while in chapter 10, He comes across like an "angel" who is robed in a cloud. In both cases, the robes and labels change, but His real identity, content, physicality, and character remain unchanged. Hebrews captures these imageries well; "They will perish but you remain, they will all wear out like a garment. You will roll them up like a robe; like a garment they will be changed. But you remain the same, and your years will never end" (Heb. 1:11–12). In Rev. 1 and 10, the robes and labels change, but He "remains the same." Hebrews further asserts that Christ came robed in human "body," but in reality He was the "radiance of God's glory and the exact representation of his being" (Heb. 10:5; 2: 14; 1: 3).

Christ Is Both Like *and* Greater than an Angel. In chapters 13, 14, and elsewhere in this study, we have argued that the Christ of Revelation 1 is presented as "one like a son of man." He especially comes through as a priest, king, or priestly-king, all of which are human characters, offices, and institutions, but in actuality, He is much more than a human character. He is greater than all the patriarchs, prophets, priests, and kings put together. In our current discussion, Revelation 10 serves to advance the same argument. Here, Christ is presented as someone like a mighty angel, but He is also greater than even an exalted angel. In other words, the divine character of Revelation 1 and Rev 10 is greater than all human and angelic characters, labels, and robes suggest. He is Jesus Christ, the very Son of God!

As seen throughout this study, these early NT issues served to morph the imageries and characters of the apocalyptic Christ. And it was the divine attempt to address these issues that the glorified Christ is packaged, labeled, and presented in varied manners in the book of Revelation.

Reasons Why the Robes and Labels of Christ Change in Revelation. As demonstrated earlier, there are sufficient evidences to suggest that

John and his church encountered real issues that challenged the origin, authority, and Christology of Jesus of Nazareth. As observed, the opponents held and proclaimed certain Jewish leaders to be greater than "this fellow," let alone the angels. It is this and other issues that shaped the language, labels, and robes of Christ. As seen throughout this study, these early NT issues served to morph the imageries and characters of the apocalyptic Christ. And it was the divine attempt to address these issues that the glorified Christ is packaged, labeled, and presented in varied manners in the book of Revelation.

John argued in a subtle, figurative, yet forceful way, that Jesus is like all Jewish iconic leaders and exalted angels of the OT Scriptures. However, at the same time, He is greater than all people and angels combined because He is God Himself! This is the argument John consistently made in all his writings, including Hebrews. Perhaps this is why Peter wrote that Jesus Christ "has gone into heaven and is at God's right hand—with angels, authorities, and powers in submission to him" (1 Peter 3:22). Paul also addressed the same issues when he wrote that "at the name of Jesus every knee [of both men and angels] shall bow" (Phil. 2:9–11). Luke quoted Peter as saying, "Salvation is found in no one else [either Jewish iconic leaders or exalted angels], for there is no other name under heaven given to men by which we must be saved" (Acts 4:12).

Summary

Therefore, Jesus holding the seven stars and seven spirits in His hand is intended to symbolically convey the fact that He is the Master of all, including the angels and the spirits of God, and that the same entities are subject to Him. If this conclusion has any merit, then we make the following observations:

1. Just as Christ was presented as "greater than" all leading Jewish iconic leaders, offices, and rituals, He is now presented as "superior to [both] angels" and the "spirits of God."

2. If all three divine beings—Christ, the Spirit, and angels—are involved in addressing the believers (especially those in Sardis), then that speaks not only of the solemnity of the message, but also of the spiritual condition of those who are being addressed.
3. There is every indication that the socio-cultural, ecclesiastical, and theological contexts of Revelation are not far removed from that of the Gospels, Acts, Hebrews, and Pauline and other Johannine writings. Using a high degree of subtlety and inference, Revelation appears to address the very issues with which the rest of the NT writings grappled.

CHARACTERS AND ISSUES

What, then, was the condition of the church that necessitated the three divine beings to address them? Did internal issues or external opponents plague this church? What exactly was the nature of the issue, and who were the opponents? In this section, we attempt to answer these questions.

Sardis is one of two churches that do not explicitly identify any external opponents[292] (the Laodicean church being the other). However, the lack of mention does not indicate the absence of opponents. On the contrary, the conditions of these two churches may indicate the results and success of the work Satan and his agents had wrought. However, what is clear is that these two churches are in terrible condition. One is described as "dead," whereas the other is "lukewarm." The "dead" were being threatened with the removal of their names from the book of life, whereas the "lukewarm" risked being "spewed out" from Christ's mouth. Perhaps the most troubling situation is that the believers in these two churches were not even aware of their own condition. Because the letter lacks any identifiable opponents, we will mine for clues that may lead to the nature of the issues and opponents among the Sardisians.

---

[292] For a thorough discussion of the similarities between these two churches, see Revelation 3:14–22.

Believers and White Robes

<u>Believers</u>. The believers in Sardis can be divided into two groups. The letter generally describes the entire church as being "dead." However, "a few" among them were commended for their faithfulness. Therefore, the following table attempts to contrast these two groups of people:

The Few	The Majority
"a few people" (3:4)	many implied (3:4)
"not soiled their clothes" (3:4)	Have "soiled" their clothes (3:4)
"they are worthy" (3:4)	Not worthy (3:4)
"will never blot out his name from the book of life, but will acknowledge his name" (3:5)	Name still in the book of life, will blot out and will not acknowledge should they continue in sin (3:5)
Live up to the reputation ... "alive" (3:1)	Name only ... "dead" (3:1)
"being alive" (3:1)	"about to die ... dead" (3:1, 2)
Wake up! (3:2)	Sleeping for they are urged to "wake up!" (3:2)
Living (3:1)	"dead" (3:1)
"deeds" are complete (3:2)	"deeds [not] complete" (3:2)
"what you have received and heard; obey it" (3:3)	Do not "hold fast"
"know at what time I will come to you" (3:3)	"will not know" (3:3)
overcomers (3:5)	urged to overcome (3:5)
"will acknowledge his name before My Father and his angels" (3:5)	Will not acknowledge their names before His Father and his angels (3:5)
"hear what the Spirit says" (3:6)	Now urged to hear again (3:3, 6)

To the majority, Christ offered a number of conditional promises. The overcomers are promised the following things: 1) they will be dressed in white and walk with Him because they are worthy, 2) their names will never be blotted out from the book of life, 3) He will acknowledge their names before His Father and angels. We will explore these statements further.

<u>Types of Robes</u>. Because references to the white robe are scattered throughout the apocalyptic narrative, the following table enlists all

occurrences.[293] The analysis of the apocalyptic garments show that there are two types of garments: 1) the gifts the believers receive here and now, and 2) the final rewards the saints will receive at the end of time.

"now"	Eschatological Garment
"a few people in Sardis who have not soiled their clothes" (3:4)	"they will walk with me, dressed in white, for they are worthy" (3:4)
"I counsel you to buy from me … white clothes to wear, so you can cover your shameful nakedness" (3:18)	"He who overcomes will, like them, be clothed in white" (3:5)
	"Then each of them was given a white robe, and they were told to wait a little longer" (6:11)
"These are they who have come out of the great tribulation; they have washed their robes and made them white in the blood of the Lamb. Therefore, 'they are before the throne and serve him day and night in his temple" (7:14, 15)	a great multitude standing before the throne and before the Lamb, clothed with white robes (7:9)
	"These are they who have come out of great tribulation; they have washed their robes and made them white in the blood of the Lamb. Therefore, 'they are before the throne and serve him day and night in his temple" (7:14–15)
"Behold, I come like a thief! Blessed is he who stays awake and keeps his clothes with him, so that he may not go naked and be shamefully exposed" (16:15)	"'and his bride has made herself ready. Fine linen, bright and clean was given her to wear.' (Fine linen stands for the righteous acts of the saints)" (19:7, 8)
	"The armies of heaven were following him, riding on white horses and dressed in fine linen" (19:14)

Analysis of the Garments. The "now" section falls into two groups.[294] First, the "white robes" are purely gifts given by Christ (see 3:18). Second, the white clothes consist of the saints' "righteous acts" (19:8). However, note that people in their own strength do not accomplish even these "righteous acts." The text is clear that all clothes are "white," "fine," and "clean" because they are "washed … and made white in the blood of the Lamb" (7:14, 15; 19:8). Stated differently, the righteous acts performed

---

[293] Note that adulterous Babylon is also "dressed in fine linen, purple and scarlet, and glittering with gold, precious stones and pearls!" (Rev. 18:16; see also 17:4). The two garments are different in many ways, some of which include the colors, the one wearing them, other articles worn with them, etc.

[294] This discussion does not include the robes that Christ, the angels, or other heavenly beings wear. It is limited to those that the saints wear.

by saints during difficult circumstances are accomplished in, by, and through the power of the blood of Jesus. Therefore, the white garments that the saints wear "now" are gifts from God. The eschatological white garments, however, are final rewards promised to the overcomers by Christ as well.

White Robes, Righteous Acts, and Heaven. John described the white robe a saint wears "now" as "righteous acts," but the white robe an overcomer receives at the end of time is also a reward for "righteous acts" (3:4, 5; 6:11).[295] This is because Jesus' end-time reward will be "according to what he [the saint] has done" (22:12). This means that the only thing the saints take from this planet to heaven is their "white robe [i.e., righteous acts or character]." However, Paul suggested that our "perishable" clothes will be transformed into imperishable ones before being taken to heaven. He wrote, "we will all be changed—in a flash, in the twinkling of an eye ... For the perishable must clothe itself with the imperishable and the mortal with immortality" (1 Cor. 15:51–53).

> The righteous acts performed by saints during difficult circumstances are accomplished in, by, and through the power of the blood of Jesus. Therefore, the white garments that the saints wear "now" are gifts from God. The eschatological white garments, however, are final rewards promised to the overcomers by Christ as well.

Defiled and Undefiled Robes. Do these white clothes represent two different gifts or just one? When a person commences his or her walk with Christ, He offers that person a spotless "white robe." However, the robe can and does become "soiled." "You have a few people in Sardis," wrote John, "who have not soiled their clothes. They will walk with me, dressed in white, for they are worthy" (Rev. 3:4). If only "a few people ... have not soiled their

---

[295] These passages will be discussed in Revelation 7:14–15.

clothes" in Sardis, that means most of the saints have already soiled their clothes. In the address to Sardis, we are not told how and why the robes were defiled, but a passage in Revelation 14 does provide some clues. "These are those who did not defile themselves with women, for they kept themselves pure. They follow the Lamb wherever he goes" (v. 4). This passage provides three crucial points.

Defiled or Soiled. First, the Greek word translated "defile [*molunō*]" is the same word used for "soiled [*emolunan*]" in Revelation 3:4.

The Cause of Defilement. Second, Revelation 14:4 provides the reasons why a white robe can become defiled. The defilement (or lack of it) comes as a result of one's association "with [the] women." If this conclusion has any merit, then it is possible that there are some shadowy women-opponents in Sardis.

Resolving to Shun the Women and Follow the Lamb. Third, the concept of a person "not defil[ing]" and keeping oneself "pure" conveys resolve and determination on the part of the saint.[296] It also suggests that the same must "follow the Lamb wherever he goes." Thus, a personal choice to refrain from associating with the (shadowy) woman *and* "follow[ing] the Lamb" are the antidotes for defilement. However, should one's robe become defiled, the same Lamb also makes His blood available for cleansing. "These [those in white robes] are they who … have washed their robes and made them white in the blood of the Lamb" (7:14).

<u>Who is This Woman?</u> If following the Lamb constitutes clothing, washing, cleansing, and making the robes white, then defiling or soiling them is equivalent to having an adulterous relationship with the woman. Who then is this impure woman?[297] Note that there is no mention of an impure woman within Revelation 4–13. The adulterous woman of chapter 17 is first introduced as Babylon in 14:8, which is four verses *after* the reference to the

---

[296] Early in Daniel's life, he was confronted with a similar situation. It was his personal resolution and God's divine power that propelled him to live an unblemished life. "But Daniel resolved not to defile himself with the royal food and wine" (Dan. 1:8).

[297] Revelation 14:4 uses the plural for woman, indicating that there is more than one, but in our discussion we will treat it as a single woman. However, when we come to chapters 13, 14, and 17, we shall see why the text uses the plural form.

ambiguous "women." To John's initial audience, a sudden reference to an adulterous woman (see 14:4) was not a mystery. By now, the author assumed that his audiences were familiar with the identity of this woman. This further suggests that the reference to impure women points right back to the "Jezebels," "Balaams," and their adulterous activities in Revelation 2 and 3.

Babylon and Her "fine linen." Previously, we have established the relationships that exist between 1) the Balaamites of Pergamum and the sea beast of Revelation 13; and 2) the Jezebels of Thyatira and the Babylon of Revelation 17.[298] Now our current study suggests that the shadowy-women-opponents of Sardis have certain "Jezebelish" and "Balaamite" tendencies. There is a possibility that we are dealing with the same woman-opponent here. Note that this adulterous woman is also "dressed in a fine linen, purple and scarlet" and contrasted with the saints of God. The saints are "dressed in white," representing their "righteous acts." These righteous acts supply the worth and value of the bride of God, while the value of the harlot is measured by her "glittering ... gold, precious stones and pearls" she wears (Rev. 18:16; 17:4).

Those Dressed in White in Sardis Are "worthy." In Sardis, most have defiled their garments. However, only "a few have not soiled their clothes." Jesus promises to them that they will walk with Him because they are "worthy [Gr. *axioi*]." The term "worthy" is used prominently in three other places as well. In Revelation 4:11, the term is used in a worship setting to describe God because He "created all things." Then in chapter 5, the same term is used, also in a worship setting, to describe the Lamb for His redemptive work (see 5:2, 9, 12). Creation and redemption are works of epic proportions. If the same term is used to describe the "few people in Sardis who have not soiled their clothes," then they obviously must have overcome uncommon opposition to keep their garments pure. No wonder "one of the elders" said to John, "These [those in white robes] are they who have come out of *great tribulation*; and have washed

---

[298] Now a sudden mention of an adulterous woman in Revelation 14:4 serves to validate the suggested relationships between Balaamites/chapter 13 and Jezebel/chapter 17. This is because up to that time, the only adulterous women discussed are those in Revelation 2 and 3.

their robes and made them white in the blood of the Lamb" (Rev. 7:14, emphasis supplied).

Then, finally, the term is used to describe the judgment of Babylon. "You are just in these judgments ... because you have so judged, for they have shed the blood of your saints and the prophets, and you have given them blood to drink as they deserve [Gr. *axioi*]" (16:6).[299] Babylon is worthy and deserving of such a bloody punishment because "her sins are piled up to heaven, and God has remembered her crimes" (18:5; see also v. 24; 19:2).

<u>White Robes and the Blood</u>. Most of the believers who have defiled their garments are asked to emulate the "few" who have not. If these robes are made clean, pure, and white by the "blood of the Lamb," then the acts of defiling and cleansing refer to one's attitude toward the Lamb and its blood. Perhaps here is an indication that one group still values the blood and its significance, whereas the other may have rejected or trampled upon it. Hebrews describes certain members of the faith community who have "fallen away" as follows:

> For *it is* impossible for those who were once enlightened, and have tasted the heavenly gift, and have become partakers of the Holy Spirit, and have tasted the good word of God and the powers of the age to come, if they fall away, to renew again to repentance, since they crucify again for themselves the Son of God, and put *Him* to an open shame. (Hebrews 6:4–6, NKJV)

Similar to the opponents in Revelation and other Johannine writings, Hebrews shows that certain people have fallen away, not just from the faith community, but also from the "Son of God," the "word of God," the "Holy Spirit," and everything else that comes with, in, from, and through Christ. If so, then it is possible that most of the saints in Sardis must have

---

[299] The text actually describes the punished as "rivers and springs of water" (Rev. 16:4). Whoever this character was, it was punished for shedding the blood of His "servants and the prophets." Then when we come to Revelation 18, we are told that the "blood of prophets and of the servants" were found in Babylon (v. 24). It is for this reason that I say the third plague was poured on Babylon and her supporters.

ceased "follow[ing] the Lamb" at the bidding of the adulterous woman, thus "soiling" their "white robes." Note that in Revelation, it is the saints who "follow the Lamb," possess the "spirit of God," hold the "word of God," and "keep the commandments of God and have the testimony of Jesus." Conversely, in Hebrews, those who have fallen away have actually removed themselves from the fellowship of the Lamb, His blood, the Holy Spirit, the words and commandments of God, and even God Himself.

<u>Summary on White Robes</u>. Imagine being in the Sardis church when Revelation was read for the first time. The elder reading has just finished the messages addressed to the churches at Ephesus, Smyrna, and Pergamum, and we are wondering if there is any message for us. However, the next message is addressed to those in Thyatira, and we become somewhat anxious. Then the elder begins the fifth message with the words, "To the angel of the church in Sardis write …." We sit in solemn awe with the realization that the great God of heaven has addressed us personally. No sound is heard as the church sits in total silence, soaking up every word, but the message ends, and the elder reads the Philadelphian message. We wish our message was a bit longer, but it was not.

However, as the elder continues to read the rest of Revelation, we follow the narrative closely, desiring to detect anything that may speak directly to us again. We then come across passages that discuss the white robes—what they are, how they are made clean and white, who gives them, who wears them now, and who will wear them later. Then when the elder reads about the great multitude in white robes that stand before God and the Lamb (see Rev. 7:9), each of us sit on the edges of our pews, and crying babies are hushed. The atmosphere is as if the assembled congregation has ceased breathing, and we can even hear our own hearts pounding.

Then one of the twenty-four elders asks John, "These in white robes—who are they, and where did they come from?" It is as if God read our very thoughts. That was exactly the same question that was running through all our minds. Then John responds, "Sir, you know." Obviously, John cannot answer, which only serves to heighten our interest because a few chapters earlier, Christ had promised *us* the white robes (see Rev. 3:1–6). At least in our own congregation, we know which believers are on that "few" list. Now we want to know if the elder can identify some of us and we anxiously wait for his response.

"These are they," the elder begins to answer his own question, "who have come out of the great tribulation; they have washed their robes and made them white in the blood of the Lamb. Therefore, 'they are before the throne of God and serve him day and night in his temple'" (Rev. 7:13–15).

The message to those in Sardis does not end with Revelation 3:6. They see themselves again in chapter 7. In fact, all of Revelation speaks to them. In this case, those in Sardis can relate to the slain saints of 6:9–11, those who endure the great tribulation of 7:14, those who stand with the Lamb on Mount Zion (see 14:1–4), and those who are "called, chosen and faithful followers" of Jesus Christ (17:14), for they are part of the "bride" of the Lamb (see 19:7, 8). If this is so, then the opposite is also true. Most believers who are described as "dead" or "dying" may have ceased following the Lamb. They are probably involved in an adulterous relationship with "the woman Jezebel" or "Babylon the Great." If the opponents had presented a "cleverly devised" substitute for Jesus Christ—possibly "his angel," "Moses," or someone else—then they may have given into those seductive teachings.

Lamb's Book of Life

Names Still in the "book of life." The promise not to remove their names from the Lamb's book of life is made, not to the few, but to the majority of those who have squandered Christ's sacrifices, "soiled" their white robes, and are in the process of falling away. In the address, this group is described as being "dead," "dying," or "about to die." Regardless of their condition, their names are *still* in the book of life! That is why it is urged upon them to "wake up," "remember," "repent," and strengthen what "is about to die."

Occurrences of Lamb's "book of life." Similar to the concept of white robes being a core part of the main messages of Revelation 4–22, the Lamb's book of life and its contents also have a similar place in chapters 12–17. For instance, in the heart of chapter 13, we are told that "all whose names have not been written in the book of life belonging to the Lamb" worshiped the sea beast (v. 8). A similar passage is also found in 17:8: "The inhabitants of the earth whose names have not been written in the book of life ... will be astonished when they see the beast, because he once was, now is not, and yet will come." Revelation 20:15 then provides the fate of those whose names are not written in or blotted out from the book of life. "If anyone's name was not found written in the book of life, he was thrown into the lake of fire." These references are summarized in the following table:

Text	Book of Life[300]
3:5	"He who overcomes will, like them, be dressed in white. I will never blot out his name from the book of life, but will acknowledge his name before my Father and his angels."
13:8	"All the inhabitants of the earth will worship the beast—all whose names have not been written in the book of life belonging to the Lamb that was slain from the creation of the world."
17:8	"The inhabitants of the earth whose names have not been written in the book of life from the creation of the world will be astonished when they see the beast."
20:15	"If anyone's name was not found written in the book of life, he was thrown into the lake of fire."

<u>The Book of Life and the Defiled</u>. As seen earlier, the divine promise "never [to] blot out the name ... from the book of life" is made specifically to those "fall[ing] away" (Rev. 3:5). It is addressed to those who are no longer following the "Lamb wherever he goes," but instead following the beast (Rev. 13:3). They have ceased worshiping the Lamb and have now begun worshiping the beast (v. 4). They have once tasted the goodness of the Word and Spirit of God, but have sacrificed all these for the seductive

---

[300] Similar literary and rhetorical styles appear in other Johannine writings. The following passages in 1 John convey a similar intent as do those in Revelation (13:8, 17:8). "No one who lives in him keeps on sinning. No one who continues to sin has either seen him or known him" (1 John 3:6). "No one who is born of God will continue to sin, because God's seed remains in them; they cannot go on sinning, because they have been born of God" (v. 9).

teachings of the beast, the woman Jezebel, and Babylon the Great. Therefore, these divine appeals seen in this context seem to say the following:

1. If those whose names have never been entered into the Lamb's book of life worship the beast, then it is tolerable.[301]
2. However, if your name (with the bulk of the saints in Sardis and others) has been once written in the book, and you have fallen away, then you should stop wondering after, following, or worshiping the beast. Instead, repent and return to the Lord.
3. If you repent and become victorious, your name will "never be blotted out" from the book of life. Your name will be acknowledged before the Father and His angels, and you will be dressed in white and walk with Christ. However, if you do not repent, your name will be blotted out from the book of life, and you will be thrown into the lake of fire.

<u>Conclusion on the Lamb's Book of Life</u>. Two conclusions can be deduced from this discussion. First, if the promise not to "blot out his name" was made to those who have actually blotted Christ out of their

---

[301] The text seems to suggest that certain names have been written in the Lamb's book of life from the foundation of the world. In other words, those who would eventually be saved, their names have already been written. And the appeal to "repent" goes specifically to them, while those whose names have not been written from the beginning will never be written now. It is as if they are destined for doom and destruction. Teachings like this seems to support the "once saved, always saved" theory. It also conflicts with other Scriptures that makes salvation open to all, and the decision whether to be saved or lost rests with all. How do we reconcile these concepts? Who are those whose names have been written but have fallen away, and who are those whose names have never been written from the beginning?

To understand those characters whose names have never been written, one must understand the character of Judas in the Gospel of John. John presented Judas as someone destined for doom and destruction. Although he was "one of the twelve," he was not chosen by Christ. He who knew the heart of humanity knew that Judas would betray him. He was of the devil, and in fact it would have been better if he had never been born! The second group of opponents who are portrayed as having a similar position are the Jews of the Gospel of John. A similar group exists in 1 John. John called them antichrists and brother-haters. These people are presented as committing sins that "lead to death," and no one should pray for them (1 John 5:16, 17). John perhaps had the same people in mind in Revelation when he implied that their names have never been written in the Lamb's book of life.

lives or "soiled their robes," then the passages in Revelation 13:8 and 17:8 are intended to appeal to the same people. It basically urges them to—because their names have already been written in the Lamb's book of life—cease worshiping the beast or its image. However, if they refuse and continue in "wondering after the beast," then their names will eventually be blotted out.

Second, if having the believers' names in the book of life is contrasted with the multitudes that rendered worship to the beast or Babylon, then that would make the latter two characters the opponents in Sardis. We reached a similar conclusion in our discussion on the white robes. This, therefore, would mean that Sardis, Pergamum, and Thyatira have the same opponents (see chs. 13–18).

Jesus Acknowledging the Saints Before God and His Angels

Jesus acknowledging the saints before God and His angels is a message that is stressed in several key places in Revelation 4–22. For illustrative purposes, three passages are sighted as follows:

<u>The Punishment of the Wicked</u>. The last of the three angelic messages of Revelation 14 reads, "He [who worships the beast and his image] will be tormented with burning sulphur in the presence of the holy angels and of the Lamb" (v. 10). This text is part of a warning that the angel issues to those who forsake God's commandment, Christ's testimony, and insist on worshiping the beast and its image. The warning finds its fulfillment in 20:11–15.

<u>The Rewards of the Righteous</u>. The saints, however, are being acknowledged and rewarded in Revelation 20:4–6. The saints consist of two groups: those who had already died by the time Revelation was read (see 6:9–11), and those who refused to worship the beast, his image, and receive his mark.

<u>Possible Acknowledgement in Revelation 5</u>. Another place Jesus appears before God and His angels is in Revelation 5, but it does not specify if Jesus actually did acknowledge His followers.

What do these passages signify? Just as the saints in other churches who may have identified certain parts of Revelation 4–22 as directly addressing their own concerns, those in Sardis may have done the same with these messages. Seeing Revelation this way shows that the entire prophecies of Revelation were comprehensible and applicable to the churches that first received it.

RELATIONSHIP BETWEEN REVELATION 1–3 AND 4–22

In this section, we build on the table we introduced in the previous chapter. There we enlisted the similarities that exist between Revelation 1–3 and 4–22. Now we add the opponents, issues, characters, and the Christ of Sardis to that list.

Revelation 1–3	Revelation 4–22
1/Ephesus Address (2:1–7)	*See also Rev. 22:2*
• Promised "tree of life" (2:7)	• "tree of life" (22:2)
2/Smyrna Address (2:8–11)	*See Rev. 12–13*
• Two wars—current war and future "ten-day" war. • War is waged against those who keep God's commandments and have Jesus' testimony • War originates from "Synagogue of Satan," and they are involved in "blasphemy" against God • Devil is described as "accuser" (2:10)	• Two wars—current 1,260 days was and a future war on "remnant" (12:17) • War waged against those with God's command and Jesus' testimony • War from dragon and beast, who are covered in blasphemous names • Satan or devil is described as "accuser" (12:10)
3/Pergamum Address (2:12–17)	*See Rev. 12, 13*
• "throne of Satan" • Christ comes with "sharp sword" to judge opponents • Rewards: white stones	• Satanic throne (13:2) • Dragon, beast, land-beast, and image have mouths/swords to kill too • Rewards: precious stones (chs. 21–22)
4/Thyatira Address (2:18–29)	*See Rev. 14, 16–18*
• Jezebel the prophetess • Prostitute, seduces saints • Faithful saints as "remnant" (2:24) • Remnant have "the commandments of God and testimony of Jesus"	• Babylon the harlot (ch. 17) • Prostitute, seduces saints • Faithful saints as "remnants" (12:17) • Remnant have "the commandments of God and testimony of Jesus" (12:17)

Revelation 1–3	Revelation 4–22
5/Sardis Address (3:1–6)	*See Rev. 13–20*
• "soiled"	• "defile with the women" (ch. 14)
• "white robe"	• "white Robe" (chs. 7, 14, 19)
• Lamb's "book of life"	• "book of life" (chs. 13, 17, 20)
• "angles"	• Angels, "his angel" (chs. 1–3, 5, 8, 19)

No opponent is mentioned in the Sardis and Laodicean addresses. However, we have agreed that a lack of mention is not a good indication of absence of opponents. Actually, there are far greater characters, concepts, and events that bind the saints of Sardis to other parts of Revelation. The concept of angels, the details surrounding the white robes, and the contents of the Lamb's book of life that are central to the prophecies of Revelation 13–17 serve as literary and thematic adhesives and bind these two materials (chapters 1–3 and 4–22) together. This leaves us with no other option but to conclude that the opponents (beast, image, Babylon) featured in 13–17 are opponents of Sardis as well.

The opponents in the seven addresses, although variously labeled and described, all relate to the beast of Revelation 13:1–10, the image of verses 11–18, Babylon of chapter 14, and the harlot and her daughters of chapter 17. There is increasing evidence that the opponents with which the early church dealt were known characters.

SUMMARY

Opponents in Sardis

The Opponents in Sardis. Concerning the address to the believers in Sardis, there is no mention of an opponent. However, when considering the entire context, an opponent does seem to emerge. If the believers did see themselves with those arrayed in "white robes" (see chs. 6, 7, 19), with their names inscribed in the "book of life" (see chs. 13–17, 20), and being in possession of God's commandment, word, and the testimony of Jesus (see chs. 6, 12–14, 20), then it is possible to identify the opponents featured in these passages as their opponents as well.

The Opponents of the Early Church in Revelation 1–3 and 4–22. We have also demonstrated that John and his audience (including those in Sardis) saw themselves as being in possession of the "word of God," the "commandments of God," and the "testimony of Jesus."[302] They could have also identified themselves with the crying (see 6:9–11), pursued (see ch. 12), and persecuted (see ch. 13). Our current study helps to develop this thesis further. In this case, the opponents, particularly the dragon (see ch. 12), sea and land beasts (see ch. 13), and "Babylon the Great" (see chs. 14–18), may have also been their opponents.

The Challenge: Identities of Those Opponents. The challenge this presents to us, however, is to identify these opponents as the early church did. In order for dualism to work, we must also discover the identities of the same opponents from our own perspective and time. Perhaps the question that needs to be answered is whether the omnipotent God used the same set of symbols, characteristics, and institutions to disclose the identities of both the early church's opponent and our end-time opponent.[303]

> *If Christ describes the church as being "dead," then it is safe to assume that "an enemy has done this," or that the believers may have given themselves up to the worship of the "beast," its "image," and "Babylon."*

Issues in Sardis

If Christ describes the church as being "dead," then it is safe to assume that "an enemy has done this," or that the believers may have given themselves up to the worship of the "beast," its "image," and "Babylon." Thus, they received the "mark of the beast" (whatever this *mark* may have been). This perhaps resulted in the "defiling" of their "white robes." To this dying church, Christ appears as the "one who holds the seven

---

[302] Refer to the discussion on "word of God" and "testimony of Jesus" in Revelation 1:9.
[303] This question will be dealt with in Revelation 12 and 13.

spirits of God." Unlike the Ephesians who fought back and disproved the claims of false teachers, those in Sardis gave into the seductive teachings of the woman and her associates. Among other things, these teachings could have included the worship of angels or setting Moses against Jesus.

Therefore, to a church that consists mostly of "dead," "dying," and "about to die" people, Christ appears to them as One having the "seven spirits." The spirits not only function as Christ's eyes, but are also "life" and life-givers. "The Spirit gives life; the flesh counts for nothing. The words I have spoken to you—they are full of the Spirit and life" (John 6:63). Therefore, Christ comes to Sardis equipped and ready to give life!

Analysis of Dualistic Method

<u>Dualism</u>. Given this situation, one must attempt to determine how much of Revelation 4–22 the seven churches (or the Sardisians in particular) actually understood. It is not responsible exegesis to deny that Revelation 4–22 was applicable to their time and context. The early church could possibly have associated their own names with this "book of life." The same could be true concerning the beasts of Revelation 13–17. We may not have answers to all the questions, but that should not stop us from asking the right questions and approaching the text in a responsible manner.

<u>Methods of Interpretation</u>. The varying concepts and characters—"white robe," "book of life," "word of God," "testimony of Jesus," "commandments of God," "harlot," "false prophets," "saints," "blood of the Lamb," "spirits of God," "angels of God," and "Lamb of God"—that form the core messages of Revelation 4–22 are also central to the seven messages of chapters 1–3. This reality should compel us to reconsider our method of interpretation and approaches to Revelation.

<u>A Responsible Exegesis</u>. As we have seen so far, scant evidence supports the attempts to divide Revelation 1–3 from the rest of the text. Both sections of the book did speak to the seven churches as they speak

to us today. Therefore, it is only proper that we seek to understand what the entire Apocalypse must have meant to the early church before we can determine what it means to us today. This is where dual-intentionalism comes in. In a dualistic approach to the prophecies of Revelation, we first try to see the whole text through the eyes of John and his initial audience before we consider what it means to us.

21.
PHILADELPHIA, PART I: HIM WHO IS HOLY, TRUE, AND HOLDS THE KEYS OF DAVID

To the angel of the church in Philadelphia write: These are the words of him who is holy and true, who holds the key of David. What he opens no one can shut, and what he shuts no one can open. I know your deeds. See, I have placed before you an open door that no one can shut. I know that you have little strength, yet you have kept my word and have not denied my name. I will make those who are of the synagogue of Satan, who claim to be Jews though they are not, but are liars—I will make them come and fall down at your feet and acknowledge that I have loved you. Since you have kept my command to endure patiently, I will also keep you from the hour of trial that is going to come on the whole world to test the inhabitants of the earth. I am coming soon. Hold on to what you have, so that no one will take your crown. The one who is victorious I will make a pillar in the temple of my God. Never again will they leave it. I will write on them the name of my God and the name of the city of my God, the new Jerusalem, which is coming down out of heaven from my God; and I will also write on them my new name. Whoever has ears, let them hear what the Spirit says to the churches. (Revelation 3:7–13)

INTRODUCTION

These next two chapters will discuss the messages addressed to the sixth of the seven churches. In this chapter, the discussion focuses on the occurrences, definitions, and significance of the three divine designations the Orator uses to identify Himself. Then in chapter 22, we will discuss the main issues, characters, opponents, and relationship that exist between the materials of Revelation 1–3 and 4–22.

JESUS CHRIST IN PHILADELPHIA

To the saints in Philadelphia, Jesus Christ appears as "the holy and true" and the One "who holds the key of David." We begin the discussion with these designations and their implications for the early church.

Jesus as the "holy and true"

The Titles of Christ in the Seven Churches. If we reconsider the table containing the list of designations in each of the seven churches, most of these titles are derived from Jesus' physicality, anatomy, appearance, wardrobe, what He does, what He holds in His hand, and where He stands. In the last two churches (Philadelphia and Laodicea), however, Jesus' self-disclosure appeals more to His inner qualities and characters, rather than His anatomical and physical features. To the Laodiceans, for instance, He identifies Himself as the "faithful and true witness," whereas to the saints in Philadelphia, Jesus presents Himself as the "holy and true." The following table summarizes this:

The Seven Churches	Designations	Comments
Ephesus	• the one "who *holds* the seven stars in His right hand and *walks* among the seven golden lampstand" (2:1)[304]	Jesus "holds the seven stars in his right hand" + "walks" among the seven golden lampstands"

---

[304] The emphases in all passages are supplied.

The Seven Churches	Designations	Comments
Smyrna	• "First and the Last, who *died and came to life again.*" (2:8)	Who He is and His deeds
Pergamum	• "sharp, double-edged sword" coming out of His mouth (2:12, 16)	Physical features
Thyatira	• "Son of God" • "whose eyes are like blazing fire" • "burnished bronze" feet (2:18)	Names and physical features
Sardis	• "who *holds* the seven spirits of God and the seven stars" (3:1)	"holds the seven spirits of God" + holds the "seven stars"
Philadelphia	• "<u>who is holy and true</u>, who *holds* the key of David. What he opens no one can shut, and what he shuts no one can open" (3:7)	"holds the keys of David"
Laodicea	• "<u>Amen, the faithful and true witness</u>, the ruler of God's creation" (3:14)	Names and characters

<u>The Occurrences of "holy and true" in Revelation</u>. In the above designation, two distinct words are clustered together to describe Jesus. In our study, we will 1) trace similar occurrences in Revelation, other Johannine writings, and the NT texts, 2) study the usage of the terms "holy" and "true" separately, and 3) assess their implication for the saints in Philadelphia and the early church.

God as the "holy and true" Judge. In Revelation 3:7, Jesus is described as *"ho hagios, ho alēthinos,"* which literally means "the Holy One, the True One." If we take the titles as they appear in the Greek, then we have three, not two, titles for Jesus Christ. They are "the holy, the true," and the one who "holds the key of David." Hence, the KJV is closer to the Greek than the NIV. However, since both adjectives are in the same case and refer to the same subject, the NIV translators have added the conjunction *"kai,"* thus joining the two words. The only other place in Revelation where a similar construction appears is in 6:10. The text reads, *"ho hagios kai alēthinos,"* which is translated "the holy and true."

21. Philadelphia, Part I: Him Who Is Holy, True, and Holds the Keys of David

Although the adjectives "holy" and "true" are separately used as titles for God (see John 7:28; 8:26), the combination—"the holy, the true" (or the "holy and true")—was "not used together ... in early Jewish or early Christian literature as attributes of God."[305] The designation in Revelation 3:7 obviously refers to Jesus. However, the reference in 6:10 is ambiguous. This is because the title is similar to the one used for Christ in 3:7, but the context prefers God. In Revelation, He who sits on the great white throne is God, and He is presented as the ultimate judge in the following judgment scenes: Revelation 19:11, 16:5–7, 18:8, and 20. Therefore, the cry of the martyrs in 6:10 seems to be directed towards *that* judge. Conventionally and functionally, this interpretation is correct, but the linguistic similarity that exists between Jesus' self-disclosure of 3:7 and 6:10 does seem to link these two characters together. We will discuss this further in the following paragraphs.

Jesus as the "holy and true" Judge. While God is the ultimate Judge according to Revelation, the text also suggests that other nameless persons "were given the authority to judge" as well (20:4). Although the identities of these judges are not revealed, when one surveys other books that are also written by the same author, it becomes increasingly clear that Jesus Christ was one of those judges. In 1 John, God as the judge is maintained, but Jesus assumes the role of an attorney who stands before the Judge (see 2:1). Then in the Gospel of John, it is clearly stated that Jesus is *the* judge. "Moreover, the Father judges no one, but has entrusted all judgment to the Son" (John 5:22: see also v. 27). Such discourses like these are impregnated with literary and theological significance.

> *While God is the ultimate Judge according to Revelation, the text also suggests that other nameless persons "were given the authority to judge" as well.*

---

[305] See David Aune, Revelation 1–5, p. 235.

The Literary and Theological Implications. What emerges here is another example of a literary construction we have seen earlier—a literary crescendo. Here, the concept of Jesus as the ultimate Judge is both intentionally and progressively crafted. In chapter 7 of this study, we have seen how certain divine titles like "Alpha and Omega," "who was, is and is to come," "eternal life," "Beginning and the End," and "First and the Last" were consistently transferred to Jesus Christ, hence making Jesus equal to God. As was discussed in chapter 7, the main reason the author used these methods was not to display his literary craftsmanship, but rather because the rhetorical and literary styles he employed were governed by the theological and ecclesiastical issues he encountered.

Since Jesus Christ, His identity, provenance, and mission were on trial, John occasionally argued, beginning with what was agreed and accepted. He then gradually developed his discourses, culminating with the disputed. Thus, we observe with admiration as John transferred each of the titles and roles of God to Jesus. The author did exactly the same with the divine title of Judge. Using literary crescendo, he transferred God's title as the Judge to Jesus as the Judge. What follows next is an updated version of the same table we saw in chapter 7.

God's titles	Jesus as God	Jesus' titles
"alpha-omega"	"alpha-omega"	
	"the true God"	"Son"
"beginning-end"	"beginning-end"	
	"first-last"	"first-last"
"eternal life"	"eternal life"	
	"eternal life"	"Jesus"
"coming one"	"coming one"	
"judge"	"judge"	["attorney"]

Further, this also has implications for the order in which the Johannine books may have been written. The manner in which the major themes are developed in Revelation and across the Johannine books shows that the books had to be written in this order: Revelation, Epistles, and the Gospel of John.

Jesus as the "holy one"

Occurrences of the Term "holy." In Revelation, the word "holy" is used to describe God's dwelling place (see 21:2; 22:19), saints (see 22:11), His own character, and Jesus' character and identity. Our brief study, however, will focus on the last two usages.

God as "holy" in Revelation. Some of the profound theological statements concerning God's holiness are found in Revelation. For instance, in a worship setting in 4:8, the four living creatures cry, "Holy, holy, holy [Gr. *Hagios, hagios, hagios*]" to the "Lord God Almighty." In another worship setting, the victorious saints cry out to God, saying, "Who will not fear you, O Lord ... For you are alone is holy [*hosios*]" (15:4). Then in the middle of the seven last plagues, the "angel in charge of the waters" is quoted as saying, "You are just in these judgments, you who are and who were, the Holy One [*hosios*], because you have so judged" (16:5). The final usage, as we have seen already, is the divine title of "holy and true" in Revelation 6:10. As shown above, two Greek words are translated "holy" in English: "*hagios*" and "*hosios*."

An Analysis of the References. First, the text is clear that only one person is holy (Rev. 15:4). There is none besides God. However, if Jesus describes Himself as being "holy and true" as well, then He must be divine and equal with God.

Second, in each of the usages, the holiness of God (and Christ) is closely linked with the concepts of worship, fear, and judgment. For instance, the four living creatures who cry "Holy, holy, holy" in Revelation 4 do so in a context and process of worship. In chapter 15, the victorious saints worship God because "his righteous acts have been revealed." The "righteous acts" referred to here is God's judgment upon those who did not "Fear Him." The angelic worship of the "Holy One" in Revelation 16:5 is actually embedded in divine judgment. Not only does the passage occur in the middle of the seven plagues, but the very reference to the "Holy One" is sandwiched between two judgment references (vv. 5 and 7). Further, other passages like the three angels' messages (see 14:6–12) do not actually use the word "holy," but the concepts of "worship," "fear" and "judgment" are clearly stated.

Third, a relationship between the above passages begins to emerge. The afflicted saints of Revelation 6:10 call upon Him who is the "holy and true [judge]" to intervene and avenge their blood. When the divine justice is finally administered, we see the "victorious saints" and the "angel in charge of the waters" crying out in gratitude, adoration, and worship in chapters 15 and 16. Such relationships show that God (and His Christ) are the ultimate Judges and all should fear and worship Them.

God as "holy" in the Epistles and Gospel of John. In the epistle, there is only one reference to a "Holy One" (1 John 2:20). In the Gospel of John, Jesus referred to God as "Holy Father" (16:11). Here it is apparent that the mention of God's holiness is less frequent than in Revelation. Inversely, when we move away from Revelation, Christ's holiness is more frequently and explicitly stated than in Revelation. This is similar to other divine titles we have seen earlier (For more discussion on this, refer back to chapter 7 of this book).

<u>References to Christ as "holy."</u> The reference to the holiness of Christ begins with His self-disclosure in Revelation 3:7. We have discussed the "holy and true" reference in 6:10 and concluded that the context favors God, but similarities in language and function support Jesus Christ as the Holy One. Apart from this, there is no other Scripture that directly supports Christ's holiness in Revelation. However, the three main concepts, namely worship, fear, and judgment, that are closely associated with God's holiness also describe Jesus Christ. For example, the Lamb is hailed as worthy and worshiped as God in Revelation 5. He is also feared as the One coming to serve justice to those who refused to repent (see 6:15–17).

Christ as "holy" in the Epistles of John. We discuss the occurrences and usages of the holiness reference to Jesus Christ in other Johannine and

NT writings. An ambiguous reference appears in 1 John 2:20: "But you have an anointing from the Holy One, and all of you know the truth." It is not clear if the "Holy One" referred to here is Jesus Christ. A second reference to the Anointer and anointing occurs seven verses later: "As for you, the anointing you received from *him* remains in you, and you do not need anyone to teach you ... just as it [the anointing] has taught you, *remain in him*" (v. 27, emphasis supplied).

It is obvious that the "Holy One" and the two personal pronouns ("him") refer to the same person. However, the Anointer is not explicitly stated. The very next verse identifies the same character as the Coming One: "we may be confident ... before *him at his coming* ... But we know that when he appears, we shall be like him, for we shall see him as he is" (v. 2:28; see also 3:2). This is a clear indication that the author had Jesus Christ in mind all along. Therefore, the Anointer and Holy One of verse 20 refer to Jesus Christ (see John 1:33; 15:26; Acts 2:33).[306]

Further, the Greek word that designates God as the "Holy One" in Revelation 16:5 is *hosios*. The reference to the "Holy One" in 1 John 2:20 is not *hosios*, but *hagios* ("*tou hagiou*"). That was the very word used in the liturgical hymn in Revelation 4:8 for God. Such rendering tears down any distinction that may exist between God and Christ, thus making Christ equal to God.

Christ as the Holy One in the Gospel of John. The apostle Peter was the first to confess that Jesus Christ is holy. During a difficult time in Christ's ministry, "when many of His disciples turned back and no longer followed him," He asked if the twelve would leave too. To this, Peter responded,

---

[306] However, if the "anointing" reference here denotes the imparting of the Holy Spirit, then in 1 John 4:13, the text says that God "has given us of his Spirit" (see also John 3:34). Therefore, the question persists: Is the anointing from God or Christ? Is this even a contradiction? As we have discussed earlier, the anointing is *and* can be both from God and Christ. According to Revelation and the Gospel of John, Christ takes from the Father the Holy Spirit and gives it to the world. Therefore, John could write, "When the Advocate comes, whom I will send to you from the Father ... he will testify about me" (John 15:26). For more discussion on the subject of anointing or the Holy Spirit, refer to chapter 7 of this book. The immediate context, however, shows that the Holy One and Anointer of 1 John 2 and 3 is Jesus Christ.

"Lord, to whom shall we go? You have the words of eternal life. We believe and know that you are the Holy One [Gr. *ho hagios*] of God" (John 6:68, 69). In 1 John, the author wrote with much hesitation, and even then, it was almost ambiguous, but in the Gospel, Christ is declared as the "Holy One," the very same title used for God in Revelation. Thus, the total number of divine designations, titles, names, and descriptions for God being systematically transferred over to Christ is increasing. To the previous list—"eternal life," "the First and the Last," "Alpha and Omega," "Holy and True," "He who was, is and is to come," and the divine "judge"—we now add the divine title "Holy One." Although we shall see more examples of this later, it is important to point out at this stage that the author eventually transfers the prominent title for God in Revelation 4—"Lord God" or "our Lord and God" (vv. 8, 11) to Jesus Christ in the Gospel of John—"My Lord and my God" (20:28).

Jesus as the "true one"

<u>Occurrences of the Term "true one" in Revelation.</u> The word "true" does not appear by itself. In most cases, the word is used in conjunction with other terms. The table below enlists the occurrences and contexts of this term:

The phrases	Biblical Text	Usage, Context
"the holy, the true [*ho alēthinos*]"	3:7	Judgment context
"the holy and true [*alēthinos*]"	6:10	Judgment context
"just and true [*dikaiōmata*]"	15:4	Judgment context
"true [*alēthinai*] and just are his judgments"	19:2	Judgment context
"Faithful and True [*alēthinos*]"	19:11	The Rider to execute judgment
"trustworthy and true [*alēthinoi*]"	22:6	The truthfulness of the testimony

Apart from Revelation 15:4, the Greek word used for "true" is *alēthinos*. *Alēthinos* means "genuine or real," as opposed to unreal or fake. The Greek for "true" as opposed to "false" is *alēthes*.[307] Whenever the word "true [*alēthinos*]," its derivatives, and other combinations are used, it is mostly in association with God as the Judge, His judgments, or the validity of His testimony. However, in two critical areas, one at the beginning and the other towards the end of the book, the title is applied directly to Jesus Christ. As we have seen earlier, the first is Christ's own self-disclosure in Revelation 3:7. Then in 19:11, the Rider on the white horse is called "Faithful and True."

<u>Occurrences of "true" in the Epistles and Gospel of John</u>. When we leave the pages of Revelation, these divine descriptions are increasingly applied to Jesus Christ. "We know also that the Son of Man has come and has given us understanding, so that we may know him [God] who is *true*. And we are in him who is *true*—even in his Son Jesus Christ. He [Jesus Christ] is the *true God* and eternal life" (1 John 5:20, emphasis supplied; see also John 17:3.). The frequent and emphatic use of the word "true" and the unique rhetoric are all intended to transfer the title from God to Jesus Christ. This is how the epistolary author achieves that.

The first reference to "him who is true" refers to God. In the second reference, the author equated both God and Christ as "true." Then in the final reference, the author described Jesus Christ as not just "true," but the "true God." This conclusion should not surprise us because we had independently reached the same conclusion with the study of the designations "Son" and "eternal life" in the same text.[308] Then in the Gospel of John we read, "Now this is eternal life that they may know you, the only true God, and Jesus Christ, whom you have sent" (17:3). Just like 1 John 5:20, this text puts Jesus Christ on equal ground with the "only true God."

<u>General Implications</u>. The analysis of the designations "the holy and true," the "holy one," and the "true one" in Revelation (and other

---

[307] See Stefanovic, *Revelation of Jesus Christ*, p. 143.

[308] We have discussed at length how the author transferred divine titles to Jesus Christ, thus making Him equal to God. Here, Jesus does the opposite. He begins with Himself as God's Son, then continues the discussion, making Himself equal with God. For more discussion on this, refer to chapter 7.

Johannine writing) reaffirms certain observations already made. Among others, here are some:

1. There was a consistent and gradual transfer of divine attributes to Jesus Christ. Thus, an intentional effort was made to equate Jesus to God. The author efficiently used a literary crescendo to achieve this end.
2. In Revelation, the divine designations, titles, and names are heavily used for God. However, if certain references are intended for Jesus Christ, then they are usually implicitly stated. It is as if the author tiptoed around those designations. Then when the same titles are discussed in other Johannine writings, they are emphatically and declaratively applied to Christ.
3. Such methodological and literary craftsmanship is not intended to merely display the author's writing skills. Rather, the author was tiptoeing around to address real issues in the early church. In other words, the theological and ecclesiastical issues that confronted the author and his audience shaped the adopted literary and methodological styles.
4. However, we have argued elsewhere that in Revelation, the contents, structure, and methods were heaven–born. The author was told to just write what he saw and heard. That means the author had less choice even in the methodology adopted in the book. He was merely the penman, but such was not so when it comes to John's later works. He had a choice. He decided what and how to write. The manner in which he

> *We have argued elsewhere that in Revelation, the contents, structure, and methods were heaven–born. The author was told to just write what he saw and heard. That means the author had less choice even in the methodology adopted in the book. He was merely the penman, but such was not so when it comes to John's later works.*

wrote his other books shows that he had a high comprehension of the material and issues of Revelation. He not only comprehended the material, but it is highly likely that all the prophecies of Revelation were applicable to him and his audience.

Meaning and Significance to the Church. At this stage, we have yet to discover the opponents and real issues that the saints in Philadelphia encountered, but the preliminary analysis of the designations Jesus used in the address seems to favor divine judgment, or more specifically, God's vengeance on the enemies of Christ and His people. We shall return to this a little later. In the meantime, we will proceed to discuss the meaning and significance of Jesus holding the "key of David" in His hands.

Jesus "who holds the key of David"

Keys of David in the OT. Apart from Jesus being "holy" and "true," He is also the One "who holds the key of David." This is a clear allusion to Isaiah 22:21–22: "I will clothe him [Eliakim] with your robe and fasten your sash around him and hand your authority over to him. ... I will place on his shoulder the key to the house of David; what he opens no one can shut, and what he shuts no one can open."

Eliakim was King Hezekiah's faithful servant who was given the robe, sash, and key to the king's storehouse, a fitting symbol of the transference of control, authority, and unlimited access to the servant. To the saints in Philadelphia, "Jesus is the One who has received full authority and has [unlimited] access to the heavenly storehouse"[309]—not just authority over the "heavenly storehouse," but also God's earthly house (see Heb. 3:1–6).

The Types and Significance of Keys in Revelation. In the vision of Revelation 1:10–20, Jesus does hold a set of "keys," but it does not include the "key of David." Instead, He has the keys of "death and Hades." Are we looking at one and the same or two different sets of keys? It is possible

---

[309] See Stefanovic, *Revelation of Jesus*, pp. 143, 144; Aune, *Revelation 1–5*, p. 235.

that the key of David is different from the ones Christ holds in this passage. This is because there are at least three sets of keys in Revelation: the "key of David," the "keys of death," and the keys to the bottomless pit (see 9:1; 20:2, 3). These keys of Christ signify that He has full control over the "storehouse of heaven," the earthly "house of God," "death and Hades," and even the "bottomless pit" and those who live in them.[310]

However, bear in mind that in Revelation, differences in branding or names is not a good indicator of differences in concepts or characters. This is because, as we have seen, a single item, concept, or character can have multiple names or brandings. Jesus Christ, the Holy Spirit, God, Satan, the opponents, saints, and a host of others all have multiple names. Therefore, it is possible that there may be a relationship between the three types of keys discussed here.[311]

<u>The Use of David in Revelation and Other Johannine Writings</u>. Apart from the Davidic keys (Rev. 3:7), there are other references to David that also demand our attention. The first is in Revelation 5:5. In response to the mighty angel's question, one of the elders assured John, "Do not weep! See the Lion of the tribe of Judah, the Root of David, has triumphed." The final Davidic reference is in Rev. 22:16. Jesus says concerning Himself, "I am the Root and the Offspring of David, and the bright Morning Star." The reasons why Jesus Christ is closely identified with David has already been discussed in chapters 13 and 14 of this book. There we have pointed out that Jesus is not just likened to all Jewish patriarchs (including David), but that He surpasses them all. Although the same concepts are reiterated

---

[310] The text allows for certain changes, especially between the actual scenes of the vision of the Son of Man (1:10–20) and the manner in which Jesus is described in the seven messages (chs. 2, 3). For example, in the vision (1:10–20), Jesus is described as the "son of man." However, the same is introduced as the "Son of God" to the saints in Thyatira. It is possible that a similar literary transformation is taking place here. The "keys of death and hades" (1:18) transforms into the "key of David" (3:7) in this message. Actually, one transforming into another is less likely because both of these keys can co-exist, just the same way Jesus Christ is both the "Son of Man" and the "Son of God."

[311] For a comparative study of related concepts, see the section dealing with the resurrection in chapter 15 of this book.

here, the focus in the Philadelphian address is about the authority and power as embodied in that Davidic key.

<u>Summary</u>. Once these names ("the holy," "the true," and "the one who holds the key of David") are assessed, a few important points stand out. First, the title "holy and true" speaks of Christ as judge and His judgments. Second, Christ having the Davidic key denotes having full authority over heaven, earth, under the earth, the bottomless pit, and those who live in each of these places.[312] Third, Christ is not only the ultimate Judge, but, according to the text, He has already administered justice. He not only has the Davidic key in His hand, but He has already opened the door through which the fledgling saints in Philadelphia were to go. As a result, we see that the afflicted saints who cried "how long?" to the "holy and true" in the fifth seal (see 6:9–11) are worshiping God in reverent fear and awe in Revelation 15 and 16.

<u>Preview of the Next Chapter</u>. However, up to this stage, we do not know the opponents and main issues in the brotherly-love church. Why does Christ come through as the "holy one," "true one," and the One having "the key of David" to those in Philadelphia? What were the theological issues in Philadelphia? Were the opponents in this locale different or the same as those in other churches? We shall proceed to discuss these and other related questions in the next chapter.

---

[312] Christ as the "Ruler of God's creation" is discussed in the address to Laodicea. Please refer to the discussion on Christ's designation in the Laodicean address.

22.

PHILADELPHIA, PART II

CHARACTERS AND ISSUES

The Opponents

The Opponents of Jewish Descent. The opponents among the brotherly-love church are described as "those who are of the Synagogue of Satan, who claim to be Jews though they are not, but are liars" (Rev. 3:9). The opponents in Philadelphia were exactly the same ones we saw in the Smyrnaean church. To help refresh our minds, we re-enter the table containing the opponents in each of the churches:[313]

Churches	Opponents	Nature of the Opponents
Ephesus	"wicked men," "false apostles"	"apostles" who claim to be sent of God, Jews
Smyrna	false Jews, "synagogue of Satan"	"Jews," as coming from the "synagogues"; thus, they are Jews
Pergamum	"throne of Satan," "Balaamites," "Nicolaitans"	possibly Jews
Thyatira	"Jezebel," "depths of Satan"	"Jezebel," probably an institution, a church perhaps
Sardis	"you are dead," "about to die," "what you have heard, received, obey it"	internal weakness; their faith is likely weakened by the Jews
Philadelphia	"liars," false Jews, "synagogue of Satan"	"Jews" from the "synagogues"; Jews

---

[313] This table first appears in chapter 17. For the Jewish nature of the opponents, see chapters 16 and 17.

Churches	Opponents	Nature of the Opponents
Laodicea	"wretched," "pitiful," "blind," "naked," "lukewarm"	Laodiceans read Colossians addressed Jew-related issues, thus Jews caused problems (Col. 4:16)

The opponents in two of the seven churches came from the "Synagogue of Satan." Both are described as false Jews and liars. The opponents in the remaining churches are variously described as false apostles, Jezebel the prophetess, the adulterous woman, Balaamites, and Nicolaitans. In our assessment, we have made numerous attempts to show that the opponents are of Jewish descent—Jews who are godly in every way, think they are serving God, but have an antichristological agenda and crusade against the provenance, authority, divinity, and Christology of Jesus of Nazareth.

> *In our assessment, we have made numerous attempts to show that the opponents are of Jewish descent—Jews who are godly in every way, think they are serving God, but have an antichristological agenda and crusade against the provenance, authority, divinity, and Christology of Jesus of Nazareth.*

The Opponents and Christ. In a church where liars and false Jews are rampant, Christ appears as the "Holy and True [one]." To put things into perspective, He is not just a *true* Jew (as opposed to the false Jews and liars), but He is also the One in whose hand is the "key of David." Therefore, the very title with which Christ has chosen to identify Himself is somewhat confrontational in nature. Let us develop this argument further.

Assessment of the Issue. The opponents were of Jewish descent, be it diaspora Jews or emissaries sent from the local synagogues or Jerusalem. However, the text disputes their claims to Jewishness and states that they are liars. The question that demands our attention is, If the opponents were real Jews (and they were), then why would the Orator (or the author) dispute that fact? The answer lies in the chosen designations of Christ. If He is presented as the authentic Jew while the opponents are not, then we must determine the standard used to test one's claim to Jewishness. There are two such tests.

The Abrahamic Descent. The first litmus test for an authentic Jew is being of pure Abrahamic descent. In one of the disputes between Christ and the Jews, the latter boasted, saying, "We are Abraham's descendants ... Abraham is our father" (John 8:33, 39). Christ disputed their claim, saying, "If you were Abraham's children ... you would do the things Abraham did ... [but] You belong to your father, the devil, and you want to carry out your father's desires" (vv. 39, 44). This passage shows that the true children of Abraham are those who "do the things Abraham did." This criterion ignores the physical Abrahamic linage and upholds his deeds and character.

The apostle Paul wrote that Abraham "is also the father of the circumcised who not only are circumcised but who also walk in the footsteps of faith that our father Abraham had before he was circumcised" (Rom. 4:12). Ellen G. White put it succinctly: "Descent from Abraham was proved, not by name and linage, but by likeness of character."[314] It is for this reason that Christ calls the Jews lairs. And inversely, Nathanael, a man "in whom there is nothing false," "a true Israelite" (John 1:47).

The Mosaic Disciple. The second test for being a better Jew is to keep the *Torah*, the "laws of Moses." In the Gospel of John, the opponents of Jesus (the Jews) accused Him of breaking the Law. They prided themselves in saying, "We are disciples of Moses!" But "This man is not from God, for he does not keep the Sabbath [law]" (John 9:28, 16; 5:28). The opponents used Moses as the standard to accuse Jesus. However, Jesus used the same yardstick to assess them. "But do not think I will accuse you before the Father. Your accuser is Moses, on whom your hopes are set. If you believed Moses, you would believe me, for he wrote about me.

---

[314] E. G. White, *The Desire of Ages*, p. 467.

But since you do not believe what he wrote, how are you going to believe what I say?" (John 5:45–47).

While the Jews used the Torah as a tool to endorse a preconceived object, Jesus talked about believing in what Moses actually wrote. The Jews merely used the letter of the law to condemn Jesus, while Jesus upheld both the letter and spirit of the law.

To the opponents, a true Jew is someone who is of pure Abrahamic descent and a good "disciple of Moses." These two criteria find fulfillment in a single requirement of the law—circumcision. Circumcision, therefore, serves a dual purpose: it connects the circumcised to Abraham and fulfills the requirement of the Mosaic Law. However, Christ raises the bar by going beyond the valley of physical linage and the letter of the law. He appeals to the character and spirit of the two patriarchs. By appealing to such a high standard, the Jews stand condemned. Paul's description of a Jew is insightful: "A man is not a Jew, if he is only one outwardly; nor is circumcision merely outward and physical. No, a man is a Jew if he is one inwardly, and circumcision is circumcision of the heart, by the Spirit, not by written code" (Rom. 2:28).

The Davidic Key. However, with the choice of His designations, especially as One having the "key of David," Christ introduces something else that sets Him apart from His opponents. His association with David is not only intended to exceed the above basic requirements, but also to put Jesus Christ on par with Israel's greatest warrior-king. That is a feat that not all Jews can claim or achieve. Here Jesus is basically saying He is not only the True Jew or One greater than Moses, but He is the "Son of David" and the anticipated Christ. This table summarizes these discussions:

Details	Abraham	Moses	David
Jews' self-disclosure	"Abraham is our father." Focus on linage and genealogy	"We are disciples of Moses": focus on letter of the law	Anticipated the "son of David"
Jews' real identity	"Your father [is] the devil": focus on deeds and character	"Moses is your accuser": focus on the faith and spirit of the law	Not all Jews can claim to be the "son of David"

Details	Abraham	Moses	David
Jesus' Identity	"the Holy and True [Jew]": "Abraham saw [my day] and was glad" (John 8:56)	"Moses wrote about me"	"holds the key of David"
Notes	Jesus: the "seed [the real child] of Abraham"	Jesus: "Moses wrote about me"; One greater than Moses	the lion of the tribe of Judah, the root of Jesse

The Saints in Philadelphia

The actual content of the message to the believers in Philadelphia can be divided into three categories. The first set of messages concerns the saints' current condition. The second and third contain a series of promises and rewards. What follows next is a brief discussion on each of these messages.

Their Current State of Affairs. Here, we will discuss certain aspects of the current conditions of the saints.

"I know your deeds." To the believers in Philadelphia, Christ begins with the formulaic statement, "I know your deeds." His address and assessment of most of the seven churches begins with this statement. This table captures these occurrences:

Churches	Christ's Address	Key Assessments
Ephesus	"I know your deeds" (2:2)	"you have forsaken your first love" (2:3)
Smyrna	"I know your afflictions and your poverty" (2:9)	"you are rich" (2:9)
Pergamum	"I know where you live" (2:13)	You live "where Satan has his throne" (2:13)
Thyatira	"I know your deeds" (2:19)	"you are doing more than you did at first" (2:19)
Sardis	"I know your deeds" (3:1)	"you have a reputation of being alive, but you are dead" (3:1)
Philadelphia	"I know your deeds" (3:8)	"you have little strength, yet you have kept my word and have not denied my name" (3:8)
Laodicea	"I know your deeds" (3:15)	"you are lukewarm" and "poor" (3:15)

A general survey of the above deeds reveals several things.

The Addresses to the Seven Churches are Based on "deeds." First, five of the seven messages begin with the phrase, "I know your deeds." Then Christ begins to assess the deeds done by the saints in each of the churches. However, the addresses to Smyrna and Pergamum commence differently. To those in Smyrna, Christ says, "I know your afflictions and your poverty," whereas the message to Pergamum begins with, "I know where you live." The poverty, affliction, and location of Smyrna and Pergamum are highlighted, instead of their deeds. However, the context shows that the afflictions and locations are also symbols of deeds—deeds not done *by* the saints, but done *to* them by Satan and his agents who live in these two cities. Therefore, in the final analysis, these assessments are all based on deeds either done by the saints or to them by the opponents.

Titles and Designations of Christ, Opponents, and Saints are "deeds-based." Second, the labels and titles that Christ gives to Himself, His opponents, and the saints are all based on what each one does. For instance, Christ says to those at Smyrna, "You are rich"; to the saints in Sardis, Christ pronounces, "you are dead"; and to the Laodiceans, "you are lukewarm." Captured in these are the identifying conditions of each of the churches. For a discussion on the deeds–based designations of each of the opponents, refer to a table provided earlier in this chapter. Then for a discussion on the deeds–based designations of Christ, refer to chapter 20.

More Blessings to the Doer of Deeds. Third, Revelation and the Bible as a whole have a lot to say about deeds and doers of deeds. As we have observed in chapter 4 of this book, Revelation pronounced blessings on those who read, hear, and keep the "words of this prophecy" (1:3). Although those reading and hearing are blessed, the ultimate blessings and rewards are pronounced to those who actually "keep," "obey," or "do" the things written in Revelation (see 22:7, 12).[315] Perhaps this was one reason why Christ's objection to the Jews' claim to be of Abrahamic,

---

[315] For more discussion on this, refer to chapter 4.

Mosaic, or Davidic linage was based on things the patriarchs had done and what the opponents were doing.

Diagnosis and Remedy for the Churches Based on Deeds. After diagnosing the conditions, all the admonitions Christ offers to each of the seven churches has something to do with deeds done, undone, or needing to be done. For example, regarding the church that fell from her first-love experience, Christ urges her to "do the things you did at first" (Rev. 2:4). To those churches doing the commands of God, Christ encourages them, saying, "be faithful ... to the point of death" or "[o]nly hold onto to what you [already] have until I come" (vv. 10, 25). Then Christ compliments those saints who are doing "more than they did at first" (v. 19). However, to the weak and dying, Christ says, "I have not found your deeds complete ... therefore, what you have received and heard; obey it; and repent" (Rev. 3:2, 3). A similar command is given to those in the lukewarm condition: "So be earnest, and repent" (v. 19). Therefore, these remedies consist of practical things that needed to be done.

> *Doing deeds of righteousness is the remedy for all spiritual maladies. The dead and dying in Sardis are promised life and healing as they put into practice the words of Christ. The poor becomes rich, the blind sees, and the naked is clothed, when Christ's words are put to practice. As the saints in each of the seven churches begin to obey and do the things they did at first—growth, strength, maturity, endurance, victory, faith, patience, and love will follow them.*

In the sacred text, the hearing, reading, and sharing of God's Word have their place, but ultimately, true religion boils down to only one thing—doing righteous deeds. This is the reason why Paul tacitly said, "Whatever you have learned or received or heard from me, or seen in me—put it into practice. And the God of peace will be with you" (Phil. 4:9).

Benefits of Doing Deeds of Righteousness. Doing deeds of righteousness is the remedy for all spiritual maladies. The dead and dying in Sardis are promised life and healing as they put into practice the words of Christ. The poor becomes rich, the blind sees, and the naked is clothed, when Christ's words are put to practice. As the saints in each of the seven churches begin to obey and do the things they did at first—growth, strength, maturity, endurance, victory, faith, patience, and love will follow them.

"I know you have little strength." Christ acknowledges that the believers in Philadelphia have "little strength." Despite this fact, they have "kept my word," "not denied my name," and "kept my command to endure patiently." Of the seven churches, only two are described as having "little strength." The table below compares and contrasts these two:

Descriptions	Philadelphia (3:7–14)	Sardis (3:1–6)
Deeds	"I know your deeds"	"I know your deeds"
Strength	"I know you have little strength"	"Wake up! Strengthen what remains and is about to die"
Reputation and character	"you have little strength, yet you have" done more	"you have a reputation of being alive, but you are dead"
Condition	In health	"dead," "about to die," "names blotted out"
Acknowledging names	"you have not denied my name" + "will make them [the opponents] acknowledge that I have loved you"	Overcomers: "I will acknowledge his name before my Father and before His angels"
Read, heard, received, kept my teachings	You have "kept my word," "have not denied my name," "kept my command," "endure patiently"	"Remember, therefore, what you have received and heard; obey it, and repent"
Completeness of deeds	"hold on to what you have until I come." Implied here: deeds completed	"I have not found your deeds completed"
Preparedness	"hold onto what you have until I come"	"I will come like a thief, and you will not know at what time I will come to you"

The Level of Strength. The admonition to the saints in Sardis—"strengthen what remains and is about to die"—clearly indicates that "what [or whatever] remains" is not much, their strength is declining at a faster rate, and if appropriate interventions are not taken, then that which remains will eventually die out. Therefore, Christ's admonition is intended to halt the diminishing faith. The Philadelphians, on the other hand, have done more despite their "little strength." Here is a situation where the saints' output rate has exceeded their actual strength or potential. To them, Christ does not prescribe any further responsibilities. Instead, He tells them to just "hold on to what you have." This graph attempts to capture the spiritual health of these two churches:

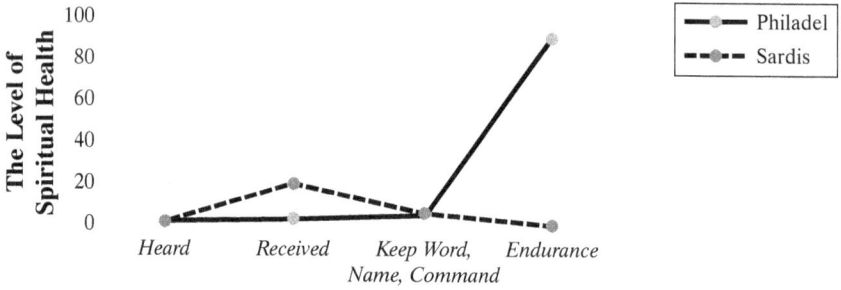

The Churches Received the Same Messages. Both churches have been introduced to the same message. Without identifying the contents of the actual messages, Christ invites the Sardisians to "remember" and "obey" what they "have received and heard." However, when complimenting the saints in Philadelphia, Christ provides a list of truths they had kept. That list includes the "word," "name," and "commandments" of Christ. It is possible that the Sardisians erred on the same truths.

The Possible Time the Churches Received the Messages. The church at Sardis is asked to remember the truths delivered to them in the past. Two conditions must exist in order for such a call to be effective. First, a call to remembrance indicates forgetfulness on the believers' part. Second, it implies a passage of time. A similar call is made to the Ephesians, where Christ urges them to remember their past experiences and repent accordingly (see Rev. 2:5). Unlike these churches, Christ does not provide any information about Philadelphia's former spiritual condition. The lack of such information, coupled with the sudden increase in faith, could suggest one of two things. Either the believers in Philadelphia consisted of mostly new converts, or satanic influence impeded their growth for a lengthy period of time. Once those impediments were removed, the church experienced a phenomenal growth. The latter scenario appears possible for two reasons.

The first reason is because her sudden increase in doing deeds of faith takes place immediately after the One who holds the "key of David" opens the door that had been shut for some time. Christ says, "See, I have placed before you an open door that no one can shut" (Rev. 3:8). Therefore, it is possible that the saints in Philadelphia lived through what appears to be a shut-door period. Afterward, we see Him who has the "key of David" opening the door, which unleashes and propels the saints into an exponential growth in spirituality.[316]

Second, the church is commended for keeping "my commands to endure patiently" (v. 10). The concept of patient endurance suggests suffering for an extended period of time for doing what is right. Despite such unfavorable circumstances, the saints refused to deny His name, word, and commandment.

---

[316] If the saints in Philadelphia had lived through what appears to be a shut–door period, then *someone* must have done that. Among other characters, the reference to "no one" could imply the "star that had fallen from the sky" (Rev. 9:1). This is because that fallen star "was given the key to the shaft of the Abyss" for a period of time. Whether there is a relationship between the "key of David" and the key to the bottomless pit is another issue, but there is a relationship between what these keys do. As soon as the fallen star opened the Abyss, thick "smoke rose from it" and darkened the "sun and the sky" and "torment[ed] the people for five months" (vv. 2, 10). Further, in Rev. 20:1–3, we see the situation reversed. There the "key to the Abyss" is no longer with the "fallen star," but in the hand of "an angel … out of heaven." The angel binds Satan and "[throws] him into the Abyss, and [locks]" him for a thousand years."

The Deeds of the Saints. The Lord praises the believers for doing two things: "you have kept my word and have not denied my name," and "you have kept my commands to endure patiently" (vv. 9, 10). As we have noted earlier, the core messages to all churches has to do with these same entities, especially Christ, His name, word, and commandments. Therefore, as evident in the table below, Christ uses the same entities to assess the health of all seven churches

Church	Teachings they were supposed to keep
Ephesus	"You have persevered and have endured hardships for **my name**, and have not grown weary" (2:3)
Smyrna	"I know your afflictions and your poverty—yet you are rich. I know the **slander** of those who say they are Jews … Do not be afraid of what you are about to suffer … Be faithful even to the point of death" (2:9, 10)
Pergamum	"Yet you remain true to **my name**. You did not renounce your **faith in me**" (2:13)
Thyatira	To the remnant who "do not hold to her [Jezebel] teaching and have not learned Satan's so-called deep secrets … Only **hold on to what you have** until I come" (2:24, 25)
Sardis	"Wake up! Strengthen what remains and is about to die, for I have not found your deeds complete in the sight of my God. Remember, therefore, what you have **received and heard**; obey it and repent" (3:2, 3). "a few people in Sardis have not soiled their clothes. They will **walk with me**… for they are worthy" (3:4)
Philadelphia	"you have **kept my word** and have not denied **my name**" and "you have kept **my commandment** to endure patiently" (3:8, 10)
Laodicea	"Behold **I stand at the door** and knock" (3:20). This church successfully shut Christ out of their doors and lives.

The issues in the seven churches and the entire Apocalypse basically revolves around the name, words, deeds, and person of Jesus Christ. In the prologue, John described "everything he saw" as "the word of God and the testimony of Jesus Christ" (Rev. 1:2). As discussed throughout this study and shown in the above table, the core issue in the seven oracles concerns Jesus Christ, His testimony, word, name, and commandments. The opponents' aimed at slandering Christ and persecuting those who follow Him. The believers are, however, urged to "hold onto what they have" and suffer for it. For further discussion on this, refer to a section dealing with the Ephesians' first-love experience in chapter 15.

"You have not denied my name." Were they expected to "deny his name"? The Philadelphian saints living through the locked-door period and suffering intensely had "little strength." Therefore, if they had denied His name, Christ would have understandably tolerated that. However, the saints endured for the sake of Christ's name. Five of the seven churches have clung to the name, word, and commandments of Christ, while the saints in Sardis and Laodicea have succumbed to the pressure.

"You have kept my commandment to endure patiently." At the time John wrote, patient endurance was a commodity that he and his churches had in common. He wrote, "I, John, your brother and companion in the suffering and kingdom and patient endurance" (Rev. 1:9). However, as we closely examine each church, we see the real condition of some of them. Most believers in two churches in particular have failed to demonstrate endurance. Further, regarding those at the verge of giving up, the author admonishes them to exercise "patient endurance" (Rev. 14:12), a quality without which none can be saved. Matthew described the same when he wrote, "But he that shall endure unto the end, the same shall be saved" (Matt. 24:13, KJV).

PROMISES AND REWARDS

Immediate Promises

Then Christ offers two sets of promises and rewards to the saints in Philadelphia: the immediate and ultimate. We shall begin the discussion with the immediate promises. "I will make them [the opponents] fall down at your feet and acknowledge that I have loved you. Since you have kept my command to endure patiently, I will also keep you from the hour of trial that is going to come on the whole world to test the inhabitants of the earth" (Rev. 3:9, 10).

"I will make them fall down at your feet." The act of kneeling before someone else's feet is a symbol of respect, worship, and submission. There are six such occurrences in Revelation. The first and last acts of worship are that of the author's own experience, where he fell at Jesus' "feet as though dead" (1:17) and then "fell at his [the angel's] feet to worship him" (19:10; 22:8). In between these are worships rendered to God and Christ by the twenty-four elders (see 4:10; 5:14). The final occurrence is the passage under study, where the opponents would fall at the feet of the saints in Philadelphia. The following table summarizes these occurrences:

Text	Falling Before God	Falling Before Jesus	Falling Before Others
John the Revelator		"fell as though dead" (Rev. 1:17)	"fell at his [angel's] feet to worship" (Rev. 19:10; 22:8)
Twenty-four elders	"the twenty-four elders fall down" (Rev. 4:10)	"the elders fell down and worshiped" (Rev. 5:14)	
False Jews			"will make them ... fall at your feet" (Rev. 3:9)

> *Falling before a divine presence is a natural response to the deity's power and glory. There is no coercion or intimidation involved here. The subject does it out of awe and reverence. Such is the case with John and the twenty-four elders' worship of Christ and God.*

Falling before a divine presence is a natural response to the deity's power and glory. There is no coercion or intimidation involved here. The subject does it out of awe and reverence. Such is the case with John and the twenty-four elders' worship of Christ and God. Further, the context makes it clear that John's attempt to fall at the angel's feet in worship was also because of his overwhelming encounter. However, we run into a problem when the worship rendered to angels in Revelation 19 is forbidden, but 3:9 seems to endorse the *worship* of saints. How, then, do we reconcile this issue?

As stated earlier, an authentic act of worship is spontaneous, and there is no external pressure. However, in the passage under study, we are told that the opponents falling at the saints' feet is not spontaneous. It is not out of reverence or awe, but forced on them. Christ says, "I will *make* them fall at your feet." Christ causes or almost forces these knees to bend.

"I will make them fall." The Greek term for "make" is *poiēsō*, which is the indicative future active of *poieō*. The term generally means "to make or do." The same verb is used almost ten times in Revelation 13. Each of their usages and meanings are as follows:

Text	Usage
Rev. 13:5	"The beast ... exercise [*poiēsai*] his authority for forty-two months"
Rev. 13:7	"He was given power to make [*poiēsai*] war against the saints"
Rev. 13:12a	"He exercised [*poiei*] all the authority of the first beast on his behalf"
Rev. 13:12b	"and made [*poiei*] the earth and its inhabitants worship the first beast"
Rev. 13:13a	"And he performed [*poiei*] great and miraculous signs"
Rev. 13:13b	"even causing [*poiē*] fire to come down from heaven"
Rev. 13:14	"he ordered [*poiēsai*] them to set up an image"
Rev. 13:15	"cause [*poiēsē*] all who refused to worship the image to be killed"
Rev. 13:16	"He also forced [*poiei*] everyone ... to receive a mark"

As demonstrated above, the term is defined variously as "exercise," "make," "perform," "cause" things to happen, and "order" or "force" someone to do something. These usages suggest heavy use of authority and force by the sea beast, land beast, and image of the beast. A similar intent is implied in Revelation 3:9. Jesus says that He "will make [order or force the opponents] to fall at your feet and acknowledge that I have loved you." Similar to the beasts of chapter 13, Christ promises to exercise His authority on behalf of His saints. The Son of David, who had earlier swung the doors open for His followers, now promises to bring the opponents to submission.

"Fall down at your feet and acknowledge." In Revelation 13, the activities of the three diabolical characters are intended to make the saints

worship the beast, its image, or the dragon. Those who refuse to comply are being threatened, persecuted, and put to death. When Christ says, "I will make them fall at your feet ... and acknowledge that I have loved you," He could either be predicting a massive conversion of the opponents or pronouncing the defeat of the opponents. Both scenarios are possible. First, the language and imagery used here is similar to that of the apostle Paul's Damascus experience. Saul was "breathing out murderous threats against the Lord's disciples" (Acts 9:1). His mission was to crusade against Christ and His followers until divine intervention made him fall down at Ananias' feet and acknowledge that Jesus is Lord. Second, God also wrought a definitive victory for Israel on the banks of the Red Sea. He crushed the pride of Pharaoh and his horsemen and made them acknowledge that "The Lord is fighting for them [Israel] and against Egypt" (Exod. 14:25). Although the Lord is able to do both, the language and context in Revelation favors another, third scenario.

Let us further illustrate this in the life of Joseph. Because of his two dreams, the jealous brothers captured and sold the dreamer. Years later, they were brought face to face with the one they had rejected. Moses recorded the account this way: "When Joseph came home ... they bowed down before him to the ground. ... And they bowed down, prostrating themselves before him" (Gen. 43:26–28). In this story, God made those who hated, rejected, and persecuted Joseph fall down at his feet and acknowledge that God loved him.

Joseph's story is similar to that of Christ's. "Therefore God exalted him," Paul wrote about Christ, "to the highest place and gave him the name that is above every name, that at the name of Jesus every knee should bow ... and every tongue confess that Jesus Christ is Lord" (Phil. 2:9–11). God promises the persecuted saints in Philadelphia that He would do exactly what He did for Joseph and Jesus. "I will make them fall down at your feet and acknowledge that I have loved you" (Rev. 3:9).[317]

---

[317] In Revelation, Christ comes through as a fighting General. The use of the name "Michael" in Revelation or "Prince Michael" in Daniel suggests this. Also, the imageries of Christ in Revelation

Final Rewards

Apart from the immediate promises, Christ mentions three ultimate rewards. These are briefly discussed as follows:

A Crown of Life. The first promise reads, "Behold I am coming soon. Hold on to what you have, so that no one will take your crown" (Rev. 3:11). The saints in Smyrna are also promised the "crown of life" (Rev. 2:10). Two things need to be mentioned concerning this promise. One, a crown is not a regular household item. It is usually found at a royal court. Perhaps this suggests what the redeemed shall become. John wrote, "[Jesus] made us to be a kingdom and priests to serve his God and Father" (Rev. 1:6). Two, in order to finally secure the crown at His coming, all the saints in Philadelphia and Smyrna (Rev. 2:10) had to do was "hold on" and "endure." This implies that the saints in these two churches are basically on the right path, and they are urged to keep pressing on.

A Pillar in the Temple. The second promise for those who become victorious reads, "I will make a pillar in the temple of my God." What does being a pillar (Gr. *stulos*) in the temple of God signify? Galatians 2:9 is the other place where the term "pillar" is used in reference to God's servants. "Peter, James and John, those reputed to be pillars [*stuloi*], gave me and Barnabas the right hand of fellowship." While Peter, John, and James are referred to as pillars of the earthly church in Jerusalem, the Philadelphian overcomers are promised that they will become pillars of the heavenly temple. In a physical structure, pillars are props, support, or the main columns that hold the edifice together. In the first century, the named apostles played an essential role in building the church of God. Similarly, the saints in Philadelphia are promised a prominent position in the temple of God in heaven.

The Names on the Gates, Foundations, and Pillars. Further, the Holy City had twelve gates and twelve foundations. "On the gates were written

---

1, 5, 6 (sixth seal), and the Rider on a white horse in 19 all portray Him as a warrior. The "sharp, double-edged sword" of Christ implies a dual role. That is, the same sword that judges and fights the opponents also protects His saints. The same is implied here.

the names of the twelve tribes of Israel." Then "the walls of the city had twelve foundations, and on them were the names of the twelve apostles of the Lamb" (Rev. 21:12, 14). In the city of God, the gates and foundations of the walls already have names. Now we are told that the "pillars" of the "temple of God" will feature the names of the overcomers from Philadelphia. However, the problem arises when we come towards the end of Revelation 21. John wrote, "I did not see a temple in the city, because the Lord God Almighty and the Lamb are its temple" (v. 22). What did this mean for the saints in Philadelphia? How do we reconcile this seeming contradiction?

Temple: The Nerve Center for Israel's Economy. What is the big deal about saints being clothed in white and serving God in His temple day and night (Rev. 7:15)? At a time when all nations worshiped stones and sticks, only Israel worshiped the true living God. Within the walls of Jerusalem was the majestic temple, which signified the very presence of this invisible God. For years, scattered saints would journey back to Jerusalem for annual feasts. Those in exile would often turn towards Jerusalem to lift their voices in prayers. With the temple being the most sacred place in Jerusalem, a "wall of separation" kept the dogs and Gentiles out. Even the regular Jew did not have excess to the temple. Only the priest had access to the Holy Place (first apartment) on a daily basis. The high priest entered the Most Holy Place once per year. Therefore, priests were the honored of all peoples. The psalmist had this in mind when he sighed, "Better is one day in your courts, than a thousand elsewhere; I would rather be a doorkeeper in the house of my God than dwell in the tents of the wicked" (Ps. 84:10).

The Prohibition of the Christian. However, following Christ's crucifixion, the Christian Jews were banned from the temple (see John 9:22; 16:1–4; Heb. 13:13–15). John encouraged them to worship "outside the city" and look forward to the heavenly "city whose builder and maker is God" (Heb. 11:10). He also told the Gentile Christians that God had made them, not the Jews, a "kingdom of priests," and they will serve God "in His temple day and night." Further, the believers in Philadelphia are promised to be "made pillars" in the heavenly temple. However, if there is no physical temple in heaven, then how or where do they serve Him?

This means that the saints will have direct and unlimited access to the living God, "because the Lord God Almighty and the Lamb are its temple." No more barriers; no more compartments; no more rituals; no more "walls of separation"; and no more Jewish priests. All the redeemed will serve God "day and night," but among them, the saints in Philadelphia are promised a prominent role. They will be made pillars in the new government of God, and as a result, they will "never again ... leave" the presence of God (Rev. 3:11).[318] It is mind-boggling to think that a Gentile dog could be made a pillar in the service of God in heaven. Such inclusivity speaks volume of God's grace!

I Will Write on Them Names. The promises to the saints in Philadelphia do not end there. Christ makes a third promise: "I will write on them the name of my God and the name of the city of my God, the new Jerusalem ... I will also write on them my new name" (Rev. 3:12). The question we must ask is, "What does all this mean?"[319]

Names on Heads and Foreheads. First of all, Revelation is saturated with names, particularly names being written on books, objects, people, beasts, and Christ. The table that follows presents a list of the names written particularly on people, beasts, and Christ:

Characters	Names Written	Comments
Overcomers in Philadelphia	"I will write on **them** the name of my God and the name of the city of my God, the new Jerusalem, which is coming down out of heaven from my God; and I will also write on them my new name" (3:12)	Each has many names. The details of the actual names are not disclosed

---

[318] Reconsider the promise in Revelation 3:11: "Never again will he leave it [temple]." The term "again" implies the addressees have once left the temple. Whether their leaving was forced on them or a voluntary step, the fact remains they did leave once already. Now they are promised that as "pillars" in the heavenly temple, they will "never" leave the temple again.

[319] For more information on the mark/seal issue, see Beatrice S. Neall, "Seal Saints and the Tribulation," *Symposium on Revelation—Book I*, pp. 245-278; C. Mervyn Maxwell, "The Mark of the Beast," *Symposium on Revelation—Book II*, pp. 41-66.

Characters	Names Written	Comments
Overcomers in Pergamum	Will give the overcomer a "white stone with a new name, known only to him who receives it" (2:17)	Same as Christ's name of Rev. 17
144,000 Saints	"Do not harm ... until we put a seal on the **foreheads** of the servants [from Israel] of our God" (7:3, 4)	Details of the seals not disclosed
144,000 on Mount Zion	Lamb on Mount Zion with 144,000 "who had his name and his Father's name written on their **foreheads**" (14:1)	Both have many names, but one on forehead, undisclosed
Rider on white horse	The Rider is "called Faithful and True ... his name is called the WORD OF GOD." "He has a name written on him that no one knows but he himself" (19:12). "On **his robe and on his thigh** he has this name written: KING Of KING AND THE LORD OF LORDS" (19:11–16)	He is "called" with first two names. His last three names are "written." Total of five names. Location of the secret name not told
Beast of Rev. 13	The Sea Beast has "seven heads ... and on each **head** a blasphemous name [was written]" (13:1)	Total of seven blasphemous names. Details not given.
Receive the mark of the beast	"He also forced everyone ... to receive a mark on his **right hand or on his forehead** ... which is the name of the beast or the number of his name ... let him calculate the number of the beast, for it is a man's number. His number is 666" (13:16–18)	A mark ... is the name of the beast/number of his name (666). It's a man's number
"Babylon" of Rev. 17	"The title written on her **forehead**: 'MYSTERY, BABYLON THE GREAT. THE MOTHER OF PROSTITUES AND OF THE ABOMINATIONS OF THE EARTH'" (17:5)	A total of four names given. They reflect her works and character
Twelve Gates of the city	"On the gates were written the names of the twelve tribes of Israel" (21:12)	Saints' names written on the Holy City
Twelve Foundation of walls	"the walls of the city had twelve foundations, and on them were the names of the twelve apostles of the Lamb" (21:14)	Saints' names written on the city wall foundations

Analysis of the Names. Second, we will provide a brief analysis of the names, titles, and inscriptions:

1. ***Names Are Either Called or Written.*** All names and designations in Revelation come under one of two categories. The names in the first category include those that were "called" but never "written." This includes the "True and Faithful" and the "Word of God" for Jesus (Rev. 19:11, 13) and "Wormwood" (Rev. 8:11), "Abaddon," and "Apollyon" for Satan (Rev. 9:11). We are not told exactly how John knew the names in this category. Whether the names were written, spoken, or impressed upon his mind, the author did not state.[320] However, the rest of the names featured in the table were "written," and John read them.
2. ***Men's Names are Rare.*** The names are written on the beast (Rev. 13), prostitute (Rev. 17), Rider (Rev. 19), worshipers of God (Rev. 7, 14), and worshipers of the beast (Rev. 13, 14, 16). However, having men's names being written on other people and things are rare, and only a few achieve that. For instance, the names of the twelve tribes and twelve apostles are written on the twelve gates and twelve foundations of the city wall, respectively. Further, the saints in Pergamum are also promised "white stone[s]" containing "new name[s]." Similarly, the mark of the beast that the disobedient receive at the end of time will also feature a "man's [name or] number."
3. ***Agents Enforce or Facilitate the "mark" and the "seal."*** The mark of the beast is essentially the name of the beast, and the lamb-like beast enforces it. The lamb-like beast forces everyone to receive it on his or her forehead or hand. The seal of God features the name of the Father and the Lamb, and it is administered by the angel from the east (Rev. 7:2, 3).
4. ***Multiple Names.*** Apart from the disobedient, the rest of the entities receive more than one name. The beast has seven blasphemous names, adulterous Babylon has four abominable names, the Rider on the white

---

[320] Concerning the total number of the "mounted troops" numbering "two hundred million," John said he "heard their number" (Rev. 9:16). Obviously, someone must have *called* them. It is possible something similar is happening in these cases.

horse has five holy names, the saints have two divine names, and the believers in Philadelphia have three heavenly names.

5. *Location of the Names.* Each of the names are featured in various places. Some of those places include the right hand, thighs, robe, heads, and foreheads, but most of them are written on either of the last two. For instance, apart from Christ's names in Revelation 19, the rest of the names are written either on the heads or foreheads.

Old Testament Background. Third, similar to Revelation, the OT features names being written on objects, people, and God.

Sign, Seal, or Mark	Parties Involved	Comments
"a mark on Cain" (Gen. 4:15)	God and Cain	"Cain is avenged seven times"
Circumcision (Gen. 17:9–14)	God and Abraham	"Covenant in your flesh"
Two onyx stones on the shoulder piece of the Ephod (Exod. 28:9–13)	The high priest before God	Aaron bore the names of twelve tribes on his shoulder as a memorial
The Breastpiece for decision and memorial (Exod. 28:29)	The high priest before God	Names of twelve tribes inscribed on each precious stone and high priest's heart
Urim and Thummim for decision making (Exod. 28:30)	The High Priest before God	On the Breastpiece, always over high priest's heart before the Lord; no sign[321]
Ten Commandments (Exod. 32:16)	By God on two tablets of rock	Obedient are "my precious possession"
Written Scripture on foreheads, wrists, and doors (Exod. 13:8–10)	God and His people	God's wishes for His people. God wanted His law to be infused in His people's lives
Seal on the foreheads of righteous (Ezek. 9:4)	God sealing the righteous on their foreheads	Placed on those who love the Lord and hate sin
Slave ear-piercing (Exod. 21:5–6)	Master piercing the slave's ear	A slave's promise to serve his master voluntarily for life

---

[321] No engraving, sign, or mark on these two gems.

An analysis of these marks and signs reveals the following:

1. **Significance of Markings.** As evident above, all forms of engraving, piercing, marking, or sealing in the OT have something to do with the unchangeable, permanent, or enduring effects of a covenant that is based on one's—not necessarily mutual—love, commitment, and devotion. For instance, a mark on Cain signified God's permanent protection and care. Circumcision indicates God's ownership. The engraving on the two onyx stones and twelve gems of the breastpiece shows God's remembrance, commitment, and unending love for His people. The Ten Commandments, which embody the character of God, prescribe the people's duty to God and one another. The art of ear-piercing and adorning oneself with written portions of the Law reveals the adorner's love and commitment to the Lord (or a master).

   > *The "sealing" in Ezekiel was a secondary mark placed only on a circumcised Jew who responded to God's love by loving Him back and hating sin. Therefore, circumcision in itself does not guarantee a relationship with God, for a sin-loving, circumcised Jew was no different from an uncircumcised Gentile.*

2. **Material of Markings.** Of the eight engravings or markings, four are done directly on the human flesh. These four include circumcision, ear-piercing, Cain's sign, and the sealing in Ezekiel. Of the remaining four engravings, three are done either on stones or precious stones. The final one consists of parchment written on with ink by a human hand. Note the differences in the signage between the first seven and the last one, as engravings on human flesh and rare gems are as enduring as God's love for His people.

3. ***Circumcision and Sealing.*** Circumcision was a physical "engraving" placed on every male Jew by divine ordinance. This mark signified the bearer as being dedicated to the true living God. In this case, the "sealing" in Ezekiel was a secondary mark placed only on a circumcised Jew who responded to God's love by loving Him back and hating sin. Therefore, circumcision in itself does not guarantee a relationship with God, for a sin-loving, circumcised Jew was no different from an uncircumcised Gentile.

4. ***Divine Engravings.*** The engravings on precious stones reveal a deeper spiritual reality. They speak of God's eternal, unchanging, stubborn, and unconditional love for His people. He said to Israel, "See I have engraved your name on the palm of my hands" (Isa. 49:16). This engraving literally took place when large, rusty nails were driven into Christ's hands and feet at Calvary. As engravings cut deeper than markings or writings do, Christ will forever carry those scares. "Jesus ascended on high from the field of conflict, bearing in His own person His bruises and scars as trophies of His victory." And through the ceaseless ages, He shall forever bear those scars.[322]

5. ***Piercing.*** In a slave–master relationship, the master pierced the slave's ear if he loved his master and wished to serve him the rest of his life. This piercing signified the sacrificing of the slave's rights and living in servitude to the master. Circumcision is what God commanded every Jewish male, but a voluntary piercing of the ears is what He requires of all His children. David had this in mind when he said, "Many, O LORD my God, are the things you have done … no one can recount to you; were I to speak and tell of them, they would be too many to declare. Sacrifice and offering you did not desire, but my ears you have pierced … [and] I desire to do your will, O my God" (Ps. 40:5–8).

Unlike in an earthly slave–master relationship, He Himself, who wants our ears pierced, was first pierced for our sins. John wrote, "one

---

[322] Ellen G. White, *Christ Triumphant*, p. 292.

of the soldiers pierced Jesus' side with a spear, bringing a sudden flow of blood and water" (John 19:34).

6. *Nature of the Markings*. Three points are noteworthy here. First, the marks and engravings were very much literal in the OT. Second, as shown above, they also had a much deeper spiritual application. Further, as seen in the "engraving" and "piercing," the same signs were also prophetic in nature. As it was in the OT, in the NT, the same signs also had both a literal and spiritual significance to the engravings. This is because Christ was literally and physically engraved and pierced for our sins, and by beholding those scars, we are healed.

Summary of the Signs. In the OT, a faith-based, covenantal relationship with a holy, unseeable God hung on these physical, tangible, and visible marks, inscriptions, and engravings.[323] These insignias were initiated by God and written on the body, hands, stones, rare gems, parchments, and other articles. They were literal, spiritual, and prophetic in nature. They all served almost the same purpose, but at different junctures of the covenantal relationship between God and His people.

For instance, the Ten Commandments, which formed the core article in the temple, bore the very handwriting of God. All Jewish ritual, organization, and government revolved around the temple, especially around these two tablets. Also, the high priest who officiated at the temple wore garments bearing engravings and inscription. Like the ten laws, these also spoke of God's compassion and care for His people. Then in obedience to His command, every person wrote out pieces of the law and wore them as ornaments on their foreheads and wrists and hung them on the doorposts of their homes. The latter signs signified the people's commitment to their God.

---

[323] The rainbow in the Genesis account also served a similar purpose. "I have set my rainbow in the clouds, and it will be the sign of the covenant between me and the earth. ... Never again will the waters become a flood to destroy all life. ... So God said to Noah, 'This is the sign of the covenant I have established between me and all life on the earth" (Gen. 9:13, 15, 17). These physical, literal, and tangible signs made the Christian God as Someone real, living, caring, and personal.

Signs, Seals, Marks, and Engravings in Revelation. Each of the signs was intended to achieve the same object, but variations in methods were for clarity, emphasis, and accessibility. In Revelation, the same is continued, but within the context of the great controversy. In other words, in the OT, the enemy and his alliances were not so apparent. However, Revelation is impregnated with polemical and competitive signs, inscriptions, and themes between God and Satan, and between the saints and the wicked. Therefore, the question is, What do the writings in Revelation mean?

The Actual Contents of the Inscriptions. Note the real contents of these writings:

i.	Philadelphia	Body: Name of God, Christ and New Jerusalem
ii.	Pergamum	White Stone: Secret Name
iii.	144,000 (seal)	Foreheads: Seal of the living God (Rev. 7)
iv.	144,000 (Mt Zion)	Foreheads: Lamb and the Father's name
v.	Rider on the White Horse	Robe/Thigh: "King of kings and the Lord of lords"
vi.	12 Gates	Gate: 12 Tribes of Israel
vii.	12 Wall Foundations	Walls: 12 Apostles
viii.	Disobedient	Foreheads: Mark, name or number of the Beast
ix.	The Sea Beast	Heads: 7 blasphemous names
x.	The Babylon	Forehead: Mystery, Babylon the Great, The Mother of prostitutes and the abominations the earth.

Names on the Saints. The names that appear on the saints include the names of God and the Lamb and the city of God. The 144,000 saints are prominently featured in two places. In Revelation 7, they are presented as having the "seal of the living God" on their foreheads. The exact inscriptions in that "seal" are not disclosed. The same group is again seen standing on Mount Zion with the Lamb, but this time, they had the Lamb and the Father's names written on their foreheads. Here it is implied that the "seal of God" consists of the Lamb and the Father's names. Therefore, if the saints in Philadelphia are promised the names of God, Christ and their dwelling place, then they are promised the divine sealing (see Rev. 3:12).

Names Blasphemed by the Beast. The inscriptions written in the "seal of God" are the "name of the Lamb" and the "name of the Father." Notice that these are the very ones that are being trampled upon by the beast and his followers. "He [the beast] opened his mouth to blaspheme God, and to slander his name and his dwelling place and those who live in heaven [including the Lamb]" (Rev. 13:6; see also 2 Thess. 2:4). Additionally, Hebrews describe those who have "fallen away" in similar language; "How much more severely do you think a man deserves to be punished who has trampled the Son of God underfoot, who has treated as an unholy thing the blood of covenant that sanctified him, and who has insulted the Spirit of grace" (10:29). Therefore, the battle must have something to do with these names. Obviously, the saints are persecuted because they cling to the very commodities which the enemy desires to obliterate (see Rev. 13:7).

Mark of the Beast. Everyone is forced to receive the "mark," "name" or "number" of the beast. If the mark stands for the name of the beast, and if it is written on the foreheads of the disobedient, then it also functions as the seal. However, this time, it is not the seal of God, but of the beast. Therefore, Christ warns those who receive the mark of the beast, saying, "If anyone worships the beast and his image and received his mark on the forehead or on the hand, he, too, will drink of the wine of God's fury" (Rev. 14:9, 10).

Significance. Both in the OT and Revelation, the inscriptions, seals, marks, and names consist of things that are physical, tangible, and visible. These are outward signs of an inward reality. Therefore, God is not arbitrarily interested in mere externalities, but concerned about that for which these marks actually stand; which are allegiance, commitment, obedience, and worship.

Names on Christ. In Revelation 19, the Rider on the white horse has many names and titles, but only one of those names is written on His robe and thigh. That name is "King of kings and Lord of lords" (v. 16). That is the same title used for Christ in Rev. 17:14. Both titles are used in the context of war. Revelation 17 talks about an impending war, one which the satanic confederacy will wage against the Lamb and His saints, "but the Lamb will overcome them because he is Lord of lords and King of kings" (v. 14).

Then in Revelation 19, that war is actually being fought, and Christ comes out victorious. "Then I saw the beast and the kings of the earth and their armies gathered together to make was against the rider on the horse and his army. But the beast was captured, and with him the false prophets ... Two of them were thrown alive into the fiery lake of burning

Sulphur. The rest of them were killed with the sword that came out of the mouth of the rider on the horse" (vv. 19–21).

Names on the Beast. The sea beast of Revelation 13 has seven heads with seven blasphemous names on them. The exact details of those names are not disclosed. However, in the same chapter, we find these words: "He [the beast] opened his mouth to blaspheme God, and to slander his name and his dwelling place and those who live in heaven" (v. 6). It is possible that some of the blasphemous names must have something to do with God, His name, dwelling place, and those who live in heaven, including Jesus Christ. As the term "blasphemy" suggests, perhaps this power claims the names, titles, prerogative, authority, and works of God and His Christ.

Apart from having the blasphemous names on his heads, when the beast opens his mouth, streams of blasphemies and lies flow out from him. Regarding Satan, John wrote, "He was ... not holding to the truth, for there is no truth in him. When he lies, he speaks his native language, for he is a liar and the father of lies" (John 8:44). Like his master, the beast not only speaks lies and blasphemies, but "there is no truth in him" at all. In other words, the lies and blasphemies are not just designations scribbled on the beast's head, or mere words coming out from the dragon's mouth, but they are actually the "flesh and blood" that make up who they are. That is their identity. As Christ's words and "flesh and blood" are one and the same, so is beast's (and Satan's) blasphemies and lies.

Names on Babylon. The four titles written on the woman's forehead were:

Mystery,
Babylon the Great,
The Mother of prostitutes
and the abominations of the earth.

Mystery and Secret Names. *Bible Works 7* defines "mystery" as "hidden things ... [or] secrets."[324] The secrets here refer to the woman's name.

---

[324] See the term "mystery" (Rev. 17:5) on *The Bible Works 7*.

Implications are that the woman has a name that is either mysterious or secretive. In other words, she has a secret name known only by her. If this is a correct assessment, then this is similar to Christ's "name written on him that no one knows but he himself" (Rev. 19:12), or the secret name on a "white stone" that is promised to the overcomers in Pergamum (Rev. 2:17).

Babylon–Mother, Satan–Father. Just as the Lamb is the bridegroom and His pure church is the bride, Satan and Babylon also assume a similar relationship. John 8:44 describes Satan as the "lair and the *father* of lies." Then in the passage under study, Babylon is described as the *"Mother* of prostitutes and the [mother of] abominations" (emphasis supplied). Babylon is not only responsible for producing "[daughter] prostitutes," but she has also conceived and given birth to all the "abominations of the world," including "lies." While the bride of Christ eagerly waits for the coming of the Bridegroom, Babylon is already in bed with Satan.

The Names Promised to Saints in Philadelphia. The final question we need to ask is, What do the names promised to the believers in Philadelphia mean? As discussed, having the names of the Father and the Lamb signifies sealing. However, the sealing in Revelation 7 and 14 does not include the "city of God." That is an extra honor placed on the saints in the brotherly-love church. Additionally, Christ promises to write on the saints His "new name." If the new name is known only to Christ Himself, then that would make the saints in Philadelphia the privileged few. Why would this church be rewarded highly like this? Although she lacked strength, she had endured incredible odds and overcome uncommon trials. Therefore, she is being rewarded handsomely.[325]

Summary on Promises and Rewards

Among all promises made to the seven churches, only a few stand out. First, Christ says to the "few people in Sardis who have not soiled their clothes" that they "will walk with me, dressed in white, for they are worthy

---

[325] Regarding the secret name of those in Pergamum, see the discussion in chapter 17.

[Gr. *haxioi*]" (3:4). As pointed out earlier, the word "worthy" is consistently applied to God and Christ, for their creative and redemptive work, respectively (see 4:11; 5:9). In a similar way, the "few" in Sardis must have overcome uncommon trials in order to be considered "worthy" to "walk" with Christ.[326] Further, God's judgment on Babylon is also described as a "worthy" one (For more discussion on these, see the section "Character and Issues" in chapter 19).

Second, the overcomers in the lukewarm church are promised, "I will give you the right to sit with me on my throne" (Rev. 3:21). Christ promises that the worthy few would "walk" with Him. Then to the overcomers in Laodicea, He would grant them the right to "sit" with Him on His throne. Then finally, the saints in Philadelphia would neither "walk" nor "sit" with Christ, but they would be made "pillars" in the temple of God and, like Gabriel, "stand in the presence of God" forever (Luke 1:19).

RELATIONSHIP BETWEEN REVELATION 1–3 AND 4–22

So many similarities exist between Revelation 1–3 and 4–22. A few of them are listed here for illustrative purposes:

1. <u>Saints in Possession of Truth</u>. First, the address to those who "kept my word" and have "not denied my name," and an admonition to "hold onto what you have" sounds a lot like those who "keep the commandments of God and have the testimony of Jesus" in Revelation 12 and elsewhere (see 6:9–12; 12:17; 14:12).
2. <u>The Opponents and Two Wars</u>. The idea of two wars in Revelation is found in both sections of Revelation. The reference to a worldwide "hour of trial" and the impending "ten-day persecution" in 3:10 and 2:10 are similar to chapters 6, 12–14, 17, and 19. Closely associated with these wars are Satan, his institutions, agents, and activities. This confederacy is heavily discussed in chapters 12–20. Considering such

---

[326] God, Christ, and the "few" saints in Sardis who have not defiled themselves are described as "worthy [*haxioi*]." However, there is a fourth group also described as "worthy."

common materials, it is hard for one to argue against the early church's comprehensibility of Revelation 4–22.

3. <u>The Name and Titles of Christ.</u> The manner in which Christ appears to the saints in Philadelphia and the choice of His designations in particular are not rare to Revelation 1–3. The concept of being "True," "Holy," and "Judge" are prevalent in the second part of Revelation (see 4–6; 14–19). Such similarities could narrow the level of differences that may exists between the two sections further. Observing this, Clinton Wahlen writes:

> In connection with the letter to Philadelphia, the description of Jesus as "holy" and "true" compares closely to that of the One to whom the martyrs under the altar cry out under the fifth seal for vindication (Rev. 6:10) ... The description of Jesus as "faithful and true" ... compares similarly to the description of the One coming on a white horse to judge righteously and make war (Rev. 19:11). Many examples, such as these mentioned in connection with Laodicea, demonstrate the close connection between the apocalyptic imagery of the letters and later chapters of Revelation ... Understanding Revelation 2 and 3 as a prophetic portrayal of God's visible church throughout history provides interpretative help for the later chapters.[327]

4. <u>The Rewards Promised to the Believers.</u> The promises concerning the concepts of names, being pillars in the temple, the crown of life, and city of God cannot be properly understood and appreciated without Revelation 4–22. These two sections (1–3 and 4–22) complement each

---

[327] Wahlen, "Letters to the seven churches: historical or prophetic? *Ministry*, November 2007, pp.13–14. As far as the material relationship between Revelation 1–3 and 4–22 is concerned, this book agrees with Wahlen. However, when it comes to the application of the seven churches, he, like all historicists, thinks the seven churches represent seven major periods throughout history. This study differs and proposes a modified historicism (a dualistic approach to the prophecies of Revelation. See Chapter 1).

other. In other words, the early saints must have understood Revelation 4–22 in order to properly interpret and appreciate Revelation 1–3, and vice-versa.

COMPREHENSIBILITY AND APPLICABILITY

In summary, we shall add these similarities to the previous list. When the two sections of the prophetic messages of Revelation are studied in this way, one cannot help but admit that the original readers did understand chapters 4–22 as being applicable to them. Therefore, we must resist the urge to divide the book based on alleged comprehensibility and applicability issues.

Revelation 1–3	Revelation 4–22
1/*Address to the Ephesians (2:1–7)*	*See also Rev. 22:2*
• Promised "tree of life" (2:7)	• "tree of life" (22:2)
2/*Address to the Smyrnians (2:8–11)*	*See Rev. 12–13*
• The two wars. The current war and a future "ten-day" war. • War is waged against those who keep God's commandments and have Jesus' testimony • War originates from "Synagogue of Satan," and they are involved in "blasphemy" against God. • Devil is described as "accuser" (2:10)	• Two wars. The current 1,260 days was and a future war on "remnant" (12:17) • War waged against those with God's command and Jesus' testimony • War from dragon and beast, who are covered in blasphemous names • Satan or devil is described as "accuser" (12:10)
3/*Pergamum Address (2:12–17)*	*See Rev. 12–13*
• "throne of Satan" • Christ comes with "sharp sword" to judge opponents • Reward: "white stones"	• Satanic "throne" (13:2) • Dragon, beast, land-beast and image have mouths/swords to kill too • Reward: precious stones (chs. 21, 22)
4/*Thyatira address (2:18–29)*	*See Rev. 14, 16–18*
• Jezebel the prophetess • Prostitute, seduces saints • Faithful saints as "remnant" (2:24) • Remnant have "the commandments of God and testimony of Jesus" (1:9)	• Babylon the harlot (ch. 17) • Prostitute, seduces saints • Faithful saints as "remnants" (12:17) • Remnant have "the commandments of God and testimony of Jesus" (12:17)

Revelation 1–3	Revelation 4–22
5/Sardis address (3:1–6)	*See Rev. 13–20*
• "soiled" • "white robe" • Lamb's "book of life" • Angels	• "defile with the women" (ch. 14) • "white Robe" (chs. 7, 14, 19) • "book of life" (chs. 13, 20) • Angels, "his angel" (chs. 1–3, 5, 8, 19)
6/Philadelphia address (3:7–13)	*See Rev. 4–22*
• "The Holy and True [Judge]" • Satan, his agents, activities and two wars • The saints and their possession of truth • Names of Christ, promises and rewards	• Holy and True Judge (chs. 6, 14–19) • Satanic agents, activities, 2 wars (chs. 12–20) • Saints possession of truth (chs. 6, 12–14) • Names, promises, and rewards of Christ (chs. 12–14, 17–19, 20–22)

23.

LAODICEA, PART I: THE AMEN, FAITHFUL, TRUE WITNESS, THE RULER OF GOD'S CREATION

To the angel of the church in Laodicea write: These are the words of the Amen, the faithful and true witness, the ruler of God's creation.[15] I know your deeds, that you are neither cold nor hot. I wish you were either one or the other![16] So, because you are lukewarm—neither hot nor cold—I am about to spit you out of my mouth.[17] You say, 'I am rich; I have acquired wealth and do not need a thing.' But you do not realize that you are wretched, pitiful, poor, blind and naked.[18] I counsel you to buy from me gold refined in the fire, so you can become rich; and white clothes to wear, so you can cover your shameful nakedness; and salve to put on your eyes, so you can see.[19] Those whom I love I rebuke and discipline. So be earnest and repent.[20] Here I am! I stand at the door and knock. If anyone hears my voice and opens the door, I will come in and eat with that person, and they with me.[21] To the one who is victorious, I will give the right to sit with me on my throne, just as I was victorious and sat down with my Father on his throne.[22] Whoever has ears, let them hear what the Spirit says to the churches. (Revelation 3:14–22)

JESUS CHRIST IN LAODICEA

The glorified Christ uses three designations to introduce Himself to the saints in Laodicea: "The Amen [Gr. *amēn*]," "The Faithful and True

Witness [Gr. *ho martus ho pistos kai alēthinos*]," and "The Ruler of God's creation [Gr. *ho archē tēs ktiseōs tou theou*]." In this chapter, we shall discuss each of these names and their significance.

The Amen

<u>Occurrences of "Amen" in Revelation.</u> "Amen" is a strong, affirmative expression meaning "truly." It is used six times in Revelation and more frequently in other NT books. The following table lists the six occurrences and their associated contexts:

The Term "Amen"	Used by	Context
"Amen" (1:6)	John	Worship and liturgy
"Amen" (1:7)	John	Worship and liturgy
"Amen" (3:14)	Jesus Christ	Title for Jesus
"Amen" (5:14)	Four living creatures	Worship and affirmation
"Amen" (19:4)	Twenty-four elders and four living creatures	Judgment
"Amen" (22:20)	John	Worship, liturgy affirmation

As evident above, each of these occurrences appears at the end of a statement of fact, thus reinforcing its validity. In five of the six usages, the term functions as an assertive particle and is used in liturgical or worship settings. The remaining reference (Rev. 3:14) is used by Christ as a title for Himself.[328] According to David Aune, this is the only place in the entire NT that "Amen" is used for Jesus' title.[329]

<u>God as Amen.</u> Aune explains that the reference to "Amen" in Revelation 3 is an allusion to Isaiah 65:16, "where the name of God is mentioned in connection with the use of both blessings and oath in the phrase ... 'he shall bless by the God of Amen.'" He further observes that the term's

---

[328] Nearly half of the occurrences in Revelation was used by the author; two were used by the four living creatures and twenty-four elders.

[329] Aune, *Revelation 1–5*, p. 255.

"connection with blessing and taking oaths probably indicates that both must be confirmed by God himself in order to be valid."[330]

<u>Jesus Christ as the Amen and Its Implication</u>. However, in Revelation, the title is attributed to Jesus Christ. Considering the overall context of Revelation, such usages are expected. This is because we have thus far seen how John consistently transferred all titles associated with God to Jesus Christ. Examples include Christ as the "Alpha and Omega," "First and the Last," "eternal," "Beginning and the End," and "who was, is, and is to come." Other divine attributes transferred to Christ include the "Holy," "True," "Holy and True," "Eternal Life," and the "Beginning One." Therefore, transferring the divine title of "Amen" to Christ is consistent with the tenor of the text. Furthermore, Paul clearly identified Jesus Christ as the "Amen": "For no matter how many promises God has made, they are 'Yes' in Christ. And so through him the 'Amen' is spoken by us to the glory of God" (2 Cor. 1:20).

Faithful and True Witness.

<u>Occurrences of Terms</u>. The terms "Faithful," "True," and "Witness," or their derivatives, appear in various combinations. There are four such usages in Revelation (For all divine designations associated with the adjective "true," refer to the discussion on Christ as "Holy and True" in the Philadelphian address). The following table captures the four occurrences:

Title	Used for
"faithful witness" (1:5)	Jesus Christ
"faithful and true witness" (3:14)	Jesus Christ
"Faithful and True" (19:11)	Jesus Christ
"faithful and true" (21:5; 22:6)	Word of God

---

[330] Aune, *Revelation 1–5*, p. 225. See also Stefanovic, *Revelation of Jesus Christ*, p. 150.

23. Laodicea, Part I: The Amen, Faithful, True Witness, the Ruler of God's Creation

<u>Jesus as the Faithful and True Witness</u>. The Greek for "faithful" is the same word for "trustworthy." It signifies the credibility, objectivity, and dependability of the Witness. The term "true" here refers to something genuine, as opposed to counterfeit or fake, and not the opposite of false. There are three implications for the usage of this title for Jesus Christ.

Three Implications of the Title. First, the use of this title implies the existence of unfaithful, counterfeit, and lying witnesses (see Rev. 2, 3; 16:13, 14; 19:20). Second, Jesus Christ is also contrasted with other genuine witnesses. Among the OT "cloud of witnesses," like patriarchs, prophets, judges, and kings, Jesus is presented as the ultimate Witness (see Heb. 12:1). The final implication relates to the credibility of a single witness. In a Jewish legal setting, a matter is established on the testimonies of two or three witnesses. This is required because the testimony of a single witness is usually considered less credible. In Revelation 2 and 3, however, a single Witness unilaterally assesses and testifies about the condition of the seven churches. That which would be rejected outright in a normal Jewish courtroom is valid in Revelation because of the quality and credibility of the lone Witness. Since the testimony is from the One who is both the "Faithful and True Witness" and "Holy and True [Judge]," as well as the Advocate and Amen, there is no need for additional witnesses.

> *In a Jewish legal setting, a matter is established on the testimonies of two or three witnesses. This is required because the testimony of a single witness is usually considered less credible. In Revelation 2 and 3, however, a single Witness unilaterally assesses and testifies about the condition of the seven churches. That which would be rejected outright in a normal Jewish courtroom is valid in Revelation because of the quality and credibility of the lone Witness.*

Further Evidences for the Implications. When the following passages are assessed, the same point comes through. "If I testify about myself, my testimony is *not valid*. There is another [John the Baptist] who testifies in my favor, and I know that his testimony about me is valid ... *Not that I accept human testimony*; but I mention it that you may be saved" (John 5:31–34, emphasis supplied). The issue becomes clearer in John 8:13–18. After Jesus declared Himself as the "light of the world," the Pharisees challenged Him. "Here you are, appearing as your own witness; your testimony is not valid" (v. 13). To this, Jesus responds:

> Even if I testify on my own behalf, *my testimony is valid*, for I know where I came from and where I am going. ... You judge by human standards; I pass judgments on no one. But if I do judge, *my decisions are true*, because I am not alone. I stand with the Father, who sent me. In your own Law it is written that the testimony of two witnesses is true. I am one who testifies for myself; my other witness is the Father, who sent me. (John 8:14–18, emphasis supplied)

Analysis of the Passages. Note the manner in which John presented the argument. He began by almost invalidating Jesus' own testimony because it lacked a seconder. Then John the Baptist was employed as the second witness. However, the Baptist's testimony was immediately dismissed as insignificant with the words "Not that I accept human testimony" (John 5:31–34).

Then in John 8, Jesus' own testimony is brought into prominence in two places ("Even if I testify on my own, my testimony is valid"; "But if I do judge, my decisions are right"). However, in order to be consistent with the law of Moses, Christ invokes His Father as the second Witness. The problem arises as those whom Jesus confronts "have never heard his [the second witness'] voice nor seen his form" (John 5:37). This would technically disqualify the testimony of the second witness (the Father) as well. That leaves us with Jesus' own testimony. This is simply because the Testifier is both the "Faithful and True Witness" and "Holy and True [Judge]."

Jesus and the Courtroom. Incidentally, the same Witness-Judge is also the Defense Attorney (see 1 John 2:1), and as if to put all disputes to rest, Jesus Christ is also called the "Amen." Just as all aspects of the Jewish sanctuary services—the temple and its furniture, every sacrificial animal and article, the rituals and services, and the priest and his garments—pointed to different facets of Christ's life and ministry, so is Christ in a courtroom setting. He is everyone and everything to whom the guilty one turns in order to receive pardon, forgiveness, and victory. He is a just and holy Judge, a defense Attorney, a true and faithful Witness, and after all is said and done, He is the Amen![331]

---

[331] To the seven churches, Christ assumes the roles of several characters (a judge, attorney, witness, etc.) and does all the associated functions. In Revelation 4 and 5, Christ is on trial, and several witnesses are brought in to testify on His behalf. Revelation 4 establishes "him who sits on the throne" as the only "worthy" One (v. 11). Revelation 5 begins with the search for Someone "worthy" to "break the seals and open the scroll" (v. 2). The "Lamb" is introduced as the "worthy" One who walks over and takes the scroll (vv. 4–7).

Following this event, a number of characters pay homage to Him in a more coordinated way. Notice especially the manner in which these are done: 1). First, the four living creatures and elders "fall down before the lamb," singing "You are worthy" (vv. 8–10); 2) Then "many angels numbering thousands upon thousands" sing, "Worthy is the Lamb" (vv. 11, 12); 3) The third set of testimonies comes from "every creature in heaven and on earth and under the earth and on the sea" who worship both "him who sits on the throne and ... the Lamb" (v. 13). What was implicit in the acts of the four creatures, twenty-four elders, and "many angels" is now clearly expressed in this single act—that Jesus is divine and equal to God; 4) After Jesus' equality with God has been established, the four living creatures agree, saying, "Amen" (v. 14a); 5) As if in agreement to these testimonies, the elders "fell down and worshiped" (v. 14b). Interestingly, the subject of their worship is not explicitly stated.

The implication is that the same people who worshiped God in Revelation 4 are now worshiping *both* God and Christ, hence making Jesus Christ almost identical with God. Here is the point: many witnesses (in this order: the four living creatures, twenty-four elders, all angels, all creatures, four living creatures, twenty-four elders) testify and make the case for Jesus' Christology and divinity in Revelation 5. Thus, the scene in Revelation 4 and 5 are intended to reinforce Jesus' Christology—the very same issue discussed extensively in the rest of the NT texts.

However, only One Witness bears all the testimony in Revelation 2 and 3. In order to do this, Christ assumes multiple roles in the process. As discussed earlier, some of the roles include the "Holy and True Judge," "the Attorney," "the Faithful Witness," and "the Amen." Two more additional thoughts need to be stated here. First, unlike in Revelation 5, in Revelation 2 and 3, the saints in the

God's Word as Faithful and True. God's word is described as "faithful and true." As seen earlier, the same adjectives are used as designations for Jesus Christ. This is not an indication of contradiction, because in Jewish thinking, the "word of God is living and active" (Heb. 4:12). The word of God has "flesh and blood." As the Scriptures say, "In the beginning was the Word, and the Word was with God, and the Word was God ... And the Word became flesh and made His dwelling among us" (John 1:1, 14). This is why Jesus Christ is called the "Word of God" (Rev. 19:13). Similarly, the title "Faithful and True Witness" can apply to both the "word of God" and the person of Jesus Christ.

Courtroom Scenes and Languages. Revelation is replete with legal and courtroom language and imagery. Thus far, the terms discussed, like "testimony;" "testimony of Jesus," "judgment," "Holy and True [Judge]," "Faithful and True witness," "throne," and "advocate," as well as the concepts of someone or something, namely the seven spirits, twenty-four elders, four living creatures, seven angels, and the Lamb, standing "before the throne," all depict a courtroom scene.

Apart from these, three other aspects about Revelation that seem to reinforce the courtroom scenario are: 1) The series of events that take place in Revelation find their origin in that "great white throne" and "him who sits on the throne." Both of these portray God as the ultimate Judge; 2) The visions and subsequent events in the Apocalypse seem to be triggered by a call for justice in the "prayer of the saints" (see 1:9, 10; 5:8; 8:3) and the "How long" cry of the slain souls (see 6:9–11); 3). There are more passages in Revelation that discuss either the judgment or the actual execution thereof. For instance, Revelation 4–11, 14–20 and most of 2 and 3 predominantly discuss judgment. Therefore, if our analysis of Revelation 2 and 3 features a lot of courtroom language, then the overall context warrants it.

---

seven churches are on trial. Second, in Revelation 5, the testimonies of the above characters are either enacted, sung, or stated, whereas in Revelation 2 and 3, the testimonies and roles of Christ are personified. For instance, Christ does not say "Amen" but that He is the "Amen"; He not only bears witness, but He is the Faithful Witness; and He not only judges, but He Himself is the Holy and True Judge.

The Ruler of God's Creation

Introduction. Jesus' third title in the Laodicean address is "Ruler of God's creation." According to Revelation, "God's creation" consists of three identifiable territories. They are the heavens, earth and under the earth, and seas, rivers, and those who dwell in them (see 5:13; 10:6; 14:7). The text in Revelation is saturated with examples showing that Christ is indeed "the Ruler" over all these and more. To illustrate this, we will consider a few examples in each category.

Jesus as Ruler over the Heavens. Jesus as the Ruler over those who live in heaven (the dwelling place of God) and other spiritual forces in higher places will be discussed separately, but here, we will assess Jesus' sovereignty over heavenly bodies. For instance, Revelation presents Jesus as having control over the sun (see 1:16; 10:1; 8:12; 16:8, 9), moon (see 12:1), stars (see 8:12; 9:1; 12:4), clouds (see 1:7; 10:1; 14:14), rainbow (see 4:3; 10:1), wind (see 7:1), sky (see 9:2), midair (see 14:6), and those that fly in them, like eagles (see 19:17) and angels (see 14:6–9).

One particular aspect that is apparent in all these is that Christ uses the same elements to accomplish His deep purposes. For instance, He whose appearance is likened to the sun (see 1:16) clothes His saints with the sun (see 12:1) and uses the same to punish the wicked (see 16:8–9). Again, we see Christ, who Himself is the "Morning Star" (2:28), crowns His saints with "twelve stars" (12:1) and punishes the "fallen [stars]" (8:10; 9:1; 12:4; 20:2, 3). The same is also true with eagles. Christ, who is like a six-winged eagle before the throne (see 4:8), enables His church by giving her "two wings of a great eagle" to fly to safety (12:14). He then uses eagles to issue a warning (see 8:13) and announce and execute punishment on the wicked (see 19:19; Matt. 24:28).

Jesus as Ruler over the Earth and Under the Earth. Jesus' rulership over the earth, under the earth, and those who live in them is another theme that is stressed (The section dealing with Jesus' authority over those "under the earth" will be discussed separately). The discussion here will cover three areas: the earth, living creatures, and minerals.

The Earth, Landscape, and Elements. A notable verse reads, "the earth helped the woman by opening its mouth and swallowing the river" (12:16). Jesus has authority over mountains and rocks (see 6:16; 8:8; 17:20), hills (see 17:9), islands (see v. 20), and deserts (see v. 3). Apart from the earth and landscape, Jesus also has authority over all the dwellers and "rulers of the earth," which we will discuss in the next section (see 1:5; 3:14; 17:13, 14; 19:15, 16, 19ff).

Christ is also in control of other earth–related elements, which include "winds of the earth" (7:1, 2), "earthquakes" (8:8; 16:18, 19), the "four winds" (7:1; Mark 4:41), "air" (16:17), storm and "flood" (12:15, KJV), and "flashes of lightning, rumblings and pearls of thunder" (4:5; 8:5).

Land Creatures. Christ cares not only for earth and its landscape, but He also has authority over the vegetation and all living things. God has special concern for "trees and grass" (7:1, 2; 8:7). This is shown in that He punishes those who destroy them (see 11:18). He has authority over the beasts of the earth (see 13:11), as well as "scorpions," "grasshoppers," "locusts," and other insects (9:3–11).

The Earth and Its Minerals. To a church that has pursued wealth, it is important to point out that Jesus is both the maker and owner of all gold, silver, and other precious stones on earth and in heaven. In Revelation, there are two types of wealth, which are heavily discussed in four places (see Rev. 4, 17, 18, 21).

The first types of stones are featured in Revelation 4 and 21. In chapter 4, stones are used to describe the appearance of God. "And the one who sat there had the appearance of jasper and a carnelian. A rainbow, resembling an emerald, encircled the throne" (v. 3).[332] Stones also describe His dwelling. "It shone like the glory of God, and its brilliance was like that of a very precious jewel, like a jasper, clear as crystal" (21:11). The city's twelve gates, which bear the name of the twelve tribes of Israel, are made of unique pearls. The city also boasts of twelve foundations, each made of "every kind of precious stones" (21:19) and inscribed with the names of the twelve disciples

---

[332] For more discussion on "precious stones," see the "Rewards" section in the address to Pergamum.

of Jesus. The walls of the city are made of jasper, and the city itself is made of "pure gold" (v. 18). The precious stones, therefore, are not only made by God, but they are also used in association with His own appearance, the gates, foundations, walls, and streets of His dwelling place, and those who live there. The precious stones, therefore, speak of the quality, purity, durability, and eternal value of God, godly people, and godly things.

The second types of stones are featured in Revelation 17 and 18. Here, the harlot is dressed in "purple and scarlet, and was glittering with gold, precious stones and pearls. She held a golden cup in her hand" (17:5; 18:16). She was not only robed in wealth, but she "longed [and lived] for" wealth (18:14). In order to acquire wealth, she has compromised a great deal, or as Revelation says, "she has committed adultery with the kings of the earth." Then with the merchants and "sea captain," she "buys and sells … cargoes of gold, silver, precious stones and pearls; fine linen, purple, silk and scarlet cloth" (18:11, 12). For Babylon, wealth is her pursuit, mission, clothing, trade, and love. However, all things that constitute wealth and luxury are part of God's creation, and this is one reason why Christ appears to this church as the "ruler of God's creation." As the Creator is adorned with and resembles precious stones, so is the counterfeit.

<u>Jesus as the Ruler Over Sea and Springs of Water</u>. Revelation is saturated with textual references showing that Jesus is both the Creator and Sustainer of the sea, waters, and all that is in them. First of all, God, through Jesus, made the "sea" (14:7), "every living thing in the sea" (16:4), "waters" (16:12; 17:15), "springs of water" (14:7), "many waters" (17:1), "rivers" (16:4), "river Euphrates" (16:12), and beasts of the sea (13:1).

Second, apart from the earthly seas and waters, Christ is also the Creator and Provider of the heavenly seas, rivers, and waters. These include the "sea of glass" (4:6), "springs of living water" (7:17; 21:6), "water of life" (21:6; 22:17), "spring of the river of life" (21:6), and "river of the water of life" (22:1). Also, Christ freely offers living water to those who respond to the invitation of the "Spirit and bride" to "Come" (22:17).

Opposed to the living waters that Christ provides, Satan and his agents counter-offer their own toxic waters. These waters include the "abominable things" (17:4), "blood of the saints" (17:6) from her "golden cup," and the "maddening wine of her adulteries—with which she [Babylonian harlot] makes the nations drunk" (14:8).[333] Those who reject Christ's gift of the "living water" and indulge in the "maddening wine" will also drink the "wine of God's fury" (14:10). In other words, to those who delight in shedding innocent blood, God will "give them blood to drink" (16:6).

<u>Jesus is the Ruler of All Kings and Principalities in Higher Places</u>. According to Revelation, Jesus is both the Creator and Ruler of the heavens, earth, seas, and springs of water. He is also the Ruler over "the rulers ... the authorities ... the powers of this dark world and ... the spiritual forces of evil in the heavenly realms" (Eph. 6:12). These rulers and authorities include all nations, kings, queens, and lords; beasts, dragons, and images; death, hades, and the bottomless pit; evil spirits, demons, and Satan. Each of these will be briefly discussed.[334]

Jesus as Ruler Over All Nations and Peoples. The following table shows most of the passages in Revelation that demonstrate Christ's authority over all peoples, nations, and kings:

Domain or Rulership	Ruler: Satan or Christ	Notes
God "created all things" (4:11)	God and Christ	*Creation*: God created all
"he was given authority over every tribe, people, language, and nation. All inhabitants of the earth will worship the beast" (13:7, 8)	Satan through the sea beast	*The Fall*: His authority was given by God to exercise it for a limited time period
"the whole world was astonished and followed the beast. Men worshiped the dragon because he had given authority to the beast" (13:3, 4)	Satan through the sea beast	*Result*: "he was given authority" by God to exercise for a limited period

---

[333] Babylon using the "golden cup" and making the nations drunk alludes to King Belshazzar's banquet in Daniel 5. The ancient Babylonian monarch used "gold and silver goblets" taken from the Jerusalem temple at the eve of its destruction (Dan. 5:2).

[334] Earlier, we argued that the spirits and angels of God are also subject to Christ. Now, the discussion here builds on that.

Domain or Rulership	Ruler: Satan or Christ	Notes
"[many] waters ... are peoples, multitudes, nations and languages" (17:1, 15)	Satan through Babylon	*Result*: All men from all nations
Blood purchased men from all nations for God (5:9)	Christ	*Redemption* of mankind
"eternal gospel ... to every nation, tribe, language and peoples" (14:6)	Christ	*The Call*: Christ's call to everyone
"great multitudes that no one could count, from every nation, tribe, people and language" (7:6)	Christ	*Saints*: Redeemed saints
Wicked as "sand on the seashore ... But fire came down from heaven and devoured them" (20:9)	Christ	*Wicked*: The wicked and their fate
Lamb overcomes all kings, rulers, peoples, and nations (17:14; 19:15)	Christ	*The War*: The Lord strikes down nations, overcomes and rules
"all the birds [eat] ... the flesh of all people" (19:17, 18)	Christ	*Wicked* during Second Coming
"leaves ... are for the healing of the nations" (22:2)	Christ	Redeemed *saints* in heaven
"The kingdom of the world has become the kingdom of our Lord" (11:15)	Christ	*Restoration*: Christ wrestles the world back

God, through Christ and for Himself, created all things (see Rev. 4:11). However, through disobedience, all "peoples, multitudes, nations and languages" have been brought under the control and influence of Satan and his demonic powers (17:15). Then, by His own blood, Christ "purchased men for God" (5:9). Therefore, He is seen calling "every nation, tribe, language and people" back to the worship of the true God (see 14:6). Those who respond to this call consist of a "great multitude that no one could count, from every nation, tribe, people, and language" (7:9). However, the number of those who reject the offer of eternal life will be like the "sand of the seashore" (20:8). The latter will then be banished from the presence of God forever (17:15–18; 19:15, 17–19). By so doing, Christ demonstrates His authority over all peoples and nations.

Jesus as the Ruler of the Kings of the Earth. Revelation 1:5 describes Christ as the "ruler of the kings of the earth." In the end of time, "ten kings" (with "ten" symbolizing perfection or totality of all end–time nations[335]) will unite against the Lamb, but the Lamb will overcome them (see 17:12) and have their flesh given to the birds of the air (see 19:18). Then after the 1,000 years are over, the same will be thrown into the fiery furnace. It is for this reason that Jesus is presented even as the "Lord of lords and King of kings" (17:14; 19:16).

Jesus as Ruler over Babylon. Babylon is variously described as an adulterous woman, the mother of harlots, a queen, or a city that sits on many waters. Through her adulterous relationship with the "kings of the earth," she has intoxicated "all the nations" and killed all apostles, prophets, and saints. Then "she boasts [saying], 'I sit as a queen; I am not a widow, and I will never mourn'" (18:3, 7). However, her authority and associated activities do have limitations. The Holy and Sovereign God will use the same kings on which she rides (now) to execute punishment on her. "The beast and the ten horns you saw will hate the prostitute. They will bring her to ruin and leave her naked ... For God has put it into their hearts to accomplish His purpose by agreeing to give the beast their power to rule, until God's words are fulfilled" (17:16, 17). Again, this demonstrates Christ's sovereignty.

Jesus as Ruler Over the Sea Beast, Land Beast, and Dragon. The first beast of Revelation 13 comes up "out of the sea," while the second beast comes "out of the earth" (vv. 1, 11).[336] The following table documents these two beasts, other beasts, reptiles, insects, and heavenly objects that come out from various locations, and their significance in the book of Revelation:

---

[335] See Beckwith, *The Apocalypse of John*, p. 700, as quoted by Stefanovic, *The Revelation of Jesus Christ*, pp. 521, 526, 527. In Daniel 7, ten horns represent ten European nations, but in Revelation 17:12, "ten nations" refer to the end–time "kings of the whole world" (Rev. 16:14). See Maxwell, *The Message of Revelation*, p. 477.

[336] It is interesting to note the area from which each of the animals are coming. The dragon was thrown out of "heaven" and "hurled down" to the earth (Rev. 12:3, 9, 10) and now assumes the title of a "king" and operates out of the Abyss (see 9:11). The "beast" of Revelation 17 "comes up out of the Abyss" and goes "to his destruction" (vv. 8, 11; 11:7).

Beasts or Characters	Location of Origin	Significance
First/leopard-like beast (Rev. 13:1)	"coming out of the sea" (v. 1)	"sea" many peoples
Second/lamb-like beast (13:11)	"coming out of the earth" (v. 11)	"earth" less people
Beast of Rev. 11:7	"come up from the Abyss" (v. 7)	"Abyss" not sea or earth
Beast of Rev. 17:8	"come up out of the Abyss" (v. 8)	Abyss
"Smoke from a gigantic furnace"	smoke rose from Abyss (9:2)	Star falls from heaven, opens Abyss/smoke rose from it/ darkens sun/sky- locusts rain down, whose tail stings like scorpions
Locusts (9:3)	Come "out of the smoke" (9:3)	
Locusts' tails	"stings like scorpions" (9:10)	
"a great star, blazing like a torch"	"fell from the sky" (8:10)	
The "fallen" star (9:1)	"fallen from sky to the earth" (9:1)	"was given the key to the Abyss" (9:1)
"angel of the Abyss [was the king of the scorpions]" (9:11)	"one who had the key," named "Abaddon, or Apollyon" (9:11)	Smoke, locusts, and scorpions' king/angel
"a third of the stars" (12:4)	"out of the sky" (12:4)	"his [Satan's] angels" (12:7)
"enormous red dragon" (12:3)	"appeared in [and from] heaven," "a star that had fallen from the sky" (9:1)	The dragon, great/fallen star, blazing torch, angel/king of Abyss, Abaddon/Apollyon

Characters Fall from the Sky. First of all, the characters that "fall from heaven" or the "sky" include "the dragon," a third of the stars, which are later identified as angels of Satan, and the "great [blazing] star" of Revelation 8 and 9.[337] Note the similarities between the fallen star (see 9:1) and the "enormous red dragon" that is thrown out of heaven.

---

[337] While these bodies fall from the sky, or heaven, the pure woman of Revelation 12 is clothed with "the sun," stands on "the moon," and is crowned with "the stars" and seen "in heaven." Of the competing locations (Abyss, sea, earth, and darkened sun and sky), this woman is presented as being in heaven. While by faith, we are citizens of heaven and daily we are moving heavenward, we also have a duty to shine like stars in this dark world (see Phil. 2:15; Dan. 12:3).

The Blazing Star. Second, the great blazing star that had fallen from heaven is given the "keys of the Abyss" (12:3, 9, 10). As seen earlier, holding the keys denotes having and exercising authority over a specific territory. For instance, Christ having the "keys of death and Hades" signifies His authority over these two places.[338] Along the same vein, the fallen star who has the "keys of the Abyss" is the same who wields authority over the Abyss.

As soon as the fallen star opens the Abyss, a series of activities follow. The character in charge of those events is an "angel of the Abyss" who also happens to be a "king." Note that the angel-king is in charge of the Abyss. Earlier we had seen the "great fallen star" being in possession of the keys of the Abyss. Therefore, it is possible that we are essentially looking at the same single character, who is also described as "Abaddon" and "Apollyon [meaning "destroyer" in Hebrew and Greek, respectively]." In other words, the "fallen" or "great blazing star" is a great fallen angel who has now become the "king of the Abyss." This sounds a lot like the "enormous red dragon" or Satan of Revelation 12. Further, his names, Abaddon and Apollyon, signify his core mission—"to steal and kill and destroy" (John 10:10).

The Dragon and His Throne. If the great fallen star, dragon, or Satan is a king and operates from the Abyss, then he must have a throne there as well. During the time of John, Satan's "throne" was located in the city of Pergamum (see Rev. 2:13). At the end of time, Satan shares the same throne with other beasts and powers (see ch. 13).

Fallen Star and the Abyss. As soon as the fallen star opens the Abyss, several activities ensue. The first activity involves smoke and locusts. Thick smoke rises and darkens the "sun and the sky." After this, locusts rain down from within the smoke. Then locusts' tails begin to sting mankind. Second, two of the beast powers of Revelation are described as coming up out of the Abyss. They are the beasts of Revelation 11:7 and 17:8. Therefore, the activities associated with the smoke, locusts, scorpions, and two beasts are directly related to the fallen star (Satan).

---

[338] See Christ having the keys of death and Hades in Philadelphia (Rev. 1:18; 3:7).

The Beast and Thrones. Unlike the above creatures (locusts, scorpions, and beasts of Reveation 11 and 17), the two beasts of Revelation 13 do not come out from the Abyss. The leopard–like beast comes up "out from the sea," while the lamb–like beast comes up "out from the earth." Despite their places of birth, Satan is still involved in their lives. First of all, just like the "mighty angel" who stands on both the "sea" and the "land" (10:2), Satan also stands on the "shore of the sea," a very convenient territory located in between the sea and land (see 13:1). Second, Satan shares his throne, authority, and power with both beasts (see vv. 2, 11, 12).[339] Third, having a throne makes each of these creatures kings in their own right.[340] Finally, at Christ's Second Coming, they will all share the same fate. The beast, false prophet (lamb–like beast), and dragon are all "seized" and "captured" by Christ and hurled into the "fiery lake of burning sulphur" (19:20; 20:2).

Christ's Authority over the Dragon. Revelation 20 paints a picture of the world immediately following the Second Coming. Christ "seized the dragon ... threw him into the Abyss ... and locked him for a thousand years" (vv. 1–3). He displays His sovereignty in unique ways. As seen earlier, Christ had offered "blood" to those who had shed innocent blood. He then scourged the wicked with the very object of their worship—the sun. He now thrusts Satan into the Abyss—the very nerve center of his operation—and locks him up for a thousand years! Afterwards, the devil

---

[339] The sea beast comes up out of the "sea." This does not come from the Abyss, but after it was conceived, the dragon offers the throne. This indicates that at its conception, this beast is not associated with the dragon. However, it was only when the beast accepted the offer of the dragon that it became diabolical. This indicates a "conversion" experience. Similarly, the lamb-like beast comes up "out of the earth." During its inception, the beast resembled a "lamb" but later began to speak "like a dragon." In their initial stages, both of these beasts were "Christian" in nature, but later they reject Christ and follow the dragon.

[340] Note that most of these creatures operate from a "throne" and have kingly authorities and powers. For instance, the dragon owns and operates from a throne (Rev. 2:12; 13:1–4). He then shares his throne with the sea beast, who in turn shares with the land beast. That is why Revelation 17 describes this union as follows: "[t]he beast...is an eighth king. He belongs to the seven and is going to his destruction" (v. 11). At the end of the age, the sea and earth beasts and the ten kings will form an alliance to fight against the Lamb, "but the Lamb will overcome them because he is Lord of lords and King of kings" (v. 14).

is "thrown into the lake of burning sulphur, where the beast and the false prophet had been thrown" (v. 10).

<u>Jesus as Ruler over Death, Hades, "under the earth," and the "Abyss."</u> Thus far, we have discussed Christ's lordship over the "heavens," "the earth," the "seas and springs of water," and "the kings and rulers in high places." We now turn to an area described in Revelation as "under the earth." The same territory is also described as "hades," "death," the "Abyss," or simply a place under or inside the earth.

Christ Has the Keys of Death, Hades, and the Abyss. Christ "hurled [Satan] down" to the earth (12:9). "Hurling" suggests a violent throw, and that is exactly what Christ does with Satan, death, and hades. The following table traces the usage of the terms "hurled" and "thrown" and their derivatives:

Actions by	Possesses Keys, etc.	Actions Done to
Michael	Strength and Might	"he [dragon] was *hurled* to the earth (12:9, 10)
Christ	Christ: Keys of Abyss	"He *threw* him [Satan] into the Abyss" (20:3)
Christ	Keys of death and hades	"death and Hades were *thrown* into the lake of fire" (20:14)
Christ	Keys of death and hades	"beast and false prophet *thrown* alive into the lake of fire" (19:20)
Christ	Keys of death and hades	"the great city of Babylon will be *thrown* down" (18:21)
Christ	Keys of death and hades	"devil ... was *thrown* into the lake of burning sulphur" (20:10)

Several things need to be pointed out here. First, note that Christ has absolute authority over the Abyss, death, hades, and the fiery lake. He has keys to each of these places (see 1:18; 20:1). Second, the Greek term that describes all divine actions, especially "hurled," "threw," or cast," is *ballō*. *Ballō* means "to throw something or someone without caring where it falls," or "to give over to one's care uncertain about the results."[341] This is

---

[341] See the term "thrown" (19:20) in *Bible Works 7*.

what Christ did to Satan when He hurled him from heaven to the earth, or when He throws him from the earth to the Abyss (see 20:3). Ultimately, the foe will be hurled into the lake of fire (see v. 10). These divine activities reveal that Christ is completely in charge, and the enemy is no match for Him.

The divine act of throwing will not only be done to Satan and his fallen angels. According to the text, Christ will do the same to the beast and false prophet. "But the beast was captured, and with him the false prophets ... The two of them were *thrown* alive into the fiery lake of burning sulphur" (19:20, emphasis supplied). Death and hades will also meet the same fate. "Then death and Hades were *thrown* into the lake of fire" (20:14). Even Babylon will receive a violent throw. "With such violence the great city of Babylon will be thrown down, never to be found again" (18:21). Surely, Christ is the Ruler over God's creation and has unrestricted power over death, hades, the Abyss, and those who live or reign in them. Additionally, this divine act is an appropriate judgment on those presently involved in throwing the saints out of the temple and synagogues (see John 9:34).

> *This is what Christ did to Satan when He hurled him from heaven to the earth, or when He throws him from the earth to the Abyss (see 20:3). Ultimately, the foe will be hurled into the lake of fire (see v. 10). These divine activities reveal that Christ is completely in charge, and the enemy is no match for Him.*

Evil Spirits and Demons. Revelation teaches that the dragon's tail "swept a third of the stars out of the sky" (12:4). Also, along with the "great blazing star" that fell from the sky, "a third of the stars turned dark" (8:12). In other places, these same spiritual beings are described as "evil spirits" (16:13) or "spirits of demons" (v. 14). Undoubtedly, these demons serve the "king" of the Abyss. Further, the text also says that

Babylon has become the "home for demons" (18:2). When the seventh plague is poured out onto the city of Babylon, the city "split[s] into three parts" (16:19). This implies that the city is made of three entities: the false prophet, beast, and dragon (vv. 13, 14). If, at the end of time, the hosts (beast and false prophet) are captured and "thrown alive into the fiery lake of burning sulphur" (19:20), then the demons and evil spirits who dwell in them are also cast into the same fire. It is like eggs in a nest, where the survival of the hatchlings is dependent on the safety of the nest. Destruction of the nest will result in an obliteration of the eggs as well. So shall it be with the beast, false prophet, and the demons who live in them.

ANALYSIS AND CONCLUSION

As seen in each of the addresses to the seven churches, Christ's self-disclosure and names reveal something about His words, deeds, and being. For a summary of these names, refer to the discussion on the sixth church (chapter 21). In the previous six churches, we have seen some specific facets of Christ's life and their implications for the churches. In our current study, we have established three things. First, we noted that Christ is the essence and embodiment of the Jewish sanctuary, with its sacrificial and priestly systems. Second, we have seen how Christ assumes the roles of several offices and characters in the Jewish judiciary system. Now, to summarize everything, Christ is presented as the "ruler of [all] God's creation," and everything is indeed subject to His authority. As discussed, the book of Revelation presents incontrovertible evidence to this effect.

24.

LAODICEA, PART II

CONTEXTUAL ISSUES

Introduction

<u>An Overview</u>. Since most of the material in the Laodicean address has already been discussed in conjunction with the previous six churches, we shall mention them for reference purposes. For example, for a discussion on the location and purpose of Jesus standing "at the door," see the section entitled "Jesus in Ephesus" in chapter 15. The discussions on other materials are summarized in the following table:

Aspects of Revelation	Location
"rich," "wealth"	See "Jesus in Smyrna," *chapter 16*.
On self-awareness	See "Opponents of Smyrna," *chapter 16*.
Comparisons of all opponents	See "Opponents of Pergamum," *chapter 17*.
The manner in which Jesus is introduced in all churches	See *chapters 17* and *20*.
The core messages and the standards used for assessing the condition of each church	See the discussion on *chapter 21*.

For further discussion on each of these points, the reader can consult the specified locations. However, our immediate concern is to assess the significance of Christ's names and titles in the Laodicean address, but first, a preliminary issue needs to be addressed. Unlike other churches, Laodicea's contextual issues are unique in a number of ways, which are stated as follows:

The Opponents—Doctrinal and Contextual Issues

<u>No Opponents in Laodicea</u>. The first unique element is that there is no explicit mention of any internal or external opponent in Laodicea. In the other six churches, the presence of opponents like Balaam, Jezebel, the Nicolaitans, false Jews, false prophets, and false apostles are explicitly stated. These characters are notably missing in Laodicea. Also, there is no mention of their parent institutions like the "synagogue of Satan" or "throne of Satan" in Laodicea.

<u>No Theological Issues</u>. The second difference is that the address does not contain any doctrinal, theological, or Christological issues. The closest we get is some ambiguous and symbolic language like "lukewarm," "nakedness," "blindness," and being in want. Whether or not these terms are a reflection of some theological or economic issues is still debatable.

<u>Doctrines of Christ</u>. Finally, the saints in the previous six churches were commended for being in possession of certain truths like faith in God and Jesus' name, not forsaking His name, being in possession of the word of God, and keeping His commandments. In the Laodicean address, these too are missing. Refer to the following table for a more comprehensive analysis of these differences:[342]

Analysis

Unlike the previous churches, there is no clear textual evidence to make the case for Judaism–related opponents or issues in Laodicea. Now—as we said it before, we say again—that the absence of these features in the text is not a good indication that they were not present in Laodicea. Like in all churches, these issues and opponents were present in Laodicea. We have sufficient circumstantial evidence to make a case for this. These evidences are divided into three groups: remote clues, similarities between Laodicea and Sardis, and other textual evidence.

---

[342] This table is cited from chapter 21 of this book.

24. Laodicea, Part II 451

Churches	Opponents	Teachings	Institutions	Teachings and Servants of Christ	Remarks
Ephesus	False "apostles" (2:2), "Nicolaitans" (2:6)	Teachings of the same twos and "practice of the Nicolaitans" (2:6)	N/A	N/A	"apostles" who claim to be sent of God, Jews
Smyrna	False "Jews, but are a synagogue of Satan" (2:9)	Teachings of false Jews and "slander" of Jesus' names (2:9)	Synagogue of Satan	"you are rich" (2:9); have "gold refined in the fire" (3:28)	"Jews" as coming from the "synagogues"; thus, they are Jews
Pergamum	Satan, Balaamites, Nicolaitans (2:13–15)	Teachings of Balaam and Nicolaitans (2:14, 15)	Throne of Satan (2:13)	"your faith in me," "true to my name" (2:13)	possibly Jews
Thyatira	"woman Jezebel," "prophetess" (2:20), "her children" (2:21), Satan (2:24)	"her teachings" (2:20, 24); "her immorality," "her ways (2:21); "Satan's deep secrets" (2:24)	N/A	"she misleads my servants" (2:20); "hold on to what you have" (2:25)	"Jezebel" is a "woman," "a prophetess," and a mother; for she has children. See "Babylon," who is a woman, a mother, and queen too (Rev. 17, 18)
Sardis	Most "soiled their garments" (3:4), no white clothes or name in book of life, for they follow the adulterous woman (Rev. 13, 14, 17, 18)	Impure wine of her adulteries	N/A	"what you have received and heard" (3:3), "few … worthy" (3:4), in "white," name in "book of life" (3:4, 5)	Internal weakness; their faith is likely weakened by the Jews
Philadelphia	False "Jews," "synagogue of Satan," "liars" (3:9)	N/A	Synagogue of Satan, "city of my God, New Jerusalem" (3:12)	"kept my word," "my name" (3:8), "my command" (3:10)	"Jews" from the "synagogues"; Jews
Laodicea	N/A	N/A	N/A	N/A	Remote clues

The Remote Clues. The first clue is the issue about the worship of angels that is addressed in Revelation and Colossians (4:16). Laodicea being closest to Colossae, the worship of angels must have been a common issue between them. The second clue concerns the consistent use of the term "overcome" or promises made to the overcomers in each of the churches. Unless there is an opposing character of some sort present in Laodicea to be overcome, the use of this term may be deemed inappropriate. Third, the inclusion of Laodicea among the seven churches in the address is revealing. Unless she was affected by the opponents and issues discussed in Revelation, her inclusion in the address is pointless. However, the truth is that no matter how hard we try to push these kinds of clues, they are merely remote clues, and there is no direct evidence to confirm each of these inferences.

Sardis[343] and Laodicea. The volume of similarities that exist between Sardis and Laodicea could indicate that they had similar issues and/or opponents. What follows next is a comparative analysis of these two churches. Again, it is important to point out that we do not have direct evidence. What we are doing here is trying to establish evidence by association.

Similarities Between Sardis and Laodicea. These two churches have several things in common. First, both churches have someone or something about which to boast. Sardis has a "reputation of being alive," but she is actually "dead." Laodicea, on the other hand, boasts about her "wealth," saying "I am rich," but she is described as "poor."

Second, Sardis has "heard and received" the message, but has not obeyed, and as a result, she is either "dead" or "about to die," while Laodicea has also heard and received the same message, but has not been "earnest" in obeying it, and as a result, Christ is "about to spit her out."

Third, the saints in both churches are accused of having issues with their articles of clothing. Sardis is accused of *both* defiling and removing her clothes, while those in Laodicea had already removed their white garments and are naked.

---

[343] For more information on white garments in Sardis, refer to our discussion in chapter 19.

1. ***Defiling***. Christ says to the faithful "few" in Sardis, "you have a few people in Sardis who have not soiled their clothes" (Rev. 3:4). The implication here is that most of the people have "soiled" their clothes. Therefore, the issue among the Sardisians is defiling of their clothes.
2. ***Removing***. Also, note that the act of *sleeping* in Revelation is akin to removal of clothes. Christ says to those in Sardis, "but if you do not wake up, I will come like a thief, and you will not know at what time I will come to you" (v. 3). Compare this with 16:15: "Behold, I come like a thief! Blessed is he who stays awake and keeps his clothes with him, so that he may not go naked and be shamefully exposed." In Revelation, the removing of clothes and the act of sleeping are synonymous.
3. ***Defiling and Removing Are One and the Same***. Note that John used two different words or concepts to describe a single act done by a single group of people. This means that, at least among the Sardisians, defiling is the same as removal of clothes, for the Sardisians are accused of both. Now the important question is, How does all of this relate to Laodicea?
4. ***Removing/Defiling Is the Same as Sleeping; Laodicea Is Accused of Sleeping***. Laodiceans are told that they "are naked" and their "shameful nakedness" is exposed. This basically means that they do not have their white garments on them. Just as Christ has called those in Sardis to "wake up" from their sleep, He now calls the Laodiceans to "be earnest" (3:19).
5. ***The Role of Revelation 16:15***. Notice that the wardrobe issues associated with the acts of defiling, removing, and sleeping in Sardis and Laodicea are held together by Revelation 16:15. The following diagram shows these and summarizes our discussion:

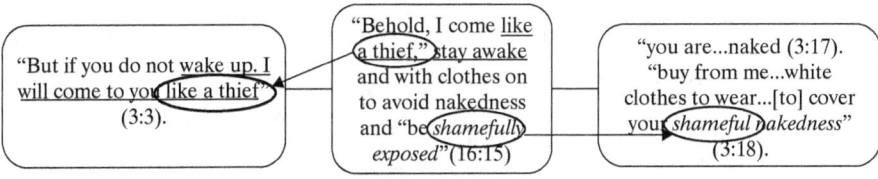

A comparative analysis of these passages shows that 1) to those in Sardis and Revelation 16:15, Christ's return is likened to a "thief," 2) the removal of clothes, sleeping, or defiling among the Sardisians is similar to sleeping and being naked in Rev. 16:15, and 3) the removal of clothes and being "shamefully exposed" in Laodicea and Rev. 16:15 are same. In this way, Rev. 16:15 serves as a link-text that connects the issues of Sardis to those of Laodicea. If Laodicea's removal of clothes and nakedness is similar to Sardis' defiling/removal, then there is a possibility that the same enemy has done this, and probably for the same reasons.

Objections to Sardis and Laodicea. Undoubtedly, there are clear linguistic and conceptual similarities between these two churches. The differences, however, are real and they outweigh any appearances of similarities.

Saints in Sardis Are "worthy." First, the saints in Sardis who have not yet defiled their white clothes are described as "worthy." "They will walk with me, dressed in white, for they are worthy" (Rev. 3:4, 5). "In John's day, worthiness denoted a distinctive qualification that made a person fit or eligible for a highly honored office. Such a qualification was based on outstanding achievements, such as prowess and bravery displayed in the battlefield."[344] In Revelation, the term "worthy" is reserved only for a few people who have "outstanding achievements." For instance, it is used to describe God for His creative deeds (see Rev. 4:11), Christ for His redemptive works (see Rev. 5:9), and Babylon for a well-deserved punishment (see Rev. 16:6). The same term is now used to describe the "few" in Sardis. As we have discussed in chapter 19, the faithful few in Sardis are described as "worthy" because they have come out of the great tribulation. It is to this group that Christ promises, "They will walk with me, dressed in white, for they are worthy." The problem, however, is that the same cannot be said for the Laodiceans.

Nevertheless, the Laodicean overcomers are promised something far superior. "To him who overcomes," Christ says, "I will give the right

---

[344] Stefanovic, *Plain Revelation*, p. 69.

to sit with me on my throne" (Rev. 3:21). Those in Sardis were promised the right to "walk with [Jesus]," while the Laodiceans are promised "the right to sit with [Jesus]." Although the term "worthy" is not used, the nature of the promise implies that the faithful Laodiceans are equally worthy candidates. Unless the opponents and issues they encountered are equal or worse, the Laodicean overcomers would never be promised the throne.

Saints in Sardis Have Earned Their "white robes." The second objection is that the white garments that the Sardisians wear are earned, while the white garments in Laodicea are bought (see Rev. 3:18). In other words, the white garments are given to the Sardisians as a result of overcoming the opponents in the great tribulation, while the same are given to the Laodiceans in exchange for "wealth." While these linguistic differences are true, the sober reality is that these white garments cost both churches something far greater than their military prowess or wealth. It cost their very own lives, for they sacrificed all, "even to the point of death" (Rev. 2:10), in order to be counted worthy of sitting, standing or walking with Christ in heaven.

Before we consider the final piece of evidence, something needs to be pointed out at this stage. As was discussed in chapter 19, the opponent in Sardis was the adulterous Babylon of Revelation 17. Thus far, the indications are that the same enemy could be at work in Laodicea as well. These preliminary conclusions compel us to reexamine the text in order to mine for more clues that may help us establish the case.

TEXTUAL ANALYSIS

Textual Evidence

When we assess the last of the seven massages, several thoughts stand out. We will briefly discuss each one.

"I know your deeds." The church at Laodicea is "lukewarm ... neither hot nor cold." She is spiritually weak, not earnest, and about to be vomited out. However, she is definitely not lazy, nor does she suffer from some common weaknesses. Christ says to her, "I know your deeds." Except to Smyrna and Pergamum, Christ begins all His addresses with this phrase. The addresses to Pergamum and Smyrna begin with the phrases "I know where you live" and "I know your afflictions," respectively. These phrases are carefully chosen to reflect the saints' greatest strength, weakness, or afflictions. Whether a church's deeds are righteous or evil is immaterial, but all churches are hardworking. The text shows that the focus of Laodicea's deeds is not religious but materialistic. Laodicea is allegedly quoted as saying, "I am rich; I have acquired wealth and do not need a nothing" (Rev. 3:17). The fact is that no one acquires much wealth by merely sleeping or dreaming. One has to work for it. Therefore, Laodicea has, and Christ is correct when He says, "I know your deeds."

<u>Lukewarm Condition of the Church</u>. The concept of Laodicea being lukewarm appears about four times in the address. The text reads, "I know your deeds, that you are *neither cold nor hot*. I wish you were *either one or the other*! So, because you are *lukewarm—neither hot nor cold*—I am about to spit you out of my mouth" (Rev. 3:15, 16, emphasis supplied).

Nearly all the characters in the seven churches—saints, backsliders, and opponents—have demonstrated uncommon zeal, determination, and perseverance in religious matters,[345] but not so with the Laodiceans (Rev. 3:19). Instead, their zeal and strength have been invested into material wealth. However, one needs to determine whether their lukewarm condition was wrought as a result of being in an adulterous (or compromised) relationship with an opponent or due to pure negligence.

Laodicea Boasts in Wealth. Laodicea boasts, "I am rich; I have acquired wealth and do not need a thing" (3:17). She may be "neither hot nor cold" on spiritual matters, but she definitely is on fire when it comes to acquiring wealth. She has bound up her life in gold and silver. Her confidence

---

[345] Refer to the previous table in this chapter. That table features the opponents, saints, and their teachings. The same table could also indicate the level of commitment that each of the personalities and institutions invested in their respective courses.

and boasting stems not only from the great wealth she already possesses, but also from her ability to acquire even more. There are other characters in Revelation that also boast about someone or something other than Christ. We shall briefly explore these boasts.

The Opponent Boasts in Judaism. Like the Laodiceans, the Jewish opponents also glory in something. They glory in their Abrahamic linage and heritage. The Jews boasted, saying, "We are Abraham's descendants ... Abraham is our father" (John 8:33, 39), and "We are disciples of Moses!" (9:28), and they hung their hopes on Moses (see 5:45). For Judaism, their relationship with God is wrapped in their genealogy and the doctrines of Moses. To them, Jesus Christ and His teachings were an intrusion that must be actively resisted. As demonstrated throughout this study, the Judaizers relentlessly persecuted the saints in Revelation. Although they were *real* Jews, Christ repeatedly described them as "false Jews," "false disciples," or "false apostles" who belonged to the "synagogue of Satan." This was because their religion was devoid of Christ. Therefore, even their doctrines are dismissed as "Satan's ... deep secrets" (Rev. 2:24).

The Sardisians Boast in Reputation. We have discussed the church of Sardis already, but consider what Christ says to her again. "You have a reputation of being alive, but you are dead" (3:3). For those in Sardis, it was neither heritage nor wealth, but their own reputation—a good name that they had built for themselves. Their reputation, which was based on their own merits, was enthroned in their hearts. Like in Laodicea and Judaism, those in Sardis have also closed their doors and locked Christ out in the process. They have "no room for" Him or His Word (see John 8:37; Rev. 3:20).

The Saints Boast in Christ. The persecuted saints in each of the churches are commended for enduring afflictions, persecution, imprisonment, and death. The only reason the faithful saints are put through the fiery affliction is because of Christ, His name, teaching, words, and commandments.[346] Though afflicted, the saints have made Christ and His sacrifice

---

[346] For more discussion on this, refer to the table at the beginning of this chapter.

their boast, delight, and joy. Although many such boasts still remain, we shall proceed to the boasting that actually has bearing on this study.

The Boastings of Babylon. No doubt these boastings are insightful, but the similarities that exist between the boastings of Laodicea and Babylonia are telling.[347]

Laodicea (3:17)	Babylon (18:7)
"You say, 'I am rich, I have acquired wealth and do not need a thing.'"	"In her heart she boasts; 'I sit as a queen, I am not a widow, and I will never mourn.'"

Babylon boasts about position, power, and authority ("queen"), marital status and adulterous activities ("not a widow"), and a life of ease and abundance ("never mourn"). As the context clearly shows, Babylon's boastings are deeply rooted in her great wealth. We shall discuss these two boastings that proceed from wealth in the next section.

Summary. All parties glory in someone or something. Surely, wealth, linage, reputation, status, and position are all worthy of one's boastings, but the greatest of all is to boast in Christ! "Let not the wise boast of their wisdom or the strong boast of their strength or the rich boast of their riches, but let the one who boasts boast about this: that they have the understanding to know me" (Jer. 9:23, 24).

Peoples	Basis of Confidence
Laodicea	"I am rich ... I have acquired *wealth*," "'I do not need a thing' But you do not realize that you are wretched, pitiful, poor" (3:17)
Sardis	"you have a *reputation* of being alive, but you are dead" (3:1)
Jewish Opponents	"I know the slander of those who say they are *Jews* and are not, but are a synagogue of Satan" (2:9, 2; 3:9)
Saints	"You have kept my *word* and have not denied my *name*" (3:8)
Babylon	"I sit as a queen, I am not a widow, and I will never mourn" (18:7)

---

[347] Notice that these two boastings are actually deeply rooted in the original boastings of Satan as recorded in Isaiah 14:13–14.

The Wealth, Clothing, and Boasting of Laodicea and Babylon

In this section, we shall discuss the relationship between wealth, clothing, and the boastings of these two institutions.

The Materials of Wealth. First, we have stated that both of these groups have excessive wealth. During NT times, the code word for wealth was "gold and silver," but a comprehensive list on what actually constituted wealth is given in Revelation 18:11–13. There are almost thirty broad categories of items attributed to wealth provided in this passage, including "cargoes of gold, silver, precious stones and pearls; fine linen, purple, silk and scarlet cloth" (vv. 11, 12). It is important to point out that the list of wealth discussed here is what Babylon has accumulated. If Laodicea also boasts of acquiring great wealth, then she must also have the same items in abundance.

The Accumulation and of Glory in Wealth. Second, Laodicea and Babylon's boasting spring from the fact that they have accumulated much of the above materials. The relationship between wealth and pride is best captured in Ezekiel's judgment against the king of Tyre. The prophet lamented, "you have increased your wealth, and because of your wealth your heart has grown proud" (Ezek. 28:5).

The Pursuit of Wealth. Third, as stated earlier, accumulation of wealth does not come by mere wishing. It requires hard work and sacrifice. One must live, breath, move, and pursue wealth in order to acquire and accumulate much. Also, it is the nature of wealth that those who have accumulated much crave for more. When the seven plagues begin to hit Babylon, a voice is heard saying, "The fruit you longed for is gone from you. All your riches and splendor have vanished, never to be recovered" (Rev. 18:14). Babylon and Laodicea boasted of what they had already accumulated and "longed for" even more.

The Clothing of Wealth. Fourth, the wealthy not only accumulate and glory in wealth, but they also clothe themselves in and with wealth. Consider Babylon, for instance. She is dressed in "purple and scarlet, and was glittering with gold, precious stones and pearls. She held a golden cup in her hand" (17:5; 18:16). Although the text does not say it explicitly, it is possible that Laodicea must have also adorned herself in "purple and scarlet." Besides, if she has removed her "white clothes," then it is possible she has adorned herself with garments of gold and silver.

The Compromise for Wealth. Fifth, Babylon's excessive wealth came about as a result of compromise. Concerning Babylon, the text says, "Fallen! Fallen is Babylon the great! ... For all the nations have drunk the maddening wine of her adulteries. The kings of the earth committed adultery with her, and the merchants of the earth grew rich from her excessive luxuries" (Rev. 18:2, 3). In verse 9, we read, "the kings of the earth ... committed adultery with her and shared her luxury." These passages show that accumulation of excessive wealth and spiritual adultery are inseparable. They are like two sides of a coin.

> *If this satanic strategy has never changed, one wonders if Laodicea's excessive wealth came about as a result of compromise and spiritual unfaithfulness. Just as the devil has successfully destroyed Balaam, Judas, the sea beast, land beast, and Babylon, he now seems to be dragging Laodicea through that familiar corridor of death.*

The dragon offered the same to the "sea beast" and "Babylon" and was successful. "The dragon gave the beast his power and his throne and great authority" (Rev. 13:2b) in exchange for worship. He did the same with the lamb-like beast (see vv. 12, 16, 17). Judas and Balaam compromised and fell on the same point. Satan even offered "all the kingdoms of the world and their splendor" to Christ in exchange for compromise and worship (Matt. 4:8, 9). If this satanic strategy has never changed, one wonders if Laodicea's excessive wealth came about as a result of compromise and spiritual unfaithfulness. Just as the devil has successfully destroyed Balaam, Judas, the sea beast, land beast, and Babylon, he now seems to be dragging Laodicea through that familiar corridor of death.

Wealth and Adultery. Sixth, Babylon boasted of being a "queen" and "not a widow." As Revelation 18:2–3 shows, she indeed has many men—all the kings of the earth. Her world was a life of compromise and adultery. The moment she accepted power, throne, and great authority from the dragon, she not only defiled her white robe (if she ever had one), but she also removed it. Then she sewed her own leaves of purple and scarlet to cover her nakedness. The point is that the moment one accepts the enemy's offer, he begins to slip into an adulterous life, and his "white clothes" begin to get defiled and eventually removed. Then clothed in "purple and scarlet," Laodicea boasts just like Babylon did: "I am rich; I have acquired wealth and do not need a thing." Perhaps we are looking at God's appeal to Babylon or another church that was at the verge of becoming *another* "Babylon."

> *Then clothed in "purple and scarlet," Laodicea boasts just like Babylon did: "I am rich; I have acquired wealth and do not need a thing." Perhaps we are looking at God's appeal to Babylon or another church that was at the verge of becoming another "Babylon."*

Wealth and God. Apart from the "kings of the earth," the Scripture also personifies "wealth" as another "master" who is opposed to God. Matthew wrote, "No one can serve two masters. Either he will hate the one and love the other, or he will be devoted to the one and despise the other. You cannot serve both *God and Money*" (6:24, emphasis supplied). This passage presents money as the second "master" on equal footing with God. Laodicea has admitted to "acquir[ing] wealth" and "not need[ing] a thing," and because she is in an adulterous relationship with wealth, Christ is heard knocking from outside.

Babylon, Laodicea, and Christ. Further, there is no such thing as adultery if the woman concerned is single, unmarried, widowed, and does not have a husband. In other words, Babylon and Laodicea would not be committing adultery with other men if they were not currently married. Paul defined adultery this way: "if she marries another man while her husband is still alive, she is call an adulterous [woman]" (Rom. 7:3; see also Matt. 19:9). However, as it is, they both have a Man. Yet in their pursuit of the "kings of the earth," they have rejected the "King of kings." Therefore, concerning Babylon, Christ laments, "I have given her time to repent of her immorality, but she is unwilling" (Rev. 2:21).[348] Instead, her response has been, "I sit as queen; I am not a widow, and I will never mourn" (Rev. 18:7). The Bridegroom declares that He has given His betrothed wife sufficient time to repent, but she is unwilling. Babylon's response is that she is not a "widow." She is not available. She is *married*. She is married to other "kings." Therefore, she sits as an adulterous "queen."

Laodicea, on the other hand, is more daring in her attitude. We saw that she is engaged in an adulterous relationship with her new man—wealth. Yet Christ (her lawful Husband) would not let her go. He is heard standing outside and pleading, "Behold, I stand at the door and knock ..." (3:20, NKJV). To this, Laodicea responds, "I am rich; I have acquired wealth and I do not need a thing" (v. 17). One wonders what *thing* is implied here.

When compared with other Scriptures, something remarkable begins to emerge. Luke, for example, told a story about two sisters' attitudes towards Jesus. The elder sister complained to Jesus, saying, "Lord, don't you care that my sister has left me to do the work by myself? Tell her to help me!" To this, Jesus replied, "Martha, Martha ... you are worried and upset about many things, but only *one thing* is needed. Mary has chosen what is better" (Luke 10:40, 41, emphasis supplied). Obviously, the "one thing" referred to here is Jesus Christ Himself.

---

[348] Paul stated the same thing this way: "'I was found by those who did not seek me; I revealed myself to those who did not ask for me.' But concerning Israel he says, 'All day long I have held out my hands to a disobedient and obstinate people'" (Rom. 10:20, 21). Interestingly, he also alluded to Israel as being like Sodom and Gomorrah (see Rom. 9:29).

A similar story is recorded in Mark. Jesus said to the rich young ruler, who had just confessed keeping the commandments from childhood, *"One thing* you lack" (Mark 10:21, emphasis supplied). Finally, when Philip told Nathaniel about finding Jesus of Nazareth, the latter said in disbelief, "Nazareth! Can *anything* good come out from there?" (John 1:46, emphasis supplied). In all these cases, Christ is consistently referred to as "a thing," "one thing," or "anything." Therefore, Laodicea has not only locked her Husband out and engaged in adulterous relationships with strange men, but when Christ comes pleading, she has the audacity to say, "I do not need [You]." However, even in the face of this utterly embarrassing rejection, the waves of mercy keep knocking on the doors of her heart. This is all because, as Christ says, "You *do not realize* that you are wretched, pitiful, poor, blind, and naked" (Rev. 3:17, emphasis supplied). As long as Laodicea does not realize it, Christ gives her the time and opportunity to repent of her adulteries.[349]

> *Laodicea has not only locked her Husband out and engaged in adulterous relationships with strange men, but when Christ comes pleading, she has the audacity to say, "I do not need [You]." However, even in the face of this utterly embarrassing rejection, the waves of mercy keep knocking on the doors of her heart.*

<u>Babylon, Laodicea, and Satan</u>. Finally, note the astonishing similarities among Babylon, Laodicea, and Satan. In boastings and pride, articles of garments and adorning, acquisition and accumulation of excessive wealth, and sins of compromise and adultery, these three characters are similar. The following table lists these similarities:

---

[349] These are the same words Christ had said earlier concerning His own tormentors. "Father, forgive them, for they *do not know* what they are doing" (Luke 23:34, emphasis supplied).

Features	Satan	Babylon	Laodicea
Boastings of the heart	"You said in your heart ..." (Isa. 14:13)	"In her heart she boasts ..." (Rev. 18:7)	"You say [in your heart] ..." (Rev. 3:17)
Acquisition of wealth	"every precious stone adorned you: ruby, topaz, and emerald, Chrysolite, onyx and jasper, sapphire, turquoise and beryl" (Ezek. 28:13)	"The merchants of the earth grew rich from her excessive luxuries" (Rev. 18:3, 16; 17:5)	"I am rich, I have acquired wealth and do not need a thing." (3:17)
Clothing of wealth	"every precious stone *adorned* you: ruby, topaz, and emerald, Chrysolite, onyx and jasper, sapphire, turquoise and beryl" (Ezek. 28:13)	"The woman was *dressed in purple and scarlet*, and was glittering with gold, precious stones and pearls. She held a golden cup in her hand" (Rev. 17:5; 18:16)	Adorned in "purple and scarlet" and precious stones too (implied)
Aim, goals, and pursuits	"I will sit enthroned on the mountain of assembly ... I will make myself like the Most High" (Isa. 14:13, 14)	"I sit as a queen" (Rev. 18:7)	"I do not need a thing" (implies that she has reached her pinnacle)

The fall of Lucifer is described as "the mystery of iniquity" (2 Thess. 2:7). No one can explain how "iniquity was found in" this perfect creature, but there are some shared features among these characters.

Pride and Boastings Go Before Fall. The first shared commodity is pride. They all boast and have something about which to boast. Laodicea boasts in wealth and the accumulation thereof, while Babylon boasts in the seat of authority she currently occupies. Satan, however, boasts in a throne he hopes to occupy in the future. Remember that pride goes before a fall.

Wealth, Beauty, Adornment, and Splendor Feeds Pride. Second, if pride goes before a fall, then the things that feed and fatten pride to a "fallable" level are 1) wealth—"You have increased your wealth, your heart has grown proud" (Ezek. 28:5). Satan and Babylon are literally adorned with "every precious stones," while Laodicea boasts of amassing wealth and being rich; and 2) beauty, adornment, and splendor. The day he was created, Satan was not only "perfect in beauty" but also "adorned" and clothed with "precious stones" (vv. 12, 13). His beauty, adornment, and splendor fed his pride and paved the way for his fall. "Your heart has become proud on account of your beauty, and you corrupted your wisdom because of your splendor. So," says God, "I threw you to the earth" (v. 17). As we saw earlier, Laodicea and Babylon are also adorned with wealth and splendor.

Wisdom, Understanding, and Skills Are Needed for Wealth Acquisition. The accumulation and display of wealth are a product of the rich person's wisdom, understanding, and skills. "By your wisdom and understanding you have gained wealth for yourself and amassed gold and silver in your treasuries. By your great skill in trading you have increased your wealth, and because of your wealth your heart has grown proud" (vv. 4, 5). Like Satan, Babylon and Laodicea's wealth is testament to their "corrupted wisdom" and "dishonest trad[ing]" skills.

A Fattened Heart Corrupts the Head. Notice that the "wisdom," "understanding," and "skills" commended here are not holy, but defiled. Satan began by being "full of wisdom" (v. 12), but pride defiled his holy wisdom. The Scriptures say, "Your heart became proud on account of your beauty, and you corrupted your wisdom because of your splendor. So I threw you to the earth" (v. 17). Once the pride of the heart is fed (by wealth, beauty, adornment, and splendor), it then corrupts or defiles the "wisdom [mind]." Once this *hardware* is corrupted, a fall is inevitable. Therefore, a fall begins in the heart and ends up in the head. Unrestrained indulgences will permanently sear and scare the conscience. The following diagram attempts to show the distance *to* and *from* pride to fall:

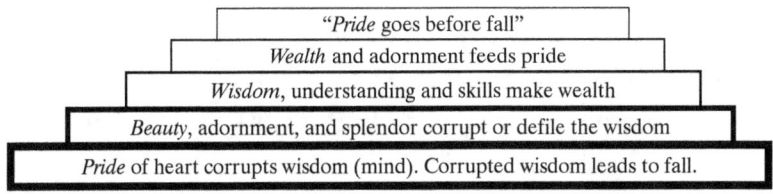

In summary, the commodities that Satan peddles are the very things for which he himself fell: pride, wealth, splendor, beauty, adornment, and the throne. According to Revelation 14 and 18, "Babylon has [already] fallen," and Laodicea is at the verge of falling. Christ's mercy was spurned and rejected by both Satan and Babylon; He now offers the same to Laodicea.

The clothing and the nakedness of Laodicea and Babylon

<u>White Clothes and Nakedness</u>. In Revelation, nakedness and indecent exposure come as a result of defiling or removing the white linen. As was discussed in chapter 19 and again here, the act of defiling and removing the white clothes signifies a life of compromise and spiritual adultery. We have thoroughly discussed these issues in the Sardisian and Laodicean addresses and Revelation 16:15.

<u>Purple and Scarlet and Nakedness</u>. However, the text does not explicitly state that Babylon ever had white clothes. Therefore, her issue has nothing to do with the defiling or removing of white garments (i.e., if she ever did have one). Rather, she is adorned in "purple and scarlet," yet she is not considered "naked." This is because her nakedness does not come until the end of the seven plagues. "The beast and the ten horns you saw will hate the prostitute. They will bring her to ruin and leave her *naked*" (17:16, emphasis supplied). In other words, Babylon's nakedness comes after the beast and the ten horns remove her purple and scarlet. Now the question is, If Babylon becomes naked after her purple and scarlet are removed, then why is Laodicea, who has removed her white, also considered naked?

<u>White Versus Purple and Scarlet</u>. By the act of removing the white garment, Laodicea puts on purple and scarlet by default, because that is what the rich wear (see Matt. 11:8; Luke 16:19). If both Babylon and Laodicea are clad in purple and scarlet, then why is Laodicea naked and not Babylon? There are two possible reasons. First, their level of awareness is different. Babylon made an intentional decision to turn away from God and turn to wealth and Satan. With the devil's enabling (see Rev. 13:3), she sets her own throne in opposition to God and boasts of being a "queen." By boasting, "I am not a widow," she is basically saying, "I do not need

a thing. I do not need another Man. I do not need God." As a result, she is covered in "blasphemous names" (Rev. 13:1, 5; 17:3). Laodicea is already exhibiting the same tendencies, but at least at this stage, she does "not realize" her real condition yet.

Second, their level or degree of wickedness is different. Concerning Babylon and Jezebel, Christ says, "her sins are piled up to heaven" and "I have given her time to repent of her immorality, but she is unwilling. So I will cast her on a bed of suffering, and I will make those who commit adultery with her suffer intensely" (Rev. 18:5; 2:21, 22). He has given time and opportunity to Babylon to repent, but she was unwilling. Instead, she "piled up" sins one upon another. Christ now extends the same courtesy to Laodicea. If she repents, she will be clothed in white again. If she does not, she will share the same "bed of suffering" with her sisters, Jezebel and Babylon.

The Implication of Christ's Name on the Issues and Opponents

To those in Laodicea, Christ introduced Himself as the "Amen, the faithful and true witness, the ruler of God's creation." Now what does this self-disclosure mean to the Laodicean church? To a pitiful church that is not aware of her true condition, Christ comes through as the "Amen, the faithful and true witness." His assessments and diagnoses are credible, and His recommendations are trustworthy. He then offers the following solutions: To a church that has slipped into a life of compromise and adultery, Christ comes offering "white clothes to ... [cover her] shameful nakedness." To a church that is engaged in the pursuit of gold and silver, He comes selling "gold refined in the fire" (Rev. 3:18). Then to a church that boasts of accumulating wealth, He comes through as the "ruler of God's creation [including wealth]"!

PROMISES AND REWARDS

The Lord's promise to the overcomers in Laodicea is, "To him who overcomes, I will give the right to sit with me on my throne, just as

I overcame and sat down with my Father on his throne" (Rev. 3:21). There are many thrones in Revelation, which can be divided into two broad categories: the thrones belonging to Satan and his associates, and those belonging to Christ and His followers. What follows next is a discussion on thrones under these two categories.

Thrones of Satan and His Associates

Throne of Satan. Satan has a throne (see Rev. 2:13). The same throne comes under different names and is associated with many different kingly characters. For instance, in Revelation 12 and 13, the throne is presented as belonging to the dragon, who shares it with the sea beast (see 13:2), who then shares it with the land beast (vv. 12–16). During John's time, this throne was located in the city of Pergamum (see 2:13). Later it was moved to the "sea," from which the sea beast reigned for "forty-two months" (see Rev. 13:5). Today, the same is located on the "earth," and the land beast rules in association with the sea beast and its image (see vv. 12–16).

Throne of the Abyss. The throne of Satan is also depicted as belonging to the "angel of Abyss." The angelic character is also a "king" and reigns from the Abyss (see Rev. 9:11). Therefore, in the end, Satan, the dragon, fallen star, angel, sea beast, and land beast share the same throne.

Throne of Babylon. Babylon boasts, "I sit as a queen" (Rev. 18:7). Undoubtedly, she sits on a throne. Of what that throne consisted, and wherever it was located, we are not told. We are, however, told that she sits and rules from both "many waters [signifying 'many peoples, multitudes, nations and languages']" (vv. 1, 15) and "deserts" (v. 3). Babylon is also depicted as sitting on both the "scarlet beast" (v. 3) and "seven heads" (v. 9). Therefore, the woman sits on several places: many waters, deserts, the scarlet beast, and seven heads.

Thrones of the Ten Horns. Just like the dragon, the ten horns (ten kings) will also give their powers, authorities, and thrones over to Babylon (see Rev. 17:12). This unified power, consisting of Babylon, the sea and land beasts, and the ten kings, will rule the world for "one hour" just before Christ returns.

Summary of Satanic Thrones. In the analysis of the satanic thrones, we find the following to be true: Satan does not have a static throne. His throne is dynamic and very fluid. The same throne that was located in Pergamum was later set up in the "sea." Today, the same throne is situated on the "land" and "many waters" and in the "desert" and "Abyss." However, in a very telling way, this throne can be manifested in many different ways. As Revelation 17 shows, Satan's throne can be a multi-headed beast or the horns of a beast, the seven hills or the seven kings; and the same can also be "peoples, multitudes, nations and languages." Essentially, wherever there is an open door, Satan moves in and establishes his throne. Therefore, at the time Christ stood and knocked, Satan was in the process of setting up his kingdom in Laodicea.[350]

Thrones of Christ and His Associates

The Throne of God and the Great White Throne. The throne of God and its details are presented in Revelation 4 and 5. God reigns from this throne. In chapter 20, we are introduced to a "great white throne." It is not clear whether these signify two different thrones or just two functions of the same throne, but what is clear is that they both belong to God. They are His thrones. The text consistently presents Christ as sitting and reigning together with His Father, "just as I was victorious and sat down with my Father on his throne" (Rev. 3:21). By the virtue of His victory at Calvary, He has earned the right to sit with His Father on His throne.

The Thrones of Christ and His Saints. Although Christ is presented as sitting together with His Father on His throne, other passages also show that He has his own throne as well. "To the one who is victorious, I will give the right to sit with me on my throne, just as I was victorious and sat down with my Father on his throne" (Rev. 3:21). Christ's throne not only has sufficient space for many to sit, but the victorious will be invited to

---

[350] A diagram comparing the satanic thrones and throne of God is found in the discussion on the Pergamum church (chapter 16).

co-rule with Him. They will also be given thrones and the authority to sit and judge (see Rev. 20:4).

Twenty-four elders' Thrones. John was also allowed to see twenty-four other thrones surrounding the throne of God. On them were seated twenty-four elders (see 4:4).

Summary of God's Throne. When considering the throne of God, one needs to pay attention to what the entire Bible teaches about this subject, for "this is what the Lord says: 'Heaven is my throne, and the earth is my footstool. Where is the house you will build for me? Where will my resting place be?'" (Isa. 66:1; see also Acts 7:49). Obviously, God and His throne are not confined to some structure. God's throne is both heaven and earth. Further, Daniel described the same throne as having fiery wheels (see Dan. 7:9). A little earlier, the prophet Ezekiel had described God's throne as a multi-directional structure with "a wheel intersecting a wheel" (Ezek. 1:16). Like the throne of Satan, God's throne appears to be agile too. It is designed to move in multiple directions simultaneously. Wherever God moves in that place becomes His kingdom. Therefore, when Christ stands at the door and knocks, He is standing with white clothes, gold tried by fire, eye salve, and also His throne. The moment a saint opens the door to Christ, that person becomes the kingdom of God (see Rev. 3:20; John 8:37). Perhaps this is one reason why Christ taught that the "kingdom of God is within you" (Luke 17:21).

> *Like the throne of Satan, God's throne appears to be agile too. It is designed to move in multiple directions simultaneously. Wherever God moves in that place becomes His kingdom. Therefore, when Christ stands at the door and knocks, He is standing with white clothes, gold tried by fire, eye salve, and also His throne. The moment a saint opens the door to Christ, that person becomes the kingdom of God.*

Significance of the Throne for Laodicea

The crucial question is, Why does Christ promise the Laodicean overcomers the "right to sit with me on my throne"? In a world of lords, kings, queens, and thrones, Laodicea probably considered setting up her own throne. Babylon has demonstrated that a life of compromise, adultery, and acquisition of wealth always paves the way for a throne. By the time Christ intervened, Laodicea had already "acquired wealth," declared herself "rich," and had said, "I do not need a thing." Also, she had defiled and removed her white clothes, a fitting symbol of compromise and adultery. And like Babylon, she is adorned in "purple and scarlet" and on the verge of declaring, "I sit as a queen." To this church, the Ruler of God's creation offers *His* throne, saying, "I will give [you] the right to sit with me on my throne" if you "open the door" and let Me come in.

RELATIONSHIP BETWEEN REVELATION 1–3 AND 4–22

The analysis of the Laodicean message serves to further strengthen the relationship between Revelation 1–3 and 4–22. Concerning Christ's names and titles, refer to chapter 21 of this book. There we have had a sweeping discussion on these names and their implications. At this stage, however, some important points are highlighted.

First, the wealth of Revelation 3 is like the tip of an iceberg because it is heavily discussed in chapters 4, 13, 17, 18, and 21. Incidentally, the entire eighteenth chapter is devoted to discussing wealth. Before anyone gets caught up in accumulating wealth, Revelation 4 and 21 puts wealth and "every kind of precious stones" in their proper perspective. God is the creator of wealth, Christ is the "ruler of God's creation [including wealth]," and we are just mere stewards of those stones and sticks (18:11–13).

Second, clothing and wardrobe issues are also discussed extensively in Revelation 4–22. The colors featured are white, red, purple, and scarlet. Whenever clothing is discussed, they are always discussed in conjunction with the issues of spiritual compromise and adultery. The defiling of clothing in Sardis (see chapters 19 and 20) and the removal thereof in Laodicea lead us directly to the adulterous woman of Revelation 17 and 18. In Sardis, the adulterous woman was the opponent, while the Laodiceans were on the verge of becoming another Babylon.[351]

Finally, apart from the current context, the comprehensive nature of Christ's title—"ruler of God's creation"—seems to have a dual role as well. The title summarizes every other title Christ has used previously. The following is an updated table showing all major relationships between Rev 1–3 and 4–22.

Revelation 1–3	Revelation 4–22
1/*Ephesus Address* (2:1–7)	*See also Rev. 22:2*
• Promised "tree of life" (2:7)	• "tree of life" (22:2)
2/*Smyrna Address* (2:8–11)	*See Rev. 12–13*
• Two wars—current war and future "ten-day" war • The war is waged against those who "keep God's commandments and have Jesus' testimony • War originates from "Synagogue of Satan," and they are involved in "blasphemy" against God • Devil is described as "accuser" (2:10)	• Two wars—current 1,260-days war and future war on "remnant" (12:17) • War waged against those with God's commands and Jesus' testimony • War from dragon and beast, who are covered in blasphemous names • Satan or devil is described as "accuser" (12:10)
3/*Pergamum Address* (2:12–17)	*See Rev. 12–13*
• "throne of Satan" • Christ comes with "sharp sword" to judge opponents • Rewards: white stones	• Satanic "throne" (13:2) • Dragon, sea beast, land beast, and image have mouths/swords to kill too • Rewards: precious stones (chs. 21, 22)
4/*Thyatira Address* (2:18–29)	*See Rev. 14, 16–18*
• Jezebel the prophetess • Prostitute, seduces saints • Faithful saints as "remnant" (2:24) • Remnant has "the commandments of God and testimony of Jesus" (1:9)	• Babylon the harlot (Rev. 17) • Prostitute, seduces saints • Faithful saints as "remnant" (12:17) • Remnant has "the commandments of God and testimony of Jesus" (12:17)

---

[351] No wonder why even Revelation 16:15 is discussed in the heart of the plagues hurled at Babylon!

Revelation 1–3	Revelation 4–22
5/Sardis Address (3:1–6)	*See Rev. 13–20*
• "soiled" • "white robe" • Lamb's "book of life" • angles	• "defile with the women" (ch. 14) • "white robe" (chs. 7, 14, 19) • "book of life" (chs. 13, 20) • Angels, "his angel" (chs. 1–3, 5, 8, 19)
6/Philadelphia Address (3:7–13)	*See Rev. 4–22*
• "The Holy and True [Judge]" • Satan, his agents, activities and two wars • The saints and their possession of truth • Names of Christ, promises and rewards	• Holy and True Judge (chs. 6, 14–19) • Satanic agents, activities, two wars (chs. 12–20) • Saints' possession of truth (chs. 6, 12–14) • Names, promises, and rewards of Christ (chs. 12–14, 17–19, 20–22)
7/Laodicea Address (3:14–22)	*See Rev. 4–22*
• "Amen, the faithful and true witness" • "Ruler of God's creation" • Compromise and adultery	• Holy and True Judge (chs. 6, 14–19) • Ruler over all, especially wealth (chs. 4, 13, 17, 18, 21) • Compromise and adultery (chs. 13, 17, 18)

Understanding these similarities, Wahlen says:

> The fact that apocalyptic imagery and ideas permeate each letter leads the reader to suspect that the churches [of Rev. 1–3] themselves are meant to be understood symbolically as well and that the letters, like the rest of the book, should be interpreted as apocalyptic prophecy. Each letter begins with language from the initial vision of Jesus in chapter 1, which itself recalls the apocalyptic language of Daniel (7:9, 13; 10:5–12). Imagery in the body of the letters, such as the lampstand being removed, the sword coming out of Jesus' mouth, hidden manna, new names, Jezebel, the rod of iron, the morning star, white garments, gold, eye salve, open and closed doors are all clearly symbolic. Closer study of these symbols reveals an intimate connection with

(and prepares readers to understand) the later chapters widely accepted as apocalyptic.[352]

The materials in Revelation 1–3 and 4–22 are indeed "intimately connected." Therefore, if we admit that the early church read and understood the seven letters (2–3) because they addressed their own concerns, then there is every indication that the later part of Revelation 4–21 also addressed their concerns. It is for this reason that a proper method of exegesis must first ask, "What did the prophecies of Revelation mean to the early church?" before asking, "What do they mean to us today?"

---

[352] Clinton Wahlen, "Letters to the seven churches: historical or prophetic?" *Ministry*, November 2007, pp. 13–14.

PART 4:
EPILOGUE

25.

CONCLUSION AND RECOMMENDATIONS

AIMS AND PURPOSES OF THE STUDY

In the summary, we shall pull together all the main thoughts that run throughout Revelation 1–3, especially as they relate to the core objectives of this study. Among others, our main objectives, as outlined at the beginning of this study, were:

1. To see the text through a *dualistic* method of interpretation, as opposed to preterist, futurist, idealist, or historical methods.
2. To show that the prophetic messages of Revelation were read, understood, and applicable to those who first received the document. Additionally, as dual-intentionalism suggests, the same prophecies could also speak to us in our time and context.
3. To determine the relationship that exists between Revelation 1–3 and 4–22, as well as that between the whole book and other Johannine books (1, 2, and 3 John, the Gospel of John, and, based on our studies, Hebrews).
4. Finally, to see Jesus as John of Patmos saw Him, for he says that "we shall see Him as he [really] is" (1 John 3:2).

What follows next are preliminary evaluations and conclusions based on the results of the study. We also offer suggestions for further study.

RESULTS OF THE STUDY

Results of Authorial, Methodological, and Literary Issues

Johannine Books. In the initial chapters of this study, we discussed authorial, methodological, and literary issues. There we stated several assumptions—the order in which the Johannine books were written, the timing of the composition of the Johannine books, and Johannine authorship of the book of Hebrews—to be true. These areas are briefly discussed in the following paragraphs.

The Order. It was proposed that the books were written in this order: Revelation, 1–3 John, and the Gospel John. We have carefully traced words, literary styles, concepts, issues, and characters in all the Johannine writings. The findings seem to confirm the above order. As an example, see chapters 7–11 of this book. However, it is important to carry out targeted studies to further reinforce these cases.

The Timing of Composition. The popular opinion holds that Revelation was the last book written at a different time to address issues other than Judaism. However, the textual evidences examined in this study show that the context of Revelation is not far removed from the other NT books. Revelation's theological and christologial issues, opponents, and timing appear to be the same as those discussed in the Gospels, Pauline, Lukan, and other writings.[353]

Johannine Authorship of Hebrews. We proposed a relationship between the Johannine books and Hebrews. We also considered the idea that John could have been the author of Hebrews. The volume of shared information, the manner in which this information was arranged and presented,

---

[353] While writing about the Hebrew cultus, Paulien wrote, "Is the cultic mentality of John typical of first century Christianity, or was John speaking to a theological minority in the ancient Mediterranean? It seems to me that the centrality of the Old Testament to early Christian thought and argumentation would lead to general familiarity with one of its central features. This is certainly true of the argumentation in the so-called Letter to the Hebrews, which requires thorough immersion in the Christian significance of the Hebrew cultus. The letters attributed to Paul and the gospels also show considerable familiarity with it. Our own lack of familiarity with these cultic practices is no argument that early Christians as a whole were unfamiliar with them. The metaphorical use of cultic imagery was probably widespread among the early Christians" (book, p. #).

the common words and concepts, Christological issues, issues concerning angels, and other literary features appear to favor this proposition. Furthermore, a careful study of these words, concepts, and subjects also shows that the Johannine books do interpret themselves very well.[354] It is perhaps an indication that a single author is behind all these books.

Dual-Intentionalism. The basic assumption of dual-intentionalism is that John and his initial audience either understood or at least *thought* that Revelation spoke to them in their local time and context. However, time has gone far past their expectations, and 2,000 years later we are still here. This being the case, how do we then approach the prophecies of Revelation? Do we conclude the entire book was addressing first-century issues and treat it like any other historical book? Or do we cling to the notion that the prophetic materials (chs. 4–22) had no relevance to the early church?

There are major inherent weaknesses in either approach. First, such approaches lack a textual basis. Second, in order to make these approaches work, one has to intentionally ignore key scientific and exegetical principles. The honest approach, even if we do not understand the materials fully, is to assume that the prophecies were written *to* the early readers. Unless otherwise stated, we must acknowledge that the author and his audience understood (or at least thought they did) the entirety of Revelation. If they did, then what did the characters, dates, symbols, institutions, powers, personalities, opponents, and issues mean to them? Afterwards, we can determine what they mean to us, for the same prophecies that spoke to them also speak to us today.

If our dualistic method helps us understand and appreciate the prophecies and reduce some of the exegetical issues, then it speaks more eloquently of the sovereignty of a God who could use a single line of prophetic material to speak to two different audiences who are separated by thousands of years. Specific details of the findings are discussed in the next section.

---

[354] Also, the structure of Hebrews is almost identical to that of 1 John. For more discussion on this, see George Paki, *The Structural and the Thematic Analysis of 1 John* an unpublished study notes.

Results of the Textual Issues

The Dual Intent of the Terms, Concepts, and Prophecies. The fundamental premise of this study was that the prophecies of Revelation, almost in its entirety, were read and understood by and applicable to the author and his initial audience. In order to establish this, we analyzed many dominant words and concepts—words, commandments, testimony of Jesus, faith of Jesus, brothers, brothers the prophets, Holy Spirit, beast, woman, etc.—and saw all of them as having a dual meaning (For further information on this, see chapters 1 and 12). From this we surmised that all characters, dates, timelines, issues, and controversies could also have a dual significance.

Relationship Between Revelation 1–3 and 4–22. Most historicists insist that Revelation 1–3 and 4–22 are different. They see the materials of 1–3 as predominantly historical in nature, addressing the issues of the first century, while 4–22 consisting of prophetic materials that speak to our time. However, we observed that the volume and quality of the relationship that exists between Revelation 1–3 and 4–22 serves to either reduce or eliminate any appearances of difference between them. The main purpose of this exercise was to determine the early church's comprehensibility and applicability of the prophetic materials (4–22). As seen throughout this book, the overwhelming relationship between these two sections of materials testify that they addressed the same issues but used different literary approaches.

Results of the Opponents and Core Theological Issues

Opponents. One surprising discovery was that the primary issues and opponents were of Jewish descent. As established throughout this book, the issues John addressed were not entirely different from the ones with which Paul, Luke, Matthew, and other NT writers dealt. For the early church, all issues were with Judaism. Similar to what Paul encountered in his ministry, there may have been some struggles with civil authorities, but they were not the primary opponents. In order for us to understand and appreciate the prophecies, we need to first see the text the way John and his initial audience saw it. We need to begin in Jerusalem with Judaism because the papacy does not come into existence until nearly 500 years later. It is not a responsible exegesis if we reduce this time period to the footnotes of our prophetic calendars. In our haste to get to Rome, we should never run past Jerusalem. Daniel was clearly told that his prophecies were not for his time. He was asked to shut the book until the end of time. John, however, was told to "read," "hear," and "keep" the "words of this prophecy" because the "time is near."

Revelation of Jesus. The book of Revelation is indeed a "revelation of Jesus." Unlike any other books of the Bible, Revelation is saturated with Jesus and Jesus-related themes. He is the Revealer, Narrator, Key Player, and Hero of the dramas therein. However, as we have seen, Jesus is also the Issue. His origin, identity, role in the OT, mission in the NT, death, ascension, relationships with the Father and Holy Spirit, role in Heaven, life, and everything about Him is on trial in Revelation.

> *It is not a responsible exegesis if we reduce this time period to the footnotes of our prophetic calendars. In our haste to get to Rome, we should never run past Jerusalem.*

In the face of this onslaught, Jesus does not shy away. He takes the issues head on. In the OT, Jesus appeared to the prophet Ezekiel as a multi-headed, multi-eyed, multi-winged creature that can move swiftly in multiple directions at the same time. However, in Revelation, Jesus is presented as the ultimate fulfillment and consummation of all OT divine characters, patriarchs, prophets, kings, priests, and judges. He is also the embodiment of all OT offices, ritual and sacrificial artifacts, judicial and legal systems, and religious systems and institutions.

In Revelation, Jesus presents His pre-incarnate role, incarnation, death, blood, book, name, word, commandments, Spirit, angels, Father, ascension, priestly role, and glorious return as the only things needed among mankind. However, in a profound way, Jesus uses the prophecies of Revelation to address the immediate issues of John and his audience and also those of our time.

Literary Characteristic. What's more intriguing is the manner in which John presented these arguments. Unlike the apostle Paul, who was more forthright in his approach, John used innuendos, allusions, and subtlety to his advantage. Nearly all prophetic materials in Revelation are enacted. One has to really "read between the lines" in order to benefit from these prophetic materials. In order to make the case for Jesus' divinity, John consistently used a device called a "literary crescendo." As we saw in chapters 7–9, John used this method to transfer all divine titles from God to Jesus. Why was such a strenuous exercise necessary? This points us back to the core Christological issue which plagued both Revelation and the entire NT. When Judaism attempted to excise Jesus from the Jewish system, the system collapsed and became obsolete. Nevertheless, Jesus "rode out as a conqueror bent on conquest" (Rev. 6:2).

RECOMMENDATIONS FOR FURTHER STUDY

Possible Areas for Further Studies

The Disclosure. The purpose of this study has been to introduce a dualistic approach to the prophecies of Revelation. This method was developed and applied particularly to Revelation 1–3. We admit that, like all other methods, the dualistic approach falls short in some fundamental areas. The pressing task for us now is to apply these principles to the weighty prophecies of chapters 4–22. Some of the specific areas that remain to be explored are as follows:

The Seals and Trumpets. The first challenge for us is to read and interpret the seals and trumpets using dual-intentionalism. The main question that remains to be answered in this section is, Just where did the early church find herself? Of the series of sevens, which of the series constituted their past, present, and future? As discussed in chapter 1, if the church saw herself as living in the "final hour," then could it be possible that from her standpoint, most of the series were in their past? This point is crucial in understanding the seals and trumpets sections of Revelation (6–11), and it remains to be explored.

The Opponents and Issues of Revelation. The view that the Jews and Judaism constituted the main opponents in Revelation remains to be strengthened, especially in Revelation 4–22. Thus far, there is no reason to postulate other opponents. If it can be firmly established that the Jews were the primary opponents (for the early church) in the Apocalypse, then these are the same issues and opponents in the other NT writings. There is much work needed to be done here.

Other Pertinent Issues. In this scheme of things, just how do we interpret the main part of this prophetic book (Rev. 12–17)? Who did the early church understand the two beasts of Revelation 13 to be?

Suggested Approaches for Future Study

How to Approach Controversial Passages in Revelation. Revelation was primarily addressed to real people who were facing real challenges. They were not supposed to be mere custodians of a body of prophetic information that did not have any relevance to them. Most interpretive issues would cease to be controversial if we approached the text with this mindset.

John and NT Tradition Before OT. As seen throughout this study, we did not study Revelation 1–3 in isolation. We heavily used 4–22, the epistles of John, the Gospel of John, and Hebrews to help us interpret Revelation 1–3. Acts and the rest of the NT books provided the general context for our study. Then when necessary, we consulted the OT books. Now the same books must also help us shed light on the major prophecies of Revelation 4–22. One must avoid being distracted by the sights, sounds, echoes, and allusions of the OT in Revelation. Every effort must be made to *make* the NT interpret the book of Revelation because the issues thereof were born in that context.

BIBLIOGRAPHY

Allen, David Lewis. "The Authorship of Hebrews: The Lukan Proposal." *Faith and Mission* 18, no. 2 (Spring 2001): pp. 27–40.

Aune, David E. *Revelation 1–5*. Vol. 52A, Word Biblical Commentary. Grand Rapids, Michigan: Zondervan, 1997.

—. *Revelation 6–16*. Vol. 52B, Word Biblical Commentary. Nashville, TN: Thomas Nelson, 1998.

—. *Revelation 17–22*. Vol. 52C, Word Biblical Commentary. Nashville, TN: Thomas Nelson, 1998.

Beale, G. K. "John's Use of the Old Testament." *Journal for the Study of the Old Testament Supplement* 166. Sheffield, UK: Sheffield Academic Press, 1998.

Black, David Alan. "On the Pauline Authorship of Hebrews (Part 1): Overlooked Affinities between Hebrews and Paul." *Faith and Mission* 16, no. 2 (Spring 1999): pp. 32–51.

—. "On the Pauline Authorship of Hebrews (Part 2): The External Evidence Reconsidered." *Faith and Mission* 16, no. 3 (Summer 1999): pp. 78–86.

Borchert, Gerald L. "A Superior Book: Hebrews." *Review & Expositor* 82, no. 3 (Summer 1985): pp. 319–322.

Brown, Raymond E. *The Community of the Beloved Disciple: The Life, Loves, and Hates of an Individual Church In New Testament Times*. New York: Paulist Press, 1979.

—. *The Epistles of John*. New York: Doubleday, 1982.

—. *The Gospel and Epistles of John: A Concise Commentary*. Collegeville, Minnesota: The Liturgical Press, 1988.

Bryne, Brendan. "The Faith of the Beloved Disciple and the Community in John 20." *Journal for the Study of the New Testament* 23 (1985).

Burdick, D. W. *The Letters of John the Apostle: An In-Depth Commentary*. Chicago: Moody Press, 1985.

Carpenter, J. Estlin. *The Johannine Writings: A Study of the Apocalypse and the Fourth Gospel*. London: Constable & Co. Ltd., 1927.

Carson, D. A. *The Gospel According to John*. Grand Repids, MI: WM. B. Eerdsman Pub. Co., 1991.

DeBruyn, Lawrence A. "Preterism and 'This Generation.'" *Bibliotheca Sacra* 167, no. 666 (April 2010): pp. 180–200.

de Kock, Edwin. *7 Heads and 10 Horns in Daniel and the Revelation*. Edinburg, TX: Edwin de Kock, 2012.

DeSilva, David Arthur. "Out of Our Minds?: Appeals to Reason (Logos) in the Seven Oracles of Revelation 2–3." *Journal for the Study of New Testaments* 23 (1985).

de Waal, Kayle B. "The Two Witnesses and the Land Beast in the Book of Revelation." *Andrews University Seminary Studies* 53, no. 1 (Spring 2015).

Ferrerro, Alberto. "Priscillian and Nicolaitism." *Vigilae Christianae* 52, no. 4 (November 1998): pp. 382–392.

Fiorenza, Elizabeth Schussler. "The Quest for the Johannine School: The Apocalypse and the Fourth Gospel." *New Testament Studies* 23 (1976–1977).

Gardiner, Frederic. "The Language of the Epistle to the Hebrews as Bearing upon Its Authorship." *Journal of the Society of Biblical Literature and Exegesis, Including the Papers Read and Abstract of Proceedings For* 7, no. 1 (June 1887): pp. 1–27.

Glasscock, Ed. "Forgiveness and Cleansing According to 1 John 1:9." *Biblieca Sacra* 166 (April–June 2009).

Geiermann, Peter. *Convert's Catechism of Catholic Doctrine*. St. Lous, MO: B. Herder, 1946.

Guthrie, George H. "Lukan Authorship of Hebrews." *Journal of the Evangelical Theological Society* 54, no. 4 (December 2011): pp. 858–860.

Hiebert, D. Edmond. *The Epistles of John: An Expositional Commentary*. Greenville, SC: Bob Jones University Press, 1991.

Hitchcock, Mark L. "A Critique of the Preterist View of Revelation 17:9–11 and Nero." *Bibliotheca Sacra* 164, no. 656 (2007): 472–485.

International Bible Society. *New International Version*. Grand Rapids, MI: Zondervan Bible Publishers, 1984.

Johnsson, WIlliam G. *"The Saints' End-Time Victory over the Forces of Evil."* in *Symposium on Revelation—Book II*. Edited by Frank B. Holbrook, Vol. 7, Daniel and Revelation Committee Series. Silver Spring, MD: Biblical Research Institute, 1992.

Kistemaker, Simon. "The Authorship of Hebrews." *Faith and Mission* 18, no. 2 (Spring 2001): pp. 57–69.

Konstenberger, Andreas J. *John*. Grand Rapids, MI: Baker Academic, 2004.

LaRondelle, Hans K. "Babylon: Anti-Christian Empire." in *Symposium on Revelation—Book II*. Edited by Frank B. Holbrook, Vol. 7, Daniel and Revelation Committee Series. Silver Spring, MD: Biblical Research Institute, 1992.

Little, Edmund. *Echoes of the Old Testament*, Vol. 41. Edited by J. Gabalda et al. Paris: Rue Pierre et Marie Curie, 1998.

Marshall, Howard. *The Epistles of John*. Edited by F. F. Bruce. Vol. The New International Commentary on the New Testament. Grand Rapids, MI: Wm. B. Eerdmans Publishing Co., 1978.

Mattill, Jr., A. T. "Johannine Communities Behind the Fourth Gospel: Georg Richter's Analysis." *Theological Studies* 38, no. 2 (May 1977).

Maxwell, C. Mervyn. *"The Mark of the Beast."* in *Symposium on Revelation—Book II*. Edited by Frank B. Holbrook, Vol. 7, Daniel and Revelation Committee Series. Silver Spring, MD: Biblical Research Institute, 1992.

—. *The Message of Revelation*. Vol. 2. Boise, Idaho: Pacific Press, 1985. https://1ref.us/10j, accessed February 13, 2020.

Mueller, Ekkehardt. "Did Jesus Emanate from the Father?" *Biblical Research Institute*. General Conference of the Seventh-Day Adventist Church, January 2012.

—. *Fornication*. General Conference of the Seventh-day Adventist Church. https://1ref.us/10p (accessed February 13, 2020).

—. "Jesus and His Second Coming in the Apocalypse." *Journal of the Adventist Theological Society*, (November–December 2000): pp. 205–215.

—. "Signs of the Times." *Biblical Research Institute*. General Conference of the Seventh-day Adventist. https://1ref.us/10k (accessed February 13, 2020).

—. "The Beast of Revelation 17—A Suggestion." *Biblical Research Institute*. General Conference of the Seventh-day Adventist Church. https://1ref.us/10l (accessed February 13, 2020).

—. "The End-Time Remnant and the Gift of Prophecy." *Biblical Research Institute*. https://1ref.us/10m (accessed February 13, 2020).

Neall, Beatrice. "Sealed Saints and the Tribulation." in *Symposium on Revelation—Book I*. Edited by Frank B. Holbrook, Vol. 6, Daniel and Revelation Committee Series. Silver Spring, MD: Biblical Research Institute, 1992.

Noe, John. "An Exegetical Basis for a Preterist-Idealist Understanding of the Book of Revelation." *Journal of the Evangelical Theological Society* 49, no. 4 (December 2006): pp. 767–796.

Paki, George. *The Two-Issue Theory of 1 John*. Study Notes.

Paulien, Jon. "Ellen G. White and Revelation 4–6." in *Symposium on Revelation—Book I*. Edited by Frank B. Holbrook, Vol. 6, Daniel and Revelation Committee Series. Silver Spring, MD: Biblical Research Institute, 1992.

—. *Facebook Commentary*. https://1ref.us/10n (accessed February 13, 2020).

—. "Interpreting Revelation's Symbols." in *Symposium on Revelation—Book I*. Edited by Frank B. Holbrook, Vol. 6, Daniel and Revelation Committee Series. Silver Spring, MD: Biblical Research Institute, 1992.

—. "Seals and Trumpets: Some Current Discussions." in *Symposium on Revelation—Book I*. Edited by Frank B. Holbrook, Vol. 6, Daniel and Revelation Committee Series. Silver Spring, MD: Biblical Research Institute, 1992.

—. "Simply Revelation—A Beginner's Guide to the Most Challenging Book of the Bible—Part 1."

—. *The Deep Things of God*. Hagerstown, MD: Review and Herald Publishing Association, 2004.

—. "The End of Historicism? Reflections on the Adventist Approach to Biblical Apocalyptic—Part One." *Journal of the Adventist Theological Society* 11 (Fall 2003): pp. 15–43.

—. "The End of Historicism? Reflections on the Adventist Approach to Biblical Apocalyptic—Part Two." *Journal of the Adventist Theological Society* 17/1 (Spring 2006): pp. 180–208.

—. "The Rhetorical Purpose of the Fourth Gospel." *Chicago Society for Biblical Research* (Trinity Evngelical Divinity School), April 1990: pp. 1–10.

—. "The Seven Heads of Revelation 17." Original Manuscript.

—. "The Seven Seals." in *Symposium on Revelation—Book I*. Edited by Frank B. Holbrook, Vol. 6, Daniel and Revelation Committee Series. Silver Spring, MD: Biblical Research Institute, 1992.

—. *What the Bible Says About the End-Time*. Hagerstown, MD: Review and Herald, 1994.

Preston, Don. K. "Full Preterism and the Millennium." *Criswell Theological Review* 11, no. 1 (Fall 2013): pp. 121–136.

Rand, Jan A du. *Johannine Persepective: Introduction to the Johannine Writings—Part I*. New York: Orion, 1991.

Rensberger, David. *1 John, 2 John, 3 John*. Edited by Victor Paul Furnish. Vol. 1 Abingdon New Testament Commentaries. Nashville, TN: Abingdon Press, 1997.

Shea, William H. *The Mighty Angel and His Message*. in *Symposium on Revelation—Book I*. Edited by Frank B. Holbrook, Vol. 6, Daniel and Revelation Committee Series. Silver Spring, MD: Biblical Research Institute, 1992.

Son, Sang-Won. "Lukan Authorship of Hebrews." *Southwestern Journal of Theology* 55, no. 1 (Fall 2012): pp. 172–175.

Stefanovic, Ranko. *Plain Revelation: A Reader's Introduction to the Apocalypse*. Berrien Springs, Michigan: Andrews University Press, 2013.

—. *The Revelation of Jesus Christ*. 2nd Edition. Berrien Springs, Michigan: Andrews University Press, 2009.

Strand, Kenneth A. "Foundational Principles of Interpretation." in *Symposium on Revelation—Book I*. Edited by Frank B. Holbrook, Vol. 6, Daniel and Revelation Committee Series. Silver Spring, MD: Biblical Research Institute, 1992.

Strecker, Georg. *The Johannine Letters: A Commentary on 1, 2, and 3 John*. Augsberg: Fortress Press, 1996.

Streett, Daniel R. *They Went Out from Us: The Identity of the Opponents in First John*. Ann Arbor, Michigan: UMI Dissertation Publishing, 2008.

Swanson, Dennis M. "International Preterist Association: Reformation or Regression?" *The Master's Seminary Journal* 15, no. 1 (2004): pp. 39–58.

Tan, Christine Joy. "A Futurist View of the Two Witnesses in Revelation 11." *Bibliotheca Sacra* 171, no. 684 (October 2014): pp. 452–471.

The Bible Works 7: Software for Biblical Exegesis and Research. BibleWorks, LLC. Norfolk, VA, 2006.

Torrey, Charles Cutler. "The Authorship and Character of the So-Called 'Epistle to the Hebrews.'" *Journal of Biblical Literature* 30, no. 2 (1911): pp. 137–156.

Treiyer, Alberto R. *The Final Crisis in Revelation 4–5.* Santo Domingo: Biblical Projections, 1998.

—. "A Book Review on *Trumpet by Trumpet* by E.R. Gane. https://1ref.us/10o (accessed February 13, 2020).

von Wahlde, Urban C. "The Johannine Commandments: 1 John and the Struggle for the Johannine Tradition." Edited by Lawrence Boadt. *Theological Inquiries* (Paulist Press), 1990.

Wahlen, Clinton. "Letters to the seven churches: historical or prophetic?" *Ministry.* November 2007.

Wallace, Daniel B. *The Basics of New Testament Syntax: An Intermediate Greek Grammar.* Grand Rapids, MI: Zondervan, 2000.

Westcott, Brooke Foss. *The Epstiles of St. John: The Greek Text with Notes and Essays.* 3rd Edition. Grand Rapids, MI: W. B. Eerdmans, 1955.

White, E. G. *The Desire of Ages*, vol. 1, Happiness Digest Series. Silver Spring, MD: Better Living Publications, 1990.

Winterbottom, D. A Russel and M., ed. *Ancient Literary Criticism: The Principal Texts in New Testament Translations.* Oxford: Claredon Press, 1972.

Wysong, Daniel and Steve Case. *Finding Jesus in the Book of Revelation.* Carmichael, CA: Involve Youth, 2014.

Yarborough, Robert W. *1–3 John.* Baker Exegetical Commentary on the New Testament. Grand Rapids, MI: Baker Academic, 2008.

We invite you to view the complete
selection of titles we publish at:
www.TEACHServices.com

We encourage you to write us
with your thoughts about this,
or any other book we publish at:
info@TEACHServices.com

TEACH Services' titles may be purchased in
bulk quantities for educational, fund-raising,
business, or promotional use.
bulksales@TEACHServices.com

Finally, if you are interested in seeing
your own book in print, please contact us at:
publishing@TEACHServices.com

We are happy to review your manuscript at no charge.

www.ingramcontent.com/pod-product-compliance
Lightning Source LLC
Chambersburg PA
CBHW060513230426
43665CB00013B/1495